Day of Reckoning

THE MIDDLE AGES SERIES

Ruth Mazo Karras, Series Editor
Edward Peters, Founding Editor

A complete list of books in the series is available from the publisher.

Day of Reckoning

Power and Accountability
in Medieval France

Robert F. Berkhofer III

PENN

UNIVERSITY OF PENNSYLVANIA PRESS

Philadelphia

Publication of this book has been aided by a grant
from the Medieval Academy of America

Copyright © 2004 University of Pennsylvania Press
All rights reserved
Printed in the United States of America on acid-free paper

10 9 8 7 6 5 4 3 2 1

Published by
University of Pennsylvania Press
Philadelphia, Pennsylvania 19104-4011

Library of Congress Cataloging-in-Publication Data

Berkhofer, Robert F., 1966–
    Day of reckoning : power and accountability in medieval France /
Robert F. Berkhofer III.
        p.   cm. (The Middle Ages Series)
    ISBN 0-8122-3796-X (alk. paper)
    Includes bibliographical references and index.
        1. Benedictine monasteries—France—History—Sources. 2. France—History—
Medieval period, 987–1515—Sources. 3. France—Church history—987–1515—Sources.
4. France—Politics and government—987–1328—Sources. 5. France—Social conditions—
987–1515—Sources. I. Title. II. Series
DC83 .B47 2004
944'.02 22—dc22   2004041492

Contents

Contents

Introduction

SINCE ENDINGS ARE OFTEN AS IMPORTANT as beginnings, let me begin with a story from near the year 1200, the end of the period covered by this book. This story concerns the Abbot Hugh of the monastery of Saint-Germain-des-Prés and the troubled career of one of his men, named Guy.

Abbot Hugh was stirring up a lot of trouble. The new abbot of Saint-Germain-des-Prés was the fifth to use the name Hugh, but the first to be so insistent about his lordship. At least, that was how it must have seemed to Guy, the mayor of the monastery's estate at Suresnes on the opposite bank of the Seine. Abbot Hugh was asking Guy to renew his oath of loyalty and acknowledge his dependent status as a serf. At first, Guy refused to do so, according to a note that recorded the affair.[1] Why did he refuse? Guy was an important man, charged with running the considerable estate at Suresnes (essentially a small village) and had power equivalent to that of many knights. To be reminded of his dependence and his low origins would have been uncomfortable and publicly humiliating at the least. But Abbot Hugh was not interested in refusals. He exercised his abbatial authority through his court, formally summoning Mayor Guy and his relations to appear.

The matter had now grown very serious. Guy knew he would be defending not just himself but his whole family at the court. In consequence, he brought fifty of his relations with him when he finally appeared.[2] Abbot Hugh was not alone either. He had gathered his monks and his other servitors. The names of forty witnesses were recorded, thirty-eight on the Abbot's side and two on Guy's. In addition to the officers of the monastery and simple brother monks, Hugh's witnesses included knights, artisans, and other mayors. It was a large, public assembly consisting of the most important members of the community. Thus, the stage was set for a showdown between Hugh and Guy.

In the end, Abbot Hugh forced Mayor Guy to submit to his authority. Guy was confronted with both verbal and written proof of his status.

Guy's own peers affirmed that he was a dependent man (*homo de corpore*) of the abbot, just as they were.[3] Abbot Hugh also had a secret weapon: an extensive written genealogy of Guy's family, tracing his descent from *homines de corpore*.[4] Although Guy was reluctant, he had little choice but to reaffirm his homage and fidelity as a *homo de corpore*. As a final piece of insurance, Abbot Hugh also made sure that the whole matter was written down in detail (from his perspective, naturally) so that his successors would remember his victory.

The submission of Guy of Suresnes to Abbot Hugh V of Saint-Germain-des-Prés was recorded in unusual detail. But how unusual was their meeting? The records surviving from Hugh V's abbacy (1162–82) indicate that Guy was not the only mayor to be summoned to renew his oath of loyalty and acknowledge his dependence. Such meetings were becoming more frequent at the monastery.[5] Hugh V was beginning to check up on all of his men—both his monks and his lay servitors. More important, he was not the only twelfth-century abbot to do so. His peers also felt the need to exercise better control over their men to insure that they behaved responsibly. They had found ways of making their men accountable to them.

What was new about this late twelfth-century event was that it combined several hitherto separate behaviors with some new ones. There are two important aspects of the story: (1) holding an agent personally responsible, or accountable, for his actions in performing the duties of an office, and (2) using written records created in monastic archives to make, justify, and record the case. Less obvious but also significant are (3) the use of records to manage the secular side of monastic estates, (4) increased attention of the religious to how the administration of monastic estates was conducted, (5) Hugh's active administration of the patrimony as part of a broader notion of ministering to his brothers, and (6) the fact that custom was no longer sufficient to manage monastic lands and income.

The humbling of Guy of Suresnes, therefore, was a complex affair, the end result of long-term strands, which had diverse centuries-old beginnings. This book explores those strands and how they became woven together toward the end of the twelfth century. The argument of the book is divided into four chapters. The first chapter looks at the period before the rise of routine practices of accountability, from Carolingian times to the mid-eleventh century, tracing strands of monastic thought and behavior in regard to reform, land, and archives. This chapter is the essential background for later chapters, which explore new ideas and practices of power and the beginnings of accountability.

The subsequent argument considers the transformation of monastic rule in the high middle ages and how the lands, texts, and ideas from the past were used for new ends. This part of the work treats three important and related changes: the use of new written aids to help administer lands; the treatment of land as an economic (not sacred) resource; and the rise of new disciplinary measures to make agents more accountable in practice. In each of these areas, substantial departures from traditional patterns of thought and behavior occurred in the late eleventh and twelfth centuries. The second chapter explores the changes in the written comprehension of monastic lands. Closely linked to changes in scribal culture, new ways of composing and storing documents demonstrate a growing concern to comprehend the patrimony in writing, not just in communal memory. The organizational structure of the new means of archival storage, the cartulary or book of charters, reveals the new concerns of their organizers and a turn to administrative thinking.

Throughout this period, the leadership of the monks—the abbot and his main officers—would be crucial as catalysts of change. Chapter 3 investigates the attempts of monastic leaders to balance ministering to their brothers with administering the monastery's resources. In particular, the chapter explores a new mode of monastic thought and behavior, which considered land as an economic resource to be exploited. The primary view of the monastic patrimony inherited from earlier generations of monks had not been economic. Religious, political, and social necessities remained extremely important in shaping monastic land; however, economic concerns began to have greater influence in the eleventh and twelfth centuries. Abbots and their closest confidantes initiated this turn to administration and fostered innovation under the guise of reform.

The most difficult obstacle faced by monastic leaders was implementation of their program. One key problem, as suggested at the outset, was accountability. In the monastic context, this meant controlling both monks to whom tasks were delegated within the cloister and lay agents who ran the monastery's estates outside it. Chapter 4 examines how abbots attempted to insist on responsible behavior from these men. Monastic tradition provided a means to discipline monks, but abbots also wanted good service from their lay servitors, who were harder to rule. Eventually, a desire for competent as well as faithful service made abbots seek more specific accountability from their men. In consequence, abbots adopted new techniques to discipline and punish them.

It was just such an attempt to insist on better service by Abbot Hugh V of Saint-Germain-des-Prés that led him to gather a public assembly to humble Mayor Guy of Suresnes. We should try to imagine the scene: Hugh was in the great hall of the monastery or on its steps under the portal, which may have depicted the Last Judgment. The abbot was surrounded by his monks, knights, and servants, as well as the holy relics of Saint-Germain. He was holding a formal audience, or to be more technical, an "audit," or hearing. Hugh also had documents with him, composed in the *scriptorium* for this occasion. Guy, faced by such an imposing array, accepted the judgment of the Abbot. He was made to profess his homage openly and swear eternal fidelity to the abbot and monks. This hearing was the sort of ritual by which agents were disciplined and accountability eventually achieved. Thus, "days of reckoning" were created as traditional days of meeting began to be used to hold agents specifically accountable for their conduct. Not surprisingly, abbots used pre-existing customary symbols and rituals to reinforce the new accountability, mixing audits with religious threats of eternal damnation and the Last Judgment. Collectively, these events show a turn to behaviors and ideas, which, while still lordly, also had recognizably fiscal, legal, or governmental elements.

*   *   *

In events such as the humbling of Guy of Suresnes, one can see the beginnings of what medieval historians call accountability, and what some historians see as the origins of modern government. Of course, modern notions of accountability do not seem to obtain in the rough and ready medieval world. Historians of modern government have not associated efficient, impersonal, and responsible behavior with medieval mayors or knights, who tend instead to be cast as the guy with the longest sword. Nevertheless, by 1250, other medieval overlords (bishops, kings, and even counts) had found ways to secure better service, ways of making their men accountable for their actions. This broader notion of accountability, of responsible behavior, is one focus of this study.

But what did accountability mean in the twelfth century? For the Middle Ages, the importance of accountability has much to do with the significance of lordship. Lordship was the dominant form of social and political organization throughout the history of medieval Europe. But lordship meant nothing without service, preferably faithful, competent service. Overlords could not realize wealth and power unless others would agree to serve them. Yet as lords tried to delegate power, especially over large areas, they discovered they could only share it. While seeking to allow their men to prosecute justice or raise money legitimately in their name, paradoxically, they often gave them free rein to extort and pillage. Overlords did not want licensed robbers (who behaved as thieves and bullies), but rather officials, who were accountable to them. Authority could not rest solely on force. Thus, disciplining and controlling agents became the great problem for lords of all ranks.

The problem of accountability is especially important in the field of medieval history because much attention has been focused on the nature of power. The recent debate began with the assertion by Jean-Pierre Poly and Eric Bournazel that a "mutation féodale" took place in high medieval France, a dramatic shift in political, social, and economic arrangements toward what appeared to be feudal relations.[6] This idea was built upon classic views of feudalism expressed most forcefully by Georges Duby.[7] Some agreed that a feudal transformation took place, though on a different chronology, preferring to emphasize the sudden changes around the year 1000, a "mutation de l'an mil."[8] Still others argued for a chronology of "feudal revolution" varying by region both within and outside France and also of varying degrees of effectiveness.[9] They argued that a new and relatively pervasive type of lordship (often called feudal) was created after 1000. At the same time, some bold scholars suggested that there was nothing feudal about medieval lordship, that there was no feudal system or feudalism because some of its cherished institutions, the fief and vassal, did not exist in the language of contemporary documents.[10] This controversy over the existence of feudalism, a concept that had been used by generations of historians, has created a bizarre situation in which some scholars completely avoided using the term. Still others insisted that such a transformation was an illusion of the evidence, not a "mutation de l'an mil" but rather a "mutation documentaire."[11] It was the sources, not the landscape of power, which shifted in the eleventh century and, thus, the argument was moot.

Naturally, a furious terminological debate ensued. Despite this debate, historians still do not understand medieval power relations very clearly. In the rush to discuss bad lordship (often equated with "feudalism"), medievalists have temporarily lost sight of its opposite: good lordship or governance.[12] Rather than focus on personal, arbitrary, or informal styles of

rule (which may or may not be called feudal), one should instead consider
how it was that by the end of the Middle Ages medieval lords had found
ways to govern. That is, lords found official and accepted ways to tax, to
mete out justice, and to administer, rather than rely upon mere force to
rule. Such governance required rulers to insist on good and faithful service; assuring such responsible service was the goal of accountability.

*   *   *

Another aspect of the humbling of Guy of Suresnes that attracts the
medievalist's attention is the prominent use of written records to reinforce
communal memory and oral testimony. Not only did Abbot Hugh produce the written genealogy of Guy's family to help make his case, he also
had the results of the meeting written down and kept for the future.
These instances of writing naturally provoke the historian to consider the
relation between oral culture and scribal culture. Elizabeth Eisenstein, in
her classic work *The Printing Press as an Agent of Social Change*, described
the shift from a medieval scribal culture to what she called book culture,
after the rise of printing.[13] The second focus of this book is a similar
but earlier problem: the relation of oral culture, a culture of memory, to
scribal culture, a culture of written records.[14]

Medieval monks had long memories. Monasteries are ideal for studying memory because they were perpetual institutions, persisting over generations of monks. Monks had a communal memory of events that informed their daily behavior (indeed, a memorial litany). They could and
did remember offenses against them. When local ruffians pillaged their
lands or stole from their estates, knowledge of the crime would be told to
the youngest novices so they could remind future generations. In short,
they knew their history.

The early monastic obsession with memory and history had a lot to
do with their later attitudes toward wealth and rule. For example, early
monks considered their estates to be both sacred and inalienable—they
should not be diminished, bought, sold, or exchanged. So they actively
remembered those who altered their lands as violators. Furthermore,
before 1000, monks viewed their land as part of their sacred trust from
God, rather than as an economic resource to be exploited. In consequence, they became obsessed with written claims to land. Thus, many
early documents were intended to describe the patrimony, to fix its contours in writing, but not, at that time, to manage it.

During the tenth and eleventh centuries, monastic history and archives were reordered as monks sought to create a useable past out of documents and communal memories from Carolingian times. Brian Stock has emphasized the increasing importance of literacy and pointed out the consequent rise of so-called "textual communities" in the eleventh and twelfth centuries.[15] Others have chosen to emphasize the importance of memory (and forgetting) in the creation and destruction of monastic documents and histories.[16] Whether the cause was the growth of literacy or the malleability of memory (or both), monastic archives, particularly in northern France, were significantly reorganized in the period before and after 1000.[17] The written remnants of the Carolingian patrimony were thus altered.

Moreover, the authentic materials left over from the Carolingian past (lands, texts, or ideas) did not constrain monastic invention. Monks forged charters to assure landholding and invented house traditions to explain the difference between their real holdings and their ideal (or desired) holdings. Besides informing the reader of monastic ideas, these inventions also demonstrate an acceptance of written documents as authoritative. Simply put, there was no need to forge documents unless the forgery served a purpose: if it could convince others about a claim or be used in place of, or to complement, oral testimony or sworn oaths. Forgery, therefore, provides a valuable clue about the importance of written records and the emergence of monastic scribal culture.[18] Monks often used forged charters in conjunction with saints' lives or narrative history in order to create myths and stories about their house. These monastic stories constitute some of the earliest revisionist history known and provide one motive driving the creation and reorganization of monastic archives, which would be inherited by later generations of monks. Monks were keenly aware of their history and, therefore, monastic historians must be aware of it as well to understand how monks used their archives to clothe innovation in the habit of tradition. Memory, writing, and authority were inextricably joined.[19]

* * *

By the twelfth century, writing and rule had become closely linked—scribal culture and accountability became mutually supporting. Investigating the relationship of memory to writing is important to accountability for a simple reason: before one could hold someone accountable, one first had to remember what had been done and be able to prove it. Written records offered an aide-mémoire that reinforced rituals of accountability. I argue that the idea and practice of accountability is fundamental to the transformation from bad lordship to good, since being accountable was what separated the thug from the tax collector, the extortionist from the lawyer, the murderer from the judge. This behavioral transformation included new documentary practices. Even so, no modern scholar of the middle ages has dealt with either the actions or the records of this process directly. Filling this gap in the history of medieval power is the overall goal of this work. Accountability—be it fiscal, judicial, or moral—was the glue that would hold later systems of governance together. Archival transformations both reflected and resulted from such new patterns of thought and behavior.

This study seeks to explain therefore how both rule and writing were conceived, defined, and practiced in medieval France leading up to the rule of Philip Augustus (1180–1223). In doing so, it attempts to avoid introducing artificial modern categories. On the one hand, the subject of power is often regarded as a secular subject. Indeed, many medievalists treat the history of lordship solely as a "secular" subject, considering only sources like royal records, which seem to lie behind the development of the nation-state. But explaining power only through such records has concealed important aspects of the shift toward governance. Few scholars have appreciated the ecclesiastical, and especially the monastic contribution to this medieval transformation of power. Yet secular and ecclesiastical power were closely linked, if not largely overlapping in this period.[20] Or put another way, the Church had a lot of influence in determining what accountability meant. On the other hand, studies of documents and their organization have tended to examine only one type of document or one archive. My study exploits the most abundant sources available for eleventh- and twelfth-century northern France, the archives of Benedictine monasteries. It uses the archives of five of the greatest houses (Saint-Bertin, Saint-Denis, Saint-Germain-des-Prés, Saint-Père-de-Chartres, and Saint-Vaast-d'Arras) and materials from others in the region comparatively. These sources encompass a wide range of materials, including charters of donation, chronicles, saints' lives, land surveys, marginal notations, and even scraps of grocery lists. These monasteries also shared certain important features. All of them were touched by similar currents of religious reform from 800 to 1200. In consequence, they were part of a learned community with shared ideas about writing, religion, and power. All of them were absorbed into the kingdom of France by 1200 and were old foundations with enormous political, economic, and religious influence. Also, despite the obvious importance of these houses, their archives are surprisingly unexplored. Even the greatest, Saint-Denis, the royal mausoleum for the French kings, has archives that remain uncatalogued today. For this reason, independent of its findings, this research is significant because it uncovers basic sources for medieval French history.

In the end, this study uses many approaches to understand problems of power in medieval monasteries. Although it examines the realities of monastic estates, it does not privilege economic explanation. While it emphasizes the use of writing to construct a usable past, it does not assume that ideas or symbols are separate from actions and behavior. Even though it takes power and rule as its focus, it does not presume that power is divorced from a social or cultural context. In short, it attempts to resist being a purely political, severely social, or contested cultural history because to do so would impose anachronistic modern divisions on both the sources and subject. Rather than attempting to pull one strand out of the medieval monastic tapestry, thus unraveling it, this study attempts instead to understand how the strands were woven into a single fabric.

I

A Fragmentary Past?
Monastic History, Memory,
and Patrimony

THE PHYSICAL AND MENTAL WORLDS inhabited by monks in 1100 were shaped by several centuries of deliberate monastic reform and unforeseen economic and political forces. This chapter highlights four important features of the prehistory of accountability from Carolingian times to 1100. It begins with the creation of the monastic estate system during the Carolingian period to 877. I examine how monastic reform was implemented, its political and economic repercussions, and immediate monastic reaction. Another important aspect of this first section is to reveal the sophisticated administrative apparatus lying behind the Carolingian monastic estate system. The next section considers the changes at monasteries after the collapse of the Carolingian system of rule from 877 to about 1000. As the public power of the kings waned, the monastic estates formed to serve it persisted in various ways. This second section also analyzes long-term monastic reaction to the effects of reform. Understanding what did—and what did not—survive is important to the later story. In both of these periods monastic estates, texts, and ideas would be created and destroyed, a process that left materials which later monks would reuse for quite different purposes.

Understanding monastic (re)constructions of their past is the goal of section three. Medieval monks had long memories and a shared history, which informed their behavior. Monastic reaction to the collapse of the Carolinigan estate system was to reinterpret past survivals in a new religious and social context. Authentic documents left over from the Carolingian past did not constrain monastic invention but rather served as raw materials for producing histories (factual and fanciful) that would be inherited by later generations of monks. Such inventions reveal monastic attitudes about their archives and governed how the Carolingian inheritance would be transmitted to future brothers.

The influence of Cluniac and Gregorian reform ideas is the subject of the fourth section. New notions of the right ordering of the sacred and secular worlds had a dramatic effect on traditional Benedictine outlook. In particular, a crucial idea was that a monastery should be exempt from ordinary episcopal control, after the model of Cluny. As monks sought to gain formal exemptions, they simultaneously developed the notion that their lands were sacred. This idea, coupled with the Carolingian inheritance, would create a new view of monastic patrimony as inviolate sacred space.

Finally, the conclusion attempts to gather these diverse strands and consider what resources (lands, texts, or ideas) were available to monks around 1100 for management. Although accountability as a routine practice may not have existed before 1100 (since there is no direct evidence), the legacies of the previous years shaped monks' attitudes and their ability to achieve it later on. I consider how these older resources were used (or not used) before 1100 and what potential they held for future monks, the subjects of later chapters.

Creation of the Carolingian Estate System to 877

Carolingian religious reform altered monastic lands and practices profoundly. The changes wrought by reform shaped contemporary monks' attitudes toward land and record-keeping and had consequences for later generations of monks. Before the historian can understand how later monks would use the lands, texts, and ideas inherited from their Carolingian brothers, one must first comprehend the original circumstances of their production. Emperors and kings reshaped monasteries to suit their purposes. In the process, their actions generated ideas of resistance and written records that monks would pass along to their successors.

Carolingian monastic reform can be divided into two phases: an early phase before and during the reign of Louis the Pious (814–40) and a later phase under Charles the Bald (840–77). The most obvious effect of early reform was to create a division between lands of the abbot and monks' portion, or *mensa conventualis*, which colored relations between the two until the twelfth century. Later Carolingian reform under Charles the Bald modified these arrangements to be more favorable to the king and his lay abbots at the monks' expense. Charles instituted a conscious policy of "divide and rule," which more clearly separated the monks' portion from abbatial lands, which were then used as rewards for loyal supporters. The documents used to effect both early and later reform were kept at many monasteries, providing evidence of methods used to divide as well as the politics of division. These documents, the lands they described, and the ideas surrounding their creation were a significant legacy of ninth-century monks to their successors.

Recently, historians have transformed their views of early Carolingian reform and the estate economy. They argue that imperial policy, as indicated by laws (capitularies) and sophisticated surveys (polyptychs), represented a system of "public" administration and taxation, which used the fiscal structures of the late Roman world.[1] This economic model required the surveying and reordering of monastic domains in order to place obligations for supporting the military on them.[2] The surveys created by this system were thus interpreted as defining monastic contributions to the public power of the Carolingian monarchs. They contend that the Carolingian system suited monasteries as large-scale landlords because it combined direct exploitation of centrally located estates (manors), using labor service and renders in kind, with cash payments from more distant holdings. Also, it seemed to make extensive use of sophisticated transport and markets to move and liquidate surplus foodstuffs.[3] Furthermore, this estate system was highly integrated with Carolingian rule, and rulers exploited and depended upon it for money and support, increasingly so in the time of Charles the Bald.[4] In short, royal power was closely linked to monastic estate administration.

Carolingian economic policy and practice were coupled with monastic religious reform from the start of Louis the Pious' reign. Early monastic reform spread through the work of Benedict of Aniane and the Council of Aix-la-Chapelle in 817, which adopted a revised Rule of Saint Benedict and implemented uniform observance of it throughout the empire.[5] Although the monks' daily routine was of primary importance, this reform touched all aspects of monastic life. One key change was the establishment of separate provisions for the support of monks (the *mensa*, or "table"), distinguishing them from the abbot's wealth. Once a part of the revenues or estates was designated to support the monks (ostensibly as a minimum), it was easy enough to regard the rest as usable for another purpose. Most often, this other purpose was to provide lands to the ruler or his designated lay abbot to give as benefices to *fideles*. In addition, monks themselves granted estates as *precaria*, holdings that were theoretically temporary (often for three lives), to valued noble protectors or legal representatives (advocates). Monks' lands were also increasingly designated to support specific monastic functions (for example, the hospital), making monastic economies more complex.[6]

Interpreting the contemporary and later importance of Carolingian fiscal documents remains a challenge. The implementation of Carolingian monastic reform is best understood by means of example. For the early phase of reform, the monasteries of Saint-Denis and Saint-Germain-des-Prés provide the best evidence. The planned size of the two monasteries was similar: provisions were made for 150 monks at Saint-Denis and for 120 monks at Saint-Germain.[7] A comparison of profession lists in the reform era reveals they had nearly the same number of monks in actuality: at most 131 monks resided at Saint-Germain in the 820s, declining to 123 in the 840s, whereas Saint-Denis had 127 monks in 838.[8] However, the fact that both shared the same abbot, Hilduin, during the period of Louis the Pious' reforms was determinative. As the new reform policies were implemented and the *mensa conventualis* was calculated, monks at both monasteries had the same guiding hand.

Both monasteries were also reformed around the same time. On January 13, 829, Louis the Pious issued an act allocating certain provisions to support the monks of Saint-Germain-des-Prés, at the request of its newly appointed abbot, Hilduin, already his archchaplain and abbot of Saint-Denis since 814.[9] It is fairly certain that Hilduin made his first attempt to define the *mensa conventualis* of Saint-Denis at a contentious synod of the archdioceses of Reims and Sens in June, 829.[10] However, the religious of Saint-Denis seem to have opposed Hilduin's reform in 829, unlike their brethren at Saint-Germain. Eventually, a similar act, which created the Saint-Denis' *mensa conventualis*, was issued after a synod in January 832, as explained below. So while the reform imposed at both monasteries was similar in substance and timing, monastic reaction to it was not.

Disputes at Saint-Denis had a long history. As related in Louis the Pious' later confirmation charter (which affirmed the synod of 832), members of the convent lived "regularly . . . although less perfectly" in 817.[11] Only a minority of the monks wished to observe the new, more

strict Rule, and so they withdrew (perhaps with Hilduin's and the reformers' encouragement) to a cell at Mours on the river Oise.[12] These
monks remained at their cell for more than a decade, near the end of
which time, between 826 and 829, a list of them was drawn up. This list,
preserved at Reichenau, included sixty-two monks, of whom ten were
deceased at the time of its composition. This number represented about
half the monks at Saint-Denis in 817.[13] The remainder of the religious,
who did not profess the new rule, stayed at Saint-Denis. Thus, the monastery was split.

It took meetings at two synods, in 829 and 832, to reconcile the
monks. In 829, some monks aired their grievances at a synod of the
archdioceses of Sens and Reims.[14] At this point, Louis and the bishops
determined which members of the convent had become "apostates" by
refusing to accept the reforms of 817 using the monastery's profession
lists. These "apostates" then swore to uphold the revised Rule in the
bishops' presence, and a new profession list was drawn up. At the same
time, Hilduin proposed new arrangements for the support of the monks,
with the condition that the "apostates" accept the more strict Rule.[15]

Unfortunately for the reformers, the involvement of Abbot Hilduin in a revolt against Louis in 830, which resulted in the temporary
loss of his abbacy and exile to Corvey until May 831, gave the dissatisfied "apostate" brethren a chance to make trouble again.[16] During
Hilduin's absence, they allegedly formed a "sworn conspiracy" (*conspir-
atio et conjuratio*) to protest the decision of 829 and reject both the new
Rule and Hilduin's plan for their support.[17] They even presented supposedly ancient privileges to demonstrate the justness of their claim.[18]
To make matters worse, they brought their protests directly to the
emperor, circumventing their abbot in violation of the Rule.[19] Such
actions, essentially a full-scale revolt, could not be ignored, and a second synod was held, in January 832, to resolve the matter. Once again,
the dissatisfied brothers were made to profess the Rule and their names
were written on a list. Moreover, two acts were issued to confirm the
arrangements, which became the final settlement. The first was an act of
Hilduin, dated January 22, 832 (later known as the *partitio bonorum*),
which divided up the revenues of the monastery to assure a minimum
of support for the monks, creating the *mensa conventualis*.[20] The second
act was a confirmation of Louis, on August 26 of the same year, affirm-
ing the decisions made at the synod as well as the arrangements in
Hilduin's act.[21]

Whether the acts of 832 were a triumph for Hilduin or a compromise with the monks of Saint-Denis, the *partitio bonorum* reflected the provisioning requirements laid out in the monastic capitulary of 817. The requirements for individual monks were translated into collective figures.[22] Even though Hilduin's act has only partially survived, the amounts allocated for the monks' basic nourishment were impressive. Overall, Abbot Hilduin intended the *mensa conventualis* to support 150 monks, servants, and guests throughout the year. Hilduin's *partitio bonorum* is, however, only part of the story. The document prescribed what provisions the monks should receive in gross figures but did not describe how they would receive them. Collecting these goods would have been a staggering task. While the *partitio bonorum* was doubtless based on surveys, it was not itself a managerial or administrative document. Luckily, one of the documents used to fashion the *partitio bonorum* survives. This document, known as the *état de redevances*, was partially preserved because it was recycled around 900 for forging a royal charter.[23] The *état de redevances*, which styled itself a *descriptio*, listed renders to be given by individual *villae*, which seem to comprise collectively the totals used in the *partitio bonorum*. Both the form and content of the *descriptio* argue in favor of this interpretation. Although the document omits renders of wheat and wine, the order of items is very similar to that of the *partitio bonorum*.[24] Furthermore, though the document itself does not give sums, a calculation of the totals (necessarily partial because of the state of the document) arrives very near to the gross amounts given in Hilduin's charter of January 22, 832.[25] A comparison of the items in common to both documents yields similar totals.

TABLE I.I. Comparison of Common Total Renders in the *état de redevances* and *partitio bonorum* (832) of Saint-Denis

Item	Partitio bonorum	État de redevances
Muids of rye	900	885
Muids of malt	450	402
Muids of legumes	300	287
Weights of cheese	330	292
Sextaria of butter	30	29

The *partitio bonorum* included, in addition to wheat and wine, totals for grease and unspecified amounts of chickens and eggs. The *état de redevances* included soap and various vegetables from gardens.

This similarity suggests that the *état de redevances* was used by a reformer at Saint-Denis (perhaps Hilduin himself) to arrive at the amounts allocated to the *mensa conventualis*. Thus, the *état de redevances* reveals explicitly the managerial sophistication implied by the *partitio bonorum* (and presumably all similar Carolingian acts).

However, the circumstances of the survival of the *état de redevances* also reveal how little such a practical document was regarded in the later period. This type of working document—one with no juridical force— quickly became outmoded and could only be made useful by recycling: to provide an appropriately old surface for a forgery. The survival of the *descriptio* is fortuitous, given its limited contemporary purpose and reduced importance in the eyes of later monks.

Although the reform and dispute at Saint-Denis are unusually well documented, the final settlement resembled policy implemented elsewhere. Abbot Hilduin made his calculations based on both the capitulary of 817 and practical knowledge of monastic estates. He applied the same methods at Saint-Germain-des-Prés when he became abbot there in 829. Hilduin's act establishing the *mensa conventualis* at Saint-Germain was very close to the *partitio bonorum* of Saint-Denis. The provisions Hilduin made for Saint-Germain were similar to those at Saint-Denis, only with a base of 120 monks instead of 150.

Although the monks of Saint-Germain received lesser amounts of some items, the proportions of the two most significant provisions, wheat and wine, were nearly identical to the proportions of brothers. Such similarity resulted from the systematic application of the Carolingian reform program by Hilduin.

But how did Hilduin, a newly appointed abbot, arrive at a practical understanding of the monastic estates of Saint-Germain so quickly? At Saint-Germain, Hilduin inherited a large and detailed polyptych for all the estates, traditionally attributed to Abbot Irminon (806–29), his immediate predecessor, and now dated to 823–29.[26] Did Hilduin use the polyptych of Irminon to help him calculate the *mensa conventualis* for Saint-Germain? Sums not part of the original survey were inserted at the end of each *brevis*, perhaps to provide a guide to rapid comprehension.[27] These sums might have formed the basis for general calculations of the type necessary for Hilduin's act of 829; however, some of the sums date to the eleventh century and were used for later purposes.[28]

Recent scholarship has stressed the importance of surveying and the redaction of polyptychs as integral components of Carolingian monastic reform. The polyptych of Irminon, by far the best surviving example, has been heavily relied on as proof. But one must be careful not to exaggerate its importance. Some specific allocations of revenues did take place in Irminon's time. For example, in the fragment of the polyptych dated 823, the revenues of estates were allocated to hospitality for guests. This entry also included benefices.[29] However, the permanent division of revenues at Saint-Germain was undertaken by Hilduin, not Irminon. Surveying and administering monastic estates were different, though related tasks. Even so, Hilduin undoubtedly benefited from Irminon's work, which allowed him to implement reform in short order, during the first year of his abbacy. Indeed, such surveys had many uses, and Irminon's ninth-century survey would continue to inspire later monks long after the Carolingian estate system collapsed.

Although surviving records from Saint-Denis and Saint-Germain offer the historian a detailed view of early Carolingian monastic reform and creation of the *mensa conventualis*, they do not provide the monks' perspective on increased royal control and the loss of lands which became abbatial. It is difficult to find contemporary evidence of monastic

TABLE 1.2.   Comparison of the *mensa conventualis* of Saint-Germain-des-Prés (829) and Saint-Denis (832)

Item	Saint-Germain	Saint-Denis	Ratio
Monks	120	150	1:1.25
Wheat[a]	1620 *muids*	2100 *muids*	1:1.3
Rye[b]	None	900 *muids*	n/a
Wine	2000 *muids*	2500 *muids*	1:1.25
Malt	None	450 *muids*	n/a
Legumes	180 *muids*	300 *muids*	1:1.67
Cheese	160 weights	330 weights	1:1.875
Lard/Grease	20 *muids*[c]	35 *muids*	1:1.75
Salt[d]	100 *muids*	2000 *muids*	1:2
Butter	4 *muids*	2.5 *muids*[e]	1:1.6
Clothing	8 villae	9.5 *villae*	1:1.66

[a] Both allocations were for the monks and their guests, but at Saint-Germain the amounts for the two were distinguished, 1440 *muids* for the monks and 180 *muids* for guests, before the total, 1620, given.

[b] The rye was allocated to the servants of the monks (*ad praebendam famulorum eis servientem*). There was no such provision at Saint-Germain.

[c] 20 *muids* of *pinguedine* or 50 *muids* from pigs.

[d] Salt was measured by its own *muids*.

[e] 30 *sextaria*. The *sextar* was usually ¹⁄₁₆th of a *muid* at Saint-Germain.

attitudes about reform, other than the victors' version of the revolt of Saint-Denis' "apostates." But the consequences of the division, both economic and political, were not forgotten by the monks. Documents from the monastery of Saint-Bertin provide a different perspective on the implementation of early reform because tenth-century monks copied their early records into a narrative of events. This codex provides some evidence for monastic reaction to patrimonial division.

The monastery of Saint-Bertin produced its first collection of charters in a book in 962, long before other monasteries in its region.[30] The monk Folquin began this work at the order of his abbot-elect, Adalolph, in 961 and the final events described by Folquin (as distinct from continuators) occur in early 962.[31] The evidence from Saint-Bertin suggests that perhaps in the 830s, but certainly a century later, the monks were sympathetic with the "apostates" of Saint-Denis and hostile to royal reform. Abbot Fridugis (820–34) was particularly disliked by Folquin, who labeled him the "destroyer of the regular life" and "unworthy of the name abbot."[32]

What were Abbot Fridugis' crimes? Fridugis presided over the reform of the monastery under his master, Louis the Pious, including dividing the estates into distinct portions for the monks and the abbot, just as at Saint-Denis and Saint-Germain.[33] According to Folquin, while the monks ran their own affairs they prospered and the Rule was observed, but during reform the *abbatia* was taken away and given to outsiders as royal benefices.[34] Fridugis reduced the number of monks at Saint-Bertin from 83 to 60 and expelled 40 monks from the church of Saint-Omer and replaced them with 30 canons.[35] Then, Fridugis divided the *villae* of the monastery into two parts. The first part was given to the religious, two-thirds for the monks and one-third for the canons, according to their numbers.[36] In creating the second part, the abbatial lands, "he reserved for his own perverse use those which pleased him the most."[37] As a result of these divisions, many monks were expelled from the monastery and estates were taken for the canons or the new abbot. The ninth-century abbot was not a sympathetic figure to the tenth-century monk.

But did Abbot Fridugis destroy the monks' revenues and usurp them or did his reform actually assure regular supplies for the brothers? Although Folquin claimed Fridugis reserved the best estates for himself, there is no evidence from the 830s indicating that Fridugis actually took an undue portion. Indeed, Fridugis's actions fit the pattern of early reform elsewhere: division of the patrimony, limits on the number of monks, and turning the abbot's portion to benefices. Such reforms may have been controversial at the time (as at Saint-Denis) but continuing resentment of the Saint-Bertin monks, even more than a century afterward, demonstrates that the consequences of dividing monastic patrimonies were to play themselves out over generations.

The hostile attitudes of Saint-Denis' "apostates" and the hard feelings that persisted at Saint-Bertin were probably not the only protests against monastic reform. Although some monks may have enjoyed the benefits of greater royal patronage, the imposition of reform from the top by the king's men, by its nature, has left few traces of discontent. Charles the Bald (840–77) exploited monastic estates even more directly than his father. Under the banner of reform—of providing adequate support for the monks—he continued to limit their numbers and reorder their holdings while simultaneously using a more fully separated *abbatia* to create benefices for loyal followers. Charles the Bald was less concerned with the monks' supply than with some monastic estates being free of obligations so that he could grant them out. His use of magnates as lay abbots was both frequent and systematic. His arrangements afforded monks badly needed protectors, but cost them lands. This trade-off was an accepted feature of later Carolingian policy.[38] In effect, Charles wished to divide monastic estates in order to rule more effectively as king.

The policy of "divide and rule" had important unintended consequences. While shoring up his own rule, Charles's division of monastic estates allowed local lords to control those lands more easily and, thus, aggrandize themselves after his death. Also, documents created to institute the "divide and rule" policy in the short-term also served, ironically, to inspire future monks to defend their lands against secular power more vigorously in the long term. These unintended consequences of Charles's monastic reform make understanding his policy vital to understanding later monastic attitudes. A combination of evidence from three monasteries—Saint-Denis, Saint-Germain, and Saint-Vaast-d'Arras—illustrates the range of political and economic consequences of Charles's policy for monks.

No monastery benefitted more from imperial and royal patronage than Saint-Denis. After the reform of 832 and during Charles's reign (840–77), Saint-Denis was drawn directly into the orbit of the monarch. In the 830s, Abbot Hilduin cemented the relationship of the monastery

and the Carolingian dynasty by literary endeavor, a combination of
historical and hagiographic material. The project's impetus came from
Louis the Pious himself in 834.[39] Hilduin responded by creating a *vita*
of Saint Denis.[40] He portrayed Saint Denis simultaneously as the author
of the neoplatonic treatise *Celestial Hierarchies* (Denis the Areopagite),
the missionary to Gaul (Denis of Athens), and the patron saint of Paris
(Denis of Paris).[41] Around the same time, two other works were written, the *Miracula* of Saint Denis and the *Gesta Dagoberti Regis*.[42] Their
author was likely Hincmar, Hilduin's young protégé and later archbishop of Reims, who worked in 834–35.[43] These works reinforced
Denis' sanctity and explained the special relation of an early Merovingian king, Dagobert, to the monastery.[44] The immediate use of these
works in the 830s was to secure the place of Saint-Denis as the chief
monastery of the ruling dynasty. The works of Hilduin and Hincmar
created an influential political myth, which the monks of Saint-Denis
would return to in later centuries.

Like his father, Charles the Bald took a personal interest in Saint-
Denis. In 862, Charles issued a charter redefining the monks' support.[45]
This charter copied the arrangements of two previous abbots: the *partitio bonorum* of Hilduin (as copied in Louis the Pious's confirmation)
and a later act of Abbot Louis, now lost.[46] The act allows the historian
to see Charles the Bald's own ideas of monastic reform. The goal of
Charles's charter was to substitute the produce of whole estates for the
renders in kind calculated by Hilduin. The entire produce of six *villae*
in the immediate vicinity of Saint-Denis replaced the foodstuffs listed in
the *état de redevances*. Separate arrangements were made to compensate
the monks for wheat and wine allocated by Hilduin. The wheat remained an annual render made to the monks by the abbot. As for the
wine, the monks gained control of many vineyards, all located in the
pagus parisiacus or at Saint-Denis, with any shortfalls in production (below the 2500 *muids* previously allocated) to be made up by the abbot.[47]

The purpose of these changes was to simplify management and
control, away from the complexities represented by the *état de redevances*
toward a system in which the monks controlled certain estates outright
—all located at or near the monastery. Conveniently for Charles, the basis
of the monks' supply no longer depended upon as many estates, and so
some could be more easily turned into benefices. Of course, the ostensible goal of the charter was to establish, once and for all, the *mensa conventualis* and confirm the monks' holdings. The division was confirmed

by a church council at Soissons the same year, and then confirmed again by Pope Nicholas I the next year.[48] After the previous struggles over the reform of the monastery, putting the matter of supply to rest would have been a high priority for all concerned. Nevertheless, Charles was not above using Saint-Denis for his own profit: he took over the abbacy for himself, placed the running of the monastery in the hands of the provost, dean, and treasurer, and left military matters to a mayor of his household.[49] The monastery, in particular the *abbatia*, had become part of his economic and military power base.

Charles the Bald's policy of "divide and rule" at Saint-Denis was used elsewhere, often with less regard for the welfare of the monks involved. The more typical effects of Charles's policy can be found at Saint-Germain-des-Prés, where the polyptych of Irminon provides a good, though incomplete survey of the undivided lands of Saint-Germain and Abbot Hilduin's act of 829 lists the *mensa conventualis*. A comparison of the two documents reveals that the establishment of the *mensa conventualis* did afford the monks some protection for their holdings, while simultaneously allowing others to exploit the *abbatia*.[50] The Carolingian estates of Saint-Germain were either around the monastery or south of the Seine and Marne within about 150 kilometers of the monastery.[51] Although dispersed over a large area, these outlying estates lay along rivers, roads, or both, and were united by transport services (carts or ships) such that they comprised an economic and administrative whole. While this estate network was not dismembered with the empire in 843, it was especially vulnerable to attacks by Vikings, who also inflicted grievous harm on the monastery itself, occupying, pillaging, and burning it in 845 and returning periodically into the 860s. Their attacks left the monastery building ruined (the monks themselves fled to the *villa* of Combs) and its estate network disrupted.[52] At this point, Charles the Bald integrated Saint-Germain into his holdings around Paris. In 872, Charles gave the monks control of five *villae* near Saint-Germain as a substitute for the majority of renders in kind allocated by Hilduin, just as had been done at Saint-Denis in 862.[53] This act also streamlined the relationship between abbot and convent, giving the lay abbot total control of other estates.[54] The same change had occurred at Saint-Denis, but the special relation between that monastery and Charles afforded it respect (and protection) which Saint-Germain did not enjoy.

Charles the Bald's practice of "divide and rule" was not limited to

Saint-Germain and Saint-Denis. The rapid way he divided the estates
of Saint-Vaast-d'Arras for his own use shows that he followed a consistent policy at all great monasteries. A close neighbor of Saint-Bertin, the
monastery of Saint-Vaast has almost no records of early Carolingian
reform but several concerning the later reforms of Charles the Bald. In
July 866, Charles the Bald obtained the monastery of Saint-Vaast from
his nephew, Lothar II, probably as part of a deal involving Lothar's
abortive divorce.[55] Thus, Saint-Vaast was a new holding and, as such,
needed to be integrated into the royal system.

The need to incorporate Saint-Vaast into his realm led Charles to
apply his "divide and rule" policy expeditiously. Charles himself became
the lay abbot and he ordered his *missi* to survey the lands. According
to the twelfth-century monk Guimann's description of the document,
the survey done in 866 was probably redacted in a standard polyptych.[56]
Next, Charles kept the best *villae* for himself as abbot and granted the
lesser *villae* to his men, after reserving some to the monks' use.[57] On
October 30, 867, Charles issued a charter allocating whole estates to the
monks' support, much as he had already done at Saint-Denis in 862 and
would do at Saint-Germain in 872. For the monks' food and drink, sixteen estates were allocated. Allocations to the *matricula, camera, porta,
hospital*, and *domus infirmorum* comprised some twenty-seven additional
estates. These allocations were proportional to the number of monks,
fixed by the charter at one hundred and twelve.[58] The provost (*praepositus*), who presumably ran day-to-day affairs of the monastery for
Charles, received considerable lands. After the estates were divided,
Charles proceeded to fix the division permanently. His initial arrangements were confirmed in 867 by Hincmar of Reims and again in 869, in
a revised version endowing anniversary meals for Charles parents' and
wife's souls.[59] These same arrangements, plus four new estates allocated
to the *domus infirmorum*, were eventually confirmed by Pope John VIII
in 875.[60] By 890, when King Odo confirmed Charles's arrangements
again, few changes had been made.[61]

Taken together, Charles the Bald's actions at Saint-Vaast show the
"divide and rule" process from start to finish. It began with surveying by
missi, who created a polyptych of the monastery's holdings. Then came
the drawing up of charters establishing the *mensa conventualis*, which
allocated whole estates to the monks' support, instead of the specific
provisions calculated during Louis the Pious's time. Next, Charles (or a
trusted *fidelis*) took direct control of the *abbatia* as lay abbot; it could

then be more easily used for benefices or to generate revenue. The tacit loss of these monastic lands was then finalized by obtaining ecclesiastical confirmations. Any difficulties the monks had were ironed out afterward. But unlike other monasteries, where reform had been begun by Louis and his abbots, Charles compressed the process at Saint-Vaast into just three years (866–69). His intent was clear: to establish irrevocably the monks' portion of the estates while using the rest for his own purposes as king.

The political agenda of Carolingian monastic reform, the increasing use of estates to reward followers, had significant consequences for monks. These policies generated unrest, especially when coupled with a religious reform program that insisted on a stricter lifestyle as the price for well-defined support for the community. Traces of this unrest existed at Saint-Denis, a relatively privileged monastery, where the "apostates" protested reform as it was imposed. Other monks, at Saint-Germain and Saint-Vaast, who were treated to a more severe *divisio*, did not leave much evidence of resistance. However, at Saint-Bertin, the hard feelings generated by early reform persisted through Charles's rule and beyond. These traces of Carolingian reform would remain extremely important after Charles's death in 877. After the decline of royal, public power, which helped guarantee such arrangements, large portions of church property were further secularized as lords took them over for themselves.[62] Although the monastic estate system created by royal reform was closely tied to kings' power and thus would decline with it, Carolingian policies would continue to influence monks long after 877.

The Consequences of Dividing Estates, 877–1000

The long-term consequences of Charles the Bald's division of monastic estates were substantial. But the exact economic and political impact of his policies is hard to discover because poor evidence makes it hard to determine which estates remained in monks' control after the Carolingian period. The surviving documents from 817 to 877 provide much more information than the fragments available for 877–1000. Fortunately, Folquin's work at Saint-Bertin provides a source for how one monastery's lands were shaped by Carolingian policy after Charles the Bald's death. This unusual source also gives clues about one community's reactions during the period 877–962. Although Saint-Bertin provides a useful case study for exploring the long-term consequences of the "divide and rule" policy, Saint-Bertin alone cannot provide a full picture of the pattern of estate survival in the late Carolingian period. The records of other monasteries show significant estate disruption. Knowing the fate of monastic lands is necessary for understanding how and why monks reacted as they did.

As already seen, Folquin of Saint-Bertin, writing a narrative *gesta abbatum* around 962, was hostile to early Carolingian reform. Although Folquin was highly critical of Abbot Fridugis's (820–34) actions, he also copied many significant documents from the time of Charles the Bald's reforms. Apparently the monks of Saint-Bertin prospered in the generation after Fridugis. They received substantial donations for their own use, notably a church at Steneland (near the main house at Saint-Omer) and some associated lands. These donations were described by Folquin in his narrative along with copies of the relevant charters. Later a subject of dispute under Abbot Hilduin (866–77), the estates and church of Steneland received detailed treatment in Folquin's section on the almonery (*porta*), to which a few of these estates were eventually allocated. In addition, Folquin copied a polyptych made in the late 850s under Abbot Adalard, an important *fidelis* of Charles the Bald. Folquin also copied Charles's charter of 877 fixing the monks' portion of the estates. Folquin took these documents and surrounded them with a story about how the monks' estates were treated in the mid-ninth century and later. Both his copies and his story preserved the memory of Carolingian reform for his contemporaries, as well providing text and motivation for patrimonial defense by his successors.

To understand the lands of Saint-Bertin (and Folquin's view), one must understand the lives of his protagonist, the monk Gundbert, and his patron, the Abbot Adalard. According to Folquin, Gundbert was a skilled scribe, who later was responsible for the renovation of Saint-Bertin's library.[63] Furthermore, Folquin claimed that Gundbert was familiar with the *computus*, an aid in chronological calculation that represented the height of arithmetical learning at the time.[64] In 828, his father Guibert placed Gundbert at Saint-Bertin as *nutritus* and donated lands to establish the church of the Savior at Steneland, reserving most of the lands for his young son's future use.[65] At this point, Folquin directed his reader's attention to his section on the *porta*, a dossier of charters concerning Steneland. In 831, Guibert and Gundbert jointly donated the family's chief *villa* of Cormont to Saint-Bertin with conditions: the benefit of the lands was to go solely to the monks and, if those in charge of the monastery tried to take them, they would revert to the heirs (Gundbert and his relations).[66] According to Folquin, Guibert himself wrote a final testament on wax tablets in 839 and divided up various holdings among Gundbert, his relations, and Saint-Bertin.[67] Folquin also recounted that Guibert, on his deathbed, put the keys of the church and buildings of Steneland into the hands of Gundbert, placing them in his custody for his lifetime.[68] Thus, writing recorded the oral and performative aspects of his bequests.

Folquin continued Gundbert's story in his *gesta* of Abbot Adalard (844–59, 860–64), who became Gundbert's chief patron. Adalard was an important follower of Charles the Bald, a son of the count of Ternois, who served as one of Charles's *missi*, as well as an emissary to Louis the German, to whom Adalard briefly defected in late 859.[69] During Adalard's rule, Gundbert rose rapidly in importance. He was made deacon and then provost of the monastery, becoming second in charge, about 853.[70] The following year, he also became a priest.[71] Around this time, Abbot Adalard ordered the creation of the polyptych describing the estates which supported Saint-Bertin's monks. Folquin copied this polyptych, composed between 855 and 859.[72] Given that Gundbert was Adalard's provost he probably participated in the polyptych's creation. He certainly had the requisite scribal and computational skills.

Although the exact nature of the Carolingian estates is important, there were also several features of Adalard's polyptych of enduring importance to later monks. Five points deserve mention. First, the *villae* described by each *brevis* were quite uniform in their composition.[73] Second, the text followed a deliberate plan. Each *brevis* contained a *descriptio* of a holding and followed a consistent order every time. This order suggested that surveyors had a programmatic series of questions to ask.[74] Third, the holdings described by the polyptych were compact and, moreover, had been so since the time of the monastery's foundation.[75] Fourth, unlike the polyptych of Irminon, Folquin wrote that Adalard ordered only those estates allocated to "the brothers use" (*villas ad fratrum usus pertinentes*) be included in the polyptych, omitting the *abbatia* and benefices; it was a practical document, describing the current *mensa conventualis*.[76] Finally, around the time of the polyptych's redaction, in 856, Abbot Adalard also confirmed Gundbert's separate personal holdings in detail.[77]

But Gundbert did not continue to prosper. Charles the Bald sold the abbacy of Saint-Bertin in 866 to a canon named Hilduin, a former supporter of his rival Lothar. Charles implemented his policy of "divide and rule" at Saint-Bertin with the installation of a new political ally as the monastery's abbot. Unlike Saint-Vaast, where little direct evidence exists of how the monks responded to Charles's reforms, Folquin's section on the *porta* at Saint-Bertin told the story of conflict between Hilduin and Gundbert (and by implication the monks) over the estates at Steneland. Folquin's explanation provided a deceptively clear view of the problem. In 867, Hilduin apparently seized both movables and lands from Gundbert, which had been given by his father and confirmed by Abbot Adalard. Gundbert's response was to list these seizures in *brevia*, which Folquin copied.[78] Folquin believed the seizures were unjust because he thought Charles the Bald had confirmed Gundbert's own lands in a charter in 866, only the year before.[79] Gundbert then departed for Rome in 868 to seek justice, probably taking supporting documents with him. In 877, Hilduin died and Charles the Bald issued a charter reallocating the monks' lands.[80] A reader was left to assume that the royal charter settled the matter.

To understand the consequences of Charles's intervention at Saint-Bertin, as well as Folquin's perspective, the historian must adopt a more critical view of the three documents Folquin copied concerning Gundbert. The text of the Steneland *brevia* suggest that Gundbert himself wrote them, since he referred to himself by name in the final passages and used a first-person verb.[81] If so, the *brevia* demonstrate that Gundbert's understanding of his holdings was sophisticated. He was able to list the type and number of precious vessels, garments, books, the number of animals (with totals by kind), the exact extent of the lands, and the renders given on specific days of the year in calendrical order.[82] Later monks' desire to recuperate Gundbert's losses for themselves produced the supposed 866 confirmation charter of Charles the Bald. This forgery was composed by later monks to resist attempts to seize the revenues of Steneland.[83] Forgery was a more subtle weapon against "reform" than the open protest used by the monks of Saint-Denis in the 830s, whose appeals and intransigence had availed them little. Fabricating a royal charter made sense after 877, since Gundbert had exhausted other defenses in his own time.

After Hilduin's death in June, 877, Charles the Bald immediately moved to quell any discontent at the abbey, issuing the genuine charter redefining the monks' portion.[84] In a lengthy justification, Charles explained that his motive was to achieve the "suitable order of that holy place" (*ordinationem illius sancti loci competentem*).[85] Charles was applying his "divide and rule" policy, reinforcing a division which had existed from the time of Adalard's polyptych, if not before. Charles's charter suggests that he intended this settlement to be final and that he was intimately familiar with the lands involved.[86] All disputes between monks, canons, and the abbots were to be ended.

What role did Gundbert's lands have in the final settlement and why did later monks care? A comparison of his lands in the Steneland dossier, the polyptych of Adalard, and imperial charter of 877 makes the importance of Gundbert's lands obvious. Many of Gundbert's lands, intended for the monks (at least in the eyes of Folquin's generation) had, in fact, been taken from them by Charles's time. Of the twenty *villae* mentioned in the polyptych, eighteen were within thirty kilometers of the monastery, the vast majority west of the river Aa and north of the river Lys, concentrated in the heart of the *pagus taruannensis*. In 856, while Gundbert was provost, Abbot Adalard's confirmation listed thirty-four places as being in his control. Many of Gundbert's holdings lay in and around the monks' holdings, sometimes directly adjacent to them, as at Wizernes.[87] A substantial part of Gundbert's holdings also lay in the valley of the river Canche and its tributaries, straddling the *pagus taruannensis* and the *pagus bononiensis*, just south and west of the convent's main holdings and centered on Cormont (Pas-de-Calais, arr. Montreuil-sur-Mer, 42 km from Saint-Omer). In 867–68, Gundbert's (and the monks') situation altered dramatically. Abbot Hilduin seized more than a third of the lands Gundbert controlled in 856.[88] The ultimate disposition of Gundbert's and the monks' lands is revealed by the charter of 877. Some estates were given to the monks in their entirety, including twelve *villae* described in the polyptych.[89] Charles was using Adalard's survey which defined the *mensa conventualis*. Of the remaining eighteen places mentioned in 877, five had been in Gundbert's control previously.[90]

What happened to the rest of Gundbert's holdings? At the height of his power, Gundbert controlled some thirty-four places in 856, but only two remained in his control before his departure to Rome in 868. It is likely that many were simply absorbed directly into the *abbatia* by Hilduin, which would explain both Gundbert's difficulty in recovering them and the desire of later monks to assert Gundbert's claims using forgery. Charles's charter of 877 tacitly allowed Hilduin's seizures of

Gundbert's lands, which were supposed to be the monks'. Folquin's later disapproval of this landgrab reflected the dismay of his predecessors; the monks' losses became Hilduin's and Charles's gains.

Folquin's story of Gundbert and the analysis of the ninth-century estates of Saint-Bertin demonstrate the economic and political consequences of Carolingian monastic reform. Charles the Bald's policy of "divide and rule" had mixed effects, which were remembered by monks. From later monks' perspective, "divide and rule" equaled lost land and lost control. The economic consequence of Charles's policy was reduction of the estates. He also systematically limited the monks' numbers and allocated whole estates (as opposed to provisions) to their support. Charles disregarded previous arrangements, such as those between Gundbert and Adalard. Charles (or his abbot) stripped away for himself whatever he wanted, leaving a carefully calculated minimum for the monks. Gundbert's dossier, the alteration of some of Charles's charters, and Folquin's copying of older records were all attempts by Saint-Bertin's monks to resist or undo the losses resulting from Charles's reform.

Charles's actions also had long-term political consequences. Folquin kept alive the memory of outside, secular control for later monks. Folquin and his tenth-century brothers could and did view the whole reform process as one continuing loss of power: first under Fridugis, then Hilduin's seizures of Gundbert's lands, and finally the less than generous *divisio* of Charles at the monks' expense. In the end, of the thirty-four places controlled by the provost Gundbert, eleven of which had been specifically given to Steneland and the monks, Folquin could only speak of one remnant (Cormont) still under their control in 962. For Folquin and his brothers, the moral of Gundbert's story was one of vanished glory and missing lands.

By the mid-tenth century, Folquin had devised a new means of defense and protest. He preserved ninth-century fiscal documents describing the monks' lands, using them as a basis for his *gesta abbatum*. He created a composite text, preserving both the documents and some memory of events behind their creation and purpose. He used them to tell a story which was biased in favor of the monks—a distinct polemical perspective. He selected documents, including Gundbert's old dossier, when they supported his view. He probably discarded others, now lost, which did not. The continued physical presence of his *gesta* at Saint-Bertin was a constant reminder for the monks of their losses. His work enjoyed such high esteem that it was kept, along with the supporting original charters, in Saint-Bertin's treasury (rather than the ordinary library) under the watchful eye of senior monks until the French Revolution.[91] Ultimately, Folquin's views and texts concerning the monks' lands provided the foundation upon which later monks would fashion their own documents about monastic estates.[92] But Folquin's tale of later Carolingian reform was also influenced by events in his time, and was just as much a tenth-century story as a ninth-century one, as we shall see.

But Charles the Bald did not do a complete disservice to the monks at Saint-Bertin or elsewhere. He left them basic holdings which were compact and proximate to Saint-Bertin. Indeed, the monks' lands around Saint-Bertin stayed together since they were near the monastery and conveniently bounded by large rivers, handy for transport, and the charters of Charles reinforced this tendency.[93] Such lands were easy to oversee since they were local and mostly consisted of complete *villae*. However, lands allocated to the *abbatia* rapidly moved out of the monks' influence, since Charles put them to immediate use himself or as benefices for his men. Indeed, even before the formal *divisio*, Hilduin had seized Gundbert's legacy for the *abbatia*.

The story of Saint-Bertin's estates, however well documented, is not the whole story of monastic lands from 877 to 1000. After Charles's death in 877, both Saint-Germain and Saint-Denis suffered at the hands of kings and would-be kings.[94] Charles's son, Louis the Stammerer, was forced to buy the support of his half-uncle Gauzlin in 879 with the lay abbacy of Saint-Denis. Charles the Fat, to solidify his power, gave the lay abbacy of Saint-Denis (along with the countship of Paris) to Odo, who eventually claimed the kingship after 888.[95] The monastery subsequently fell from royal (Capetian) favor until the early twelfth century.[96] The monks, overtaken by the decline of the empire, ended up with more localized holdings. Meanwhile, in 892 the lay abbacy of Saint-Germain passed into the hands of Robert, brother of King Odo, who treated Saint-Germain as a "lucrative benefice."[97] No doubt, the Viking siege of Paris in 885 justified the lay abbots' exploitation of its lands in return for their protection.[98] Robert, in turn, passed on the lay abbacy to Hugh the Great, who was apparently particularly brutal in his treatment of Saint-Germain, since even a royal charter as late as 1061 had harsh words for him.[99]

Nevertheless, the *mensa conventualis* of Saint-Germain remained somewhat stable. Of the eight *villae* allocated in their entirety to the monks by Hilduin in 829 and the five added by Charles in 872, they kept control of ten through the tenth century. If lands had been allocated for the support of Saint-Germain's monks in 829, or, more importantly, for their use by the time of Charles the Bald, they were likely still to control the lands in the latter half of the tenth century. Even so, by then the monks at Saint-Germain had already lost several whole *villae*. In these cases location was the paramount factor: *villae* located far away from Saint-Germain (Quillebeuf, Chalo, Couvin) were lost.[100] In contrast, the highly organized and unified estates near Saint-Bertin, perhaps an exceptionally concentrated *mensa conventualis*, seem to have been very durable. Most of the estates of 877 were still recognizable to Folquin at the time of his writing in 961, even if many belonging to Gundbert had been seized.

Was Saint-Bertin's situation unusual? The evidence from other monasteries shows that it was not Saint-Bertin's loss of estates that was exceptional, but rather their retention. At Saint-Germain, control of lands in the *mensa conventualis* was greatly compromised. Estates such as Combs, allocated to the monks by Charles the Bald in 872 and seized by lay abbots, became royal benefices. Such benefices blurred the line between the monks' and abbot's (the king's) estates and moved them beyond the monks' control. Thus, the ancient patrimony was dismantled: just four or five of the thirteen *villae* which Charles originally allocated to the *mensa* remained even nominally in the monks' control by 1025.[101] Apparently the rich estates of the Carolingian period had been lost. The story seems to have been similar at Arras, where the twelfth-century monk Guimann of Saint-Vaast claimed that he could recognize only a fraction of the lands he saw recorded in Charles II's polyptych of 866.[102] Unfortunately, no narrative recorded this decline from the monks' perspective, as at Saint-Bertin.

The loss of estates after 877 can be traced not just in great monasteries but in small ones as well, such as Saint-Père-de-Chartres. Like their brethren elsewhere, the monks at Saint-Père also saw valuable lands slip away during the tenth and eleventh centuries. Founded in the middle of the seventh century, the early history of the monastery remains obscure because of successive devastations in the ninth and tenth centuries, which destroyed its Carolingian documentary record. Subsequently, a fire in 1078 destroyed most of the remaining documents. This fire motivated the abbot and a particular scribe, named

Paul, to copy the remaining documents or to reconstruct lost documents by consulting the memories of the oldest monks. The resulting work, a cartulary of Saint-Père in the form of a *gesta abbatum*, preserved a handful of texts for the period before the year 1000.[103]

What can be pieced together of Saint-Père's early history demonstrates that violence and misfortune were all too frequent. The first of several Viking raids in 857–58 resulted in the bishop of Chartres's death and, according to Paul, the destruction of everything around the city.[104] This attack followed hard upon what Paul described as a hostile takeover by Bishop Eli of Chartres (ca. 840), who seized the monastery's movables and distributed its lands to his men as benefices.[105] Could this have been the convent's memory of Carolingian monastic reform? After these two tragedies, the monks were left with the barest necessities.[106] By the tenth century, virtually nothing remained of the Carolingian monastery or its archives, which Paul attributed to the neglect of the treasurer and the lack of writers.[107] Bishop Aganon of Chartres successfully refounded Saint-Père around 930, and from this point forward Paul was fortunate enough to have charters (or memories of monks) he could use in writing his text. Paul chose to place the surviving documents in rough chronological order based on the rule of abbots. The first two books, however, concerned the two bishops who refounded the monastery, Aganon and his successor Rainfred (954–60).[108] Indeed, the religious at the restored monastery were not initially monks, but regular canons from the cathedral at Chartres, who did not adopt the Rule until after Aganon's death in 954.[109]

What can be learned from the *liber agani* and *liber ragenfredi* about Saint-Père's tenth-century lands and Paul's perception of them? The first important evidence is Bishop Aganon's foundation charter and Paul's commentary on it. The foundation charter provided only the vaguest description of Saint-Père's restored lands, which included a vineyard and lands near Chartres in the valley where the monastery stood.[110] Paul's commentary on the charter demonstrated how frustrating the lack of early charters must have been to eleventh-century monks: he wrote out the status of the lands in his own time, including descriptions of holdings and how they had been given.[111] While Paul's description reveals only the situation at the end of the eleventh century, it suggests that the holdings had been completely altered since the tenth century. Lands seized by Bishop Eli in the 840s and given as benefices were probably impossible to restore, so Rainfred gave the monks twelve

prebends of the cathedral in perpetuity instead.[112] Two charters of Rainfred list lands given to the monks: holdings within and outside the city
of Chartres, vineyards around the monastery, five churches (and associated lands and tithes) and nineteen holdings within the *pagus carnotensis* ranging in size from one to eight *manses*, and another three holdings
immediately outside it.[113] These holdings were small in comparison to
the other monasteries under consideration, but they were local and
fairly compact.

Other documents transcribed by Paul suggest how Rainfred
selected new estates for the monks of Saint-Père. Descriptions were preserved on two rolls (*rotuli*) that survived the fire of 1078. Paul explained
that these rolls contained descriptions of the holdings of the former
canons (*ad canonicos pertinere*), as well as lands added by Aganon and
Rainfred.[114] The first roll contained a list of possessions, essentially a
survey, which described *villae*, including *manses*, as well as the peasants
(*agricolae*) by name and the renders or rents they owed.[115] The second
roll included a list of rents and renders supplying food or paying for a
church's illumination.[116] Yet, Paul remarked that the customs (*consuetudines*) in these rolls were very different from those in his own time.[117]
These documents predated Rainfred's charters, perhaps by many years,
and almost certainly were written at Chartres's cathedral.[118] Furthermore, though some of places mentioned on the two rolls appeared in
Rainfred's charters, there were substantial differences.[119] These records
probably came with the bishops' grants and served as symbolic (if not
actual) replacements for the lost records of the monks' predecessors.

But none of the tenth-century documents described the monks'
Carolingian holdings. The monks' ninth-century lands had been seized
by Bishop Eli or disrupted by invasion. The charters that described those
lands were probably destroyed at the same time, since the monastery
itself was reduced to rubble, forcing Bishop Aganon to rebuild it.[120] The
bishops provided new lands, new buildings, and new texts when the monastery was refounded. Although Paul tried to write a continuous history
from the refoundation in 930 to the fire in 1078, he found his task difficult. The fact that Paul could not recognize lands described in the earliest surviving documents suggests that the patrimony had been further
disrupted between 930 and his time. Paul was forced to add his own
descriptions, to salvage what he could from the remains of the archives.

Although the patterns of estate survival from 877–1000 suggest that
monasteries lost control of substantial lands, the evidence does not

allow a precise reconstruction. Control of estates certainly eroded under the rule of lay abbots or other "protectors." These clues suggest that monks were on the defensive in this period. On the other hand, monks themselves could voluntarily initiate land transactions, which might temporarily (or permanently) diminish their control of estates. Though such transactions were only a small proportion of grants, monks could exchange land or make temporary gifts in *precaria*, thus moving lands out of their immediate control to reinforce social ties with the local aristocracy.[121] Precarial grants or gift-exchanges could benefit monks, even at the cost of land control. Thus, the pattern of estate survival tells only part of the story of how tenth- and eleventh-century monks used and defended the resources of their Carolingian past. For the other part of that story, one must consider the monastic ideas and archives in the tenth and eleventh centuries.

Memory and Archives Around the Millennium

Lands, texts, and ideas all survived from the Carolingian monastic world. It was not just the pattern of survivals from the ninth century but also attempts at preservation during the tenth and eleventh centuries that determined the resources available to twelfth-century monks. By the late tenth and early eleventh centuries, a more active defense of the patrimony would determine how monks viewed their lands and archives. This defense took many forms, including *vitae* and *miracula*, monastic histories, and copying old charters, all of which preserved the monks' past while selectively emphasizing certain favorable aspects of it. The trail of surveys, charters, and stories generated by the "divide and rule" era provided materials with which later monks could reconceptualize their landholdings. The need for patrimonial defense caused monks to invent traditions for their houses. These new traditions were composed of older texts and ideas, legacies from Carolingian times, but assembled in new ways.

The use of past texts in new compilations was, however, sometimes insufficient for monks' purposes. If traditions could not be discovered by licit means, then some monks resorted to illicit ones. The modification or outright forgery of older texts could supplement or even replace authentic texts in monastic histories. Archives were altered, and so the Carolingian past was only partially preserved in text and in memory. But

a more selective recalling of the past could be useful in preserving patrimonial lands or, if brazen enough, in asserting new claims clothed in
the garb of tradition. Thus, exploring the ideas and texts of tenth- and
eleventh-century monks is vital for two reasons: to understand how
traces of the Carolingian past survived and to understand common
monastic attitudes about patrimony passed on to later generations.

A common defense was to rely on the patron saint. While royal or
episcopal protection was often ineffective (or even exploitative) in the
tenth and eleventh centuries, divine authority, in particular the protection of the saint, was constant. Indeed, there was an increasing tendency
in northern hagiographic literature of the eleventh century to describe
despoilation of monastic lands. Mentioning land seizures in detail in a
vita preserved the monks' memory of the event, since a *vita* was often
read on the saint's day and had the effect of publicizing misdeeds. Likewise, *miracula* could assert the intervention of the saint to defend the
monastery and castigate those who despoiled it.[122] The fiction was given
force at many monasteries by having the charters of donation placed on
the altar (above the relics), or by keeping them with relics in the treasury, as happened with Folquin's work and original charters at Saint-
Bertin. Relics of the patron not only helped overcome the losses of lands
and records from the ninth and tenth century, but also helped eleventh-
century monks maintain a connection to the past and preserve influence
in the present. Indeed, on some occasions, monks could successfully
recover lands with the threat of divine intervention.[123] Hagiographic
texts kept the memory of misdeeds and the certainty of punishment at
the forefront of monks' (and others') minds. In addition, texts which
described the acquisition (*translatio, furta*) or discovery (*inventio, reve-
latio*) of relics could be deployed to reinforce the holy status of particular locations.[124] A related tactic was liturgical cursing, damning those
who interfered with land donations. Using curses to protect property
was common in tenth- and eleventh-century northern France.[125] Insert-
ing such curses in charters was another way monks defended their patrimony more aggressively by using writing.

Monastic literary endeavors were not limited to *vitae*, relic stories,
or even curses. Monks like Folquin of Saint-Bertin and Paul of Saint-
Père turned to their archives and found records of property to copy. By
resuscitating older documents, such as the Steneland dossier or the rolls
of Chartres, and using them to describe lands the monks should possess,
Folquin and Paul could draw attention to the differences between the

real and ideal holdings by demonstrating that the monks had (at some point) rightfully held those lands. After such a demonstration, the march toward justice (and presumably restitution) was viewed as possible. If monks had held land once, they were supposed to hold it perpetually, excepting a voluntary grant. Preserving and copying of these documents, therefore, became an important task. If older records could be used to represent a past ideal patrimony, then perhaps it could be made real once again in the present.

Beyond copying older documents, the pattern of events needed explanation to show the paradox of the real and ideal patrimonies unequivocally. Hence, the arrangement and presentation of documents within a narrative also took on importance. A composite text often told a story in which the main actor and hero was the monastery itself, or a rough equivalent in the form of a patron saint, the convent, or a particular brother, like Gundbert. These stories, constructed out of both charter and narrative materials, as well as communal memory, became the history of the monastery. In western Francia, which to become the kingdom of France, this tendency became widespread in the eleventh century, and transformed the role of monastic archives, as Georges Declercq has observed: "Here, the archival memory had hitherto essentially been organized in the form of collections of originals, but now the need of the monastic reform movement to create a useful past resulted in the composition of historical or commemorative cartularies in which charters and diplomas became part of a narrative aimed at interpreting the past in light of concerns of the present."[126]

While such histories begin to become more plentiful in the eleventh century, few survive from northern France in the tenth century. One exception is the *gesta abbatum* of Folquin of Saint-Bertin, which served as an inspiration for future generations of Saint-Bertin's monks. A valuable source for the period of transition in the tenth century, Folquin's book is worth exploring in detail because it illuminates the beginnings of the transformation of "archival memory" described by Declercq. Uncovering the reasons why Folquin undertook his work in 961 explains a great deal about its form and content. He offered his own explanation in his prologue. First, he wanted to make known the deeds of the abbots (*gesta abbatum*). Second, he wished to describe the *possessionum traditiones*, the "traditions" of the possessions: what the faithful had handed over and the records of those donations, especially if written in charters.[127] The importance Folquin attached to the possessions

became apparent at the end of the prologue, where he remarked that
"we have heaped up a codex of little pieces of parchment in the body of
one book so that, if by chance anyone should be desirous of investigating the possessions of this place, he might have recourse to it."[128] So
Folquin combined a narrative history of the abbots to 961 with transcriptions of charters or briefer summaries of them, often with witnesses or circumstances spelled out. Folquin believed this work to be
part of his original mandate, claiming in his conclusion: "I have ful-
filled, with the aid of the Lord, the tasks which you had ordered, most
blessed and most beloved lord-father Adalolph, comprehending in one
book the *traditiones* of the faithful with their charters and also the deeds
of the abbots (*gesta abbatum*)."[129]

Thus, Folquin's work was historical (recording deeds of the
abbots), commemorative (about faithful donors), and preservative (copying charters). Faithful representation of both the archives and communal memory was important. For all these purposes, accuracy and
orderliness in writing was desirable. Folquin himself emphasized the
importance of truthfulness by confessing at the end of the work: "I
speak the actual truth, of which I am myself a witness (*teste*), that nothing has been written here other than what I could discover in the examples of the ancients and what I could learn in the utterances of virtuous
men."[130] But did Folquin protest too much? To say that Folquin was
conscientious is not to say that he was disinterested or unselective,
merely that he was copying charters and relating events without any
obvious bad faith. Indeed, the project was carried out in good faith, but
it was the good faith of a monk writing in the interests of his brothers.
He was trying to fashion a particular past, one useful in his own time.[131]

Folquin's motivations were two-fold: natural inclination and immediate political circumstance. Folquin's natural inclination was typically monastic. Until 961, Folquin's place at Saint-Bertin, as a young,
junior monk who held no major position, would have been like the
other monks. Only in 961 did Folquin have the confidence of the abbot-
elect and become charged with the custody of the *scrinium*, the records
and treasures of Saint-Bertin.[132] The political circumstances in which
Folquin undertook his work also governed his execution of it. Folquin
may have shared the highly polemical views of his patron Abbot
Adalolph, as writers of *gesta* often did.[133] Adalolph had been elected
by the monks to resist the heavy-handed reform of Count Arnulf I of
Flanders. Just before 961, Saint-Bertin had been reformed from outside

by Count Arnulf, under the supervision of Gerald of Brogne and two abbots, Hildebrand (950–54), the nephew of Arnulf I, and Reginald (954–61).[134] In this political context, Adalolph's ordering Folquin to write a *gesta abbatum* made a great deal of sense: he wanted to glorify the position of abbot and assert the monks' independence from comital domination. Similar concerns about comital reform had inspired the monks of Saint-Peter's, Ghent, to construct a similar defensive *gesta abbatum* in 945.[135] Folquin himself was cautiously critical of Count Arnulf. At the end of November, 961, Arnulf visited Saint-Bertin. While there, Arnulf seized some Rhenish wine for his own use and gave the brothers the church of Petresse (near Calais) in compensation, an act which Folquin himself subscribed. Folquin later wrote that the count gave the church "lest he be seen to incur the ill-fame of a thief (*raptoris*)," a thinly veiled slander.[136]

The other part of Folquin's work was to preserve the *traditiones possessionum*, literally the written "deeds" (*traditiones*) of the monks' lands. He believed that the archives of Saint-Bertin were imperiled. Were it not for the efforts of Gundbert, the monks' library would have deteriorated, obscuring the memory of past attempts at secular control.[137] Gundbert's life was, therefore, both a model and a motivation. It was this aspect of Folquin's work, preserving the community's "traditions," which would have greater significance to the brothers after 962. The seeds of earlier monks' resistance to Carolingian reform could now bear fruit, and it was Folquin who would tend them.

One can only speculate about the documents available at the time of Folquin's writing. In his prologue, he claimed to preserve all the documents that survived his predecessors' neglect and were not claimed by fire or age. But there were many more acts than the monk wrote down. In 1779, Charles DeWitte viewed a handful of originals from prior to 962 that Folquin did not copy.[138] If comparable monastic archives are any guide, there were probably many more extant in the tenth century, despite Viking raids. Other monasteries, like Saint-Denis, produced hundreds of charters in the Carolingian period, and there is no reason to consider Saint-Bertin an exception.[139] In addition, substantial modification of acts had taken place before Folquin's time, though he himself only minorly altered the forty-seven acts he copied.[140] Futhermore, it was the narrative, more than the charter copies, that was the scribe's weapon.[141]

Folquin's assertion of the monks' right to their possessions and their independence, in extreme instances, approached a legal argument.

In the highly charged political climate, altering well-known documents could have been very dangerous. Nevertheless, Folquin was not above making events fit into his argument, but he did so either by exercising discretion in selecting documents (a discretion which cannot be reconstructed) or by commenting directly on events. Certainly, Folquin felt justified in implying that Count Arnulf's seizure of wine was an act of rapine. Therefore, when Folquin offered the reader his personal confession of truthfulness at the end of the work it was a kind of testimony, for he was a "witness" (*teste*) to events. Folquin was not the only witness. He could also call upon his brothers. He was familiar with the methods of verification used on charters and so he imitated their form at the end of his work to suggest veracity to the contemporary reader.[142] Since he had relied on the monks' memories, listing their names added further credence to his writing. His list of the forty-five monks at Saint-Bertin functioned as a kind of witness list for the whole book.[143] Recording the charters faithfully served their interest in a general way by preserving their *traditiones*.

Folquin also served his brothers' interests by adding a supplement to his *gesta abbatum*, containing more of Saint-Bertin's charters. These documents were mainly Gundbert's dossier, but Folquin thought they were more than this: the charters concerned the estates designated to support almsgiving. Such groups of charters would reflect the estates allocated to a particular activity or function, which he called a ministry (*ministerium*).[144] In the midst of his dedication to Adalolph, Folquin explained why he had undertaken this additional work to buttress the monks' position: "Indeed I have taken care to write down separately the remaining charters assigned to support the diverse ministries, so what had been distributed to each ministry could be inquired after with an easier search."[145] These remaining (presumably lesser) charters were to be included to help monks in the future. Understanding of Folquin's intent is impeded by the transmission of his manuscript. Only the section on the almonery (*porta*) remains. The only evidence that Folquin completed the other "ministries" was that he described his project in the past tense (*curavi . . . inscribere*). Whether Folquin simply failed to complete the project or whether the rest of it was lost remains a mystery.[146]

The completed section on the *porta* reveals the continuing influence of Carolingian reform texts. Folquin chose to group charter copies by *ministeria* as a result of the documents he had inherited. Other than Gundbert's dossier, the most obvious source was the polyptych of

Abbot Adalard. Folquin's introduction to the polyptych revealed his own understanding of its structure. Folquin wrote that Adalard had ordered the *villae* which sustained the brothers described "without those which were distributed to other *ministeria*."[147] Since the polyptych lacked a description of the *ministeria*, Folquin thought it incomplete. The charter of Charles the Bald establishing the *mensa conventualis* also could have inspired Folquin. Folquin was aiming toward a composite work on *ministeria*, and though the final product was his own, it was a mélange made from various Carolingian sources.[148] On the other hand, Folquin, writing in the mid-tenth century, did not use words like *ministerium* with the precision that the ninth-century authors of the polyptych knew from capitularies.[149] Even so, the polyptych's omissions worried Folquin: the charters he organized by "ministry" were an important supplement, simultaneously preserving the claims of Gundbert (and the brothers) and collecting documents organized by a particular activity, by almsgiving.

Folquin's project was not "administrative" in any managerial sense, but concerned "ministering" in a broader sense. Though Folquin's work showed marks of his own thinking, it tended to be unoriginal in its description of the monks' lands, since it relied mainly on documents from 820–77. Folquin preserved older fiscal documents, but his compilation did not constitute a new survey of estates or describe the managerial situation in the tenth century. Indeed, for the period after 877 leading up to his own time, Folquin wrote less about land and more about great political events (such as the election of King Odo) or religious ones (the life and death of Saint Folquin). Only six of his forty-six charter copies dated from the period of 877 to 962. On the other hand, only seventeen copies were imperial or royal diplomas and, unusually, twenty-nine were private charters.[150] Folquin's goals were to give the brothers a continuous, if polemical, history (*gesta abbatum*) and to commemorate donations (*traditiones* in a broad sense).

Folquin's work helped shape and preserve communal memory. His material was continuously reused at Saint-Bertin. For example, in the 1050s, Abbot Bovo produced an *inventio* of Saint Bertin's relics, in an attempt to reconcile the monks and canons of Saint-Omer and assert his own agenda.[151] Later monks at Saint-Bertin certainly considered Folquin's text valuable enough to recopy his *gesta abbatum* completely before starting their own.[152]

By the eleventh century, the need to defend the monastic patrimony overshadowed other concerns. Resentment of the actions of lay abbots or lordly protectors, the usurpation of the *mensa conventualis*, and the rise of proprietary possession all contributed to monks' sense of urgency. Another way to try to assure control of the monastery's lands was to seek further confirmations from popes, kings, and counts, a time-honored practice. As an added measure against lesser lords, Carolingian judicial immunities could be recopied and reconfirmed at the same time. Original imperial and royal charters were not just the most solemn and legally authentic documents in the monks' possession, they also contained useful information.[153] For example, those which established the *mensa conventualis* often had clauses within them guaranteeing the permanency of their arrangements. These clauses could later be modified or reinterpreted to afford the monks some theoretical protection against lay abbots. In seeking to store and copy their diplomas, as Folquin did at Saint-Bertin, monks also preserved a lot of the information related to the *mensa conventualis* and the earliest fiscal records. These copies, along with surviving original charters, became the materials monks used to defend their patrimony. During this defense, texts, ideas, and even lands were reshaped and placed in the context of a more ideal invented past.

The monastic response to secular or abbatial domination was to milk older documents for all they were worth, especially the charters of Charles the Bald and his father. Reconfirmation (and alteration) of older documents, especially immunities (which granted theoretical freedom from public exactions and royal agents), had already become a common practice in the later tenth century. For example, at Saint-Bertin, the immunity granted by Charlemagne, confirmed by Louis the Pious, and reaffirmed by Charles the Bald in 874, was confirmed again in the charter of Lothar, supposedly from 962, but which the monks had actually forged after 965.[154] The monks at Saint-Denis did much the same thing, by improving a charter of Charles III (allegedly granted in 898) which reconfirmed their immunity.[155] Indeed, the monks of Saint-Denis made a virtual industry of the production of royal diplomas, including at least half of the known acts supposedly granted by Charles the Bald to the monks.[156] In combination with general confirmations of lands, monks hoped such immunities would help prevent abuses based on the pretext of doing justice or public exaction.

But such immunities were no defense against kings or counts who were also lay abbots. Instead, monks tried to insist on the unalterability of the *mensa conventualis* to protect themselves against such abusers. Almost every Carolingian act establishing the monks' portion had clauses indicating that the arrangements made in it were not to be changed. These clauses had existed from the beginning of Louis's reforms, in his charters establishing the *mensa conventualis* at Saint-Germain and Saint-Denis.[157] They also existed at Saint-Bertin, having been included in the immunity obtained by Abbot Fridugis in 830.[158] Charles the Bald repeated these clauses, with slight variations, in his acts for these monasteries.[159] Indeed, Charles included such boilerplate clauses in his acts redividing the *mensa conventualis* at most monasteries as a matter of practice.[160] Such clauses were intended to emphasize the finality of Charles's arrangements, which the king also sought by means of ecclesiastical and papal confirmations.

Later monks easily reinterpreted Carolingian clauses of unalterability for their own purposes. At Saint-Vaast, where Charles divided the monastery's holdings in 867, he had included such a provision. Charles provided multiple assurances which were typical: confirming previous arrangements by royal authority, guaranteeing that none of his successors would reduce the *mensa*, and that they would not put the land to other uses, especially not as benefices or by placing exactions on them for military purposes.[161] The only unusual variant in this act was Charles's description of his successors. At Saint-Denis and Saint-Germain, Charles merely referred to his successor abbots,[162] but at Saint-Vaast he had written "none of our successor kings and abbots" (*nemo successorum nostrorum regum vel abbatum*). Such usage was not strange because Charles was both king and lay abbot (*rex et abbas*) of the monastery, as he was elsewhere. But by 890, a misunderstanding in Odo's chancery altered this phrase in his reconfirmation of Charles' arrangements at Saint-Vaast to read "none of our successor kings and counts" (*nemo successorum nostrorum regum vel comitum*).[163] Whatever the royal chancery had meant, this phrase could (and would) allow later monks to interpret the whole clause as meaning that their land (the *mensa conventualis*) was unalterable by kings and counts. Willful misinterpretation of such clauses occurred elsewhere and was reinforced by interpolation.[164] As will become clear, such willful misinterpretation was common in the tenth and eleventh centuries.

Ideas of immunity and unalterability, once given currency in a community of monks, must have died hard, even though they were almost certainly ineffective. Continual repetition suggests that such clauses, even when altered, did not afford much protection. Certainly, the counts of Flanders were not impeded from dominating Saint-Vaast in reality. The counts and lay abbots certainly did as they pleased at Saint-Bertin. But the more outside interference with monastic holdings occurred, the more coveted such protections would be and the more monks wished to keep them. As late as 1075, a charter of Abbot Heribert confirming lands of the *mensa conventualis* at Saint-Bertin made a similar provision, asserting the *mensa*'s unalterability and binding successors not to usurp the lands.[165] Such inherited ideas changed the content and context of monastic libraries in similar ways. Archives and communal memory would be further altered by how northern French monks chose to keep and fabricate documents in the eleventh century.

New Ideas of Patrimony in the Eleventh Century

The selective modification or reinterpretation of Carolingian documents was already a growing trend by the end of the tenth century, when a new level of polemical discourse was achieved as a result of Cluniac reform. Reformers' ideas about independence provided new tactics for monks. One of the hottest issues by 1000 was episcopal control over monasteries. As a result, a goal of many eleventh-century reformers was to acquire a new kind of document, a papal exemption. Exemptions (in theory and eventually in practice) removed the monastery from diocesan control. Such documents were innovations inspired by the foundation charter of Cluny, which placed the Cluniacs under the exclusive authority of Rome.[166] The success of the Cluniacs inspired other monks to assert their independence. Eleventh-century monks quickly discovered older records in their archives, which looked like, or could be made to look like, exemptions.

This heightened desire for exemptions, not the actual state of the patrimony, was one driving force behind monks' decisions to keep or reuse documents in the eleventh century. For their struggles, monks produced polemical dossiers to argue before synods and at the papal court. The demands of these dossiers helped determine exactly which documents (and ideas within them) would be preserved from the Carolingian past. Thus, these dossiers reveal contemporary monks' views of their patrimony as well as what records they kept and how they kept them. Reformers' attempts to achieve monastic exemption from episcopal power occurred in two waves: the first, initiated by Abbo of Fleury and the Cluniacs themselves in the 990s and continuing into the early decades of the eleventh century; the second, stimulated by Gregorian reform and assertions of papal power from 1060–75.

In the 990s, Abbo of Fleury engaged in a long campaign to assert monastic independence. First, he collected a series of canonical texts to support papal primacy over French bishops. These were used, ultimately, to obtain a papal exemption for Fleury in 997 from Gregory V.[167] Abbo's efforts were coordinated with those of Cluny's monks to have some of their lands declared exempt at the Council of Anse in 994.[168] Abbo was the leader of a Cluniac monastic faction arrayed against the episcopate, whose ultimate success included a complete papal exemption granted by Gregory V to the monastery of Cluny in 998.[169] Abbo's success provided not just the texts (his collection for monastic exemptions was adopted directly into the *74 Titles* and other later Gregorian canonical collections) but the polemics by which other monasteries could also obtain exemptions.[170]

Abbo had aid from many sources, since his endeavors generally benefited monks in need of help against their bishops. During a dispute at Saint-Denis in 993 or 994 between the bishop of Orleans and the monks over their control of tithes, Abbo became the monks' defender. As a result of this case, he began to revise his decretal collection.[171] At Saint-Vaast, where successive bishops of Cambrai-Arras were attempting to discipline Abbot Fulrad and open fighting erupted between 992 and 1004, the monks produced two false charters to support their cause: a pseudo-privilege of Vindicianus, bishop of Cambrai-Arras (ca. 669–93), protecting their lands from episcopal interference, and a false confirming bull of Pope Stephen II (752–57). [172] Significantly, all seven places mentioned in the forged episcopal privilege were in the *mensa conventualis*, at least as described in Odo's 890 confirmation of Charles the Bald's act.[173] The monks of Saint-Vaast thus claimed they had had an exemption virtually since the monastery's foundation. The false bull of Stephen II confirmed the arrangements in the equally false privilege of Vindicianus, justifying itself by citing a doctored version of Gregory the Great's letter *Quam sit necessarium*, which Abbo later incorporated in the final version of his letter collection. The letter was one of four key decretals which ultimately allowed Abbo to justify monastic exemptions on canonical grounds.[174] Thus, the Saint-Vaast forgeries helped Abbo obtain an exemption for Fleury in 997 and for Cluny the following year.

Unfortunately for Abbot Fulrad, Count Baldwin V of Flanders intervened and asserted his (and the bishop's) control at Saint-Vaast. Abbo's
work was the first of a new breed of argumentative collection, providing model texts for opposing bishops and falsifying ancient privileges, a
model that was widely disseminated over northern France.

Thanks to Abbo of Fleury, the monks at Cluny were fantastically
successful. The declaration of the Council of Anse in 994 listed twenty-
two of their holdings as being inviolate (*inviolabiter*).[175] The monks
built upon this base by obtaining confirmations from the king of Burgundy and an exemption from Gregory V in 998, which included an
extensive list of holdings, seventy-eight in all. According to Barbara
Rosenwein, these lands constituted the "special property" of Cluny and
the list was repeatedly reconfirmed throughout the eleventh century.[176]
Rosenwein argued that this "special property" had religious and, more
importantly, social significance because it had been at the nexus of gift-
exchange relations by which Cluny allied itself to the local aristocracy
during the tenth century. The most important effect of the exemption
(and confirmations) was to publicize these relations, naming friends,
just as later letters of Benedict VIII in 1021–23 publicized enemies.[177]
Interestingly, the "special property" of Cluny in the immediate vicinity
of the monastery had diminishing ties to the local aristocracy and
increasing economic importance after 1000. Such lands had lost some
of their social meaning and were later integrated into Cluny's patrimony.[178] Furthermore, the frequency of exchange transactions declined
in the abbacy of Odilo (994–1049), with almost all his exchanges concentrated in the years 994–1010. Part of this decline Rosenwein attributed to the movement toward "seigneurial incorporation" around Mâcon
around 1000, observed by Georges Duby, but also to a conscious policy of unifying holdings near Cluny prior to the privilege of 998.[179]
She concluded from the overall decline in the volume of land transactions after 1000 that "The pancartes drawn up at the end of the tenth
century attest to the consolidation that took place then and mark the
end of a phase."[180] This redefinition of Cluny's local property as inviolate, holy ground continued throughout the eleventh century, becoming
fixed in space, liturgy, and documents.[181]

What Rosenwein observed as the end of a phase of patrimonial
consolidation was also the start of archival manipulation at Cluny. The
earliest cartulary of Cluny, Cartulary A, was begun under the direction
of Abbot Odilo in the period after 1030.[182] Just as land consolidation

was completed and the "special property" was confirmed as inviolate, a new documentary resource was being created. Although Cartulary A continued to be compiled throughout the eleventh century, much of its content was part of an older, mid-eleventh-century project, a self-described *narratio* organized according to the reigns of early abbots.[183] Therefore, the original project had historical and commemorative elements like the *gesta abbatum* of Saint-Bertin.[184] Even though it did not contain as much narrative as Folquin's and Paul's works, Patrick Geary argued that the acts written into the cartulary were changed so that they told a story the monks wanted told. To do so, the monks both copied and altered documents.[185] The Cluniacs were simultaneously preserving the past and inventing traditions.

Other monasteries adopted the tactics of Cluny and Abbo as disputes arose with their bishops or as their abbots realized the benefits of siding with the reforming popes in the eleventh century. Starting with Pope Leo IX in 1049, monks began to have a new forum in which to seek independence: regular synods in Rome. By the time of Pope Alexander II (1061–75), these synods occurred almost every year.[186] These meetings offered judicial opportunities to raise general grievances against bishops (such as simony) and also a chance for monks to make their cases for independence. Monastic communities had stories about their Carolingian past, which they could now deploy in their own defense. Resentment of secular domination at older monasteries, like that of Folquin of Saint-Bertin, and the survival of useful texts from an earlier period provided monks with the motive and opportunity to follow in Cluny's and Abbo's footsteps. Exemptions became the lens through which older documents, including but not limited to Carolingian immunities, could be focussed to create a theoretically inviolate patrimony. Knowledge of Cluny's exemption and how Abbo achieved it spread quickly, becoming common knowledge in northern France. The texts themselves, with explanatory marginalia, were soon diffused in Normandy and the Parisian region.[187] By 1057, even the monks of Saint-Bertin had obtained a bull from Pope Victor II citing the appropriate, now canonical, texts.[188] By the late eleventh century, the monks of Saint-Germain used original Merovingian documents to fabricate an "exemption" charter of Saint Germain himself, which later served as evidence for obtaining a papal exemption in 1107.[189]

Some monks were willing to do whatever it took to obtain such privileges. The monks of Saint-Denis, already adept inventors of documents, produced one of the most spectacular efforts. In the 1060s the monks produced a dossier to defend themselves before the papal court. This dossier, entirely fabricated, later became the basis of a codex of papal privileges, canonical arguments, and royal charters known as the *Privilegia ecclesiae Sancti Dionysii*.[190] The initial purpose of the dossier was to acquire a papal exemption to help Saint-Denis resist the authority of the bishop of Paris in the 1060s.[191] This conflict had been simmering since the dispute of 994.[192] The dossier included a large number of forged papal bulls, modelled on those commonly used to obtain exemptions, including a doctored bull of Leo IX from 1049.[193] The monks achieved their goal and Alexander II issued the desired exemption for them on May 6, 1065.[194]

Obtaining a papal exemption was not the only patrimonial goal for eleventh-century monks; they also sought to have their ancient charters reconfirmed. Again, the monks of Saint-Denis led the way. They sought to have their ancient Carolingian (and even Merovingian) immunities confirmed, along with a veritable host of other charters. These supposedly ancient diplomas were also forged, using the physical materials of authentic texts (papyri and parchments) the monastery possessed and the monks' knowledge of the Carolingian chancery. Even before the drive toward an exemption in 1061–65, the monks of Saint-Denis had created new documents of King Dagobert based on their intricate foundation myths inherited from Hilduin and Hincmar. These documents were easily incorporated into their new dossier in 1065.[195] Previously doctored versions of Charles the Bald's acts also reappeared.[196] The monks were subsequently successful in having these documents confirmed, along with the papal exemption, by Philip I in 1068.[197] The monks even went so far as to create a series of Anglo-Saxon royal acts to assert claims to lands in England lost in the Norman Conquest in 1066.[198] Copies of these fake acts were then bound together in one codex with the canonical material, concluding with copies of the two confirmations of Alexander II and Philip I. It was a major achievement of preservation and invention, as well as archival destruction.[199] Thus, the monks of Saint-Denis asserted their independence not only with their exemption but also with reconfirmations of their lands.

Monks also created narratives to preserve and defend their patrimony, which could be used to support dossiers presented in synod or at Rome. One of the more effective tools, as seen in the case of Folquin, was history, in the form of *gesta*. Such histories had many purposes, but one of them was almost always to reinforce the patrimony's defense by providing an appropriate context for ancient documents, such as foundation charters (real or invented) or ancient diplomas.[200] The appeal of forging foundation stories or foundation charters was very great for most monastic communities. Foundation myths were powerful devices for adjusting the relationship of monastic communities to outside powers.[201] Origins could be constantly reinvented. These concocted origin stories often created or justified a liaison with powerful patrons, either spiritual or temporal, who could afford the monks protection or status. For example, monks of Saint-Germain used the *vita* of Droctroveus (thought to be their first abbot) to reinforce the "foundation charter" of Childebert I, created between 1002 and 1015, to defend their estates at Issy from royal lay abbots.[202] By the late eleventh century, these texts were woven together by the monk Gislemar with the earlier universal chronicle of Aimoin of Fleury to create a history of Saint-Germain.[203] Such activity laid the groundwork for obtaining a papal confirmation in 1107.[204] After 1078, when Paul of Saint-Père-de-Chartres was struggling to overcome the fire that destroyed his archives, he too collected his foundation documents into a *gesta*, so that his successors would have the advantages of communal memory of their origins to draw upon. By 1106, the monks of Saint-Père had obtained the requisite papal privilege.[205]

All of these efforts were given new impetus, new texts to draw upon (such as Abbo's collection), and a new polemical stance by the success of Cluniac reform. Hagiographic literature, especially *vitae*, were also rich in supporting material. Just as confirmations could publicize allies and enemies, a *vita* or the *miracula* of the patron saint, read aloud on the saint's day, or a *gesta* that preserved the legends and history of the monks, could serve much the same purpose.[206] It was no accident that keepers of records, relics, and treasures, like Paul and Folquin, were chosen to write these texts. Their (hi)stories could contribute to a sense of institutional identity among monks by reinforcing their communal memory.[207]

Regardless of the success or failure of these defensive measures (and regardless of the reality of monastic lands or archives), they helped create an ideal view of the monastic patrimony as inviolate, unalterable by outsiders, and independent of them. In particular, the *mensa conventualis* was supposed to remain fixed, stable, and permament, excepting only new gifts. This tendency to view lands as a fixed territory grew even at monasteries like Cluny, which had no ancient *mensa conventualis*, but where a carefully defined "special property" was created out of a fluid gift-exchange system. By 1095, Pope Urban II was declaring a "sacred ban" at Cluny, a fixed area which was sacred and consecrated space.[208] Oddly enough, the more the estates changed in reality, the less changeable they were thought to be ideally. This perspective inevitably altered the perceived relationship of documents to lands, as well as ideas about both.

Traditional Patrimonial Management

But what about managing obsessively protected patrimonial lands? By 1000, several factors discouraged using written instruments to survey or to aid in administering monastic estates, as had been done during Carolingian monastic reform. First, Charles the Bald's reforms concentrated estates locally and reduced the need for complex calculations of renders from larger numbers of widely scattered holdings. Monks subsequently entrusted such estates to servitors, who would be responsible for bringing their produce to the monks.[209] Second, one must acknowledge the success of Carolingian reform in creating stable supplies. The existence of the *mensa conventualis* guaranteed a minimum of provisions for the monks and provided little incentive to change, so long as they proved sufficient. However suspicious monks may have been of the goals of the abbot or king in the ninth century, the stability of the *mensa conventualis* served their needs. The extraordinary continuity of these arrangements at Saint-Bertin until 962 shows that the efficacy of this estate system, if left intact, could be formidable. Third, eleventh-century monks were not simply passive continuators of late Carolingian practices; they defended them aggressively. The result was an outpouring of hagiographic literature, histories, and charter copies aimed at defending the patrimony. Eventually, a desire to assert the inviolate nature of holy space also encouraged monks to fix that space in texts and territory.

All three of these factors, combined with a pious reluctance to exploit the patrimony for gain, produced a common mentality of patrimonial lordship among eleventh-century monks. Maintenance of stable (even fixed) resources to assure adequate supplies for the brothers in perpetuity was the goal.[210] From a modern economic perspective, this type of management was particularly wasteful; the guarantee of a minimum but steady supply of certain items, such as grain, leather, or wine, was more crucial than maximizing the production of estates.[211] The shared conditions of all great houses led to common solutions which eventually became the everyday practices of patrimonial lordship by the eleventh century.

Yet common solutions created common difficulties for eleventh-century abbots and monks: controlling and overseeing their estate managers. For ecclesiastics who did not live communally, the solution was to live at the estates (as prebends) or to visit them in rotation, a practice also adopted by lay lords. Such a solution was not possible for monks, confined as they were to their cloister, with their specific needs for food and clothing. The unique demands of the monastic profession were intensified by economic and political changes from 877 to 1000. Monks' lands became more compact and local, as a result of Charles's divide and rule policy, the rise of nearby lords, or by choice, as at Cluny around 1000. As a result, early eleventh-century monks clung to practices established in the ninth century during the creation of the *mensa conventualis*. The more compact their holdings, the more effective old practices of patrimonial lordship would be, since some oversight of estate managers was possible from the main house. By the eleventh century, these arrangements had been in place for some time. Moreover, these managerial practices had become usual, they became *traditiones* (if favorable) or *consuetudines* (if unfavorable), which is to say they were endowed by repetition with the force of tradition or custom.

Practices of traditional patrimonial management relied heavily on communal memory but also used some writings as memory aids. The prevalence of this style of patrimonial lordship explains why so little evidence of new written instruments of monastic administration, especially surveys, can be found before 1100: older documents were used to complement memory. As long as the established management system worked and remained relatively stable, keeping track of domains and revenues was possible by memory aided by older texts. A river or prominent hill could act as a guide to location or boundary of a holding. Boundaries were rarely recorded in northern French monastic charters in this period. Even at Cluny, where they had once been recorded, charters start to omit mention of bounds.[212]

If memory failed, older documents which recorded time-honored obligations or simple donation charters might serve as reminders. Oliver Guyotjeannin traced numerous instances of monks in northern France updating older documents with notations to aid in describing the patrimony. One example are glosses written by Paul of Saint-Père to clarify a convention of Count Eudes of 1024 regarding the use of an estate fifty years after the event.[213] More telling are the numerous notes added to Carolingian polyptychs as a means of updating their content, including six instances in the polyptych of Irminon at Saint-Germain from the late tenth and early eleventh centuries.[214] The careful, even obsessive preservation of some Carolingian documents at Saint-Bertin by Folquin was symptomatic of a larger monastic view: such texts were sacred, as the relics had always been, and as the physical environs of the monastery were increasingly viewed. Subsequently, Folquin's writings were kept with the relics. Paul of Saint-Père found the community's older documents in their "sacred archives" (*scrinia sacra*).[215] Writing and written documents were enormously important to the patrimony.

Even so, eleventh-century monks do not seem to have conceived of "administering" their lands using writing or trying to make them more productive, as long as their particular needs were met. The administrative mentality which could have motivated the production of new written instruments for land management simply did not exist. The writing and document production that did exist was directed to other ends: securing the inviolacy of the monks' lands and their independence. This goal encouraged, even demanded, obsessive preservation and forging of ancient documents. The place of writing in this monastic mentality was to support the idealized patrimony and not to act as an instrument of management.

Thus, the monastic scribal culture that had evolved from Carolingian times to 1100 had little interest in what I call accountability. Commemorative, historical, and polemical concerns dominated archival production while patrimonial management remained traditional. While older documents could be reinterpreted, their immediate usefulness for determining the monks' actual patrimony was much more limited. A practical appraisal of the monks' managerial resources is sobering. By 1100, all the monasteries under consideration (perhaps even Saint-Père) had documents from the age of Carolingian reform, either polyptychs or charters establishing the *mensa conventualis*. Recent scholarship, which emphasizes the public nature of the Carolingian administrative system, has also stressed the durability of its fiscal categories, the *mansus* and *villa*.[216] But these documents—in either originals, altered copies, or borrowings—often bore little or no relation to monks' actual holdings in 1100. Notes updating older documents provided a support for communal memory but did not provide a realistic assessment of actual landholdings. Later monks, like Guimann of Saint-Vaast, could not recognize more than a fraction of the names listed in polyptychs.[217] Often, the estates had been substantially reduced (or usurped) over the years, leaving smaller holdings, near the monastery. Such reductions affected the monks directly. Even at Saint-Bertin, where the holdings seem to have been less disrupted, one list indicated that the number of monks had fallen from sixty in Fridugis's time (eighty-three before reform) to forty-seven in Folquin's and as low as eight by the time of Abbot Roderick (1017–43).[218]

What monks did have was a tradition of patrimonial management they had inherited and malleable documents and memories. Their documents, both real and forged, could assert ancient claims to large areas, as at Saint-Denis. Monastic use of archives to protect the patrimony also transformed the role of documents.[219] Older documents could be "preserved" in a new form as part of a history or *gesta abbatum* (for commemorative reasons) or in a dossier (for polemical ones), though one should not insist on too fine a distinction. Sometimes documents were not even organized in textual form but simply arranged physically in the *scriptorium*, as indicated by dorsal notes found on surviving originals.[220] They also could be lost in various ways, such as the fire at Saint-Père. Nevertheless, Carolingian documents which did survive (for whatever reason) often had no clear relation to the real patrimony until incorporated into communal history.

Conclusions

In short, early twelfth-century monks inherited no written instruments for land management. Monastic scribal culture in the tenth and eleventh centuries was directed toward other ends. Indeed, interest in creating such managerial documents may have been fading for a long time. Already in the mid-tenth century, Folquin included no new survey or estate descriptions in his codex for Saint-Bertin. In a pinch, ancient surveys of the *mensa conventualis* could be used to check on the minimum amounts of renders. It may be that monks simply relied on these older documents, such as the polyptych of Saint-Germain, which shows some evidence of reuse in the eleventh century. Such continuing use was more likely in the Empire, where traditional patrimonial management (and archival resources) show stronger continuity from Carolingian administration.[221] Like Folquin, eleventh-century French monks were excellent storytellers and polemicists—they were good at forgetting and remembering selectively—but they were not land surveyors.

As social and economic conditions changed in the later eleventh century, however, traditional patrimonial management was no longer adequate. The depredations of lesser lords continued to disrupt the integrity of the patrimony. Reductions in the frequency and quality of pious land donations meant that monks could not use economic growth directly to offset these losses. This trend may have been more acute at older Benedictine houses, such as Saint-Germain and Saint-Bertin, whose records show few acts of new donation after 1000.[222] Cluniac and Gregorian reform further complicated economic relations with lay magnates as well as bishops. For example, reforming popes insisted that laymen relinquish possession of churches and tithes, which had once belonged to monasteries, creating "new," though contested streams of revenue.[223] All of these changes magnified the common difficulty of managing estates locally and, even more so, at a distance. Establishing when and how monks first perceived these problems as managerial, and not just religious or social, is difficult. The idea of the monastic patrimony as fixed, holy, and inviolate territory continued to be influential after the eleventh century and it masked any managerial impetus. Nevertheless, twelfth-century monks used the lands, texts, and ideas they inherited for new economic, administrative, and disciplinary purposes. But when did traditional patrimonial management give way to ideas of changing and improving land and when did monks first record this shift in recognizable form? When and how did monks begin to administer their resources using written records? How were archives deployed to achieve accountability? These are questions that only later monastic documents can answer.

2

Written Comprehension of Land and Signs of an Administrative Mentality

CHANGES IN THE PATTERN OF traditional management at the end of the eleventh century are hard to detect because management practices were largely unwritten. A common tendency in historical thinking has been to search exclusively for "administrative" documents, like surveys, to prove the rise of new managerial ideas about the patrimony.[1] But this method mistakes the document for the more important underlying behavior. A survey was the culmination of a lengthy process, the product of monks thinking, acting, and then writing "administratively" about a monastery's lands and revenues. Such administrative thinking and doing had several components. The first was a territorial (in addition to a social or religious) comprehension of land and the ability to write down that comprehension in descriptive form. The second was the ability to vary the kinds of income from estates or to alter the composition of lands. The third was the desire or need to do so, which led to an acceptance of change. An inclination to improve holdings and income allows a pattern of exploitation for gain to be established.[2] When all three were present, the traditional style of managing the patrimony could be changed to one influenced more by administrative or economic concerns.

In order to determine when and why monks began to manage their patrimony in new ways, one must answer two basic questions: how did twelfth-century monks understand their lands and how did they record that understanding? Few new administrative or fiscal documents seem to have survived from the eleventh century. Even so, there are some written traces of managerial thinking in eleventh-century monasteries. These traces include updates of charters and old surveys to reflect current conditions. The polyptych of Irminon saw extensive reuse as what Olivier Guyotjeannin has called a "support de la memoire," literally a

physical support for new text which was added occasionally in the tenth
and eleventh centuries. These updates included diverse short items, all
of which were to supplement the descriptions of the original survey.[3]
But these efforts were quite modest, literally marginal additions.

As seen in Chapter 1, the eleventh century was a time of invention
during which the applications of writing diversified. Monastic reformers frequently adjusted the relationship of archives, memory, and patrimony. Patrick Geary perceived the historicizing of monastic archives as
manipulating or even obliterating memory of the Carolingian past.[4] In
contrast, Laurent Morelle contended that the reduction or distortion
of monastic archives in the eleventh century must be examined on a
case-by-case basis and that such "hypercritism" of sources is often unjustified.[5] Morelle's successful reconstruction of archives at three monasteries in northern France from various "mediators" (inventories,
chronicles with charters in them, cartularies) shows that books of copies
often mirrored archival organization rather than negating it and so he
argued that the prevailing ethos was one of preservation.[6] In my view,
one must weigh the considerable effort that both copying (on individual sheets or in groups) and organizing (of originals or in cartularies)
required. Such rewriting was not a casual undertaking or the product of
accident, though one must always measure how deliberate (and polemical) the transformation of archival memory was. The distinctions we
make between hagiographer, historian, archivist, and copyist should be
applied with great care and must be subordinate to explaining further
the physical and mental aspects of this archival transformation. For
the purpose of the present study, one must ask: did these documentary
practices show any concern with administering or accountability? Already, we have seen no strong administrative bent in monastic activity
before 1100 and likewise, no direct evidence of accountability, even for
the sophisticated Carolingian estate system.

Could there be more administrative material which is now lost?
Discovering the full effects of selective memory on archives is difficult
because distortion and even destruction accompanied invention. However, some evidence of the selection process does remain. Morelle, using
a 1098 inventory from the monastery of Saint-Riquier, explained the
selection process used by the monk Hariulf in preparing his 1104 chronicle of the monastery. He discovered that of sixty-nine documents listed
in the inventory, Hariulf transcribed less than half (thirty-three). Furthermore, Hariulf's pruning of the documents became even more severe

for the period from 1007 to 1098: he used only fifteen of forty-eight known pieces.[7] Had only Hariulf's chronicle survived, historians' view would be constrained by his selections, as is the case at other monasteries. Moreover, no surveys or other obviously fiscal documents were in the inventory. The inventory of 1098 listed only those charters that survived the eleventh century at Saint-Riquier, by which time the Carolingian heritage was already much reduced and contained no polyptychs. As was true elsewhere, the scribes of the eleventh century do not seem to have emphasized administrative documents. So, in searching for written comprehension of monastic lands, it is necessary to resort to indirect methods of analysis.

Papal Confirmations and Enumerations

Fortunately, evidence for monks' written comprehension of their patrimonies can be found within documents which have not usually been viewed as relevant to administration: confirmations. As Barbara Rosenwein argued in the case of Cluny, such confirmations often had a social function, the publicizing of friends and enemies, which had the result of making confirmations more specific about people than about lands.[8] Donors and their continuing relation to the saint were the most important aspect of such confirmations. But this social meaning of land attenuated under stresses which encouraged monks to view their lands as an inviolate patrimony, leading them to seek confirmations that would fix its composition.[9] However rich their social meaning, confirmations would also contain lists of lands, as they did at Cluny in 998 and thereafter. Thus, the growing obsession with establishing inviolate monastic estates in the eleventh century provides the historian with valuable clues. The increasingly frequent confirmation of holdings and privileges by popes, kings, and lesser lords, coupled with the growing desire to preserve these confirmations, insured that monks copied them and that they survived. These confirmation charters provide the first glimpses of an increasingly written comprehension of the patrimony and they allow some understanding of monks' view of their lands.

Diplomatic studies of papal confirmations and their lists of possessions, the *enumeratio bonorum*, reveal three important trends in the late eleventh and twelfth centuries. First, Dietrich Lohrmann observed that the *enumeratio bonorum* was frequently supplied by the beneficiary,

meaning that the grantor often had no specific knowledge of their accuracy.[10] This tendency was particularly true for papal confirmations, since
the pope was frequently operating at a remove from local events and
was dependent on information sent to him. Giles Constable also observed this trend and agreed that papal confirmations with an *enumeratio bonorum* tended to become *pancartes*: documents that collected
and confirmed in one charter properties acquired over many years.[11]
Second, as a result of beneficiaries providing lists and a desire to avoid
disputes, Constable argued, the papal chancery started employing new
phrases at the head of the *enumeratio bonorum* by the end of the eleventh
century. While older lists of properties tended to be introduced by simple phrases like *id est* or *videlicet*, the new form, adopted apparently by
Urban II in his travels through France, was *propriis vocabulis* or *propriis
nominibus*.[12] In this way, the popes indicated that they had not verified
the claims to possessions that had been supplied, a formula which
became standard in the papal curia by the 1130s when the introductory
wording was fixed: *In quibus hec propriis duximus exprimenda vocabulis*.[13]
Finally, both scholars observed changes in the internal structure and
content of the *enumeratio*. Lohrmann found that in some confirmations,
especially pancartes, information about donors was frequently preserved,
as were terms of donation and donation groups.[14] He also discovered a
tendency in geographical lists to change from a traditional organization
by Carolingian *pagus* to listing places by diocese.[15] Such groupings,
often recopied in later confirmations, could be detected by the connect-
ing text in the lists, which Constable demonstrated for the monastery of
Beaume-les-Messieurs.[16]

While both Lohrmann and Constable studied the *enumeratio bonorum*, they warned against using such lists without caution. Both stressed
that confirmations, especially papal confirmations, cannot be easily used
as indicators of real possession.[17] Indeed, Constable even questioned the
wording of the description of properties, arguing that taking terms
such as *ecclesia* at face value would lead to misunderstanding the complex nature of most holdings.[18] Such difficulties, combined with the
monastic tendency to exaggerate claims, made any conclusions about
patrimonial lands very uncertain. As a result, he argued that such lists,
especially in the case of monasteries, could only reveal claims to particular properties rather than the actual state of the possessions.[19] They reflected the ideal rather than the real state of affairs.

Confirmations were not administrative documents, but collectively they do offer a chance to understand changing perceptions of the patrimony over time. Significantly, it was the monks themselves who often provided the information necessary for composing them, petitioning higher authorities to confirm their work, as at Cluny.[20] Monks and abbots gathered such information and then sent it to the pope, as lists, groups of originals, or dossiers, as the monks of Saint-Denis had done to obtain their exemption.[21] As a result, papal confirmations reveal aspects of the patrimony that the monks or abbot thought necessary to confirm, as well as how and when they began describing their lands in written form. Since monasteries sought reconfirmation frequently, usually repeating and sometimes varying their petitions, they produced series of documents that allow the historian to detect the changing patterns in written comprehension of the patrimony over time. Petition and repetition thus provide the means to understand monks' changing priorities. So, although confirmations offer only indirect proof of monastic understanding of lands—since their understanding of the patrimony for confirmatory purposes was not the same as understanding it for management purposes—confirmations still provide a good gauge of the written component of territorial understanding.

For the purpose of revealing monks' written comprehension of their lands, papal confirmations come in three varieties. These varieties are based on the relative content of the *enumeratio bonorum* rather than on documentary form or internal structure. The first kind is the "general" confirmation, which reaffirms the possessions of a monastery as a whole with little or no enumeration of possessions. The second confirmation type is the "incremental" confirmation, which either confirms particular holdings by name (often relating their history or donors) or confirms new or added holdings by name in an *enumeratio*. The third variety is the "explicit" confirmation, which lists holdings in detail in the *enumeratio*, providing a list which purports to describe the entirety of the monks' possessions, ancient and recent. It is worth noting that the rest of the confirmation besides the *enumeratio* was frequently independent of it. Privileges (such as the abbot's right to wear a miter or an exemption) could be included in any of the three types of confirmation, though the listing of privileges tended to become more elaborate as the enumeration of possessions became more explicit.

An analysis of all confirmations, including originals, cartulary copies, and forgeries for the period 1000–1200 for the five monasteries under consideration reveals three important trends. First, the content of land descriptions did move toward greater specificity over the course of the eleventh and twelfth centuries. Second, enumerations of places in incremental and explicit confirmations were a decidedly twelfth-century phenomenon. For all five monasteries, only general confirmations were sought before the end of the eleventh century. The shift to more explicit lists of holdings reveals, albeit indirectly, a more descriptive written comprehension of the patrimony in the twelfth century.[22] Third, the timing of changes in the *enumeratio* varied significantly from monastery to monastery. These variations suggest that local circumstances played an important role in requests for enumerations, even if monks may have been generally inspired to seek confirmations by a common current of reform, the papal chancery, or distant brothers. Thus, it is worth considering when these changes in the *enumeratio* occurred at each monastery.

At Saint-Bertin, the first papal confirmation after the year 1000 was a general confirmation granted in 1057.[23] This document granted an exemption to the monks and cited the now standard canonical texts first gathered by Abbo of Fleury.[24] No places were specifically named, though the privilege was to apply to all the monks' holdings.[25] By the end of the eleventh century, in an attempt to forestall simoniacal activity on the part of the diocesan bishop, Urban II took Saint-Bertin under his protection and guaranteed by name the liberty of churches controlled by the monastery in two bulls in 1095 and 1096.[26] Such privileges, while

TABLE 2.1.   Land Enumerations in Papal Confirmations, 1000–1200

Monastery	General	Incremental	Explicit
Saint-Bertin	1057	1095	1139/1145
Saint-Germain	1107	1122	1176
Saint-Denis	1049/1065[a]	1122	1148
Saint-Vaast	1021/1024[b]	1102	1164/1170
Saint-Père	None	1106	1127

General = first confirmation, no *enumeratio bonorum*; incremental = first mention of places by name; explicit = lengthy *enumeratio bonorum*.
This table includes confirmations known, in whole or in part, through copies, forgeries, or originals. Confirmations are the bulk of extant papal documents before 1150: 17 of 25 (Saint-Bertin), 6 of 8 (Saint-Germain), 11 of 20 (Saint-Denis), 8 of 12 (Saint-Vaast), and all 5 surviving documents at Saint-Père.
[a] 1049 confirmation of Leo IX, interpolated to support bid for exemption; see Chapter 1.
[b] Confirmations of Benedict VIII, probably of a general nature, interpolated before 1109; see below.

a product of the reforming spirit of the pope, were a natural extension of the previously granted exemption. The first bull specifically named some twenty-eight churches by diocese, eleven of which also included some mention of the church's *villae*.[27]

During the twelfth century, papal confirmations of the possessions of Saint-Bertin continued to become more and more descriptive. In 1107, Pascal II issued a very detailed confirmation, listing thirty-seven places and fisheries along the river.[28] The Saint-Bertin monks kept their confirmations up to date, as Abbot Lambert did in 1114, asking the pope to confirm lands and altars recently acquired in an exchange with the count of Flanders. The *enumeratio* included the terms of the agreement, including donors, rents, and tithes associated with the six new properties.[29] These new holdings were later incorporated into a larger incremental confirmation of possessions in 1119 which the monks sought from the new pope, Calixtus II.[30] The details of new gifts or acquisitions continued to be confirmed in subsequent charters, eventually amalgamated in the extensive listing of forty-nine properties in the confirmation of Innocent II in 1139 and the slightly modified confirmation of Eugenius III in 1145.[31] By this time, the telltale cautionary phrase, *in quibus hec propriis duximus exprimenda vocabulis*, had been included by the papal chancery. Thus, the monks of Saint-Bertin had or made lists of some holdings by the end of the eleventh century, to which they added as necessary during the first half of the twelfth century, eventually taking a consolidated list to the popes in 1139–45.

The behavior of the monks of Saint-Bertin was not unusual. The surviving papal confirmations of the other monasteries indicate that monks at Saint-Bertin received incremental confirmations earlier than some, perhaps because of disputes over churches with their bishop, but that a similar drive toward explicit listings of lands occurred elsewhere. The monks at Saint-Germain-des-Prés did not receive their first papal confirmation after the millennium until 1107, and then only received a general confirmation of possessions without specifics.[32] This confirmation was the monks' exemption, for which they had produced a dossier which included a fabricated charter of Saint Germain.[33] Another papal confirmation was not sought until 1122, which listed by name two churches recently acquired.[34] Such precision was unusual and popes continued to issue the monks general confirmations of possessions until mid-century, though other privileges became more numerous. In 1150 and 1163, the pope granted two confirmations containing incremental

listings of Saint-Germain's holdings, confirming formerly disputed
lands.[35] Only in 1176 did the monks receive an explicit confirmation of
their possessions, in which thirty-nine churches and their appurtenances
in nine dioceses were named.[36] What had the monks of Saint-Germain
taken to the popes? As the text of most of these confirmations made
clear, the monks continued to take their old confirmations (or copies)
to the popes for renewal. Each pope made direct reference to his predecessors' confirmations, usually copying clauses of the confirmation
in their entirety before any privileges were added.[37] They petitioned
and repetitioned constantly with each new pope. Apparently no list of
possessions was taken along with these confirmations until 1176. By
contrast, the monks of Saint-Bertin had a list of churches in a confirmation by 1095, had submitted a variety of lists starting in 1114, and had
acquired an explicit confirmation by 1139.

The monks of Saint-Denis did more than simply take their old
confirmations to the pope; they manufactured new ones to serve their
purposes. The first confirmation after 1000 granted to Saint-Denis was
in 1049 by Leo IX, which contained a general confirmation of possessions, although the charter was later interpolated and its original text
is now uncertain.[38] However, the monks of Saint-Denis sought a general confirmation as part of a campaign to acquire an exemption from
Alexander II at the synod of 1065.[39] As explained in Chapter 1, this
exemption resulted from the monks' active solicitation. They composed
a dossier of sixteen fabricated documents (including the interpolated
Leo IX confirmation) which they took to Rome. This dossier was later
incorporated into the codex called *Privilegia ecclesiae Sancti Dionysii* in
1068.[40] While the 1065 confirmation of Alexander II was very precise
about the pseudo-history and privileges of Saint-Denis, it still included
only a general confirmation of possessions. One document copied by
the monks into their dossier at the same time, an interpolated confirmation of Nicholas II dated 1061, contained specific mention of the disputed holding of Lebraha in Alsace, supposedly granted in Carolingian
times by Abbot Fulrad, but nothing more.[41]

Apparently satisfied with these efforts, the monks of Saint-Denis
did not pursue any more confirmations in the latter half of the eleventh
century. They received their next confirmations in 1102 and 1119, from
Pascal II and Calixtus II, which again contained only general confirmations of their possessions and stressed their exemption.[42] From the
Calixtus II confirmation of 1119, it is clear that the monks were still

bringing prior confirmations to papal attention, since the document referred directly to both the pseudo-bulls of Stephen and Zachary in the *Privilegia* as well as the authentic acts of Leo and Alexander II establishing the *libertas* of the monks. It was not until 1122 that Saint-Denis received an incremental confirmation, which listed only the church of Cergy, given by Louis VI.[43] In 1129 and 1130, Saint-Denis gained final papal approval of control over the nunnery of Argenteuil.[44] Soon thereafter, in 1131, the monks sought another charter, an incremental confirmation with an *enumeratio* of five holdings newly acquired by Abbot Suger around Metz, six places in the bishopric of Orléans, Argenteuil, the county of Vexin, and the town of Saint-Denis.[45] Finally, in 1148, the monks obtained an explicit confirmation, joining the 1131 list with twenty-one other holdings in France and England, beginning a series of similar confirmations thereafter.[46] Despite preservation and extremely elaborate invention of documents in the mid-eleventh century, the monks of Saint-Denis did not seek an explicit confirmation of their lands until the mid-twelfth century. Earlier monks directed their energies toward obtaining an exemption, however between 1119 and 1148, the motives of the monks had shifted.

At Saint-Vaast, the surviving papal confirmations provide more difficult evidence of the written comprehension of the domains. The first papal confirmation granted after 1000 bears a date of 1021.[47] This document was altered subsequently, though the beginning and end were left intact, which suggests that the known copies came from a genuine confirmation of 1021 with an interpolated middle section, no earlier than the second half of the eleventh century.[48] Though the monks of Saint-Vaast had been in the midst of Abbo's and Cluny's attempts to gain an exemption, their initial failure and a lack of further evidence leave the content of the original a matter for speculation. The doctored version, however, contained interpolated clauses intended to establish possession of specific holdings, including a list of fifteen places with considerable detail about mills, which it claimed had been given for the monks' use. These clauses were almost certainly written by someone familiar with the language of Carolingian charters establishing the *mensa conventualis*, since it listed lands allocated to various monastic needs in similar ways.[49] Several of the mills were the subject of mid-twelfth-century disputes, suggesting that the interpolator may have been working at that time.[50] The only other early confirmation was dated 1024, though it was a twelfth-century forgery. This charter was forged sometime around 1109, at the moment Saint-Vaast was reformed from Cluny, in order to support the independence of a monastic priory at Haspres.[51] It also contained a list of fifty-five places held by the monks, a remarkable set of written claims.[52] Had the monks been keeping track all along?

Authentic confirmations dating from the early twelfth century also show increasing specificity in enumeration, especially of altars and churches controlled by the monks of Saint-Vaast. A confirmation of the rights and possessions of the monastery by Pascal II in 1102, which granted an exemption, also contained a list of forty-five altars.[53] Disputes between the monks and the new cathedral chapter at Arras generated a flurry of papal documents in the second decade of the twelfth century, at least two with limited but specific lists of possessions in 1112 and 1119.[54] By 1135, the monks were careful to obtain a confirmation of their exemption from Innocent II (citing their pseudo-Vindicien charter written in the 990s as well as the earlier confirmation of Pascal), which relisted their altars and added three of their priories, Haspres, Berclau, and Gorres.[55] This confirmation not only shows that the monks were taking older confirmations to the pope, but also included the new introductory phrase, indicating perhaps some doubt in the papal chancery about the monks' claims. The exact same lists were reconfirmed by Eugenius III in 1153.[56] By 1164, however, papal confirmations began to include more detailed lists of holdings in addition to the now standard lists of altars, some thirty-seven holdings in all.[57] The process culminated in the lengthy bull of 1170, which confirmed churches, landholdings, tolls, privileges, and whatever else the monks could think to include.[58] Both confirmations included reference to a spate of earlier charters, including the pseudo-Vindicien and the false bull of Stephen adopted by Abbo of Fleury, as well as the authentic confirmations of Pascal II, Innocent II, and Eugenius III. Since the beginning of the twelfth century, the monks at Saint-Vaast had sought out confirmations that included enumerations. By the third quarter of the century they had obtained explicit confirmations that exceeded the level of detail present in confirmations at either Saint-Germain or Saint-Denis.

No papal confirmations for the monastery of Saint-Père survive before 1106. Nevertheless, the confirmation charter of 1106 granted the monks there papal protection and affirmed a limited list of sixteen possessions, including six altars granted by Bishop Ivo of Chartres and six prebends granted by the tenth-century patron, Bishop Rainfred.[59]

It also included a variation of the increasingly standard introductory phrase, "in quibus hec propriis visa sunt nominibus annotanda." Furthermore, the confirmation contained no reference to any prior papal document or any document besides episcopal charters. Such lists (or the charters that contained them) were almost certainly prepared at the monastery first and then taken to Rome. The monks were taking advantage of what records they had to secure a papal confirmation, which were few if the description in Paul's *gesta* of the fire of 1078 was accurate. Paul himself had made some lists of possessions, but while more exact about the boundaries of holdings, they did not cover a greater number of places (see below). However, in a papal confirmation of 1127, the monks' list had become more extensive, fifty-six churches in all, probably encompassing most or all of what they controlled.[60] It was in the intervening period (1106–26) that the brothers must have been working more actively on their own behalf.

The process of petitioning the pope had been the same for most monks, who provided their own lists or dossiers for confirmation. The petitioning process already had a long history in 1100: the monks of Saint-Denis took an elaborate dossier to Rome in 1065 and the monks of Cluny had done so in 998. The reformed papacy encouraged such expansion of its influence.[61] Although papal documents in the late eleventh and twelfth century included a *petitio* as a matter of course, formal similarities should not obscure important differences in the content of monastic requests. Local circumstances at each monastery caused monks to take more specific lists of possessions to the popes for confirmation. Variation in the chronology of incremental and explicit confirmations reinforces this point. Monks in different locations faced different challenges and, consequently, the chronology of explicit papal confirmations varied from monastery to monastery. The final transition from incremental to very explicit confirmations can be dated for each of the monasteries roughly as follows: Saint-Bertin, 1095–1139; Saint-Denis, 1122–48; Saint-Germain-des-Prés, 1122–76; Saint-Père-de-Chartres, 1106–27; Saint-Vaast, 1102–64 (see Table 2.1). Moreover, the content of explicit confirmations also varied considerably. Some monasteries wanted confirmations that listed churches, others specified mills, still others included *villae* or town boundaries. Different groups of monks had different priorities.

The chronology of papal confirmations offers a rough guide to changing monastic perceptions of their landed patrimony and the use of writing to express them. In particular, the date of the first explicit confirmation at each monastery suggests a time before which the monks had prepared a detailed list of holdings to take to the pope. While these lists were usually a collection of names of churches and villages, they sometimes included more elaborate descriptions of rights and properties, as at Saint-Vaast in 1170. However, these lists of possessions for confirmations were not administrative instruments, such as surveys, even though they may have had a territorial organizing principle, such as the *pagus* or, increasingly, the diocese. Furthermore, these confirmations did not represent the real state of the patrimony, but rather what the monks wished it to be, an idealized patrimony. The claims of the monks of Saint-Denis to the nunnery of Argenteuil in 1129 were just as invented as those of the monks of Saint-Vaast for the independence of the priory of Haspres in 1109. Nevertheless, even forged papal confirmations that contain lists of holdings demonstrate that monks had the capacity to write down patrimonial claims, as well as some appreciation of the importance of doing so. Although early monastic petitions were principally motivated by desire for an exemption or *libertas*, changes in the descriptive content of confirmations signal a movement toward a territorial comprehension of land expressed in writing. It remains to discover exactly when, how, and why this change took place.

Local Confirmations and the Chronology of Change

Although papal confirmations suggest a movement toward written description of land in the twelfth century, greater precision is possible. Royal, episcopal, and comital confirmations help to date changes in the written perception of the patrimony more accurately by filling in the (sometimes lengthy) gaps between papal confirmations. While these other confirmations may offer a better opportunity to understand the real as opposed to the ideal patrimony, they are less certain evidence of the monastic mentality, since they were the joint products of monastic intentions and of authorities who were more familiar with local disputes. The king, the count, and especially the diocesan bishop had a much greater stake in local monastic affairs than the pope. Granting an exemption from regular jurisdiction to a monastery could be of some benefit to a pope, but it could ruin a bishop. Local authorities could be enemies as well as allies. Consequently, a monastery received royal, comital, or episcopal confirmations depending on its location, importance, and local politics. Even so, it is still possible to find evidence of changing perceptions of the patrimony in these confirmations by distinguishing those which offer extensive and detailed lists of holdings from those which do not. Monks still sought to have extensive lists of lands included in these confirmations, although the authorities involved might be less inclined to confirm them and harder to fool. In consequence, these charters allow the historian to identify more precisely the time when specific descriptions of holdings became desired or required at each monastery.

Episcopal and comital confirmations corroborate the early parallel development of detailed enumerations in papal confirmations at Saint-Bertin. The confirmations granted by the diocesan bishop, the bishop of Thérouanne, moved from general confirmations of possessions toward increasingly specific confirmations at the same time papal confirmations became more exact. In 1040, a general confirmation was issued which contained no names of holdings.[62] The next confirmation, in 1075, named three altars specifically.[63] By 1097, just after the confirmations of Urban II, a confirmation of the bishop of Thérouanne listed twenty churches in the diocese belonging to Saint-Bertin, the same churches in the same order listed in the pope's confirmation.[64] In this case, the bishop's list was derived from the prior papal confirmation. This trend toward explicit listing of possessions in the bishops' confirmations ceased at the end of the eleventh century, as Saint-Bertin was increasingly removed from diocesan jurisdiction and became subordinate to Cluny as part of an attempted reform in 1099.[65] As a result, the twelfth-century monks sought episcopal reconfirmations only for possessions lying outside the diocese. For example, in 1125 the monks obtained a reconfirmation from the bishop of Tournai of the liberty of four churches in his diocese, which had been previously confirmed to the monks by Pascal II in 1119.[66] The monks were using their papal confirmations to obtain more explicit local episcopal confirmations. Although clearly derivative, these early episcopal confirmations show that concern with listing lands at Saint-Bertin began around the turn of the twelfth century.

Confirmations granted by the counts of Flanders to Saint-Bertin provide more revealing, if more complex evidence. Many early comital documents concerned the possession of the *villa* of Arques, which the count and the monastery had disputed since the mid-eleventh century.

The detail in these confirmations was particular to Arques, and the controversy masks the existence of any general impetus toward more specific listings of possessions. The first two comital acts concerning Arques were granted in 1093 and 1119, the second much more detailed about the monks' rights than the first.[67] Evidence that the monks desired greater specificity than the count would provide in 1093 can be found in a forgery perpetrated by the monks and dated 1102. Apparently dissatisfied with the 1093 charter, the monks of Saint-Bertin fabricated another which granted them the right to erect mills near Arques and enjoy their profits, probably between 1102 and the confirmation of 1119.[68] Although the monks did not acquire this right explicitly in 1119, they did obtain freedom from comital exactions at Arques and the customary rights of lordship there, which may have included the right to erect mills.

These deceptions at Saint-Bertin were only the beginning. A comital confirmation of 1147, which confirmed a fairly detailed list of holdings, was insufficient for the monks and they interpolated details of their own, especially concerning Arques, resulting in an explicit confirmation of many lands and dues.[69] By this time, the fabrications by Saint-Bertin monks had reached a level of detail which suggests they were thinking very carefully about their possessions. Still, the dispute over Arques had not ended, and by the latter half of the century the monks felt compelled to forge two charters, supposedly from 1056 and 1093, to establish an even longer and more detailed history of possession.[70]

The altered and forged comital confirmations for Arques show the monks' desire to have more detailed descriptions of their holdings. Starting sometime between 1102 and 1119 and continuing with increasing ardor after 1147, the monks manufactured confirmations which a disinclined count would not produce. In the same period that episcopal and papal confirmations became more explicit in their lists of possessions, the monks created comital documents of increasing detail, a process they perfected toward mid-century. Thus, the evidence of papal, episcopal, and comital confirmations at Saint-Bertin points to changes in written comprehension of the patrimony beginning in the last decade of the eleventh century and into the first quarter of the twelfth century, a period nearly identical to the rule of Abbot Lambert (1095–1124). These efforts were rewarded slightly later, between 1125 and 1150, when the monks received increasingly explicit confirmations from all authorities.

While nonpapal confirmations of possessions were less abundant at the other four monasteries, they still provide crucial evidence for dating the shift to a written comprehension of the patrimony. At Saint-Vaast, episcopal and comital confirmations help clarify the evidence of papal confirmations just as they did at Saint-Bertin. In 1098, the new bishop of Arras confirmed the monks' possession of twenty churches in the diocese of Arras, naming each altar, and the same list was confirmed four years later in the papal exemption of 1102.[71] The division of the diocese of Cambrai-Arras into two bishoprics in 1093 certainly motivated the creation of a specific list of churches in the diocese of Arras. Soon thereafter, a dispute between the monks of Saint-Vaast and the canons of the new cathedral of Arras over the boundaries of the "old" and "new" town of Arras (occupied by the monks and canons respectively) was adjudicated by the bishop in 1112 at the pope's order. As a result, the pope confirmed the boundaries of possessions prepared by the bishop and monks, though the dispute would continue for many years.[72] These two lists represent the start of detailed enumerations of Saint-Vaast's possessions, though the close involvement of the bishop in confirmations ceased after this point, as Saint-Vaast underwent attempted reform from Cluny beginning in 1109. The altar list and the boundary description were combined in papal confirmations in 1135 and 1153, showing that once the bishop and monks had drawn up these lists, they were put to repeated use.[73]

A few other confirmations help clarify the monks of Saint-Vaast's ideas in the third quarter of the twelfth century. By the time an explicit list of the monks' possessions had been taken to the pope in 1164, episcopal confirmations for Saint-Vaast, even those from other dioceses, were extremely precise. For example, the bishop of Cambrai's confirmation before 1167 of the monks' possessions at the priory of Haspres (the subject of dispute during the reform of 1109) enumerated all the dependent churches and tithes of that priory.[74]

Evidence of comital acts offers little help at Saint-Vaast, since no comital confirmations of landholdings survive from this period. However, disputes with the count of Flanders over the tolls of Arras and the monks' exemption from them, beginning around 1148, indicate that the monks took measures to define their economic privileges more precisely at that time.[75] Although movement toward comprehension of the lands in written form began in the early twelfth century, the consolidation of these various partial lists of possessions began between 1135 and 1153 and culminated with the papal confirmations of 1164 and 1170 obtained under the guidance of Abbot Martin (1155–1184).

For the monasteries of Saint-Denis and Saint-Germain, proximity to Paris made the kings of France the most important confirming authority. At Saint-Denis, the monks sought out royal confirmations in the eleventh century in the same fashion they sought out papal confirmations: using forgery. Just as they had fabricated papal documents in a dossier to gain Alexander II's exemption in 1065, they fabricated royal documents to obtain a confirmation from Philip I in 1068.[76] Once they had obtained this general confirmation (and relations with Philip I soured), the monks did not receive further confirmations until the twelfth century. In 1144, the monks received from Louis VII an explicit reconfirmation of their possessions and rights in and around the town of Saint-Denis, just a few years before the explicit papal confirmation of 1148, a pancarte summarizing the Saint-Denis claims.[77] The one was preparation for the other, since, unlike other monasteries, Saint-Denis had a more willing ally in the king than the pope. But these two confirmations were the end, rather than the beginning, of the reshaping of the patrimony undertaken by Abbot Suger (with the assistance of Louis VI) during his abbacy (1122–51). Although Louis VI only confirmed particular acquisitions for Saint-Denis, the volume and frequency of these acts indicates the close relationship of king and abbot: Louis's chancery issued at least nineteen acts for Saint-Denis during his twenty-seven-year reign.[78] Abbot Suger played a significant role in shaping these charters. In 1122, for example, the new abbot obtained a reconfirmation of the grants Louis VI had made in the previous decade, including the rights to the markets at Saint-Denis (within specified geographical boundaries), the church of Cergy, the vines at Rueil, and freedom from tolls.[79] In 1124, in an act almost certainly composed by Suger himself, the king took up the oriflamme banner from the altar of Saint-Denis (and with it the county of Vexin from the Saint), while simultaneously granting the monastery control over the fair of Lendit.[80] The language of these grants was later repeated in the papal confirmation of 1131.[81] Louis VI and Suger worked virtually hand in glove to reshape the domains of Saint-Denis until Louis's death in 1137.[82] This elaborate reshaping was then recorded and fixed in the royal and papal confirmations of 1144 and 1148 during the latter phases of Suger's rule, after the king's death.

In contrast to Saint-Denis, the monastery of Saint-Germain is remarkable for its paucity of royal confirmations. Despite (or perhaps because of) royal tutelage, the monastery received very few acts from kings in the eleventh century and virtually none at all from the 1070s until the reign of Louis VII (1137–80).[83] Indeed, no general confirmation of lands and privileges was issued before the reign of Philip Augustus. Just as the pursuit of explicit papal confirmations was retarded at Saint-Germain, so were other types of explicit confirmations. Louis VII confined himself to issuing charters concerning particular disputes, nine in total, all granted after 1157.[84] Episcopal charters, also concerned with individual cases, show a similar gap, with only one issued between 1100 and 1150.[85] However, between 1150 and 1176, the monks obtained at least four episcopal confirmations of individual holdings.[86] Many of the holdings or churches mentioned in these royal and episcopal charters later appeared in the explicit papal confirmation of 1176.[87] The appearance of these confirmations in the third quarter of the twelfth century provides additional evidence of a new desire to list possessions before 1176, late in the time of Abbot Hugh V (1162–82).

Popes and kings paid even less attention to the small monastery of Saint-Père-de-Chartres than they did to Saint-Germain. It was the bishops of Chartres who refounded and sustained Saint-Père. Their confirmations provided the documentary security which the monks sought. In the late eleventh century, the monks of Saint-Père received a few incremental episcopal confirmations of their holdings, either of individual churches, as in 1084, or small groups of holdings, such as the confirmation in 1093 of their six prebends.[88] Although the monks only received confirmation of a single holding from Louis VI in 1115, they received an explicit confirmation of thirty-seven of their diocesan possessions from the bishop of Chartres in 1126.[89] The bishop even issued a second confirmation of three newly acquired churches on the same day.[90] The episcopal confirmations of 1126 thus prepared the way for the explicit papal confirmation of the next year, which incorporated all forty holdings in its *enumeratio*.[91] Like Suger and the monks of Saint-Germain, the monks of Saint-Père laid the groundwork for papal confirmations by acquiring prior local confirmations in the years after 1100. For the first time since their tenth-century refoundation, the monks at Saint-Père began acquiring papal and royal documents. The crucial period of activity for Saint-Père was during the first quarter of the twelfth century, the abbacy of William (1101–29).

The chronology of change derived from royal, episcopal, and comital confirmations shows that attempts to list holdings more explicitly did not occur at the same time at every monastery. Monks at Saint-Bertin and Saint-Père were already seeking explicit confirmations in the first quarter of the twelfth century, when the monks of Saint-Germain were only seeking general confirmations. Monks at Saint-Denis sought explicit confirmations in the second quarter of the twelfth century, those at Saint-Vaast in the third quarter, and those at Saint-Germain not until the last quarter of the century. This divergent chronology (and beneficiary redaction) suggests that local circumstance at each monastery, rather than general conditions (or changes in diplomatic practice), was the immediate cause of more explicit written comprehension of the patrimony during the twelfth century. However, a movement toward explicit listing of lands in confirmations took place at all five monasteries sometime in the twelfth century, which implies that common factors ultimately led monks to enumerate possessions. While proximate causes were different, the long-term influences were similar.

What particular circumstances contributed to an increasingly written comprehension of the patrimony at each monastery? At Saint-Père, the initial motivation for seeking out new, more explicit confirmations was similar to the reason Paul starting copying charters into a cartulary: the fire of 1078. The loss of some of the monastery's archives created an unstable situation. The monastery was left open to disputes or usurpations with little defense in the way of documents, a fact the scribe Paul recognized. His work was a direct response to this disaster, providing a means for the brothers to remain informed and vigilant: "It is necessary for all to know about the properties by means of which provisioning and clothing are administered to them, so that they may repel the ambition of sacrilegious men, which always terrifies simple men with disputes and threats in order to wrest something away from them."[92] The unfortunate fire, combined with the threat of ambitious men making claims, offered a perilous prospect, especially for such a small monastery. Such archival misfortune urgently demanded a response. So Paul set to his work, probably finishing around 1087, by which time he had copied and organized the monastery's documents into a *gesta abbatum* of sorts.[93] The monks were thus poised to seek out more explicit confirmations, beginning with their bishop and proceeding to Rome.

At Saint-Bertin, at least two factors were important. The continuing struggle with the counts of Flanders over Arques, beginning as early as 1093, certainly encouraged the monks to define their rights and possessions more closely. Another crucial element was religious reform, or the threat of it, from outside the monastery. After Abbot Lambert had tried to give the care of Saint-Bertin to Cluny in 1099, reform of the convent (by importation of Cluniac brothers) proceeded in 1101.[94] The monastery was then split by a dispute over independence. Even though Pope Pascal II's bull of 1107 did not fully resolve the question, it did affirm the rights of the brothers with a specific confirmation of possessions. The specificity of this confirmation may have been prompted by the effort to resist Cluniac control. As mentioned above, some of the more recalcitrant monks were trying to resist reform at the priory of Haspres before 1109, fabricating older confirmations using the new formulas of the papal chancery. Although Pascal II considered making Saint-Bertin a dependent monastery of Cluny in 1109, Abbot Lambert had changed sides and in 1112 was already agitating, with the aid of the bishop of Thérouanne, for the monks' freedom to choose their own abbot.[95] By 1116, although Lambert was ordered by the pope to obey Abbot Hugh of Cluny in matters of discipline, the general independence of Saint-Bertin was confirmed.[96]

Saint-Bertin's drive to create a written description of its patrimony was undoubtedly influenced by inconsistent papal policy. After Lambert's death, Honorius II once again gave the Abbot of Cluny, Peter the Venerable, the care of Saint-Bertin in 1125, though he forbade him to install his own abbot.[97] At the same time, the pope ordered the monks of Saint-Bertin to obey Peter.[98] In 1132, Innocent II apparently restored the total independence of Saint-Bertin, following the election of Abbot Simon.[99] But Simon was deposed by the pope in 1136 when the abbots of Cluny once again gained the upper hand.[100] Finally, in 1139, the pope restored the independence of the monastery, after forty years of contradictory decisions, in a document that included an explicit confirmation of possessions based on earlier lists.[101] During this time, the use of the monastery's estates was a pressing issue, since the ostensible purpose of the reform was to change the monks' lifestyle, including their personal control of estates.[102] Furthermore, the monks had been insistent on the inviolability of the *mensa conventualis* as recently as 1075 and had a fierce tradition of asserting their claims, inherited from Folquin's time.[103] Such controversy would have encouraged the monks to protect their patrimony carefully.

Similar influences can be detected behind the increasingly written

comprehension of the patrimony in other monasteries. During the early
years of his abbacy, Suger chose to reform the lifestyle of his brethren
at Saint-Denis. Evidence for this reform is sparse, though some believe
it was prompted by Cistercian criticisms after 1123, specifically those
of Bernard of Clairvaux.[104] Whatever the reason, this reform began in
the 1120s and continued throughout Suger's abbacy.[105] Although his
control of the monastery was never as severely challenged as Lambert's
was, pressure for reform may have moved Suger's thinking toward
greater strictness and discipline. This reforming spirit would guide him
in later endeavors to improve the patrimony. It was reform from within,
not from outside, which was the crucial factor at Saint-Denis. At Saint-
Vaast, it was the nature of the monks' possessions and rights which
encouraged increasingly careful consideration of the patrimony. Pos-
sessing extensive economic rights within Arras, a rapidly growing city,
the monks of Saint-Vaast were constantly confronted with competing
claims, sometimes by the counts of Flanders but more often by the
canons of the new cathedral at Arras. The continuing disputes with the
canons over the boundaries of the "new" and "old" town promoted
greater definition of the monks' possessions and privileges. At Saint-
Germain, several of these elements—sudden change, external or internal
reform, and the challenge of competing lordships—may have played a
role, though no single cause is easily discerned.

The different local circumstances which led monks to an increasingly written comprehension of their patrimony affected the expression
of that understanding. At Saint-Père, when disaster struck and required
a quick response, Paul embarked on a project which was a variation on
the traditional *gesta abbatum*. Other monks faced gradual challenges and
responded more slowly, building up a more explicit store of documents
over time as a repetition of the same problems prodded them into
action, as was done at Saint-Bertin. Still others undertook new writing
projects as a result of considered planning, usually led by a forceful
abbot, such as Suger. All the written responses represented departures
from previous thinking, though some were more radical than others.
Everywhere, the ideas lying behind traditional patrimonial management
were changing, as an increasing consciousness of insufficiencies in older
arrangements took hold. Now that the timing and some of the political,
economic, and religious reasons behind this shift have been discovered,
the next step is to determine the strength and effectiveness of the written response.

The Production of Codices and Cartularies

One way to find signs of a managerial or an administrative mentality is to examine the rise of new methods of organizing written records. The organization of records is often valuable evidence of the purpose or intention of the organizer. In the period between 900 and 1100, a common means of organizing became the pancarte, which grouped several related charters in a single text. The extensive use of the pancarte shows that monastic reconsideration of written records was continual. Pancartes could contain reminders, record later modification of acts, or group acts for convenience. Thus, pancartes were a modest way to collect and organize charters.[106] In the period after 1000, the great new means of organizing archival documents was the codex. Although dorsal notes on early surviving originals show that charters had been organized in various ways before 1000—in boxes, in cubbyholes, in bundles or in rolls—and would continue to be thereafter, copying charters in books became a prominent new means of organization.[107] As seen in Chapter 1, Abbo of Fleury's campaign for exemptions also promoted the widespread adoption of the ad hoc dossier for particular causes around the millennium, a practice foreshadowed perhaps by Gundbert's dossier in the ninth century. Eventually, charters concerning land began to be grouped in codices in various ways. The production of these books offers another way to investigate monks' written comprehension of their land.

In the late eleventh and twelfth centuries there was an explosion of book production in northern French monasteries. Regardless of how originals had been ordered, the book offered a new way to organize charters for different ends. The earliest efforts incorporated charter copies in historical and hagiographic narratives, as happened at Saint-Bertin in the mid-tenth century. Eventually, a new form of book composed predominantly of charter copies, the cartulary, became widespread. Georges Declercq counted at least thirty-one such codices in Western Francia before 1100, most from monastic institutions in the second half of the eleventh century.[108] Various explanations have been given for this turn to codification of archives in France in the eleventh century. Observing that the rise of cartularies occurred first in Eastern Francia during the ninth century, Patrick Geary attributed their rise to the imposition of Carolingian power in that region. For Western Francia, he argued that their development was retarded by the practice of keeping originals in archives, but that "East and West, cartularies and

Traditionsbücher were reborn in the tenth and eleventh centuries as part of the concern for reforming the past in light of present needs."[109] Michel Parisse posited an alternative explanation for the gap between East and West, attributing it to differences in monastic estates: in the East monks had to keep track of large numbers of private charters for hundreds of small pieces of land, whereas western monks' lands were great estates unified by ninth-century reform. By the late tenth century, however, the decline of the Carolingian estate system left western monks faced with similar conditions and they had to keep track of many smaller holdings.[110] In contrast, Georges Declercq argued that a shift in the status of documents explained the difference of East and West, especially the persistence of the probative value of the private charter in France. He connected the rise of cartularies (and other new written forms of codification) with the simultaneous decline of older charter practices and the rise of beneficiary redaction, which empowered monks to adopt new ways of organizing writing.[111]

Most likely, it was a combination of these various factors with local circumstances that led to increasing use of the codex to organize charters in late eleventh-century French monasteries. The goal of traditional patrimonial management was to assure a fixed and steady supply for the monks and, as a result, the overwhelming impulse was to preserve and protect the stability of the patrimony. Consequently, authoritative confirmations initially had the highest priority for abbots and monks, who resisted transactions which reduced or altered their landholdings. Yet there were events significant enough to jolt the monks out of the stable routines of traditional estate management, such as reform, new local competition for land, and natural disaster. Combined with the pressure of seigneurial disruption, the rise of small donations, and changes in documentary practice, such events threatened stability severely enough that abbots and monks strove to achieve a different written comprehension of their patrimony. Thus, while there were common parameters governing the writing of cartularies in northern France, the timing and nature of their production varied from monastery to monastery.[112] My analysis of confirmations indicated that changes in the written comprehension of land occurred at different times at each monastery. Significantly, new codices or cartularies were also drawn up around the same time at these monasteries. Reviewing the circumstances surrounding the production of codices at each of the five monasteries reveals the important role played by abbots in the archival changes taking place.

The evidence from confirmations at Saint-Bertin points to the abbacy of Lambert (1095–1124) as the time when concern grew about creating more explicit written descriptions of the landed patrimony. Soon after he became abbot in 1095, Lambert encouraged his young student, Simon, to begin a *gesta* modeled on the earlier work of Folquin, which also would incorporate charters from the archives. Simon probably continued working on his task until 1123, when Abbot Lambert fell ill and became paralyzed.[113] By this time, Simon had finished his labors on the four abbots before Lambert, covering the years 1021–94, a work later incorporated as the first book of a combined *gesta abbatum* by his anonymous continuators.[114] After 1123, Simon became involved in the running of the monastery; in 1127, he became abbot of Auchy and subsequently abbot of Saint-Bertin itself in 1131. Simon was forced to retire from the abbacy because of the influence of Cluny in 1136.[115] In residence at Ghent from 1137, Simon was able to spend his twilight years composing a *gesta* of Lambert, in which he related the abbacy of Lambert in detail and his successors until 1145, just three years before Simon's own death.[116] This second work was a true memorial for Simon's teacher, but, unfortunately, humility caused Simon to relate virtually nothing about his own rule. Thus codex production and the quest for explicit confirmations proceeded at the same time.

At Saint-Vaast, evidence of land description in confirmations points to the third quarter of the twelfth century and the time of Abbot Martin (1155–84) as most significant. In the latter part of Martin's abbacy, the monk Guimann began to compose his massive cartulary. The career path of Guimann can be found in the necrology of Saint-Vaast: he became a priest by 1160; in 1175 he became cellarer, in charge of the monks' provisioning; later he was given two important provostships; and he died in 1192.[117] Guimann began writing his cartulary in 1170, as he indicated in his dedication to Abbot Martin.[118] Since the plan he announced in the prologue remained incomplete, Guimann may well have continued to write until his death in 1192. As cellarer, scribe, and right-hand man of Abbot Martin, Guimann was intimately familiar with the actions of Martin and played a major role in his move toward actively administering the patrimony. His cartulary was part of Martin's plans.

Abbatial action and the making of a cartulary were linked in other monasteries. At Saint-Germain, a connection between cartulary writing, the quest for explicit confirmations, and abbatial initiative can be firmly established. The earliest cartulary of Saint-Germain, known to French historians as the "cartulaire + + +" or "cartulary of three crosses" because of the design of its fifteenth-century binding, was begun in the late twelfth century, in the abbacy of Hugh V (1162–82), and continued after his death. A collection of charters with few narrative elements, the cartulary of three crosses was produced by unknown authors and reworked several times, probably in the early thirteenth century, prior to the production of subsequent cartularies. Nevertheless, the clustering of many acts before Hugh V's death in 1182 implies that much of the cartulary was composed late in his rule, around the same time Hugh obtained the monastery's first explicit papal confirmation in 1176.[119] All indicators point to a refurbishing of the *scriptorium* during Hugh V's rule.

At Saint-Père-de-Chartres, the composition of a codex preceded the quest for more explicit confirmations. The monk Paul began his work (a *gesta abbatum*) prompted by the fire in 1078, which destroyed virtually all the monastery's archives except two rolls and a handful of charters.[120] Paul continued to labor until the eighth year of Abbot Eustache, 1087. Thereafter, he or anonymous continuators added to his initial work until the beginning of the twelfth century.[121] The early composition of this book may help explain why the monks could take detailed lists of possessions to the pope, when they sought out papal confirmations in 1106 and 1127. The papal confirmation of 1106, for instance, mentioned the prebends Bishop Rainfred had allocated to the monks in his charter of 954, which Paul had copied in the second book of his *gesta*.[122] Paul and his brothers had already embarked on reconstructing and ordering their archives and had largely finished by 1100. The way had already been prepared for more active abbots, such as William (1101–29) and Udo (1130–50).

The monastery of Saint-Denis produced no cartulary in the time of Abbot Suger (1120–51), when its confirmations became more descriptive. In the eleventh century, the monks had produced the fraudulent dossier, the *Privilegia ecclesiae Sancti Dionysii*, but once they had achieved their desired end, royal and papal confirmations of their immunity and their exemption, they seem to have lost interest in creating codices of charters. Although no cartulary was compiled at Saint-Denis under Suger, it would be absurd to insist that this lack demonstrated the failure of the monastery to produce a codex with an administrative end. Saint-Denis had at least one book that could serve this function: Suger's own *gesta*.[123]

Suger's writings on his own deeds represent the epitome of new administrative thinking. Suger began composing his work in 1145, immediately after his acquisition of a specific royal confirmation in 1144 and just prior to obtaining explicit papal confirmation of the monastery's possessions in 1148.[124] Indeed, the connection between the texts has been noticed. Giles Constable identified at least six of the newly acquired possessions described in Suger's work among the twenty-two possessions listed in the confirmation of 1148.[125] The two documents, together with Louis VII's confirmation of 1144, formed the capstone of Suger's efforts to reshape the patrimony. More important, the form and content of Suger's book demonstrated a strong administrative bent in the abbot, who reformed the monks, repossessed lands, and renovated the church of Saint-Denis with surprising vigor. His deeds show a new administrative mentality at work.

Cartularies as Organizing Tools

At Saint-Denis the influence of an administrative mentality in Suger's writing was obvious. But how influential was the rise of administrative thinking at other monasteries? The organizational schemes of twelfth-century cartularies sometimes reveal the influence of territorial and administrative thinking as it took hold. The goals of commemoration and preservation continued to pervade all cartularies, but in the twelfth century new ends are also evident. The arrangement of charters in cartularies—the pattern used to put the book together—provides good evidence of the purposes of the monks who constructed them. In twelfth-century cartularies, the order and arrangement of charters shows whether monks still perceived their patrimony traditionally (and hence were copying charters because of concerns about the inviolate nature of their estates or social relations to donors), or whether they were trying to administer their lands (copying charters to aid in that process). Sometimes these cartularies demonstrate that the lands of the patrimony were understood as part of a broader notion of the saint's possessions, which included movables, books, and even relics. The grouping of documents by estates, the notation of changes in landholding since a charter was written, or even the inclusion of surveys, ancient or contemporary, could all indicate administrative concerns.

Cartularies (or codices with charters in them) had many purposes because they evolved from older forms of books. The purposes of early composite works included the historical, commemorative, and the polemical, or even just simple preservation. However, these works are significant because their organization reflects monastic thinking about the value and use of the documents they contained. There are three main patterns of organization in monastic cartularies in the eleventh and twelfth centuries. The first is organization by chronology: cartularies that place charters in order based on when they were composed. The influence of historical and literary genres on such works was substantial and has already been discussed in Chapter 1. The most important influence was the *gesta abbatum*, like that of Folquin, which grouped charters according to the rule of various abbots and incorporated them to a greater or lesser degree in a narrative context. Organizing by date or reign of kings was also influential, as in annals or chronicles, like that of Hariulf of Saint-Riquier. The second pattern was organization by grantor. The most common grantor-based pattern was to begin with papal documents, then royal diplomas, and then alternate between ecclesiastical and secular authorities of lesser rank. Cartularies organized by grantor were influenced by the dossier, popularized by Abbo of Fleury, and exemplified by the two halves of *Privilegia ecclesiae Sancti Dyonisii*, which gathered forged papal and royal charters to obtain authoritative confirmations. Both forms of organization could be and were used to defend the patrimony, and their construction was deliberate and purposeful. When they contain charters that have descriptions of land, such works allow the historian to see how the monastic view of the inviolate patrimony became more territorially explicit. On the other hand, neither form of organization was particularly helpful for managing land.

In the twelfth century, charter collections increasingly departed from the early forms, allowing the historian to see when the idea of the patrimony as fixed inviolate territory began to be influenced by a more managerial view. The third pattern was to organize charters by geography. These cartularies ordered charters based on the location of lands mentioned in the documents and could use a variety of schemes including by estate or by terrain (physical or sacred). Thus, the physical structure of these cartularies helps reveal how their organizers mentally constructed the space around them.

The organizational schemes of monastic cartularies provide valuable clues about changes in monastic thinking. An analysis of the cartularies produced at the five monasteries in northern France shows that some authors remained preoccupied with traditional concerns and others were more interested in administering their land. The books produced at Saint-Bertin and Saint-Père-de-Chartres were of the first type, organized by chronology. The cartulary at Saint-Germain-des-Prés was of the second type, organized by grantor. The works of Guimann of Saint-Vaast and Suger, however, were of the new type, organized by geography. Thus, the cartularies of the five monasteries represent a spectrum of monastic thought.

At Saint-Bertin, Simon consciously followed the model of Folquin (and the wishes of Abbot Lambert) in constructing his *gesta abbatum*. As a result, he organized more traditionally, by chronology. He used a similar alternation between narrative and charter copies, each being, as he aptly put it, "separate in one volume." In this way the charters, and later confirmations of them, served the purpose of averting controversy and assuring peace, as well as aiding memory and publicizing the good deeds of the previous abbots.[126] This work was part of a traditional defense and commemoration of the patrimony. Simon's original project, the *gesta* for the period 1021–95, must have mirrored Folquin's text even more closely than the surviving copy, which was cut down by Simon's continuators and became the first "book" of a rewritten *gesta*.[127] Fortuitously, the Bollandists preserved a description of the original *gesta* of Simon. Their description indicated that the manuscript originally consisted of thirty-eight chapters, followed by two "books of rents" that concerned estates of the monastery, containing details of rents and renders which vassals paid, and also a catalogue of the library of Saint-Bertin and a brief genealogy of French kings.[128] François Morand proved this manuscript existed, discovering in the later copy of the *gesta* a table of contents for the thirty-eight chapters.[129] Unfortunately, no copy of the two books of rents or the catalogue of the library survives. The fact that they once existed indicates that Simon was following Folquin closely, perhaps inspired by the form of Folquin's final section on *ministeria* and his copying of Gundbert's charters.[130] These lost books may have been intended to serve managerial instead of historical and commemorative purposes.

Simon's later work, the *gesta* of Lambert and his successors, had mixed purposes as well. This work grouped charters relevant to the abbots' rule at the front of the work and related events at the back.[131] It was a hybrid of cartulary and *gesta*. None was better suited to this task, for Simon had been Lambert's chief minion and later became abbot himself. Simon's writing expanded as his knowledge grew, for the second work, even though it lacked finishing touches, was 117 chapters long—nearly three times the length of the first. It was a virtual handbook of Lambert's rule. The scope of this work demonstrates that Simon had been influenced heavily by the rule of Lambert and wished to record his actions in detail.

Likewise, Paul and his continuators at Saint-Père organized their cartulary chronologically. This chronology was not strict, as in an annal, but rather a rough grouping of charters under the times of the bishops and abbots, like a *gesta abbatum*. Paul organized the first two books of his cartulary by this principle, under the deeds of Bishops Aganon and Rainfred. Paul even named the books the *liber hagani* and the *liber ragenfredi* in his prologue.[132] However, after the *liber ragenfredi*, the monk did not strictly organize by the rules of abbots, though the pattern was sufficiently strong to encourage Benjamin Guérard to edit (perhaps overzealously) the cartulary in accordance with this plan.[133] Paul was influenced by traditional concerns, by a desire both to preserve charters after the fire of 1078 and to incorporate them into a narrative of events that would preserve a history of the monastery. While the narrative sections of his work throw some light on the rule of early abbots, the form of his work was understandably more defensive than that of Simon of Saint-Bertin. The time in which the influence of an administrative mentality would be felt at Saint-Père had not yet come.

Evidence of traditional impulses can also be found in the form of the cartulary of Saint-Germain-des-Prés. Saint-Germain's cartulary of three crosses was organized by grantor. Containing no narrative at all, the cartulary arranged copies of charters by the status of the grantor— popes, kings, other lay lords, bishops and other ecclesiastics—and then miscellaneous acts. This structure was a variant on the more common pattern of popes, kings, bishops, counts, and others, alternating between ecclesiastical and secular authorities by rank.[134] It was, in essence, a massive dossier. This type of scheme provided quick reference to all the charters granted by a particular authority and would be especially useful when petitioning for new confirmations, as the monks did frequently. Such a codex was difficult to use in an administrative way, since it was hard to find charters relevant to particular lands within it. This hierarchical form arose from the obsession with defending the inviolacy of the extant patrimony. Given the severe challenges to their patrimony, such a written response was a useful strategy. This pattern broke down in the end sections of the cartulary, in which some documents were grouped by estate, suggesting that administrative thinking at Saint-Germain emerged later or was a weaker influence than traditional concerns.

Much stronger administrative influence on codex form is evident at Saint-Vaast. The monk Guimann had planned his cartulary in four sections: *de privilegiis et immunitatibus*; *de bonis mobilibus et immobilibus*; *de hostagiis*; and *de diversitate districtorum*.[135] Guimann completed the first three of these sections but only part of the fourth before his death in 1192. The very large cartulary was a hybrid of two different organizing schemes, by grantor (part one) and geography (parts two, three, and four). The first section, *de privilegiis et immunitatibus*, contained a series of papal, royal, comital, and episcopal charters confirming the rights and possessions of the monastery. It was a dossier, par excellence. The series began with the supposed exemption of Bishop Vindicien of Arras and concluded with the lengthy explicit confirmation of Alexander III from 1170, containing some thirty-seven confirmations in all.[136] Unfortunately these charters do not supply a continuous body of evidence for the monastery, since a large gap existed between the 1030s and 1100 and virtually all the early documents were forged. If this section were the only available part of the cartulary, it would demonstrate less influence of administrative thinking than the cartulary of three crosses does for Saint-Germain.

By contrast, sections two, three, and the lengthy though incomplete section four of Guimann's work were products of different concerns. These parts of the cartulary contained a description of the patrimony, which began with the holy relics of the church of Saint-Vaast and radiated outward: to the church building and its grounds, to houses in the city and the market, to suburban holdings and beyond to rural estates. Section two, *de bonis mobilibus et immobilibus*, described the "goods" of the church of Saint-Vaast and its buildings and possessions within the town of Arras.[137] The organization was not by chronology or grantor, but rather by geography. The size and detail of this section demonstrate both what Guimann's notion of "space" was and how meticulous he was in recording it. Guimann began inside the church itself, writing down long lists of relics lodged in the sanctuary, under the altar, or in reliquaries, consisting of literally hundreds of relics. In addition to the relics, he listed all the liturgical vessels, ornaments, robes, and even valuables left in the church as pledges "so that we will include everything."[138] Also listed in this section were the possessions of Saint-Vaast within the walls of the old *castrum*, in Arras-town where the monastery lay, which included two churches and various outbuildings.[139] In addition, Guimann included comital and abbatial charters explaining tolls and duties, as well as three detailed toll lists of his own. These toll lists functioned virtually as schedules, covering everything from taxes on moneylenders to duties on eggs, fowl, pigs, and cows, and even stall rents for the market.[140] He was extremely thorough, and for every possession or right which was granted, he provided both the charter and a corresponding enumeration of the exact details of arrangements he composed. Such a structure both justified the monks' rights and explained their practice. Intimately familiar with details of everyday transactions as cellarer, Guimann did not hesitate to record all that he knew.

Even more remarkable than the second section of Guimann's cartulary were the third and fourth, *de hostagiis* and *de diversitate districtorum*. The first part of *de hostagiis* described the ancient custom of *hostagia*, a rent-payment that all householders in Arras had to make to Saint-Vaast.[141] Although this section did contain a few charters granting control of specific buildings, the bulk of it comprised a massive survey of all *hostagia* collected by the monks. This survey enumerated all that was owed and how it was collected. A typical entry included the household from which the payment was collected, the officer of the monastery who collected it, and how much was collected. Guimann grouped these entries by areas within Arras, from which each monk made collections. The collection was clearly both systematic and thorough, beginning in the *castrum* and radiating outward around the town in a clockwise pattern.[142] The fourth section, *de diversite districtorum*, extended the geographic pattern of the third, attempting to provide all the lands of Saint-Vaast outside Arras with a copy of their charters and a description of their holdings.[143] By far the longest part of the manuscript, it began in the *suburbium* of Arras and radiated further outward. Presumably, Guimann had intended to treat the furthest holdings last.

An enormous amount of effort went into preparing the second, third, and fourth sections of the Saint-Vaast cartulary, probably requiring years of Guimann's life. The historical value of the text is great, despite its poor transmission in fifteenth- and sixteenth-century copies.[144] The organization of Guimann's cartulary provides the best illustration of what patrimony meant to twelfth-century monks at Arras. Guimann viewed the patrimony as a continuum, both spatial and conceptual, from the saint's relics to the revenues of distant estates. Sacred space and physical space were unified. The cartulary not only provides a basis for exploring his view of the patrimony of Saint-Vaast, but also demonstrates the rise of new, more administrative concerns alongside older ideas. Simply put, Guimann's work contained a comprehensive land and revenue survey, a lengthy and detailed written instrument of administration. The structure of the cartulary therefore reveals Guimann's perception of the domain as an economic resource, not just a traditional, fixed patrimony.

The work of Suger at Saint-Denis was also organized by space, but according to a different plan. The work had two parts: one which described the lands of the monastery and another which described the rebuilding of the church of Saint-Denis. In the first section, Suger treated the lands in an order based on estates. From Saint-Denis, the touchstone of his mental geography, Suger proceeded in a counter-clockwise fashion to describe nearby holdings to the east, Tremblay and Argenteuil with its holdings (ch. 2–3). Then, he treated the holdings of Saint-Denis in the near parts of the county of Vexin to the north (ch. 4–9). Next, he moved west of the Seine, to holdings clustered in the valley between the river and the forest of Yvelines (ch. 10–13). Moving from southwest back to east, Suger then described groups of holdings in Beauce (ch. 14–19), in Gâtinais (ch. 20–22), near Brie (ch. 23–24), near Meaux (ch. 27) and in Lorraine (ch. 28), and finally outward to northern holdings in further parts of the Vexin and Normandy (ch. 29–30), completing the spiral.[145] This list of holdings was far from complete and, for the most part, local.[146] After describing the estates, Suger proceeded to describe in detail his renovation of Saint-Denis, which was his overall goal. The church was the most important part of the patrimony and any spatial organization scheme would include it. Suger's geography, like Guimann's, was both sacred and mundane.

Written Instruments of Administration

Guimann's survey of the lands and revenues of Arras was not the only written instrument of administration in twelfth-century cartularies of northern France, although it may be the most impressive. Whether the form of a codex revealed a strong or weak influence of administrative thinking, certain documents within it could individually be considered written evidence of administration. These written instruments provide more direct access to the workings of monastic administration which confirmation charters and charter collections do not. Some of these documents were supplemental to the administrative process, such as memory aids in the form of lists of lands or fiefs, which could either serve as the basis of a nonadministrative document (e.g., an explicit confirmation) or for action. Others were integral to the actions carried out by monks, such as a survey. Surveys and surveying were not new, of course, and models from the Carolingian period did survive into the twelfth century, usually polyptychs or other documents inspired by them. As a result, both new and old documents, especially Carolingian fiscal documents that were recopied, can provide evidence of growing administrative concerns.

Typically, written instruments in twelfth-century cartularies list land or revenues in two different ways. They recorded either what a monastery ought to possess (usually called "prescriptive") or what it currently did possess (usually called "descriptive"). It is important to bear the distinction in mind because the nature of a document limits historical reconstruction of the monastic administration. Documents that enumerate what ought to be paid or possessed usually provide indirect access to administering, showing its goals. Such categories must be used with caution because descriptive documents, when no longer current, could become effectively static or prescriptive. By the eleventh century, Carolingian polyptychs were effectively static for monks, since they were by then fixed lists of what the *mensa conventualis* should be (or had been), regardless of how they had been used earlier. As argued in Chapter 1, surveying and reallocating lands usually accompanied the redaction of polyptychs in the ninth century; however, most of this process was difficult for eleventh-century monks to recover since few written traces of their composition survived. Documents containing such static lists were not practical instruments of administration, but records or reminders of its results. In series, these records can reveal changes in the patrimony to the historian, as confirmations sometimes can, but they offered only a crude instrument of administration to monks. Documents describing current conditions had more immediate practical uses. Therefore, surveys that described the current disposition of the patrimony (as Guimann's did) provide a better opportunity to study the administrative mind at work.

Both static and current descriptions of possessions had their uses. Guimann's list of *hostagia* gave immediate access to where, when, by whom, and from whom payments were gathered at Arras. Such a document offered the possibility of an accounting, holding someone accountable for revenues based on written records of payments. Accounting required both static (prescriptive) records and current (descriptive) records, since it was not one or the other which provided the crucial information, but rather the difference between the two. This was the genius of Guimann's section on *hostagia*: he provided both the charters, which established the right to collect and what should be paid, and a list of payments collected, which indicated what had been received. Together, they offered the possibility of finding what still needed collection, from whom, and who had not done the collecting, as well as bringing them to account.

What remains is to identify the existence of surveys and other written instruments of administration besides those of Saint-Vaast. The chronological boundaries already established indicate when to look for these documents in archives and codices. Of course, Suger's work on his administration of Saint-Denis is one source of information, although it reveals more about the abbot's attitudes and deeds than about his written instruments, since it does not contain surveys. Suger certainly took effective and extensive actions to augment the possessions of Saint-Denis, but did he ever survey the domains of Saint-Denis? One piece of evidence is a copy of a charter of Matthew le Bel from 1125, which lists his holdings and all those of his liege *milites*. Matthew listed his forty-one knights and their combined lands, some fifty-five holdings, including churches, tithes to mills, and other dues.[147] The level of detail probably exceeded any amount Matthew would have provided without Suger's prompting. Another example is that Suger claimed that he would append a list of castle guards from fiefs he had purchased at Toury in *De administratione*, though no trace of it exists.[148] Perhaps Suger had decided to survey the whole of the Saint-Denis domains, but no other trace of such a survey survives. It is equally possible that Suger simply requested the information he needed on an ad hoc basis, such as the list of knight service. If Suger had been as well informed about other lands of the monastery, it would help explain his success as recorded in *De administratione*. By the 1140s, Suger had a firm idea of both what he ought to receive and what he did receive, since he prided himself on the increment or improvement he had achieved at each estate.[149] Therefore, it seems likely that he employed various unknown written instruments to achieve his ends.

The contents of Guimann's cartulary and Suger's work illustrate the new administrative mentality, which became increasingly prevalent in the twelfth century. At other houses, the traces of written instruments are less dramatic but still significant. Enough documents survive to show that other monks and abbots also felt the spur to action. At Saint-Germain, which had had extensive written records of possessions in the Carolingian period, such as the polyptych of Irminon, no complete survey or administrative treatise has survived from the twelfth century. On the other hand, the monks made use of the polyptych during the eleventh century by writing supplemental notations on it. These include descriptions: an inventory of movables, notes on the customs of villages, a charter of donation, serf genealogies, and even a new *brevis* in the eleventh century written in Carolingian form, suggesting admiration for the old survey.[150] But by the time of Abbot Hugh V, other kinds of documents were clearly being used for administration. A number of documents, all current descriptions of holdings, had been composed by the second half of the twelfth century. These included handlists of current estates, descriptions of new acquisitions (such as the estate of Samoreau), and rents.[151] These documents were used in conjunction with the charters obtained from Louis VII, which confirmed the renunciation of various exactions or rights over land possessed by the monks.[152] Together they indicate a tendency toward territorial consolidation and perhaps also a nascent administrative mindset.

At Saint-Bertin and Saint-Père, the monasteries where a traditional patrimonial mentality held sway early in the twelfth century, the monks also reused and added to older written instruments. At both monasteries, descriptions from an earlier period were kept and copied into new codices. Simon of Saint-Bertin recopied all Folquin's work, including its Carolingian fiscal documents (the polyptych of Adalard, charters of Charles II, and Gundbert's dossier). Furthermore, inspired by Folquin's section on *ministeria*, Simon even went so far as to produce lists of rents, though they are now lost because Simon's successors did not recopy them in their more traditional *gesta*. He also commented on charters. Intending to create a single codex, the monks who copied Simon's work after his death in 1148 also copied Folquin's in its entirety (making convenient spurious additions at the end). They created a composite book, beginning with Folquin, followed by Simon's first work (which they edited), then the work of Simon's later years, and finally concluded with their own continuation.[153] These reworkings prove the continuing perceived utility of the older work for later monks. On the other hand, the anonymous twelfth-century monks were aiming at a history of the monastery, rather than creating handbooks for future abbots. They had a greater interest in presenting an ideal picture of patrimony. So, even though there is some evidence that written instruments of administration might have appeared under Simon at Saint-Bertin, the later monks did not preserve them. The compact arrangement of their estates and relatively stable possession, combined with the drive for independence from Cluny, may have made the creation of new administrative instruments less pressing. Preserving the older documents in a historical (and political) context was far more important at Saint-Bertin.

Following the fire of 1078, Paul of Saint-Père preserved whatever he could in his work. In so doing, he copied ancient surveys of the domains, even though they had no understandable connection to the domains he knew. Nevertheless, Paul was inspired by these documents, or rather their insufficiency, to create lists of his own. Adopting the practice of making narrative comments after charters, as Folquin had done and Simon did later, Paul produced lists of lands he knew the monks possessed. He placed these lists after all the oldest documents, effectively updating the documents for his readers and making their descriptions current. For example, after the foundation charter of Aganon, Paul described the location and extent of lands currently held by the monks, alterations since the time of Aganon, and gifts which had been added and by whom they had been given. Furthermore, Paul described these holdings in detail, including boundaries such as roads and area measurements. He followed a spatial pattern in his land lists, beginning with those possessions east of the river, then moving to the town itself, followed by the western side of the river, and then outlying possessions.[154] In another case, following the fragments of the alleged polyptych of the ancient canons, Paul proceeded to supplement what had been listed with his own description of the true extent of the monks' possessions.[155] These descriptions, including the names of *manses* and locations, were what he claimed to know from destroyed documents and from the monks of his time.[156] Each time he encountered an older list of possessions, he was reminded of its insufficiency and stimulated to produce a description which rectified it. Thus, Paul strove simultaneously to preserve older documents and yet to describe the domains as they were in his day. His actions may have been inspired by the commonplace defensive attitude about patrimony; however, his work of organizing and supplementing the archives also provided a strong base for future administrative efforts.

Conclusions

The obsession with the past and the desire to keep lands fixed and stable were the hallmarks of traditional patrimonial management. Changes were to be resisted or, at best, accepted when forced upon the monastery. As present concerns became more pressing because of disaster, reform, or changes in the local political landscape, monks began to perceive the importance of having descriptions of their lands. The rediscovery or reuse of static descriptions from the past, followed by a realization of their inadequacies in the face of continuing difficulties, led monks in the direction of current descriptions. Once they had both old and new documents, monks could compare what they should possess or receive with what they possessed or received in actuality. The difference between the ideal and real was thus brought into sharper focus. In addition to surveys, static and current descriptions in narrative form, handlists of holdings or acquisitions, and collections of annotated charters all aimed at providing a comprehension of this difference. Such written comprehension became more necessary as pressure on land mounted and the challenges of neighbors grew, as at Arras.

But understanding the difference between the ideal and the real domain and acting upon it were not the same thing. Monks had long had the ability to exchange, purchase, or even sell land to alter the income and composition of their domains. The psychological acceptance of change also had to occur. Once change was accepted as possible, even as useful, it became conceivable to view lands as a resource to improve upon rather than a fixed patrimony. Monks had long possessed the ability to administer, but in the twelfth century they found (or rediscovered) that they wanted to increasingly. As with so many innovations in the Middle Ages, changes in mindset usually proceeded under the guise of "reform" or "tradition," which made them easier for contemporaries to accept but harder for historians to recognize. Under this guise, the difference in the real and ideal could then be acted upon, as

Suger did at Saint-Denis by improving revenues or Hugh V of Saint-Germain may have done by repossessing old lands.

As abbots and monks began to alter their lands, the need for written comprehension of them increased since memory would no longer suffice as a means to comprehend the estates and collect their revenues. The charters solicited and the books produced at northern French monasteries indicate when the monks and abbots began becoming more interested in describing their current holdings. Annotating charters of transactions, making handlists, and arranging charters by spatial schemes all served this purpose. To aid themselves in their managerial tasks, the bolder abbots and monks created prospective documents or compilations of documents, intended to have a functional role in the new monastic administration. Unlike the charters which survive from the time of traditional patrimonial management, the written instruments produced by these administrators in the twelfth century provide an opportunity to study their plans, activities, and techniques at the ground level.

3

Ministering and Administering: Abbots as Catalysts of Change

THE EVIDENCE OF TWELFTH-CENTURY confirmations indicates a growing monastic concern to list and describe holdings more specifically. These descriptions of monastic patrimony suggest that monks were beginning to think about their lands in new ways. They also worked hard to copy and arrange charters in collections and books. The form of these books departed increasingly from older patterns, showing more interest in managerial matters. The twelfth-century cartulary served not just to preserve archives or commemorate deeds but also to inform readers about the monastic estates and, sometimes, to help manage them. Cartularies often show a growing concern with organizing records of land transactions, not just confirmations. Even if the structure of a cartulary did not obviously reflect managerial or administrative thinking, documents copied in it sometimes demonstrate a movement away from the traditional management and steps toward more dynamic use of the patrimony. Although an overall increase in literacy might explain this rise in written records, increasing variation in the kinds of documents also points to a new mentality at work.

As demonstrated in Chapter 1, the reasons to alter the patrimony before 1050 were primarily social or religious, not economic. In the earlier period, many transactions that altered estates were voluntary and designed to reinforce ties with neighbors. Other changes were forced on monks, either in the form of usurpations or uneven exchanges sought by putative protectors, such as the royal masters of Saint-Germain. At some monasteries, evidence of these changes is scarce. Among the few surviving charters and charter copies of Saint-Vaast there are only a handful of donations and confirmations between 1030 and 1090. Despite an aggressive campaign for an exemption in the mid-eleventh century, the charters of Saint-Denis reveal only a few donations and judgments defending the monks' possessions.[1] If any other kinds of documents existed, accident or the monks' process of selective remembering has left no trace. By contrast, twelfth-century monks compiled and kept cartularies more systematically, which protected archival resources. Cartulary production accompanied the trend toward more specific land description in confirmations and reinforced it by copying charters containing land transactions. These later monks had adopted new goals and used new schemes to write them down.

These new concerns became important at different monasteries at different times and seem to have been accompanied by attempts to manage more dynamically. Although not all communities changed their attitudes or practices, some monks moved toward actively administering their patrimonies. In particular, three changes were important and need to be examined in detail. The first change was viewing land as an economic resource, which required modifying earlier views about the patrimony as fixed and sacred. Once land was viewed economically, monks could exploit it more systematically. The second change was using writing to help manage and keep different kinds of records of all resources, not just land. More dynamic management required more dynamic archives. The third change was an altered working relationship of abbot and chapter. Abbots needed aid to manage resources, leading to increasing consultation with the monks. The prime movers in these changes were abbots, who combined their traditional role as minister to their brothers with the new role of administrator of the patrimony.

Monastic Land as an Economic Resource

Whatever its origin, land given to monks (or their saint) was usually regarded as belonging to them permanently. This view lay behind the aggressive defense of the patrimony in the eleventh century and was what made alienations and loss of monastic land so horrifying to monks of that time. Although lands belonged to a monastery forever in theory, monks could lease or temporarily give away land (by *donum in precaria*, for example). Despite such temporary grants, there was a strong tendency to insist on reacquisition of the land, or at least confirm ultimate monastic control over it, because of the religious or social importance of land. This pattern was particularly strong at Cluny, as Barbara Rosenwein observed, where land given to "Saint Peter" returned time and again to the monks' control.[2] The deliberate sale or permanent exchange of land was rare and, therefore, such acts offer particularly good examples of actions which had been given serious consideration and undertaken with a definite purpose.

Religious and political necessities remained extremely important in shaping monastic estates but they are not the whole story. Even though religion and power continued to shape monastic patrimonies, economic thinking began to have greater influence in the eleventh and twelfth centuries. In general terms, this makes sense because a tremendous economic boom took place in Europe in the eleventh and twelfth centuries. Population was growing, trade expanding, money was becoming more common—and people were becoming more interested in counting it.[3] The overlay of economic utility distinguished lands with important social or sacred meaning from others that could be permanently exchanged, altered, leased, or even sold to achieve economic ends.[4] The change in thinking was crucial, but this mode of thought and action had become so pervasive in the later Middle Ages that its importance has often been overlooked. Exploring the timing and extent of this movement toward using monastic land as an exploitable economic resource helps show changes in monastic mentality, changes which led to behavior which ultimately may be called administrative.

The most direct and surely the most copious sources of evidence are charters transferring land. The first question to consider is whether the number of monastic land transactions increased in the twelfth century. A simple count of land transactions appears to bear out this trend; however, an investigation of the volume of land transactions is clouded by two a priori evidentiary problems. First of all, an increased amount of copying, often in the form of more durable cartularies, assured greater survival of all charters starting in the late eleventh century. So, the apparent rise in charters could simply be a shift in recording practices rather than a real change in behavior. Second, selective remembering during the period before 1100 emphasized documents such as confirmations, which were not transactional. Thus, the increased volume of transactional charters may be an illusion of documentary survival.

On the other hand, there are some important patterns in charter survivals. Laurent Morelle observed the rising importance of the abbatial charter, which appears to be issued in greater numbers and preserved with greater zeal starting already in the eleventh century.[5] Interestingly, acts issued by abbots who sought more explicit confirmations of land seem to survive at a higher rate than they did earlier. For example, at Saint-Vaast, only sixteen abbatial acts survive for the seventy-nine year period of the abbacies of Alold (1068–1104), Henry (1104–30), and Gautier (1130–47), whereas seven survive from the abbacy of Wéry (1147–55) and eighteen from the time of Martin (1155–84), a total of twenty-five in thirty-seven years.[6] Such an increase in evidentiary material does not constitute decisive proof. Nevertheless, the period of greatest abbatial activity at Saint-Vaast between 1000 and 1200 seems to coincide with the time of Abbot Martin, who had other archival concerns. A similar correspondence between the specificity of confirmations and survivals of abbatial documents occurred at Saint-Denis, where virtually no abbatial charters survive from the eleventh century but at least sixteen survive from the rule of Suger (1122–51).[7] In other cases, however, little discernible increase in abbatial charters (or keeping them) occurred. At Saint-Bertin, despite the production of a *gesta* dedicated to him, Abbot Lambert seems to have issued few more charters than his predecessors. Abbot Simon, who wrote his cartulary after his retirement in 1136, included no acts of his own previous abbacy.[8]

An examination of the distribution of abbatial charters and notices within the rule of individual abbots sometimes offers a more revealing perspective. The distribution of surviving acts of Martin of Saint-Vaast is quite uneven: only six acts in the fourteen years of his rule leading up to the time he ordered Guimann to begin his survey of holdings in 1170, but twelve in the fourteen subsequent years.[9] This chronological distribution could have been the result of Martin's greater interest in "administrative" matters, although again it may be an illusion caused by the increased survival rate of his charters because they were copied in the cartulary he ordered produced.[10] What is certain is that such abbots did order their own (and their predecessors') charters to be collected, copied, and organized into cartularies along with confirmations. This documentary push demonstrates increased interest in preserving and using these documents, even if a general increase in land transactions cannot be proved definitely.

Even if the increase in transactional documents is an illusion of documentary survival, there is corroborating evidence of increased concern with land management. In addition to the quantity of land transactions, the quality of land transactions must also be considered. One common method for determining changes in monastic thinking has been to examine the dispositive clauses of land charters and look for

new types of transactions, especially the buying, selling, and mortgag-
ing of land. Several scholars have noted the rise of mortgages at the
end of the eleventh century in connection with the First Crusade in
1095. The need to finance and equip these expeditions certainly required
mobilizing the greatest source of capital in medieval Europe: land.[11]
While this sudden mobilization of capital may be a watershed from
the perspective of economic history, one must question whether such
transactions were viewed as normal or extraordinary. Certainly, monks
benefited from being lenders, but there is little direct evidence that it
altered their overall view of their estates. Instead, one should focus on
the selling of monastic lands. While selective buying could promote religious, political, or economic ends, selling off land was anathema to
monks concerned with establishing a sacred and inviolate patrimony.

Permanent alteration of the patrimony, especially the rare selling of
land, provides a clue to larger shifts in monastic attitude. Changes in the
kinds of transactions some abbots initiated demonstrate an increased
willingness to regard their lands as exploitable resources. Although the
language of most eleventh- and twelfth-century monastic charters does
not yield simple typologies such as "sale" or "purchase," close reading
of such acts often reveals arrangements which effectively buy, sell, or
otherwise permanently transfer lands or revenues. In a very few cases,
however, the language of a charter's dispositive clauses includes verbs of
buying and selling (*emo* and *vendo*). Most of these overt sales and purchases occur after 1120. Interestingly, these charters were usually composed within the same periods as the increasingly explicit confirmations
analyzed in Chapter 2. At Saint-Vaast, none of the abbatial acts before
the time of Abbot Martin (1155–84) used these verbs but in Martin's
time two did, and significantly both were sales rather than purchases.[12]
Although there were no sales recorded at Saint-Denis, Abbot Suger
bought many properties, often for large sums, in a concerted attempt to
build up Saint-Denis' estates.[13] Abbot Hugh V of Saint-Germain (1162–
82) also bought numerous properties to supplement the monastery's
estates, which were eventually listed together (see below).

Relying on such typologies is dangerous. The change to using
terms like sale or purchase without an attempt to disguise them may
have been less a change in action (lands had been permanently trans-
ferred before) than a change in conception (the acceptance of the idea
of sale or purchase). In particular, the rare use of the verb "to sell"
(*vendo*) was significant. Monks had long been aware of sales, although

they did not favor them. Many later abbatial charters approved sales by subordinates or describe sales of holdings prior to the time the monastery acquired them. Such land transfers, which even included sales between tenants or vassals of the monastery and third parties, were approved and recorded in notices, even though the rent received by the monastery did not change.[14] But the awareness of buying and selling (especially by laymen or other religious groups) did not mean that such practices were accepted when it came to the monastic patrimony or the saint's land.[15] The verb "sell" (*vendo*) would not have been used if all monastic land was insistently viewed as inalienable, sacred patrimony. First, some lands had to become less sacred than others.[16] The overt use of the terms "sale" and "purchase" may have been less an innovation in transactions than the gradual erosion of habitual reluctance to apply such terms to monastic land.

Such transactional analysis of dispositive clauses, while good method, does not seem to yield much evidence of economic thinking, indeed quite the reverse. One of the reasons why classifying monastic transactions is so difficult is that during the eleventh and twelfth centuries the form of charters was not fixed. This problem has been made famous by Dominique Barthélemy, who labeled it the "mutation documentaire" in order to contrast it with what he believed was the overblown "mutation de l'an mil."[17] From a diplomatic perspective, the eleventh and twelfth centuries in France witnessed the rise of the private charter, combined with a profusion of small grants to monasteries. These charters have become notorious for their long preambles and lack of fixed form.[18] The variable wording of monastic charters from 1000 to 1200 is both an evidentiary curse and a blessing. Such variability makes any transactional analysis of acts highly speculative. Indeed, classifying such acts into categories such as "buying" and "selling" begs the question whether those who composed them thought in such ways: obviously they did not, at least in a modern sense. On the other hand, the lengthy preambles of these charters, which tend to be truncated with the rise of formulae and notices in the thirteenth century, provide rich evidence about monastic motives. But such evidence, while it can explain the reasons for particular transactions or a series of seemingly unrelated charters, also tends to emphasize religious or political goals over economic ends. In searching for innovation, the historian must not assume documentary change is tantamount to social change.

Economic Reform

Here it is best to keep in mind a fundamental question: were some monastic land transactions motivated by a purpose that was identifiably economic? To answer this question, it is necessary to reconstruct, wherever possible, the pattern of landholding at a monastery and consider carefully whether individual transactions or an overall pattern of transactions (implying the existence of a guiding plan) had economic, or partially economic motivations. One must go beyond documentary form to content and context. By examining the geographic and social context of transactions, the problems caused by relying on typologies can be avoided. Difficulties caused by the scattering of estates, attempts at consolidation, or movement from farming to leasing can only be understood spatially. In particular, abbatial acts are important, for in these acts one can discover planned and intentional exploitation for gain.

One does not have to rely on charter typology to establish the growing importance of economic ideas. In some cases, it can be shown that the motivation for particular land transactions was explicitly economic in nature. The surviving abbatial charters for the monastery of Saint-Vaast strongly demonstrate the increasing prevalence of transactions based on efficiency of exploitation from the middle of the twelfth century. A charter of Abbot Wéry from 1152 explained that the abbot ceded (*concedo*) land to the collegial church of Saint-Laurent-au-Bois, which had requested it, because it had long been unoccupied and "although it is subject to our estate of Ponz, it is less convenient (*minus habilem*) to farm because of its remoteness from that estate."[19] This transaction was not literally a sale, but it effectively removed the land from Saint-Vaast's control and was justified on economic grounds.[20] Wéry acknowledged the request of the religious at Saint-Laurent because "that land was necessary to them and easier to farm."[21] Often religious and economic purposes worked hand in hand: Wéry followed this grant with another to encourage the religious at Saint-Laurent to become monks. In 1155, Wéry granted Saint-Laurent deserted land in the *villa* of Bouzencourt for a rent of two *solidi*, with two conditions: that if any tithes were eventually gathered there, they would belong to Saint-Vaast and that if the religious became monks, the rent would be abolished completely. Obviously, the religious were being given an incentive to take up the habit but, regardless of their decision, the monastery gained revenue from previously unproductive lands.[22] The abbot was planning for the future, for agrarian expansion and a new church.

Even in cases in which the economic utility of transactions was not immediately apparent in charter language, a spatial reconstruction of estates shows that many of Abbot Martin's transactions at Saint-Vaast had economic motivations. One of the chief motivations was to simplify and assure receipts from distant or disputed estates. In order to avoid difficulties of collection from the dependent priory of Haspres (Nord, Valenciennes, 45 km from Arras) which arose in the time of Abbot Wéry, Martin made at least two attempts to lease out lands attached to the priory in order to obtain more steady rents and renders.[23] Both of these holdings, Neder-Overhembeek and Kattem, were located far away from Arras (more than 150 km, in modern-day Belgium, north of Brussels).[24] Inconveniently located lands were also sold outright. In 1176, Martin sold five measures of land at Bergues (Nord, Dunkerque) to the monastery there for eleven marks.[25]

In addition to land sales, Martin made attempts to acquire new holdings conveniently located near older ones around Arras. In 1176, Martin acquired an allod at Ficheux (8 km from Saint-Vaast, adjacent to many other holdings) from the monastery of Saint-Vincent of Senlis in return for an annual rent of six pounds.[26] Permanent exchanges with other churches also built up estates in local areas. For example, in 1178, the monastery acquired lands at Acheville near Oppy (10 km from Saint-Vaast) from the church of Hénin-Liétard in return for two and a half *mancoldi* of grain. Just the year before, the monks had exchanged twenty-four *mancoldi* of grain to the monastery of Marchiennes for the tithes of Oppy and the nearby village of Neuvireuil (10 km and 12 km from Saint-Vaast, respectively).[27] All of these transactions had the effect of simplifying and consolidating the monks' estates, as well as reducing transport costs. Such deals with other religious groups to consolidate estates worked both ways and became increasingly common in the second half of the twelfth century just south of Arras.[28]

There were three important aspects about these land transactions at Saint-Vaast. First, almost all of them were arrangements with other churches and they were intended to be perpetual, effectively permanent alterations in the estates.[29] Second, transactions for the purpose of consolidating estates were new to this monastery, if not within the overall history of monastic landholding. Third, their cumulative effect suggested a guiding hand at work. Suddenly, in the time of Abbot Martin (and possibly starting in the time of Abbot Wéry), thinking about the lands as dynamic resources had become more prevalent at Saint-Vaast. Sales of the monks' land occurred which formerly would have been bitterly resisted. Holdings that had remained unchanged for generations were suddenly being vigorously exploited. Economic thinking about the patrimony was taking hold.

Even if lands did not enter or leave a monastery's control, their receipts could be reorganized for economic purposes: efficiency of exploitation and managerial ease. Considerable effort was devoted to reorganization at Saint-Vaast. Small holdings were granted in return for rent or renders, often to churches, either in order to spare the trouble of farming them directly or to acquire particular produce.[30] Other holdings were granted on terms with the intention of having renders delivered to a more convenient or central location. In 1167, Abbot Martin gave the lands at Écourt-Saint-Quentin (21 km southeast of Saint-Vaast) to the monastery of Marchiennes for an annual rent of two *mancoldi* of grain, which were to be rendered at Biache-Saint-Vaast, 12 km from Saint-Vaast but on the river Scarpe and easily accessible.[31] In addition, he assured the amount and quality of important renders in kind, such as grain. In 1178, Martin allowed the *majorissa* of Riencourt (25 km from Saint-Vaast) to sell one-third of her land to two priests, who agreed to render annually two *muids* of wheat and one *mancoldus* of peas; however, if the land was insufficient to raise these amounts, the priests had to make up the difference themselves. Furthermore, if the grain produced by the lands was inferior, they had to provide grain of better quality from their own stores.[32] Even more complex leases or mortgage arrangements could be made.[33] Collectively, Martin's actions demonstrated a desire to arrange for better, more consistent, or more convenient receipts.

Often it was reorganization, rather than land transactions, which played the more important role in economic reform. Such was the case at Saint-Denis. Abbot Suger concentrated on improving extant estates and also striking a balance between revenues in coin and in kind. After hard-fought battles to recover lands or to remove the oppressive lordship of local castellans (often with royal assistance), Suger worked even harder to improve estates.[34] His own description of his actions in *De administratione* makes reconstructing these enterprises fairly straightforward. For example, at Tremblay (an estate located 15 km east of

Saint-Denis), the counts of Dammartin customarily received a tallage of 5 *muids* of grain, but in fact exacted at will. Suger bought off the count's claims for an annual payment of ten pounds in order to use the land in peace. Then he built a new grange at the entrance to the village, which received the harvest of four ploughlands held in demesne and also the share of the tenants' crops, the *champart*. Suger also surrounded the village with a wall and built a fortified house near its church. All in all, Suger's efforts succeeded in raising the renders from 90 to 190 *muids* of grain.[35]

Suger improved many other estates similarly. At Villaine, the gains were dramatic: the revenues were raised from twenty pounds to one hundred, of which twenty-four were permanently allocated to building the church at Saint-Denis.[36] Producing wine was a particular concern of Suger's, in order to avoid having to borrow money to purchase it for high prices at the Lagny fairs. As a result, he replanted lands with vines or acquired new ones for vineyards assiduously.[37] In addition, Suger also put vacant land to use. In 1145 he founded a new village at Vaucresson as part of a continuing attempt to encourage population growth around Saint-Denis, in order to raise (indirectly) revenues from mills, tolls, and the markets.[38] As a result of this plan, Suger managed to raise the combined revenues at Saint-Denis substantially. At Saint-Denis itself, where the urban economy was already growing when he took office, the revenues increased nearly 60 percent, while in newly developed areas, he reported greater gains in *De Administratione*, often raising revenues two- or threefold, and, in some cases, as much as tenfold.[39] This increase, which Suger did not hesitate to claim credit for, was the result of a concerted, long-term plan of reorganizing and rationalizing domain exploitation.

The economic reforms at Saint-Denis and Saint-Vaast accompanied an overall religious reform initiated by their abbots. At Saint-Denis reform began in the mid-1120s when Suger initiated a sweeping change in the routine at Saint-Denis. A new ordinance, modeled on Hilduin's 832 act, was part of this reform, the first phase of which must have been complete by 1127, when Bernard of Clairvaux praised Suger for its effects in a letter.[40] This reform was crucial and, although the new customary which recorded the changes Suger adopted has been lost, historians have made inferences about its content.[41] Giles Constable argued that Suger's ongoing reform was in the tradition of "strict black Benedictine monasticism" rather than that of new monastic orders.[42] Constable characterized Suger's reform as having three important elements. The first was improving orderliness and quality of the monks' lives, which included such measures as better provisioning, both for the brothers and the sick, and changing the choir to be more comfortable. Second, Suger increased the length and amount of liturgy, adding a daily mass of the Holy Spirit and weekly offices for the patron Saint Denis and the Virgin, as well as various anniversaries (notably Charles the Bald). The third feature was "a concern for conspicuous display, both in charity and in building and decoration."[43] This part of the reform included lavish giving on anniversaries such as Suger's own, as well as the elaborate ornamentation of the church with precious metals and stones. This reform was as effective in improving the state of religiosity at Saint-Denis and earned Suger approval, even from Bernard.

In Constable's view, besides the religious reasons for reform, Suger had two other motivations, which placed him firmly within the Benedictine tradition. First of all, Suger associated the monks' "liturgical intervention for the welfare of outsiders with the economic support owed them by society."[44] As proof of this point, Constable cited Suger's second ordinance of 1140 for Saint-Denis, which discussed his duty as minister to the monks:

To provide for those who are dedicated to the service of Almighty God . . . and to care for and protect from all molestation the contemplatives who are truly the arc of divine atonement. . . . Embracing their religion with my entire soul, I implore beseechingly the prayers of religious men, both in order that they may provide more devoutly and effectively for us in spiritual matters and [that] we, by providing for them in temporal matters, may most devoutly take care to sustain [and] foster them with provisions.[45]

Second, according to Constable, Suger associated strictness and austerity of monastic lifestyle with freedom, heeding the warning of Abelard that "the less regular an abbey was the more it would be subject to the king and of use . . . for temporal gain."[46] Suger expressed this view himself when he warned the monks of Longpont about their lifestyle in a similar vein: "It is sure, O servants of God, that you live only from [your] labors and nourishment or that you are supported by alms. The stricter your life and support, the freer it should be."[47] For Suger, both prosperity and freedom were intimately associated with religious reform. He had learned the lessons of *libertas* that Cluniac reform of the eleventh century had taught, then drew his own conclusions about what needed to be done.

Suger's reforms may have altered the routine of monks at Saint-Denis, but their behavior was still very much that of traditional Benedictine monks. Suger's religious reforms and attitudes fit well within the general movement toward reform found in older Benedictine houses in the 1120s. Indeed, Suger's reforms were intended to be a return to the principles of Benedict of Aniane and the Council of Aix in 817, which were reaffirmed in a general council of abbots from the archdiocese of Reims in 1131. More specifically, Suger borrowed the form and language of his three most important reform acts, the ordinances of 1124 and 1140 and his Testament of 1137, from Carolingian models: Abbot Hilduin's reform of 832 and Abbot Fulrad's testament of 777.[48] The survival and revival of Carolingian reform was part of Suger's plan.

Even so, Suger's program differed in important ways from the Carolingian model of reform. The need for provisions and the debt crisis inherited from Abbot Adam encouraged Suger to supplement the *mensa conventualis* from the abbatial lands, some of which had been removed from the brothers by his predecessors.[49] In general, the old Carolingian system based on whole *villae* no longer functioned well because of broader transformations in the rural economy. Gifts often no longer came as entire *villae*, but in miscellaneous collections of lands, rents, or rights. The traditional farming out of estates at fixed rates did not allow the monastery to profit from growth. Moreover, where estates had been divided, oppressed by advocates or mayors, or impoverished, granting them out to religious houses or consolidating them as new holdings afforded an opportunity to remove these difficulties.[50] Only by looking beyond traditional management to treating the patrimony as an economic whole could Suger match revenues to needs, achieve the increases he sought, and build as he planned. His vision of religious reform and a general desire to promote order and the cult of the saint were also expressed in a managerial tendency. As a result, he initiated the first comprehensive economic reform of Saint-Denis and its estates since the ninth century.

A similar religious reform occurred at Saint-Vaast somewhat later. Abbot Martin modified the practices of the brothers by taking the opportunity of a legatine visit in 1175 to issue a new customary.[51] In addition to liturgical changes, Martin probably also sought a reunification of the *mensa conventualis* and the *abbatia*, which may explain the increased number of acts transferring lands after 1174.[52] This reform undoubtedly followed the general principles laid down in the Council of

1131, which had become well known. Martin may have been preparing the way for such a reform as early as 1170, when he ordered Guimann to begin his codex describing the possessions of the monastery. Such a description was vital to any attempt at reorganizing the domains. It was also no accident that comprehensive changes followed upon the explicit confirmation which Martin had obtained from the pope in 1170.[53] Increased security and enhanced authority allowed the abbot to begin sweeping plans to reform the community, almost fifteen years into his rule. Guimann's meticulous descriptions provided knowledge the abbot needed to make economic decisions about landholdings to assure proper support for the monks.

Suger and Martin may have been exceptional in their reforming zeal but other abbots also changed their thinking, if less rapidly. The idea and practice of exploitation for gain could be gradually adopted. Even though no overall plan of economic reform was implemented at Saint-Bertin, the handful of Abbot Lambert's charters that survive show the growing influence of economic motivations on individual transactions in a more conservative monastery. In 1096, Lambert sought justice in the court of Count Robert of Flanders against Baldwin of Salperwick, attempting to regain a rent of three pounds which his predecessor had granted to Baldwin's grandfather. Eventually, Lambert settled for buying out Baldwin for five marks and this deal was written down. Lambert's intent in this accord, as the document stated, was to restore the rent to the *mensa conventualis* (it was originally allocated to the cellary), from which it had been granted without the assent of the advocate or the brothers.[54] In 1104, Lambert bought off a cleric named Everard for four marks, in order to regain undisputed use of other lands.[55] He also obtained recognition of a rent of four *rasaria* of grain from the abbot of Andres in 1105.[56] These actions were clearly motivated by the desire to recover rights foolishly granted away as much as by a desire for economic reform. They were also attempts to improve the monastery's long term finances.

Economic plans were less important to Abbot Lambert than his ambitious religious reforms. Faced with recalcitrant monks, Abbot Lambert sought to submit Saint-Bertin to the control of Cluny, provoking dissension in the house and causing disputes well into the time of Abbot Leo (1138–63). Continuing struggles over the reform of the monks' behavior and factional opposition facing the abbots made any further changes all but impossible. The political stability and communal agreement needed to implement needed economic reforms simply did not exist in the first half of the twelfth century at Saint-Bertin. Controversial religious disputes preempted other considerations. Fortunately for the brothers, the relatively compact domains allowed for the preservation of some of the Carolingian estate system, the memory of which had never been completely lost. A list of lands in the *mensa conventualis* existed in an act of the Abbot Heribert as late as 1075.[57] Folquin's *gesta* had been remembered, kept, and used as a model. The impulse to preserve control of the old *mensa conventualis* had been strong, and served to slow the erosion of estates even as it maintained traditional ideas of management. So, despite early and detailed written confirmations of land, the monks of Saint-Bertin did not make the leap to economic reform as smoothly as other monasteries.

The rearrangement of landholdings to achieve greater convenience and to improve farming and revenues was not a wholly new idea. Indeed, the actual methods for doing so in the twelfth century may not have been all that different from those used in the ninth or eleventh, save perhaps the form or wording of the documents. What was remarkable was the greater intensity of such doings at some monasteries—the willingness to make new arrangements with an eye toward gain. The goal was more than achieving sufficiency, which had been the ostensible object of establishing the *mensa conventualis* in the ninth century, or patrimonial inviolacy, which was the battle cry of the eleventh century. The goal was to rationalize exploitation to increase revenues as much as possible. It was increase itself, often for religious ends, that was the obsession of Suger. Indeed, his treatise on his own administration was not an attempt at a comprehensive survey, but rather concentrated on the *incrementum* or *augmentatio* he achieved at each place. These increases were channelled into improving the lives of the monks and building the massive new church. At Saint-Vaast, the goals were not so baldly stated, but were similar: the lands were rearranged and patterns of renders altered for the sake of improvement rather than just need alone. Even the idea of inalienability of church land, which had grown up around the *mensa conventualis*, had eroded, and when sales could bring improvement, they occurred. Some twelfth-century monks, unlike their eleventh-century counterparts, had a more intense and active interest in managing their land, in exploiting it for gain. This fundamental shift in attitude had profound consequences for monks' behavior and their written records.

Record-Keeping and Surveying

One part of economic reform was the keeping of more and different records about land and revenues. Indeed, more descriptive record-keeping became necessary as the increasingly complex arrangements of landholding and managing meant that monks could not rely on memory alone. Such arrangements were more frequently written down—literally overwriting the Carolingian estate system. Charters may have been produced more frequently and were certainly better preserved in the form of cartulary copies. But copying charters in books, especially in light of the obsession with inviolacy and exemption in the eleventh century, was nothing new in itself. What was new was the creation and preservation of new types of documents—surveys and lists—and new structures of cartularies and codices for purposes related to management of land and revenue. While these books owed much to their commemorative and historical predecessors, they were not imitations but rather attempts to produce new written instruments for a new form of administration, based on revenue and not estate allocation. Different monasteries reached different levels of achievement depending on their motivations and circumstances. Two of the most successful and dramatic twelfth-century attempts to codify new managment ideas and practices were those of Guimann at Saint-Vaast and Suger at Saint-Denis. More limited but still important achievements occurred at other monasteries, where traditional concerns (or more concern with tradition) lessened the effort put into managing and, consequently, preparation of memory aids for managing. Still, these new documents provide glimpses of what may have been widely diffused notions of economic reform.

The most impressive of the new books devoted to the subject of domain management was Suger of Saint-Denis' *gesta* about his abbacy. The work was not an attempt at a comprehensive survey of lands, but rather a description of the efforts Suger had made to rationalize the exploitation of his monastery's estates. It was not a managing tool in itself, but an explanation of the results of management. Thus, it provides direct evidence of both Suger's deeds and his motivations.

Suger's explanation of how the monks persuaded him to write *De administratione* provides a window onto the new monastic mentality:

In the twenty-third year of our administration, when we sat on a certain day in the general chapter, conferring with our brethren about people and private matters, these very beloved brethren and sons began strenuously to beseech me in charity that I might not allow the fruits of our so great labors to be passed over in silence; and rather to save for the memory of posterity, in pen and ink, those increments (*incrementa*) which the generous munificence of Almighty God had bestowed upon this church, in the time of our prelacy, in the acquisition of new assets as well as the recovery of lost ones, in the multiplication of improved possessions, in the construction of buildings, and in the accumulation of gold, silver, most precious gems and very good textiles. For this one thing they promised us two in return: by such a record we would deserve the continual fervor of all succeeding brethren in their prayers for the salvation of our soul; and we would rouse, through this example, their zealous solicitude for the good care of the church of God.[58]

Several elements stand out in this explanation. First of all, consider Suger's description of himself, the abbot, in consultation with the brothers in general chapter. More than the standard literary *topos* of a command performance in a prologue, this portrayal had political ramifications. It was not the lordly abbot, but the abbot as governing superior who took counsel from his brothers, which was emphasized.[59] Second, Suger mentioned discussing private matters, suggesting that he and the brothers were conferring about nonreligious business. This passage provides a hint that such sessions took place regularly. It was this image of consultation, perhaps self-serving, that Suger wished to stress.[60] Third, the object of the exercise was important. Initially, it was couched in terms of preserving the memory of Suger's deeds, so a commemorative concern was present. However, Suger specified this general concern: what was to be written down for posterity were the *incrementa* (increments or increases) which had been achieved in his time. Unwilling to violate the convention of humility, Suger attributed these increments to God, but he was not loath to spell them out. He did not describe the totality of the monastery's possessions—he did not make a static survey—but rather he listed the acquisitions, improvements, and accumulations he had achieved. For his labors of writing and (by implication) administering, Suger would receive the reward of prayers for his salvation and would encourage his brothers by example. Thus, his material gains were transformed into spiritual gains following the logic of his religious principles.[61]

The interplay of these elements produced a striking book, the form of which further reveals Suger's view of his enterprises. Although written out as a continuous work, *De administratione* consists of two distinct parts.[62] The first concerns the management of lands. After his introductory words, Suger explained his efforts to improve revenues in and then around Saint-Denis, concentrating especially on the "augmentatio," the enlargement of revenues, which he had achieved.[63] This enlargement led to the "incrementum," the exact amount of increase, usually specified in detail. Suger would repeat this pattern (*augmentatio* then *incrementum*) throughout his description of properties. As noted in Chapter 2, the estates were described following a spatial scheme. This scheme was for local estates and it did not include distant holdings in Champagne, Lorraine, Aquitaine, or England. Such omissions make sense when one considers Suger's goal of describing the *incrementa*, for those faraway properties could not be managed on a day-to-day or even a monthly basis and were not areas Suger could easily administer.

Such a comprehensive, well-organized, and precise document was not the work of a single instance of writing. Suger undoubtedly based his book on practical documents in which he had previously collected the details of holdings. One source of inspiration may have been the old surveys or charters from the Carolingian period, which still existed in the Saint-Denis archives.[64] As a young monk, Suger had been assigned to the *armarium* at Saint-Denis, and in *De administratione* he mentioned uncovering various documents by rooting around in old records.[65] He also collected new documents that served his purposes. One such document is the 1125 charter of Matthew le Bel, a major vassal of Saint-Denis. In this document, Matthew listed the fiefs he and his men held, stating that he did so as the liege man of Abbot Suger and the convent and at their request.[66] This charter was far from a simple list of place names: it contained an enumeration of fifty-five fiefs held by forty-one men, describing land, churches, tithes, and details of rents and renders.[67] It was a list of knight-service, usable for military purposes, but it also could have been used like a survey of possessions and revenues, which led at least one biographer of Suger to conclude that the abbot had surveyed all the holdings prior to the reform of 1127.[68] While such a conclusion is too extreme, Suger probably seized upon opportunities to write down details and later reused such documents to compose *De administratione*. He was a list maker by inclination. Moreover, the list survives because later monks thought it valuable enough to copy it into the *Privilegia Sancti Dyonisii* in addition to the *Cartulaire blanc*.[69]

The second part of Suger's *De administratione* concerned the various stages of building and ornamenting the church at Saint-Denis. The church's movable and immovable wealth were linked to a larger notion of treasure or goods of the saint and so this transition was normal. In fact, the elaborate building project represented the culmination of Suger's managerial work: "The increases of the revenues (*reddituum incrementis*) having been assigned in this manner we turned our hand to the memorable construction of buildings."[70] The augmentation of the domains and the increments obtained by years of work had been transformed into the church and thus made sacred. So, Suger described the richness (both artistic and material) of the church—the paintings, hangings, and sculptures—for they had become sanctified to the glory of God. At the same time, his work was a personal devotion, and he did not hesitate to have his name placed in many prominent locations.[71] Indeed, Suger was perhaps pricked by his conscience for putting his name so many places. In the last lines of the work, after a brief passage devoted to his anniversary, he baldly concludes: "For late and scanty penance cannot atone for so many and so great [sins] as I have committed, nor for the enormity of my crimes, unless we rely upon the intercession of the universal Church."[72] This conclusion, resembling the standard humility *topos*, might have also been tacit acknowledgment that not all Suger's contemporaries (such as the more ascetic Bernard) might have agreed with his enterprising spirit.[73]

De administratione proves Suger had a global vision of the monastery's economy. Although the book was written after twenty years of rule, clearly omits setbacks, and may exaggerate the coherence of Suger's plans, it still shows long-term thinking and a new mentality at work.[74] Rather than a static survey of the monastery's possessions, it was a description of a dynamic and active manager. Just as Suger did not hesitate to bring force (even royal force) to bear against the "evil customs" of oppressive advocates, he did not hesitate to break customs of the manor, changing rent and farming arrangements to suit his plans.[75] In *De administratione* the historian has the most direct access to the new, aggressive economic spirit of twelfth-century abbots, for it is the *gesta* of a successful manager.

This aspect of Suger's abbatial style has not failed to attract the attention of historians. Michel Bur did not hesitate to distinguish Suger's active interest in increases from prior monastic endeavors: "The program is clear. The abbot did not seek to draw up a complete polyptych of the possessions, but to free up monetary resources (treasure) from the increases in production in case of need and, in ordinary times, to achieve an augmentation of revenues by judicious exploitation. It was population and economic growth which interested him."[76] Suger was well versed in the history (both written and unwritten) of his monastery, and *De administratione* was a description of his plan of action, of his "ministering" to his church, which used older documents in new ways. This long-term plan distinguished Suger from other lords, in the view of Giles Constable: "Suger stands out among his contemporaries in both ecclesiastical and secular positions for his farsighted and aggressive economic policy, of which he left a unique account in *De administratione*."[77] It was not just his plan but his successful execution of it which Constable noted, for "he pursued the economic advantage of Saint-Denis with energy, imagination, and occasionally a touch of opportunism."[78] In contrast, Lindy Grant viewed Suger as more typical of contemporary Benedictine abbots in his aims and even his writings, although very successful on a practical level.[79] In addition to freeing estates from advocates and improving them, Suger acquired mortgaged property during the Second Crusade, secured land by multiple confirmations of popes and kings in France, Lorraine, and England, and solicited confirmations of supposedly ancient rights of lordship and justice under dubious title. While Suger's goals may well have been typical for a Benedictine abbot of his time, his own understanding of the monastic archives and economy led him to extraordinary success.

While no other surviving twelfth-century French work is as directly revealing about land management as Suger's *De administratione*, many other documents provide evidence of the transformation of monastic administration. For Saint-Vaast, we luckily have copies of the cartulary compiled by Guimann, the cellarer of Saint-Vaast, one of the most detailed surveys for any monastery in the twelfth century.[80] As argued in Chapter 2, the organizational structure of this cartulary shows the mixing of older ideas of sacred patrimony with newer economic thinking. The first part contained copies of confirmation charters, from the mythic founding of the monastery until 1170, organized chronologically. The second and much longer part, *de bonis mobilibus et immobilibus*, revealed new thinking. It was a comprehensive inventory of all the monastery's possessions. The cartulary's organizing principle was to start at the center of the church and move outward to the furthest possessions, in a combination of listing, surveys, narrative, and charter copies. Guimann began by describing the body of the patron saint, Vedastinus, and then proceeded to describe the possessions in the following order: the relics in the *scrinium*; the precious "treasures"; the pledges left in the church; and a recently returned relic, the head of St. James.[81] Then he moved outside the main church to describe the churches and buildings within the walls of the old ninth-century *castrum* of Arras, including the monastic school. Next, he provided extensive schedules of tolls owed in the markets of Arras-town for each good, as well as the rent owed on each stall in the marketplace.

After these items, Guimann described the *hostagium*, a ground rent owed by every house in Arras. This massive listing included the name of each householder, the rent paid, and the monastic officer to whom it was paid—all listed by the route used by the surveyors who recorded the information.[82] As Guimann explained, this survey was to be updated to assure proper collection of rent. It is worth quoting his remarks in full on this point, since they reveal his motives:

Concerning *hostagia*, that is the rents of houses: since evil-doing has grown, with the result, often after a long passage of time and the change of generations,

TABLE 3.1.   Conceptual Outline of Guimann's Cartulary

I. Privileges and confirmations (in approximate chronological order from foundation to 1170)

II. *De bonis mobilibus et immobilibus*
   1. Church of Saint-Vaast:
      • body of Saint-Vaast
      • relics kept in *scrinium*
      • "treasures" (vessels, gold, vestments)
      • pledges
      • head of St. James
   2. Inside the *castrum* of Arras-town:
      • churches
      • rents on buildings
      • monastic school
   3. Tolls and marketplace of Arras-town

III. *De hostagiis* (ground rents of Arras-town)
   This description begins at the *castrum* and has lists of rents of the streets of the "old" town of Arras, apparently following the paths of collectors.

IV. *De diversitate districtorum* (lands around Arras)
   This description begins with the *suburbia* and proceeds to more distant holdings, listed in patterns which suggest paths used by surveyors. When Guimann died in 1192, this section was incomplete.

that those who owe *hostagia* inquire why they owe them, a liberty which they do not have nor ought to have and strive to usurp for themselves, I deemed it proper and necessary to specify the places themselves, in which and for which they owe, and the people who owe by name, praying that these names which are written down may in no way be erased, so that in future times they may also reveal how much gain or loss the revenues have suffered. Moreover, he who has the *breves* ought to change the names of those owing in his charters according to the deceases and successions of generations, so that whatsoever happens to the inhabitants, either through death, sale, transfer, or division, the said charter (well conceived in all respects) will name and single out the places themselves and no occasion for fraud or other errors will remain.[83]

Guimann intended his work to be followed and used by his successors. His survey of *hostagia* was to insure that the monks received their due. His description was a prospective one: updating the document was the key to collecting revenues owed and reducing evasion from payment. After completing this massive work, Guimann proceeded to describe the landholdings outside of Arras itself, listing in surveys their tenants, rents, renders and relevant charters, 151 places in all, before the manuscript abruptly ends, unfortunately incomplete.[84]

By starting with the reliquaries and proceeding to the details of tenancies, Guimann combined the traditional reverence for the sacred patrimony and the treasures of the church (on which the monks' lives were spiritually and politically centered) with a newer, more ambitious spirit of making sure every penny owed was recorded and then extracted. He also considered the pressures of population and politics on the monks' holdings. He mixed charters with practical, working documents intended to be used in revenue collection. Whole sections of the patrimony, now viewed as challenged but exploitable economic resources, were described in previously inconceivable detail. The documentary foundation of confirmations thus supported the edifice of inventories and collection lists. Newer, economic thinking had been added on top of older notions.

Although Suger's and Guimann's writings were different they shared a common impulse and common ideas. Both emphasized the role of the sacred. In both, the physical location of the monastery was an important organizing principle in their writings. Guimann, perhaps the more traditional monk, began his description with the church and its patron saint (in particular the treasury and sacristy), the foundation of the spiritual and economic well-being of the monks, and moved outward to the furthest holdings beyond the immediately sanctified environs of the church. His geography was a sacred geography. Suger, on the other hand, wrote in the spirit of a builder, explaining all the work and effort which culminated in the great church. His spirit was less commemorative and more celebratory; the church was the product of labors made holy by their end. Yet neither monk was ever far from the spiritual: both included *miracula* in their works; both lovingly described sacred vessels and other church treasures; both exalted the relics of saints.[85] These elements of their works show the continuing importance of sacred space and the attachment to tradition. Never was the patrimony fully detached from these demands. The social and religious concerns which had preoccupied monks since the tenth and eleventh centuries always mitigated the turn to economic thinking in the twelfth. Guimann still copied confirmations assiduously and Suger worked hard to obtain new ones. The new economic and administrative mentality was an overlay, a nuance in behavior rather than a sudden shift to a totally new paradigm of thought. Suger's and Guimann's works were two different variations of the same Benedictine reform spirit, offering a slightly different balance of shared religious and economic elements.

Yet, the new economic thinking was systematic and purposeful. Guimann not only recorded what was owed but to whom it was paid. The list of *hostagia*, for instance, named the monastic officer who received revenues as well as the amount being collected. Offices or ongoing activities, such as the cellary, were assigned streams of revenue rather than being assigned whole estates (as had been done in the charters of Charles the Bald). Taken as a whole, Guimann's work reveals that the new system was as much one of allocation (or reallocation) as it was collection.[86] This innovation was really as complicated as Suger's estate improvements, which often allocated new revenues to specific purposes, such as building or wine production. This new method of allocation attempted to substitute support from specific sources for the generalized support of the *mensa conventualis* which had been modified in recent reforms. As a result, nothing less than a complete change in the revenue distribution of the monastery took place at Saint-Vaast and Saint-Denis. Although revenues could be (and had been) collected without written instruments, allocation of revenue streams, especially from many sources to many different purposes, was harder to achieve by memory alone. Thus, the new revenue allocation system was a written system. New written instruments, like Guimann's survey of *hostagia*, were required to record it, as well as to guard against abuse within and outside the cloister. It could be used to check on rent payers and monastic collectors; it made accountability possible.

There were many other written records which show traces of the turn toward economic thinking and the new system of monastic revenue allocation in the twelfth century. Record-keeping and surveying included more than book-length projects. Indeed, a proliferation of surveylike documents occurred at monasteries other than Saint-Denis and Saint-Vaast. Unfortunately, overreliance on formal typologies by historians and local variations in structure, content, and wording have concealed the essential similarity of purpose in these documents. Using broad and flexible terminology to characterize these varied documents is helpful. What they all shared was a desire to write down (in greater or lesser detail) the material and often the spiritual wealth of the house. This impulse began in the late eleventh century, as we have seen, with a desire to preserve holdings and the memory of control over them, or to collect charters in cartularies. Often, monks next moved toward listmaking or the creation of static surveys in an attempt to describe possessions more fully in the twelfth century. These documents, as Guimann observed, could became outdated and then would require revision or resurveying of a more active sort than was needed for confirmations. Perhaps the best name for this sort of document was a commonly, though loosely, used medieval phrase: *descriptio bonorum*, a description of goods. Surviving documents of this type were usually inserted in bindings next to other book-length projects to which they pertained, such as a history of the house or *gesta* of its abbots. Sometimes, monks assembled the descriptions with a particular economic purpose in mind or as a practical aid. Occasionally, these descriptions were grouped or linked in a rough organizational form. Less frequently, an entire system would be laid out comprehensively, as in Suger's and Guimann's works.

At Saint-Germain, which had a surviving polyptych from the Carolingian period, no complete survey or administrative treatise existed in the twelfth century. Updates were added to the old document until they grew insufficient. Abbot Hugh V (1162–82) had a substantial number of descriptions composed during his rule, all related to administration in some degree. These documents took the form of lists and were attempts to comprehend better the true extent of the possessions. The most important was a list of all fiefs held from the monastery, which headed a quaternion added to the cartulary of three crosses.[87] Dating from the last years of Hugh V, 1176–82, this list includes the names and holdings of fiefholders ranging from counts to men who held small pieces of land. Hugh or his subordinates kept this list current, as shown by additions concerning the estate of Samoreau, acquired in an exchange in 1176.[88] This survey was the first to be recorded at Saint-Germain since the polyptych of Irminon, about 350 years earlier.

The list of fiefs was the longest of a series of similar documents from the same period, which suggest a possible push to reform land management by Abbot Hugh during his rule. These other documents included a detailed list of fiefs held by Geoffrey Pooz and his vassals, mentioned briefly in the longer list of fiefs and reminiscent of the list Matthew le Bel supplied to Suger in 1125.[89] Another document contained an enumeration of Hugh V's new acquisitions, including the entire estate of Samoreau, listing what had been bought, from whom, and for how much. Two copies of this list of acquisitions were bound into the endpages of a late twelfth-century decretal and letter collection.[90] Another list in the cartulary of three crosses contained the names of all householders at Saint-Germain who paid rent to the monastery, perhaps as the householders at Arras did, though only the number of houses for which they owed was written down.[91] In addition, monks composed several genealogies of mayors, in conjunction with efforts to force mayors to acknowledge their service to the monastery.[92] All these documents were more humble than those of Guimann and Suger, but all of them had practical purposes and aided Hugh and his subordinates in comprehending and administering Saint-Germain's lands and revenues. Indeed, they may give some insight about the documents Guimann and Suger used to create synthetic treatments of their patrimonies.

The transition from older surveys to new types of written descriptions for economic exploitation is nicely illustrated by the monastery of Saint-Pierre-le-Vif of Sens. In the early twelfth century, under the abbacy of Arnaud (1096–1124), the monks of Saint-Pierre composed a codex that began as a universal history and chronicle of Saint-Pierre and eventually included copies of many documents in their archives. The survival of the original manuscript, which remained a working document for many years, provides an opportunity to study directly how twelfth-century monks compiled their records.[93] The work consisted of 138 folios, divided into two parts, the chronicle (fols. 1–104) and miscellaneous associated documents (fols. 104–38). The chronicle was divided into four sections: a chronicle in the form of a universal history (the birth of Christ to 1100); a parallel chronicle of Sens (675–1096); annals of the abbacy of Arnaud (1096–1124); and a later continuation of the annals (1124–80 and beyond). The second part contained, in a jumble, various charters, excerpts of letters, canons of councils, liturgy, and lists which were related to events in the chronicle and were written down to supplement it.[94] Among these were a list of relics and four groups of fifteen lists of rents and renders from the monastery's holdings, which were essentially surveys.[95] The editors of the chronicle dated the first cluster of lists to the first years of the twelfth century; the second cluster to the abbacy of Arnaud (1096–1124); and the last two clusters to a time within roughly a generation of the second.[96]

These lists of rents and renders provide evidence of several important aspects of land management at Saint-Pierre-le-Vif. They also throw light on the abbacy of Arnaud, who ordered the chronicle compiled and very likely had a hand in producing its text.[97] Prior to 1096, the domains of Saint-Pierre seem to have been organized by the monastic estate system prevalent at many monasteries since the Carolingian period. The first cluster of three surveys enumerate the rents in the abbot's hand, in effect describing the *abbatia*, including the rents paid, who owed them, and the times of the year at which they were owed.[98] These documents suggest that Saint-Pierre had adopted the division between the *abbatia* and the *mensa conventualis* in an earlier period.[99] In addition to these surveys of the abbot's rents, the second cluster of surveys included a list of a rent which "came into the hand of the lord Abbot Arnaud," which is to say new rents he acquired or increases on rents from old holdings.[100] This list was intended to supplement or update the first group of surveys of the abbot's lands. Abbot Arnaud, therefore, seems to have been active in managing his portion of the lands and having a written description of them prepared.

The fifteenth and final survey in the Saint-Pierre-le-Vif manuscript (fol. 138v) contained a list of customs (*consuetudines*) at Sognes which enumerated both renders in kind and cash rents.[101] The holdings at Sognes had also been the object of an earlier survey of the abbot's rents. The initial survey of Sognes was followed by an explanatory note, which indicated that the list was made for the purpose of obtaining the subscription of the former (now deceased) mayor (*maior*) of Sognes, who was presumably responsible for collecting rents for the abbot. This subscription seems to have been for the purpose of verifying the rents.[102] The second survey of Sognes, written down later, included few of the individuals listed in the first survey of Sognes and recorded a substantial decline in money rents. How this change came about is a mystery, but it is clear that the abbot or his successor maintained an up-to-date record of obligations.[103] The later survey of Sognes also provides a clue to what must have been an increasingly active attempt to keep records current at Saint-Pierre: it concludes with the description of the rents of a man who died without heir, whose land probably reverted to the abbot's control.

The other surveys in the Saint-Pierre manuscript also offer evidence of an increased interest in having a practical record of revenues. Some include sums of rent, presumably for use in a more global calculation of revenues (nos. 10 and 14).[104] Most were probably notes composed by surveyors, which were intended for later compilation in a more elaborate document, which was lost or not completed.[105] One of the lists of lands (no. 9), which described holdings by units of area, was clearly intended to be included in an act granting the lands to a priest.[106] The extremely high number of entries in this list, twenty-five in all, the small size of the holdings, and the dispersal of them in the region around Sens indicates either that the rights and possessions of the monks were scattered, as fragments of formerly unified *villae*, or that the abbot had some reason for granting the lands in bits and pieces. In either case, a precise written list would greatly aid the management of the holdings because of their fragmentary nature.

Even though the primary purpose of the Saint-Pierre codex was historical, certain administrative and managerial concerns were incorporated. Abbot Arnaud probably preserved the old system of *abbatia* and *mensa capitualis*, for which static surveys, frequently redone to keep current, were enough. Doubtless the project strongly reflected the character of the bibliophilic Arnaud, who, forseeing his approaching death (*providens vicinitatem mortis*), was most concerned with the preparation of a catalogue of the library, which he had had written down to assure the preservation of sacred books. Indeed, as the chronicle pointed out, "At all times it was the highest purpose of his mind to relieve himself [of the distraction] of almost all secular business."[107] Arnaud's decided preference for books of a religious or historical nature represents an important strand of monastic thought. Surveys, though practical, were mundane and so monks like Arnaud esteemed them less than other writings as objects for devoted work. Furthermore, the surveys of Saint-Pierre did not describe the monastery's holdings completely, not even all the abbot's revenues, and there was no attempt to be systematic in written presentation. Arnaud and his monks certainly possessed the skills necessary to create systematic surveys, but preferences for "holy" writing may have retarded movement toward a system of revenue allocation precisely because such a system emphasized a new (and disliked?) type of procedure and written instrument. Not every abbot shared the zeal of Suger and Martin for combining economic and religious reform.

Similar traditional views were probably held by the monk Paul of Saint-Père-de-Chartres, whose insertion of lists of holdings in his work was a response to the loss of many of his monastery's land titles in the fire of 1078. Despite the magnitude of his project and its continuation as a charter collection by other monks, the transition to a written description of lands for management purposes did not occur until generations after 1100. By the last quarter of the twelfth century, the monks of Saint-Père had begun to produce another cartulary, organized on quite different principles. This cartulary, the *Codex Argenteus*, had four books.[108] The first book contained charters of general importance, such as papal confirmations, and also those pertaining to the cellary. It included documents relating to revenues and, most importantly, provisioning of the cellary itself. Charters in the other three books were organized geographically, listing estates in three directions around the monastery of Saint-Père, grouped by provostships (*praepositurae*), and secondarily by chronology within each estate. The *praepositurae* were groups of estates from which revenues were collected by designated monk provosts (*praepositi*).[109] Some of these sections even contained brief notes or descriptions of holdings, for example, a *descriptum* of the fief of one Guerricus, which listed all of his men and what they owed.[110]

The organizational scheme of the *Codex Argenteus* suggests that the influence of the new administrative mentality had become paramount at Saint-Père. The monks transcended the obsession with title (a dossier organized by grantor) or history (chronology or deeds of the abbots). The pattern of organization was based on either revenue allocation for specific needs, like the cellary, or how revenue was collected (*prepositurae*). The cartulary was intended for future use in administration.[111] By contrast, the concern in Paul's time was preserving past records of the patrimony, and, at most, describing the present situation. His desire for mere preservation was characteristic of the traditional style of monastic management and writing.

Many late eleventh- and early twelfth-century compilations, like those of Saint-Père-de-Chartres and Saint-Pierre-le-Vif, were based on reuse of older book forms, but change to new organizational schemes did gradually occur in the twelfth century. The rise in managerial comprehension of possessions, in particular the exploitation of land for increased income, was paralleled by a slow shift in record-keeping emphasis from preservation of title—all important when land should never be lost—toward recording the actual state of the land and keeping track of changes in the revenue. As was the case with so many medieval "reforms," monks looked to old exemplars for inspiration to make what were essentially new records. Suger rooted through Saint-Denis' archives to his advantage. Guimann of Saint-Vaast acknowledged the inspiration of the polyptych of Charles the Bald in the prologue to his work.[112] They were probably more innovative, or more bold, than other monks. Their predecessors Simon of Saint-Bertin and Paul of Saint-Père just copied older documents, such as polyptychs, into their works and appended their own lists of holdings to make them reflect the changed state of the domains. Arnaud of Saint-Pierre, a contemporary to Suger, ordered the writing of surveys to describe the current state of a system which had been put into place in the ninth century. The monks of Saint-Germain admired Irminon's polyptych for more than 300 years, but did not compose wholly new descriptions until the time of Abbot Hugh V. Eventually, the new modes of thinking, the new system of revenue allocation, and the new descriptions would reshape the practices, holdings, and archives of many Benedictine monasteries.

The profusion of cartularies in northern France in the thirteenth century testifies to the rising popularity of this form of archival organization. For example, Bernard Delmaire counted fifty-three surviving cartularies in the thirteenth century for the Nord and Pas-de-Calais area, as opposed to just seven from the twelfth.[113] In addition, by the thirteenth century, the view of land as an economic resource was often translated directly into the organization of documents within cartularies. Many of these cartularies were similar to the *Codex Argenteus* of Saint-Père. The *cartulaire blanc* of Saint-Denis was certainly the most elaborate of these cartularies, grouping 2,500 charter transcriptions by offices and estate groups.[114] At Saint-Germain, the monks eventually produced a cartulary organized by the pattern of estates suggested in

Hugh V's surveys, the so-called *cartulaire AB*.[115] At Saint-Bertin, the brothers created a variety of thirteenth-century cartularies, organized by geography, of which only later copies survive.[116] There are traces of continuations of Guimann's work at Saint-Vaast from the early thirteenth century.[117] The older forms of organizing cartularies by chronology or by grantor persisted, since defending the patrimony would always be an important concern, but new, alternative schemes also developed to suit economic or administrative ends.

The Turn to Administration

What circumstances motivated certain northern French abbots and chapters to adopt economic ideas and practices of exploitation of land and to keep different records about them? Why did others fail to do so or only do so much later? Sometimes financial crises could precipitate a move toward new ideas and practices after challenges from outside the cloister made their adoption useful. Frequently, however, such conditions could exist for a generation or longer before any substantial change in internal administration could be effected. It was often the intervention of a reform-minded abbot that mattered most. Certainly this was the case at the monasteries with the most developed "administration," Saint-Vaast and Saint-Denis, where Abbots Martin and Suger led the way. Internal and external pressures could encourage an abbot to adopt a new way of thinking about the patrimony, to combine religious and economic reforms, and to order the compilation of new records. In these cases, abbots were the catalysts of change.

The monastery of Saint-Vaast provides a good example of how important a strong abbot could be in overcoming long-term reluctance to adopt the new practices. The tremendous explosion of population in and around Arras in the twelfth century put significant pressure on the Saint-Vaast monks' ability to maintain and keep track of their revenues. Proof of this increase can be found in the rapidly growing number of new parishes and the extensive road building in and around Arras.[118] Guimann himself complained about the difficulties the burgeoning population caused the monks in their record-keeping (see above). The problem from the monks' perspective was that the households of Arras were multiplying and dividing while the monks' fiscal units remained constant. Formerly, the payment for a household came from a single source, now multiple individuals had to render the same amount. As Guimann notes, this state of affairs made collection difficult and avoidance easier. Worse yet, new sources of rents were not being exploited.

Changes in the physical and political environment of the monastery exacerbated the monks' problems. In the late eleventh century, Arras was divided into two settled areas, city and town. The monastery of Saint-Vaast was located in the town. In 1093, a new bishopric was created in Arras-city.[119] Between 1100 and 1111, the count of Flanders fortified Arras, and the new fortifications physically divided the already divided lordships of bishop and abbot, the city and the town.[120] However, the bishop and abbot were not the only powers in Arras. The count's castellan also resided in Arras-town, and by the late twelfth century, there was a nascent urban commune, which was to become a powerful force in the thirteenth century.[121] Twelfth-century Arras was a welter of competing lordships and interests. The relationship of people and space was changing rapidly and these changes certainly impinged on the monks' own sense of their surroundings.

If these competitive conditions had existed since the late eleventh century, why was there so little response by the monks until the time of Abbot Martin (1155–84)? One reason was that the monks were preoccupied with defending their interests. The obsession with rights and the defense of the patrimony led to a mentality of preservation, not exploitation. The traditional view dominated, like that of Paul of Saint-Père and Arnaud of Saint-Pierre. A new mode of thinking was required to reshape the economy of the monastery, a spirit of improvement. Religious reform often provided both the justification and the opportunity for more sweeping reform. Economic reform was tied to religious reform and usually needed a vigorous and secure abbot with the will to effect it, such as Martin, who doubtless borrowed from the common rhetoric and practices of abbots at other houses. Even then economic reforms came second. Most of Martin's main administrative activity (including land transactions, Guimann's writing, and issuing more abbatial charters) occurred only after he secured a comprehensive explicit papal confirmation in 1170, after fifteen years of rule.

The situation was similar at Saint-Denis, except that Suger was more aggressive in economic matters. But Suger would not have been willing to effect economic reform without the pressure of circumstance. Perhaps the public prodding of new monastic reformers, such as Bernard of Clairvaux, had its influence, but there were some internal problems created by Suger's predecessors. Many of the holdings of the monastery were encumbered by debts at disastrous interest, including the tolls of Saint-Denis, the *villa* of Montlignon, and the holdings at Vernouillet, which had been in gage forty years.[122] Many lands had been rented on foolish terms, such as the rich holdings at Beaune-la-Rolande, which had been granted by Abbot Adam to the monastery's *servientes* for an annual payment of thirty pounds to cover a bad debt.[123] Worse still, many of the debt payments were for mortgages which contributed nothing to paying the principal. Indeed, the situation may have been comparable to the difficulties caused by the tremendous debt incurred by the monastery of Cluny in the same period.[124] The problem of debt was exacerbated by the persistence of secular lords exacting at will from the monastery's estates, including the monastery's advocates, as at Tremblay, Corbeil, and several other holdings.[125] Even the rapacity of the monastery's own mayors reduced income, especially in the Vexin, where force had to be used.[126] Such delapidation of the monastery's lands provided endless opportunities for the reforming abbot.

One must also ask why certain monasteries, which experienced conditions similar to Saint-Denis, failed to achieve comparable economic or managerial reform. At Saint-Bertin, the instability of the abbacy retarded the shift to administration. Although Abbot Lambert (1095–1124) finished the rebuilding of the monastery started by his predecessors in 1106, his primary goal was to institute religious reform of the brothers, who held private property in violation of their vows and kept servants supported by revenues allocated to the poor. In 1100, he harangued the brothers about their failure to live according to the Rule, even though he had taken ill. This speech had the effect of alienating the brothers and, his authority compromised, Lambert resorted to more extreme measures. He secretly sought the aid of Count Robert of Flanders and his wife Clemence, but the monks were forewarned by the canons of Saint-Omer and Thérouanne: they seized him and forced him to forswear his plan. Lambert then arranged to secretly visit Cluny under the guise of a mission to Rome and submitted himself to the abbot of Cluny.[127]

A struggle for control of the monastery began and the chapter was divided between those who wished to overthrow Lambert's authority and those who supported him. Unlike Saint-Denis, where Suger could boast of reforming the religious practices of his monks peacefully, religious reform impeded economic reform at Saint-Bertin.[128] This division in the chapter festered throughout Lambert's rule and became acrimonious during the elections of his successors. The subsequent abbots of Saint-Bertin had only loose control over their monks and were not in a position to institute economic reforms, since religious reform was so hotly disputed. Furthermore, the status of later abbots was uncertain, since Cluny continued to claim control over the abbacy. Indeed, the question of the abbot's and the monastery's independence was debated in the papal courts until the abbacy of Leo (1138–63). Although this dispute about Saint-Bertin's independence explains why the monks sought out confirmations relatively early and often, it also explains why no parallel development of the estates occurred. The abbots' field of action was constrained, resulting in few new abbatial acts (though many were issued by the bishop of Thérouanne or count of Flanders) and even less alteration of the lands. Thus, the compact and local domains Saint-Bertin had enjoyed in the Carolingian period remained, although battered, largely unaltered in the first half of the twelfth century. Fortunately, such a domain could be handled (or mishandled) by traditional management techniques apparently well enough to support the monks.

The consequences of the disputes at Saint-Bertin are evident from the form of Simon's cartulary. He was more concerned with politics and propaganda than with administrative practices. Descriptions of resource management in the present or the past served primarily as a moral tale about neglect or abuse, which explained the threat of subjection (to the count of Flanders or Cluny) because of laxity. Unlike Suger, Simon wrote nothing of his own abbacy, even though he lived many years after being deposed. The dispute over the spiritual and practical control of the monastery was all-consuming. A move toward producing written documents related to administration was delayed well into the latter half of the twelfth century.

Conclusions

Local conditions often explain when monks began managing their lands better and keeping improved records of their efforts. Demographic change, lordly competition, rival religious powers, and religious reform all were important. But local variations in timing should not obscure the common solutions and responses of monks. By the late twelfth and early thirteenth centuries, emerging monastic systems of revenue allocation

and estate management were actually quite similar, as cartularies organized by estates or offices indicate. These books show a new monastic
mentality about the land as an economic resource and a desire to administer it, widely diffused under the guise of reform. They reflect a body
of ideas and practices that persisted over time. Nor should variations
obscure the importance of an energetic abbot committed to change.
Their common response, like Suger's, was linked to traditional black
Benedictine monasticism and a return to Carolingian ideas, but with
substantial differences in the area of economic reform.

In the final analysis, many Benedictine abbots began to think
administratively in the twelfth century, which is to say they were
increasingly concerned about "ministering" to their brothers and their
patrimony. Such an expanded notion of "ministering" included altering
monastic estates for more effective exploitation, revenue allocation
for specific purposes, and more comprehensive record-keeping to control revenue. Of course, twelfth-century monks and abbots thought of
their problems within different categories than historians do, such as
reform, *augmentatio*, or simply a reaction to the evils of others. Such
categories were broad and flexible, allowing monks to incorporate new
ideas within the framework of old notions. The very flexibility of these
notions allowed for the acceptance of change. Since medieval monks
and abbots thought in these categories, they must be respected when
considering monastic actions and/or justifications. What remains to be
seen is how these administrative notions would be implemented, how
ideas and practices of accountability came to be used, and how effective
they would be.

4

Discipline and Service
Inside and Outside the Cloister

THE TURN TO ADMINISTRATIVE thought and behavior, even if initiated by a forceful abbot, required others to cooperate. At the same time that abbots were rearranging monastic holdings for better exploitation and keeping better records of revenues, they were also reordering internal administration and trying to discipline and control their followers. Abbots were simultaneously the heads of religious houses and powerful lords, connected by ties of allegiance and kinship to laymen outside the cloister. Those serving abbots and acting as their agents were a wide spectrum of people both inside and outside the cloister. Inside the cloister, these agents ranged from monastic officers, often highly literate and familiar with the internal workings of the house, to monks who collected revenues for estates, to lesser brothers or members of the monastic *familia* who carried out vital daily tasks. Outside the cloister, abbots had various kinds of lay associates and followers, ranging from largely independent advocates, who could protect or exploit monastic lands, to knights who fought for the abbot, to mayors and bailiffs who helped collect revenues from estates, to serfs who worked them. Even a visionary administrative scheme would founder without the cooperation of these various servitors. Therefore, reforming abbots desiring change sought not mere cooperation from their servitors, but effective and useful cooperation. Thus, implementing any administrative or managerial scheme also demanded accountability to make service effective.

It was one thing for the abbot to organize the monks themselves, but quite another to control the laymen who ran the monastery's estates. In the case of monks serving as agents, usually as provost (*praepositus*) for the abbot, the religious authority of the abbot buttressed his lordship. The abbot could expect a more responsible form of behavior from monks and had various censures he could use under the Rule to obtain it. But the same behavior could not always be obtained from laymen, especially powerful advocates and knights, but also humble mayors and bailiffs, unschooled in the monastic culture of authority and hierarchy. Yet subordinating or resubordinating these men was a way to restrain abuses, assure the proper doing of justice, and monitor the collection of revenues. How could they be held to a higher standard of behavior and performance? How could they be made more accountable for their actions? To insure useful cooperation, twelfth-century abbots would employ new methods to monitor and discipline their subordinates both inside and outside the cloister.

In the Cloister: Sharing Power and Monastic Offices

Changes in monastic managerial practice led to changes in personnel. The new system of allocating revenue, rather than whole estates, for particular purposes meant that the abbot often needed help in managing the domains. Although customary practices pervaded abbatial rule, the need to evaluate and describe revenues in coin and in kind, manage receipts, make payments, and interact with the community became more pressing as lands came to be exploited for gain. The tendency of the abbot to rule in an associative fashion increased as the more complex way of running the domains required increasing delegation of power. Reform notions bolstered these ideas and abbots increasingly sought the assent of the chapter for matters which were thought to require it. The individuals who filled the role of go-betweens were the monastic officers, who occupied crucial intermediate positions. Placed in charge of revenues and given specific duties, they were responsible to the abbot for their conduct. As members of the community familiar with everyday affairs, they also were his best counselors and the de facto representatives of the brothers.

While monastic officers had existed from the Carolingian period, indeed since the Rule of Saint Benedict, tracing the relation between the ninth-century officers and their twelfth-century counterparts is highly problematic. The problem is not merely evidentiary but also conceptual. It is difficult (but possible) to trace the existence of monastic officers, for example the cellarer, throughout the period in question. There was a monk called the cellarer at every monastery examined so far from 750 to 1200. But what that monk did, how he behaved, and whether a distinction was drawn between him and the "cellary" as an office is an open question. Certainly, the increasing definition of such offices in the twelfth century was related to prevailing canon law ideas (themselves changing rapidly), though the realities of practice were also important.[1] Furthermore, when and how a monastery absorbed such ideas and behaviors must be explained.

In northern France, evidence for the rising importance of officers and offices is abundant at Saint-Denis. In many of his acts, Abbot Suger used language that distinguished officers from their duties or "office." In his testament of 1137, he distinguished between the "cellarer" (*cellerarius*) and the "brothers of the chamber and cellary" (*fratres de camera et cellario*). This wording implied that there were a number of monks who carried out tasks under the cellarer and indicated also an idea a "cellary" and "chamber." In the same document, Suger differentiated the capicer (*capiciarius*), who functioned as the monastery's sacristan, and the *capicio*.[2] These wording shifts suggest growing numbers of specialized officers, assistants, and spheres of responsibility within the monastery. Suger also allocated revenues directly to offices in his charters. In 1137, at the same time he issued his testament, he assigned revenues from the estates of Berneval and Carrières to the treasury (*thesauro*) in order to fund the decoration of the church.[3] As part of his ordinance of 1140, Suger designated revenues for the capicery and infirmary.[4] These allocations were permanent and intended to provide support for the expanded activities of these offices. Indeed, the thirteenth-century *Cartulaire blanc* of Saint-Denis grouped some charter copies by offices and the earliest charters for each office began to be issued during Suger's abbacy.[5] Reading backward in later cartularies at other houses yields similar clues about when the shift to expanded use of offices took place. For example, most of the early abbatial documents pertaining to the cellary in the *Codex Argenteus* of Saint-Père, composed in the late twelfth century, date to 1101–29, the time of Abbot William.[6]

Suger also delegated important matters to his officers, who would act on his behalf. In 1136, he authorized one of his loyal followers, the chamberlain (*camerarius*) Peter to meet with the bishop of Liège and resolve difficulties concerning the church of Grand-Axhe. Peter eventually issued a charter for the lands of Grand-Axhe in the name of the abbey.[7] Suger had surrounded himself with monastic officers who were skilled in administering, including Hervé the prior (his right-hand man), Thouin the subprior, Odo of Deuil (his eventual successor), and, by the 1140s, a younger group including William the cellarer, Geoffrey the capicer, and William the precentor. These officers joined other close confidantes skilled in writing—all named William—William the secretary (Suger's eventual biographer), William the notary, and William Medicus of Gap (a later abbot), who seem to have been members of Suger's immediate household.[8] Whenever Suger delegated authority, which happened increasingly in later years, it was usually to these officers and confidantes.

Although Suger trusted these men more than other monks, he was still careful to employ the rhetoric of consultation with the monks at large. At times, he stressed the associative relationship between abbot and chapter in his charters. Especially in matters concerning the chapter, Suger would consult with the brothers collectively and their communal assent would be recorded in the resulting charter, usually with the formula *communi assensu nostri capituli* or some variant. Some acts needed assent more than others. In particular, the creation of anniversaries (especially Suger's own), acquisitions, or permanent allocations of revenues to offices needed assent.[9] As Giles Constable observed, this consultation had both a practical and political aspect: "This increasing departmentalization was balanced by an emphasis on consultation, which both legitimized decisions and prevented excessive decentralization. Suger may in fact have ruled with an iron hand but in the written records it appears well concealed by the velvet glove of consultation."[10] The new rhetoric of consultation was required because the presumptive inviolability of the monks' portion (*mensa conventualis*) demanded capitular assent as a guard against abbatial despoliation. Both changes and additions to the brothers' lands (which could only benefit them) seem to have needed assent.[11] Likewise, when Abbot William of Saint-Père (1101–29) and his successor, Abbot Udo (1130–50), established their anniversaries, they stressed the assent of their chapter.[12]

Often the monks' assent would be accompanied by other changes in form. In some acts, Suger used the term *minister* instead of *abbas* to refer to himself, stressing his role not as autocratic lord or superior, but as governor, office-holder, or caretaker—a "minister" in both the religious and administrative sense.[13] Taken together, these new usages implied that Suger shared his power with the chapter, or was at least required to consult it when making important decisions.[14] Another related formal change sometimes appeared in the dating of Suger's charters. Some charters were dated from the *annus administrationis* of Suger:

in the year of his "administration," a phrase with a spectrum of meanings.[15] These formal usages constituted a new style of charter, indicative of a new rhetoric and practice of shared power.

The witness lists of Suger's charters also demonstrate the increasing importance of officers, who appear more and more frequently in his acts. Acts which concerned the chapter directly or which included revenue allocations to specific offices had the most extensive subscriptions of officers.[16] Suger's testament of 1137, with its new dispositions of the monastery's resources, had the most extensive witness list. The testament had a total of fifty-seven witnesses, including forty-eight monks and visiting ecclesiastical dignitaries, and listed eight officers of Saint-Denis: the prior, sub-prior, precentor, chancellor, treasurer, capicer, infirmarian, and cellarer.[17] As officers became associated with the rule of the abbot, they became heads of real offices, controlling revenues, overseeing particular activities, and even making written records. It soon became unacceptable to alter revenue allocation without consulting them. This process may have been accelerated at Saint-Denis by Suger's long absences at the royal court, especially during his regency. Dealing with the complexity of the new revenue management was hard enough when the abbot was present, but absences necessarily required delegation, beyond simply relying on the prior, as his predecessors had likely done.

Charter evidence from other monasteries shows a pattern similar to that at Saint-Denis. Three of the same new formal features were present in the charters of Abbot Martin of Saint-Vaast. The first was the title of the abbot in the charter protocol. Up until Martin's time, the standard term had simply been the *abbas*, but in half of Martin's acts, the word referring to the abbot was *minister*.[18] The term *minister* was often accompanied in the protocol, or elsewhere in the document, by a phrase indicating that the monks had collectively assented to the charter, usually some variant of *communi assensu nostri capituli*. Just as at Saint-Denis, these acts were the ones which closely touched the brothers' livelihood. But the most dramatic change was the inclusion of officers as charter witnesses. An examination of all surviving abbatial charters of the monastery of Saint-Vaast to 1200 shows a movement toward including monastic officers as witnesses in the second half of the twelfth century. Certainly, the handful of acts surviving from the rule of Abbots Aloldus, Henry, and Walter (1068–1147) do not include many monastic witnesses at all, and even the prior appears only once.[19] Only one act, a charter from 1102 freeing two serf brothers to marry who had been men of the cellarer, contained other witnesses who were officers: the cellarer himself, the *edituus*, as well as a deacon. The language of this charter is especially interesting, as the men were said to be "belonging to the *ministerium* of the cellarer" (*ad ministerium cellararii pertinentes*).[20] This act was exceptional at the time but pointed to what would later become the rule: in matters concerning a subordinate, the abbot increasingly felt the need to consult.

By the time of abbots Wéry (1147–55) and Martin (1155–84), the abbot often had his monastic officers and other important men of Saint-Vaast witness charters. In particular, charters which resulted in permanent changes in the lands, such as sales, exchanges of land and revenues, or leases in perpetuity to ecclesiastical corporations, may have required officers as witnesses. Even the endowment of anniversaries needed witnesses from the convent. Officers appear as witnesses in seven of eleven acts of these types, whereas they only appear once in Martin's other seven acts.[21]

The presence of officers as witnesses indicates not merely that the abbot had an increasing obligation to gain assent from the chapter as a whole, but also that the practicalities of management impelled him to include monastic officers in his decision making about the permanent disposition of land. For example, the lease of the distant lands of Kattem had as witnesses the three priors of Saint-Vaast, the treasurer, cellarer, chamberlain, almoner, and the guest-master, as well as many other monks.[22] These same officers all received revenues directly, according to Guimann's list of *hostagia* and possessions. The reason for having these officers as witnesses was simple: once Abbot Martin had delegated significant economic responsibilities to these men, the need to consult his subordinates about permanent changes in land holding (and prove that he had consulted) became increasingly important. Indeed, his new customary of 1175 spelled out the expanded role officers would have in revenue management.[23]

Once in place, the system of consultation fed on itself: as the day-to-day tasks of running the domains became more complex, abbots shared power with monastic officers. Abbot Martin of Saint-Vaast was increasingly required to delegate power, to assign duties to his officers. As he did so, his tendency to rule in an associative, consultative fashion also increased. Indeed, the chapter or certain officers at Saint-Vaast may have been able to act of their own motion, as the existence of notices about land in the name of the *ecclesia* with mention of assent (but without mention of the abbot) may indicate.[24] Likewise, while renovating the dilapidated library of Saint-Père in 1145, Abbot Udo assigned specific revenues from many different offices. Udo's act stressed the assent of the chapter.[25] It also emphasized the role played by the monastic officers, who were instructed to pay specified amounts (a detailed list by office was appended) on a yearly basis. Udo was making sure that the officers did their duty and that none fell short.[26] During his rule, he also kept written descriptions of allocations to offices such as the chamber and the capicery.[27] Such record-keeping reflected the need to monitor revenues more closely.

A search for similar language in the abbatial charters of other monasteries reveals that the system of relying on officers was not implemented at every monastery so easily. For example, during the twelfth century there is only one use of the term *minister* to refer to the abbots of Saint-Bertin and only a handful of acts which contain capitular assent.[28] The hostile relationship of abbot and chapter in the early twelfth century explains the rare use of the term. The term *minister* was used in an act of Abbot John II (1124–31), though in unusual circumstances. John was the immediate successor of Abbot Lambert, a former regular canon, installed by the partisans of independence with the aid of the count of Flanders and the bishop of Thérouanne over objections of the Cluniac faction.[29] His act of 1126 concerned arrangements for celebrating his anniversary. This act had, for the first time at Saint-Bertin, explicit mention of the abbot as *minister* and the assent of all the brothers. Abbot John II emphasized that the monks consented to his action and further specified that the provisions the monks would receive in return for their prayers would be "administered" (*administrabit*) by the brother who held the procuration of the church of Lissuge. Although John had a personal interest in his anniversary, the participation of the whole chapter was emphasized by the phrase *communi totius capituli assensu*.[30] Clearly, the abbot was uncertain if the monks, who were divided against him, would faithfully undertake the care of his soul. Therefore, John made explicit the role of the chapter in his charter and also deemphasized his role as superior by using the term *minister*, while simultaneously leaving no doubt how the gifts he gave for the monks' benefit would be managed. The gifts of food became part of the monks' table (*mensa*) and those breaking the terms of the charter were to be anathemized, a penalty clause which evoked the politics of an earlier time.[31] The de facto power of the chapter was being recognized, in a rhetoric designed to appease it, while assuring John's salvation.

Abbot John II of Saint-Bertin's rhetoric, unlike Suger's, was one of weakness, not of new found strength. No other abbot of Saint-Bertin needed to resort to such measures; indeed, assent of the chapter played little role in other abbatial acts and then only in exceptional circumstances.[32] However, the sudden appeal to the new style of abbatial charter in the 1120s shows that a shared rhetoric of rule existed in the Benedictine world, a rhetoric adopted to greater or lesser degrees by twelfth-century abbots depending on circumstance. As seen at Saint-Denis and Saint-Vaast, these linguistic changes reflected changed behavior. Abbots tried to associate their brothers with their rule more closely and delegate important responsibilities to them. Within the cloister at least, the nature of good service had changed.

Outside the Cloister: Oaths of Fidelity

Although abbots were able to rely with some confidence on monastic subordinates, lay agents who oversaw the rural estates were another matter. Controlling lay agents was a problem abbots shared with other great lords. The first priority in controlling these men, as it was for all lords, was fidelity, which is to say faithful service. Abbots had various ways to assure the faithfulness of their men, some of which were the same means used by lay lords. The most common way to encourage faithful service was to insist on a solemn oath of fidelity from lay servitors. Most of them were already theoretically men of the monastery, having done homage (perhaps by placing their hands within the abbot's) and having sworn fealty. However, once they received power over estates, these men set up minor lordships of their own in the shadow of the abbot's power at many monasteries in the tenth and eleventh centuries. Such men had gotten "out of hand," often exercising a violent and predatory quasi-lordship of self-aggrandizement which abused the peasants on the monastery's lands.[33] The problem was forcing such men to acknowledge the oaths they had given, or extracting new ones, as a precursor to assuring better service.

Frequently, the solution was to confirm the status of the man involved, who was usually called a *major* (mayor) or *villicus* (bailiff).

These men had almost all originally been of low or servile status in the Carolingian period.[34] Even in the twelfth century some were still exchanged as serfs. In 1107, for example, Godescalc, the mayor of Champol, and his wife and progeny were pawned by three brothers to Abbot William of Saint-Père-de-Chartres for money to go on crusade.[35] Escaping from their servile status was often what such men were trying to do in order to become independent. But once a man acknowledged his dependent status or that he held his land originally by a servile tenure, the abbot—as his lord—could usually expect him both to do homage and to swear fealty again. It was a short, but crucial, step from fealty, a one-time general pledge of faithfulness, to renewing fidelity periodically. Eventually, abbots demanded a more specific pledge of faithfulness about their servitors' duties as mayor or bailiff. In this way, common lordly methods of restraining men edged slowly toward abbatial expectations of proper (and even official) behavior.

The legal status of lay agents was an important means of disciplining and controlling them. The subordinate status of men like mayors could be asserted in a variety of ways. Abbots could insist on control of marriages and on the servile status of a mayor's wife.[36] In the latter half of the twelfth century, abbots often took to writing such important matters down. When Abbot Thibaut of Saint-Germain (1155–62) exchanged female serfs with Abbot Odo of Saint-Denis (1151–62), both his and Odo's charters insisted that the woman of Saint-Denis (Hersinde, who was given in marriage to John, mayor of Rue) was released from her servitude to Saint-Denis and placed into that of Saint-Germain.[37] Abbots like Odo routinely exchanged serfs to facilitate marriage, but having written notices of servile marriage became more important after Adrian IV's decretal on marriage in 1155, which allowed a serf potentially to become free if he or she married a free person.[38] The purpose of such notices was twofold. First, they provided a record of dependent status. Second, they assured that descendants could not escape their parents' servility, causing loss of revenue and services—a problem that was exacerbated if the parent was a mayor. In effect, the notice served to assure that mayors could not escape an abbot's control and get "out of hand." That such men could not always successfully be restrained shows that abbots were justifiably concerned.

Controlling their lay agents impelled abbots to regulate mayoral marriage carefully even before 1155. Abbot Udo of Saint-Père-de-Chartres

summoned Robert, mayor of the town of Saint-Père, to his court
"because we suspected that he wished to withdraw from our lordship"
and then made him swear publicly on holy relics that he would not
take a wife without the assent of the abbot or chapter.[39] On top of the
oath, Robert was made to find men to pledge the enormous sum of one
hundred pounds on his behalf.[40] Abbots also carefully watched the
spouses of mayors' children. Gallesius, future husband of the daughter
of Albert, mayor of Emprenville, and his father were made to swear
fidelity publicly to the abbot.[41] Additionally, his bride, provided she survived him, was made to promise not to take another husband without
the consent of the monks.[42] The object of such occasions was to incorporate the new husband into hereditary obligations (and oaths) of the
girl's father, the mayor. In cases where the wife was not servile, it was to
remind mayors of their dependent status and their oaths. Writing such
promises down prevented them from being forgotten and provided the
monks with proof should a dispute arise.

More direct ways existed of extracting oaths from mayors than
monitoring their marriages. Abbot Udo's predecessor, Abbot William
(1101–29), found that harsher methods were required to control the
behavior of his mayors and bind them to oaths. William imprisoned
both Mascelinus, mayor of Reconvilliers, and his brother Tiedard because of Mascelinus's many offenses against him.[43] But imprisonment
was not a long-term solution and William chose instead to bind Mascelinus "with the chain of oath."[44] Although William did not specify
the exact nature of his offenses, the oath made them clearer. Mascelinus
promised that, without orders from the monk in charge (presumably a
praepositus), he would not buy or sell the monastery's land; that in matters of justice, he would obey the wishes of the monk; he would not
take exactions from peasants; and he would do service with his horse
when called. Moreover, he and his brother had to find pledges to support their oath, thirteen men pledging a total of four hundred and
eighty pennies.[45] Mascelinus had abused his powers and seems to have
set up a minor quasi-lordship for himself and, through this detailed
oath, the abbot sought to check his power. William used his power as
lord to discipline Mascelinus in the way any lord might. Such ad hoc
methods may have been employed as needed, but few were written
down; in this case the abbot kept a record of the oath because of the
pledges and to discourage future misbehavior by Mascelinus.

In general, more extensive record-keeping helped support an abbot's insistence on the dependent status of his mayors and, consequently, assure their faithful service. Abbot Hugh V of Saint-Germain (1162–1182) was particularly zealous in insisting on and in recording his men's status and their new oaths of fidelity. Evidence for his actions is contained in four notices of oaths of fidelity copied in the cartulary of three crosses. These four notices appear together at the head of a quire which also contained the list of fiefs of Geoffrey Pooz and next to one with the lists of holdings acquired by Abbot Hugh.[46] The first notice contained the oaths of William, mayor of Esmans, who swore fidelity as a servile man, or as the document puts it, *sicut homo de corpore*.[47] The second was an oath by another mayor, Robert of Celles.[48] The third notice recorded the oaths of husbands of two mayors' daughters, who swore fidelity *sicut homines nostri de corporibus*.[49] The fourth contained an oath of fidelity by the wife of a mayor's son, who swore *sicut femina sancti germani de corpore*.[50] These brief notices reveal little more than that Hugh obtained acknowledgements of fidelity and dependent status from these mayors and their relations in a public assembly before the monks and many lay witnesses, including some other mayors, whose names were recorded. However, their appearance in the cartulary surrounded by lists of fiefs and land acquisitions suggests that they may have been part of new administrative push by Abbot Hugh.

Were these the only documents we possessed, we would know very little of the context of these oaths of fidelity. However, a copy of the fuller notice of the oath of Guy, mayor of Suresnes, fortuitously preserved on the endsheet of a book of sermons, provides more information.[51] Although the oath has already been described in the introduction, it is worth reviewing in the context of related documents. According to the notice, Guy wickedly denied himself to be a man of Saint-Germain, whereupon Abbot Hugh admonished him to appear in his court with his relatives.[52] Hugh gathered other *homines de corpore*, and they affirmed that Guy ought to be the abbot's man, just as they were.[53] At this point, "seeing himself to be guided less than cautiously or wisely in refusing to acknowledge our lordship,"[54] Guy accepted the judgment of his peers. He publicly professed his homage (*homagium*) and his fidelity as a dependent man (*homo de corpore*) and swore to be faithful forever to the abbot and monastery. How Guy's peers reached their decision goes without remark in the notice, but Abbot Hugh probably had to show them some proof of Guy's status. A clue to how he may have done so also survives on the *verso* of the endsheet: an extensive genealogy of Guy's family, tracing his descent from *homines de corpore* through five generations.[55]

These records reveal that Abbot Hugh tried to keep his hold over Guy by insisting on Guy's unfree status and on a new oath of faithful service and he wanted to be certain no one forgot it. The large public assembly included all the monks and forty witnesses, as well as at least fifty of Guy's relatives and, therefore, guaranteed that the whole community would know.[56] Writing up the notice helped to insure that future generations would remember. The existence of three other similar genealogies, especially one gathered with the notices of fidelity in the cartulary of three crosses, suggests that Guy's case was not exceptional but rather part of a concerted campaign by Hugh to insist on the fidelity and dependent status of his men.[57] Abbot Hugh V was taking advantage of previous record-keeping at Saint-Germain, servile genealogies added to the polyptych of Irminon throughout the tenth and eleventh centuries.[58] Copies of similar genealogies for "liege men" at Saint-Vaast indicates that other abbots attempted such an exercise and that men of a higher status may also have been subjects of scrutiny.[59]

The notice of the fidelity of William, mayor of Esmans, shows that Abbot Hugh's extraction of these oaths also had a strong disciplinary purpose. After having already sworn fidelity once in the presence of four monks and ten other witnesses, William "after a long time" (*post longum vero tempus*) was again summoned before Abbot Hugh to answer as a *homo de corpore* for his misdeeds.[60] William at first denied the homage and (in particular) the fidelity which had been previously witnessed. However, after taking counsel with his friends, he recognized both.[61] Indeed, even his son Milo, who had previously refused to do the abbot's bidding, pledged fidelity to the abbot and monastery after consulting with his father, brothers, and friends.[62] Such matters had a broad significance in the community. For this reswearing of fidelity by father and son, ten monks, thirty-six others (including two other mayors), and at least four men on William's and his son's behalf were present. Abbot Hugh had forced William to appear for his misdeeds, insisted on his lordship over him, extended his control over his son, and did so in the most public way possible. Thus, Hugh insisted that a one-time oath of fidelity by his mayors was insufficient and that continuing faithfulness in both word and deed was required.

Lay Agency: Oaths of Office and Duties Owed

Although abbots made men like William of Esmans swear their fidelity, less is known about the actual content of the oaths they swore. Unfortunately, the notices of Abbot Hugh's time focused more on the publicity of the oath than with recording its contents. Often, the issue of fidelity, rather than a specific kind of fidelity, was stressed. Yet the exact wording of the oath was crucial, since it constituted the actual relation of abbot and man. Dependent status provided an avenue for lordly discipline but that was not all the reforming abbots wanted. They also wanted service more like the official behavior of monks they had come to expect. One may safely suppose that the service of men such as Guy of Suresnes or William of Esmans dissatisfied Abbot Hugh, but Hugh's exact notion of proper service was not written down.

Although no further evidence is available at Saint-Germain in Hugh's time, similar situations existed at other monasteries in the twelfth century which provide evidence of abbatial expectations of good service. One of the most interesting instances of abbots enforcing a dependent man's oath occurred at Saint-Bertin in the early twelfth century. In 1107, Abbot Lambert entered into an agreement with his *ministerialis*, also named Lambert, about the *ministerium* that the lesser Lambert exercised over the village of Poperinghe. The agreement was written down and survives in an original as well as a copy in Simon's cartulary.[63] The story it told is worth recounting in detail, since the nature of the *ministerium* was the main issue. The accord explained that the monastery held the *villa* of Poperinghe peacefully from the time of its donation by Count Arnulf until Odo de Reningelst obtained the *ministerium* of the *villa*. Then, during his time, Odo had raised "bad customs" (*pravas consuetudines*) there.[64] Upon Odo's death, his son Lambert "came to Abbot Lambert, asking him to give back to him what his father had held from him, namely a certain fief in lands (*feodum in terris*) and the *ministerium* of Poperinghe, and offering money for the *ministerium*."[65]

After consulting with the monks in chapter and his men, the abbot returned the land to Lambert, but he did not wish to give him the *ministerium* of Poperinghe, because of the great injustices and confiscations which his father Odo had perpetrated.[66] Abbot Lambert then specified Odo's crimes: he plundered the men of the monastery unjustly and against the will of the monastic provost (*praepositus*) of the village; he took tallages without the judgment of the count's *scabini*; and he took all the profits of justice which belonged to the abbot for himself, although he was entitled to only a tenth. In order to avoid such problems with Odo's son, the abbot, in the presence of the monks and his knights, "merely commended (*commendavit*) the *ministerium* to the custody of Lambert and thereby made no grant from it in any way to him, on the condition that he would only have this custody as long as he pleased the abbot."[67]

Abbot Lambert took pains to distinguish the de Reningelsts' hereditary lands (the *feodum in terris*) from the *ministerium* of Poperinghe, in effect asserting that the *ministerium* was an office held by faithful service. Subsequently, Lambert de Reningelst was made to promise in the presence of those assembled to refrain from the crimes of his father: never to extract tallages; not to take money without the assent of the provost or the judgment of the *scabini*; and not to take more than his share of the profits of justice. In addition, he had to promise not to engage in many other activities which had doubtless been problems for the abbot in the past: not to accept accusations unless they were made publicly before the provost and judges; not to reconcile a complaint without the provost; not to buy land in the village without the permission of the abbot even though his father may have collected their rents; and not to impress horses without the abbot's permission. In addition, Lambert's share of redemptions of military service for comital expeditions was specified. All other exactions to repay costs of mounting an expedition from Poperinghe were to belong to the abbot, not the *ministerialis*. Lambert also had to promise not to commit any sort of misdeed (*iniuria*) in the village or to interfere in the collection of abbatial revenues there without being advised (*monitus*) by the abbot's provost.[68]

The elaborate description of the promises made by Lambert de Reningelst provides enough information to determine what Abbot Lambert intended. The promises spelled out what Lambert de Reningelst was, and was not, allowed to do as *ministerialis*. His power was constrained and certain activities, especially the most abusive bad customs of his father's pretended lordship, were placed out of bounds. Arbitrary and unjustified exactions under the flimsy guise of "justice" or "protection" were particularly condemned. Lambert was made to consult with the abbot's provost and he was not to act on his own in matters of justice and war. This arrangement allowed for monastic oversight of his activities. In addition, his hereditary lands were distinguished from his *ministerium*, which he held at the abbot's will and only for continued proper behavior.[69] His promises constituted, in effect, an oath of faithful service for what was certainly a more narrowly defined *ministerium*: an oath of office.

In the long term, the oath of Lambert de Reningelst was very important. Abbot Lambert intended to restrain his excesses, which were growing in the shadow of his own authority, by making the privileges (and profits) of his man more contingent on good behavior. The agreement they reached was no small matter, for Poperinghe was the largest *villa* held by the monks outside of Saint-Bertin itself and was experiencing rapid economic expansion in the twelfth century: a ripe location for the rise of a new pseudo-lord.[70] Moreover, the ritual surrounding the agreement was important. The agreement took the form of a publicly sworn oath: twelve laymen (of Lambert de Reningelst's status) witnessed the agreement as well as the entire chapter of Saint-Bertin. Abbot Lambert made the promise as public as possible and intended for it to be remembered by the whole community associated with Saint-Bertin. It therefore served an exemplary as well as a practical purpose.

Despite the turbulent situation of Saint-Bertin's abbacy in the first half of the twelfth century, the promises Lambert de Reningelst made were remembered for a long time. In 1151, Count Thierry of Flanders confirmed the agreement between Saint-Bertin and its *ministerialis* in Poperinghe, who by then was Raoul, son of Lambert de Reningelst.[71] The Count specifically mentioned the prior agreement and reiterated that the *ministerialis* was entitled to only a tenth of the profits of justice.[72] The arrangements adopted in 1107 were to continue in force. In 1177, the monks sought papal confirmation of the arrangements at Poperinghe.[73] In this confirmation, the monks did not seek to confirm the more recent agreement with Raoul or the comital charter of 1151, but rather the original agreement between the two Lamberts in 1107. This fact suggests that the less specific charter of 1151 somehow seemed insufficient. Soon after, in 1179, the monks obtained another confirmation from Thierry's successor, Count Philip.[74] This charter contained a more detailed reiteration of the basic agreement and also extended it to cover all the *ministeriales* of Saint-Bertin. What had been an individual accord for Poperinghe in 1107 had become a general practice of monastic rule by 1179.

Even though the language remained the same forty or even seventy years later, some aspects of the original arrangement were still open to reinterpretation. Although Abbot Lambert insisted on the nonhereditary nature of the *ministerium* in 1107, this provision received no mention in the count's charter of 1151. Was the monastery satisfied with the service it had received, or had Raoul simply managed to inherit his father's position? Apparently a little of both, since his enjoyment of the *ministerium* was not disturbed in 1151. By 1179 there was no room for doubt about nonheritability of the *ministerium*, at least in theory. Count Philip asserted that the nonhereditary terms by which Lambert de Reningelst held his *ministerium* in 1107 applied to all *ministeriales*. Indeed, the language of his charter elevated this principle to the status of "law": "We authorize that law (*eandem legem*) to hold for other *ministeriales* of the church, such that none of them have his *ministerium* either by hereditary succession or in fief, nor in any other way than that which it pleases the abbot or church to grant."[75] Perhaps the papal confirmation of 1177 helped to endow the agreement with the flavor of "law," although it would be unwise to insist on a rigid definition of language in these charters.[76] In any event, between 1107 and 1179 what had initially been an ad hoc (though serious) negotiated agreement became the model for routine expectations of all ministerial behavior at Saint-Bertin. Ministerial responsibilities were distinguished from fiefs or hereditary positions, although sons often followed their fathers in practice, as the case of the de Reningelsts shows. An attempt was being made to put the idea of office into effect among lay overseers of the monastery's lands. Moreover, this idea had moved from the realm of verbal agreement to written records of abbot-agent relations. By 1179, the charters of both count and pope expressed a new notion of proper service.

The relations between the abbots of Saint-Bertin and the de Reningelst clan exemplify the struggle of abbots to control lay agents in the twelfth century. This case illustrates four important elements in the process of extracting more specific oaths from lay agents. First, abbots wanted to separate the landholdings of the man from his duties, functions, or powers as an agent of the abbot. The former was the *feodum in terris* at Saint-Bertin; the latter was the *ministerium*.[77] This distinction had the effect of separating personal holdings and monastic property. The second element was the abbot's insistence on the nonheritability of functions performed by the man as his agent. His duties or "office" were not heritable, which created a greater dependency of service and emphasized that these duties were contingent on abbatial authority. Abbots could also achieve the same end by insisting on unfree status, as Abbot Hugh did at Saint-Germain, which in itself implied nonheritability, or at least service owed at the lord's will. The third element was to define the proper behavior of the agent, although often only what should not be done was stated. In trying to prevent abuses, while simultaneously augmenting income, abbots sought to impose limits (even if merely instructions not to repeat past misdeeds) on their agents' power to exact and judge. Abbots were trying to delegate but not give away power. Consequently, the terms of granting power became more specific. Fourth, in addition to imposing behavioral restrictions directly, abbots also sought to subordinate lay agents to monks, usually provosts. Monks provided oversight of laymen, could be more easily controlled, and had notions of proper conduct more like the abbots' own. Although implementing any of these four changes did not require writing, it often helped to provide a record of events, be it the public audience of the abbot, the man's acknowledgement of his dependent status, the oath-swearing of the man which limited his power, or an instance of discipline. Writing was a powerful aid in assuring better service.

Signs of similar shifts in thought and behavior, countermeasures to the growth of lay agents' proto-lordship, can be found at other monasteries in the twelfth century. Signs of treating *feodum* and *ministerium* separately appear in the early twelfth century at Saint-Vaast-d'Arras. One of the monastery's advocates, Count Arnold of Cleves, wrote to Abbot Henry in 1120 to explain how he made the abbot's local man, Theodore, forswear both his *ministerium* and a *feodum* in money he received. Although Theodore was generally accused of having "maltreated the things of his lord" (*male tractando res dominorum suorum*), his protestations in his own defense also included his claim never to have "prosecuted justice for the abbot of Saint-Vaast beyond the bounds of his *ministerium*."[78] Whatever the nature of Theodore's misconduct, it was apparently his failure to perform as an officer which provided the advocate a convenient excuse for removal (see further below).

Ministerium was not the only way to express the concept of office which abbots were seeking to impose on lay agents. At the monastery of Saint-Père-de-Chartres, abbatial charters already tried to distinguish between investing a mayor with his mayorship (*majoratum*) and the land he received in the time of Abbot William (1101–29).[79] By the time of his successor, Abbot Udo (1130–50), the phrase *majoratum officium* was routinely used to express the duties of the mayor.[80] The duties of lay agents were being increasingly conceived, like those of monastic provosts, as "offices." Abbots were seeking better service from both groups with whom they shared their power.

One need not and should not, however, rely only on the wording in charters spelling out agents' duties to prove how important notions of "office" had become for abbots. Requiring oaths from lay agents sometimes was less important than defining who could hold a *ministerium* in the first place. Nonheritability of mayoral or ministerial position was often the most controversial aspect of abbot-agent relations. The abbatial charters at Saint-Père-de-Chartres, for example, increasingly insisted that mayorships were not heritable. The late eleventh-century charter of Abbot Eustace (1079–1101) implied that even if Albert, sole son of Martin, mayor of Emprenville, survived him, he would receive the mayor's house and lands (*majoratus villicationem*) only if his father did not misbehave and then only for his life.[81] The monks maintained control of Albert and the mayorship by not allowing his daughter to marry without her husband swearing fidelity.[82]

Abbot Udo (1130–50) was particularly insistent that mayorships were held only for life. When granting the mayorship of Champol to his man Berengar, Udo made sure Berengar had no doubts about his position:

I, brother Udo, humble abbot of the monastery of Saint-Père-de-Chartres . . . wish all to know . . . that Berengar, son of Godescalc, recognized in our chapter and swore upon the holy relics there that, because he claimed nothing by heredity in the mayorship (*majoratu*) of our village of Champol, he ought not to claim or to have anything by feudal right (*feodaliter*) or by birthright. We have commended to him the office of the said mayorship (*majoratus officium*) for as long as he shall live, on this condition, that neither he nor his descendents should ever make a feudal claim (*feodaliter*) of anything in respect of heredity or birthright in regard to this office.[83]

Although the precise meaning of Udo's use of *feodaliter* is vague, the overall thrust of his meaning appears clear: Berengar was not to inherit and his heirs were not to do so either. That Berengar was the son of Godescalc (and had been given in pawn in 1107) left no doubt about his unfree status. Abbot Udo took other opportunities to reinforce the notion of nonheritability of mayorships. In a collection of fiscal documents, he noted under the item for *Achiacus* that the land there was held, with the *majoria*, only for the life of the mayor.[84] When the once-imprisoned Mascelinus, mayor of Reconvilliers, came seeking freedom for his daughter, Abbot Udo seized his chance. In granting her freedom, Udo agreed not to hold a grudge "if neither she nor her heirs in descent of the aforesaid Mascelinus her father, could reclaim anything under any circumstance by heredity."[85]

Abbots also tried to prevent arbitrariness by limiting the power of their agents to exact and judge. These powers were the first ones lay agents arrogated to themselves and, when unchecked, they infringed on the abbot's own lordship. Although the abbots of Saint-Père may have cowed Mascelinus into promising better conduct by imprisoning him, limitations on mayoral behavior usually resulted from some degree of negotiation. Abbot Martin of Saint-Vaast and his mayors of Esclusiers and Bihucourt came to agreement over the mayors' taking of *corredium* (the custom of procuring meals that belonged to the monks) only through arbitration, including at least one other mayor as arbiter.[86] Extracting promises was naturally easier upon the initial appointment of a new mayor. At Saint-Père, Abbot William extracted quite explicit promises from Geoffrey of Arrou, when he made Geoffrey mayor of newly acquired land at Bois-Ruffin.[87] He limited Geoffrey's power to fine to 20 *denarii* and all pleas were to be resolved before the monk in charge and according to his wishes.[88] The woods there were to be open to all for their pigs, but Geoffrey was allowed to take other animals he found there, provided he returned any lost beasts to their owners. Finally, the charter noted that since Geoffrey wanted to place his man on the land, if Geoffrey failed to amend wrongs that man committed (when thrice-warned), Geoffey's man would be ejected.[89]

William's successor, Abbot Udo, was even more insistent (and specific) in his charters. Around 1140, Udo made Odo, mayor of Germignonville, reswear fidelity because of injuries he had done to the monastery.[90] Not satisfied with just an oath, Udo also had an agreement in two copies, a chirograph, drawn up between himself and Odo. The use of the chirograph may itself suggest that a negotiation transpired; its content certainly does. In this act, Abbot Udo explained that Odo admitted that "he had seized many things under the pretext of a fief over our church" and forswore doing so again in a public audience held by the abbot.[91] Odo's wife and heirs also had to abide by his promises. In return, Odo and his heirs were granted a *feodum* of twenty *solidi* beyond what he received as mayor. Such concessions were necessary to achieve peace.[92] Indeed, mayors already in place may have been harder to discipline, as they could pretend to have their position as a *feodum* or to hold it *feodaliter*, which is to say they could claim to inherit. Nevertheless, the abbot wanted and received assurances, since such hereditary claims ran directly counter to the new monastic sensibility about agents.

Abbot Udo had other means of control over Mayor Odo written

into his agreement with him. If the renders on which Odo's twenty *solidi* fief were based (the pasturing of pigs in the forest) declined, so would the amount he received. Odo was not to collect himself but only to receive his twenty *solidi* (or whatever was available) from the monk who was provost of the area at a particular time.[93] There would be no pretense of acting independently after the fashion of a lord. The agreement also restricted various other activities: the type and amount of grain Odo received was specified; the land he held remained limited to that held by his father, prior to Odo's claims to hold a fief; Odo had to allow the provost to judge all pleas and forfeitures of land. Finally, the chirograph specifically mentioned that Odo and his heirs could not in future claim more of a fief (*feodum*) than had been specified in the agreement.[94] Abbot Udo did not simply define Odo's holdings more closely, but also established the oversight of a monk as a check on his behavior. Thus, Odo was subordinated to both the abbot and the provost of his area.

Subordination of mayor to monk, usually a provost, while an important part of most monastic land management, is sometimes hidden from the historian. For example, in 1113, Louis VI freed one of his serfs to marry the daughter of the mayor of Toury, a substantial estate of Saint-Denis under threat from Hugh of Le Puiset, because a new mayor was needed to defend the estate.[95] Despite being a youthful provost of Toury at the time, Suger did not explain at all what kind of relationship he had with the mayor in his later description of Toury in his *De administratione*.[96] Why Suger omitted the event in his otherwise lengthy entry remains a matter for speculation.[97] Suger was clearly familiar with such matters. In 1134, a charter of Bishop Bartholemew of Laon recorded a donation by Robert de Montaigu of land at Petras to Saint-Denis, which specified that the land would be free of any of the bad custom (*prava consuetudine*) to which it had been subjected by Odo, mayor of Saint-Denis, and his nephew, Jobert. Furthermore, future disputes between the parties were to be settled by the provost for the area around Petras.[98] This act implied subordination of the mayor, and the monks of Saint-Denis later copied it into the *Cartulaire blanc*, but one does not know what Suger thought about it or about the actual relations of the various parties. Eventually, the mayor of Toury's duties and his subordination to a provost (especially in matters of justice) were spelled out in detail by Suger's successor Odo in 1159.[99]

The motivation for subordinating mayors to monks was obvious in other cases. Abbot Udo of Saint-Père probably insisted on subordination whenever possible because of difficulties like those in the time of his predecessor, Abbot William. In one case, a dispute arose between Germund, mayor of Pomeria, an estate belonging to the capicery of Saint-Père and Conan, the capicer. When Conan resisted Germund's attempt to have his nephew succeed him as mayor, Germund proceeded to destroy the village in retaliation. Later, after peace was made, Germund made amends. The list suggests the extent of the damages he did: he rebuilt the burned houses of the monks; he returned the horses, cows, and other chattels he had taken; and he handed over to Conan a tithe he had seized.[100]

The relations between mayors and monks were often just as rocky as relations between mayors and abbots. The violent nature of this kind of dispute must have reinforced Abbot Udo's (and other abbots') desire to provide for more thorough monastic oversight of mayors. Indeed, by the later twelfth century, such oversight became routinized at Saint-Père, as were the terms by which a mayor received his *majoratum*. In 1180, Abbot Stephen told Milo of Mendreville explicitly how he held the mayorship and what his relation to the sacristan would be. Besides the routine insistence that he would hold only for his lifetime, Milo was to hold the *majoratum* as his father did: he would have his house without rent and would render part of his crop from the land he worked. When the sacristan sent his man to collect and count his share of the crops, Milo would receive only half the right of pasturage. Should the sacristan choose instead a fixed rent of two *solidi* and ten *denarii* in a given year, Milo would receive all the pasturage. Finally, the monks would give Milo bread and wine, like other mayors, when he brought the monastery its rent.[101] Such explicit arrangements evolved out of a desire to eliminate the problems created by subordinating mayors to monks, who now served as intermediaries for abbots, and to whom abbots had delegated important aspects of their authority.

Men "Out of Hand" and Problems of Accountability

Enforcing precise arrangements with each mayor was easier in theory than in practice for twelfth-century abbots. Insisting on nonheritability of mayorships, limits of mayoral power, and oversight of mayors by monks was a difficult task. Such countermeasures to the aggrandizement of lay agents had to be applied constantly and even then were not always fully effective. Abbots increasingly had their men swear publicly, on relics, in the presence of many witnesses, and had oaths written down. Communal memory buttressed the strength of such oaths and thus gave monks an advantage over others in implementing such techniques of discipline. Written records increasingly provided proof of such agreements and their terms. Thus the rise of scribal culture aided abbots, as the increasingly instrumental use of writing helped achieve administrative ends. Oversight by monks tried to insure that these agreements would be properly kept by lay agents. Both memory and writing reinforced abbatial discipline, since constant repetition of disciplinary measures was necessary to keep abuses in check. But the abbot and his monks had to be ever vigilant.

One would be right to be suspicious of the effectiveness of these disciplinary measures. While many historians have critiqued the rhetoric of lay usurpation in monastic charters as a product of ecclesiastical bias, it is important to realize the nature of this "bias." Monks and their abbots had different notions of proper behavior and service. By portraying laymen as violators of church property, these charters may provide poor evidence of lay ideas, but they are good evidence for monastic mentality—an increasingly administrative mentality, seeking to rationalize land management and demanding accountability of agents. Implementing such shifts in behavior was difficult and met with resistance. Only strong abbots could do so at first, though the desire to achieve accountability was widely prevalent in all the monasteries examined. But were their methods effective?

The difficulties of applying disciplinary measures to lay agents should not be minimized. The complexities of the peculiar letter sent by Saint-Vaast's advocate, Count Arnold of Cleves, to Abbot Henry show that using such measures in practice was not easy.[102] As discussed above, Arnold's letter accused Theodore (both *minister* for Betuwe and *servus* of the abbot for an annual *feodum* of twenty pennies) of having maltreated his lords' holdings (*male tractando res dominorum suorum*).[103] Theodore had been called to answer for these unspecified misdeeds by the monastery's previous advocate, Count Arnold's father. Theodore attempted to avoid the old count and when he finally appeared before him, he denied ever being a *servus* of Saint-Vaast and claimed he had never prosecuted justice "beyond the bounds of his *ministerium*."[104] Oddly, Theodore tried to escape his dependent status (and the abbot's lordship) while simultaneously claiming he had acted properly as the abbot's *minister* in Betuwe. Count Arnold's father arranged to have Theodore removed from the *ministerium* (the *feodum* is not mentioned) and soon after died. The new count, Arnold, then summoned Theodore, who cleverly deceived him into restoring the *ministerium*.[105] At this point, the abbot's provost, William, objected to the reinstatement of Theodore and produced letters which justified the previous removal by Arnold's father.[106]

Count Arnold then proceeded to put the matter to rest. Arnold made Theodore and his heirs agree to forswear (*abjuravit*) both the *ministerium* of Betuwe and the *feodum* for a twelve-pound payment.[107] On the appointed day, Theodore and his heirs appeared before the count, the provost, and the *familia* of Saint-Vaast, received the payment and gave back the *ministerium* and the *feodum* to the provost and again forswore both. Then, Theodore accepted four-and-a-half *manses* at rent from the church, as a member of the abbot's *familia*, and, like it or not, he received them from his own nephew Theodore, now the abbot's new *minister* of Betuwe.[108] Although Theodore had been removed from the *ministerium*, he retained some land and his nephew acquired the *ministerium* despite (apparently) no claim of heredity. One wonders if the abuses of his uncle's time continued and if dislodging Theodore made his nephew's service any different.

A critical aspect of Theodore's case was the intervention of William, provost of the abbot. Had he not intervened or failed to produce the letters relating to the previous removal, Theodore probably would have succeeded in retaining his position. This intervention illustrates the weakness of relying solely on oaths to discipline lay agents. Oaths could be conveniently forgotten by agents once those who imposed them were no longer on the scene. The complementary role played by writing was extremely important. Agents could not be held accountable for their actions and disciplined if no one could remember what they had promised.

Even when armed with written records, abbots sometimes found themselves at a loss when dealing with their agents. Mayors and other men of the monastery often tried to act as independent lords. In the time of Abbot Martin of Saint-Vaast, Achard, mayor of Esclusiers, sold off the monks' rent of fifty eels to the monks of Saint-Eloy without the abbot's permission. Then, after Achard was caught out by Abbot Martin and Guimann, Martin had to guarantee Saint-Eloy the payment through the monk at Vaux-sur-Somme. If Achard did not produce the rent, even when ordered by the monk (which was virtually assumed), the monk of Vaux was to pay Saint-Eloy himself and take measures against Achard.[109] This Achard was the same mayor who had been taking meals for himself at the monk of Vaux's expense.[110] Such men behaved like minor lords and often flouted the monks' expectations of their subordination.

The discipline and control of lay agents in charge of monastic estates was not always as effective as abbots would have liked. Although many abbots sought to assert an alternative model of administrative rule, their model was not the dominant one. Lordship, especially oppressive, self-aggrandizing quasi-lordship of men like mayors, was often a nearly intractable problem. In particular, any attempt to prevent sons of these men from inheriting their power (nominally their duties) was routinely frustrated. Despite specific oaths abjuring any hereditary claims, the de Reningelst family of Saint-Bertin held the position of *ministerialis* of Poperinghe from before 1107 (when Lambert replaced his father Odo) to 1151 (when Lambert's son Raoul took over) and well into the thirteenth century, when various descendants became the hereditary "justiciers" of Poperinghe.[111] Even though the abbots of Saint-Bertin could not check hereditary claims by the de Reningelsts, in 1192 they did negotiate a detailed agreement which placed thirteen separate restraints on their behavior, especially in fiscal and judicial matters.[112] At Saint-Père (and elsewhere), the situation seemed little different. Albert, Mayor of Emprenville, inherited from his father, as did Berengar, son of Godescalc of Champol, and Milo of Mendreville. Occasionally, one can even find women bearing the title *majorissa*.[113] But the threat of non-inheritance, even when not realized, remained a useful negotiating strategy for abbots. In order to get the abbot of Saint-Père to agree to his brother Simon's inheritance before going on crusade, Herbert, son of the mayor of Ymonville, had to confront charges of damaging the estate and agree to a very specific definition of his receipts as mayor.[114] Thus, the familial *majoratum* and abuses of power were restricted in scope.

Abbots' increasing insistence on specific oaths of service and on rituals (and writing them down) demonstrated their desire to redefine the service of their lay agents. However, achieving more official behavior in practice was difficult. The persistence of actual heritability of mayorships, despite repeated acknowledgements of nonheritability by mayors, proves this point. On the other hand, inheritance was not a great problem so long as continued dependency and relatively good behavior could be assured. Indeed, as the dispute between the Mayor

Germund and capicer of Saint-Père showed, flouting mayoral expectations of inheritance could have disastrous consequences. Fidelity remained the basis for service. A strategy of accommodation guaranteed a certain rudimentary stability in income and peace, without exploiting the lands to their fullest potential. Checking the abuses of lay agents was one thing, but systematically redefining their service was another. Implementing accountability on a practical level required additional tools to be effective.

Audits and Accountability

Reforming abbots used many related methods to control their men. Abbatial insistence first on fidelity and dependent status, then on the renewal of fidelity, and eventually on oaths with more specific terms slowly led to increased control of unruly lay agents. Monastic oversight of lay agents, usually in the form of mayoral or ministerial subordination to a provost, reinforced occasional abbatial demands of good behavior. The next step toward accountability was routine monitoring and evaluation of the efficacy and reliability of these men. As abbots sought to exploit their estates economically, they developed the tools with which to perceive the gap between what they were owed and what their men brought in. Abbots' attempts to extract the difference had to compete with their men's desire for self-aggrandizement. In consequence, implementing change was extremely difficult. Still, meetings of abbots and agents became less occasional and more routine. Meetings became audiences before the abbot and, by implication, his court. At these meetings, abbots attempted to discipline and control agents for specific practical purposes as well as to make an example of them in front of their peers. One of the most important of these purposes was the collection of revenues, whose potential was only just being realized. Monks began to keep written records of these meetings to assist in this process. New and more descriptive surveys also aided in this goal. Thus, the "audit" slowly developed, in which agents were held fiscally accountable for their actions.

Audits could be either oral or written, but the vast majority of audits must have originally been oral and so little written evidence of them survives. Even when aids were employed, such as an abacus or counting sticks, they have left little permanent evidence. Audits grew out of the more general lordly audiences and distinguishing between the audit and the meeting itself may be overly rigid. Suger, for example, was a master of the audience but surprisingly we have no evidence of his having used a written audit in the more restricted sense. He began his *De administratione* with the claim that his brethren approached him in general chapter while he conferred with them about "people and private business."[115] This claim had the effect of portraying him as both the abbot consulting with his brethren and as lord holding an audience. It was a dual role familiar to all abbots. Likewise, when Matthew le Bel claimed that he was "asked by lord Abbot Suger and the whole convent" to list his fiefs and vassals in 1125, such a request likely came during an audience or at least in a public assembly.[116] Yet despite the careful way in which Suger presented in his book the *incrementum* he achieved at each holding during his rule, he almost never mentioned either mayors or provosts (except himself) and never described anything like an audit of them. Indeed, Suger mentioned a mayor only once, in passing, as having usurped lands belonging to the abbey at Beaune-la-Rolande.[117]

In general, improved revenues were far more frequently mentioned by Suger than any audits he may have conducted. Such omissions are especially frustrating in Suger's case, given that there is plentiful evidence that he had detailed knowledge of the abbey's estates from personal experience, since he had served as provost at Toury and Berneval early in his career.[118] In addition to his precise calculation of revenues, he mentioned that he had the ancient and ruinous customary renders in kind (*consuetudines*) enumerated at Monnerville, before remitting them.[119] Suger probably conducted a contemporary survey of the *consuetudines* or else relied on older documents (perhaps even those produced in the Carolingian period) for a listing of what was owed.[120] But lacking any surviving surveys or evidence of an audit of any kind (such as wax tablets), the historian can only speculate about Suger's actual relations with the men who ran Monnerville for him.

Part of the purpose in developing new, more accurate written surveys of possessions was to determine the extent of wealth and whether what was owed (or what should be owed) was paid. Just as confirmations moved toward listing holdings in more detail, so too did surveys change from static lists of rents and renders to more descriptive current documents. The movement to increasingly accurate surveys or records of revenues shows an enhanced concern not just with exploitation of land, as argued in Chapter 3, but also with monitoring lay agents of the domains. Monitoring or auditing the performance of such men through oral and written means was a crucial step toward making them more accountable for their actions.

Suger's contemporary, Abbot Udo of Saint-Père-de-Chartres, began to keep detailed records of revenues and payments in addition to his other written records. Later monks copied various samples of these records in the later *Codex Argenteus* as a composite document.[121] Several of the items they copied pertained to the holdings of mayors whom Abbot Udo (and abbots before and after him) tried to control. The list of revenues of the chamberlain included six pennies from the grange of Mascelinus, the once-imprisoned mayor of Reconvilliers.[122] The revenue listing of the capicery had three payments in coin by the mayor of Mendreville and a note for him to deliver the *champart* owed when requested. This description of crop sharing foreshadowed the more specific relation between the mayor of Mendreville, Milo, and the sacristan (the superior of the capicer) spelled out in 1180.[123] All the revenues of Pomerata, which had been the subject of the contemporary dispute between Mayor Germund and the capicer, were listed, including the tithe, *champart*, and other revenues.[124] Even the minute rents of Champol were mentioned, where Berengar was mayor.[125]

This section of the *Codex Argenteus* also included longer descriptions of revenues for specific estates, resembling miniature surveys, or *brevia*. These descriptions had lists of rents owed by individuals, when and to whom they were paid (including payments to mayors), and collective totals of payments.[126] The detail of these lists indicate that the disputes between Udo and his mayors probably had a more concrete nature than suggested by the oaths and agreements previously examined. Indeed, taken together with all the other lists he made, they suggest a wide-ranging effort by Udo to monitor both his men and the collection and distribution of revenues. Keeping track of the fiscal obligations of mayors in written records represented an attempt by Udo to more effectively discipline and control the mayors of Saint-Père. It was a step toward fiscal accountability.

Guimann of Saint-Vaast compiled an extensive set of lists attempting to monitor collection and distribution of revenues for Abbot Martin. The sheer size and detail of these lists suggests he expended a great effort to assemble and write down the information. The final and incomplete section of Guimann's work, *de diversitate districtorum* (effectively a massive survey) contained a series of *brevia* interspersed with charters, listing the possessions of Saint-Vaast outside of Arras and the detailed obligations of those inhabiting them. These *brevia* followed a fairly standard order of presentation, beginning with a general statement of the monastery's rights and possessions in each place, such as the church, manor house, profits of justice, ovens, tolls, mills, and tithes. Next, they usually proceeded to list the lands held by farmers and the payments rendered for them. Finally, the *brevia* included a list of larger landholders: the vassals of Saint-Vaast, their own men, and their fiefs.[127] The *brevia* thus formed a logical extension of the *hostagia* list for the town of Arras which they followed in Guimann's cartulary.[128]

Although rather different in form and content from those in the polyptych of 866, which Guimann said he had before him, these *brevia* may have been inspired by a systematic element in it.[129] Like the list of *hostagia*, the survey of the districts contained both general statements of what was owed and lists of specific payments by individuals. For example, even though the survey clearly stated that the residents of the *suburbium* of Arras near the gate of Puniel owed twelve pennies and two chickens for each *curtil* of land every year, the *brevia* recorded actual obligations paid by every person for their *curtils*, frequently at different rates.[130] Thus, the survey served as both a prescriptive document and a description of the payments actually made.

Evidence for the relations of Abbot Martin with his lay agents can often be found in the part of each *brevis* listing larger landholders. Included amongst these men were the laymen who acted for the abbot, the *villici* or bailiffs, and a description of their holdings and privileges. These entries usually specified the revenues of a bailiff, which always included his bailiwick (*villicatio*), the monastery's part of each estate, and the collection of rents and fines. The *villicatio* was similar to what the *majoratum* was at other monasteries, and the bailiffs acted as mayors did.[131] At Saint-Vaast, the *villicatio* consisted of one-third of the customary payments for land or farming, as illustrated by the entry of the village of Vic, in which two bailiffs, Peter and Stephen, shared the *villicatio*, each receiving a sixth of the payments.[132] The *villicatio* included fines they also received for doing justice. Bailiffs also usually possessed land of their own and had their payments for them listed with other lands. The most humble bailiff seemed to have little more than a *curtil* or two and a fraction of the *villicatio*. Some of the more powerful bailiffs had their own vassals. For example, Walter of Arras, both a bailiff and a cleric, had five *vavassores*, including Wibert, another bailiff, and Baldwin, a knight.[133] Thus, the entries for bailiffs indicate that these men varied widely in power, but the form was consistent enough to indicate that Guimann tried to record their duties systematically so as to monitor their activities better.

The formulaic nature of Guimann's entries suggests that some system of estate administration was already in place by his time. Abbot Wéry had probably already started reshaping the monastery's domains before Martin's time, as the pattern of land transactions suggests.[134] Furthermore, it seems likely that the division of revenues, one-third to the agent and two-thirds to the monks, had already been fixed by custom when Guimann began surveying. The thoroughness of preexisting arrangements should not be underestimated just because they were not recorded in sufficient detail for the historian to reconstruct them completely. For example, the descriptions of the judicial customs for Saint-Vaast's large allodial properties, listed under the title *de generali placito* in Guimann's work, show a rather complex interaction between the abbot and his local men.[135] Only the abbot or his provost could come to judge in the allodial lands and then he did so surrounded by the local *scabini* and according to the *lex placiti*. Men would then bring claims to be heard and they would be judged by the abbot in consultation with the *scabini*.[136] Such meetings were, in effect, a great judicial audience, the procedure for which had long been agreed upon. Although the abbot only possessed fines of justice in these allodial properties, their payment was carefully specified: one-third went to a *major placiti* and two-thirds to the abbot, unless a man of the abbot was involved, in which case the whole fine went to the *major*.[137]

The two-third/one-third split of revenues between abbot and *major* or *villicus* throughout Guimann's *de diversitate districtorum* shows that the division of responsibilities and payments had been established in principle by Martin's time. On the other hand, Guimann intended to describe the monastery's holdings clearly and one must not mistake his desire to create an orderly work (or orderly records) for the existence of actual order. The consistency of his *brevia* prove that he was systematic, but not necessarily that administration of the monastery's estates was so.

Although the normative aspect of Guimann's survey hid much of the wrangling necessary to produce it, disputes and the disciplining of bailiffs left their marks. A notice from 1169, added to the end of the entries for Berneville, explained one such instance involving Baldwin, bailiff of Simoncourt.[138] The notice explained that for a long time

Baldwin had held the payments, renders, and tithes of a church in the nearby hamlet of *Gorghechunz*, claiming that it was his fief, a claim Abbot Martin denied.[139] As Guimann described it, the result was similar to instances of mayoral discipline at other monasteries: after being summoned to "Christian justice" (the abbot's court) and "for fear of God and with the counsel of his friends," Baldwin realized that "it was illegitimate and against reason" for a layman to hold things belonging to a church, and so he gave them back to the monastery.[140] Martin had higher expectations of his bailiffs than his predecessors did. By ordering Guimann to survey the monastery's holdings, Martin took steps toward disciplining and controlling his bailiffs. Resolving such disputes and recording their resolutions must have been one goal of compiling so complete a description of obligations.

Guimann's survey offers little direct evidence about audiences or audits, because its *brevia* were the product of public assemblies rather than part of the process of holding them. Guimann and his assistants probably toured the estates and made inquiries at each *villa* about what was owed. The order of the *brevia* in Guimann's work suggests possible routes of surveyors through the estates, up and down river valleys, in loops around Arras.[141] These inquiries certainly included testimony by lay agents of the monastery in addition to the use of older normative documents documents which Guimann copied. Guimann's explanation of how he surveyed at Bailleul shows the oral component of auditing:

Although in the village of Bailleul the diversity of customs in lands and rents of Saint-Vaast creates much confusion, because Saint-Vaast has nothing except jurisdiction (*districtus*) in its free allods, we who are the preservers of the rights of our church consign to writing the truth of customs and rents which has been clearly investigated and proven by the testimony of mayors.[142]

Thus, Guimann used oral testimony, probably in a public assembly, to determine rents being paid, and to go beyond the charters, which indicated what was theoretically owed. In short, he conducted something like an on-site audit.

Such inquiries doubtless proved difficult, and not simply because of the passage of time or the resistance of bailiffs. The survey at Bailleul resulting from Guimann's inquiries allocated various payments into three separate lists of revenues for the vestiary, the infirmary, and the treasury of Saint-Vaast. It often recorded different payments by the same individuals, such as the bailiff Godfrey, under these separate lists.[143] One wonders if the peasants or the bailiff could have kept such a complex network of payments straight to begin with or whether Guimann and his surveyors simply imposed it on top of existing payments. In any event, the structure of the survey of Bailleul offers no direct information about its later use.

Nevertheless, the detail and apparent precision of Guimann's *brevia* made them nearly ideal aids for auditing or accounting. First of all, Guimann went beyond a general statement of what was owed to describe individuals' payments. This description allowed the monks to identify and extract renders from nonpayers. Second, there are signs that Guimann intended his work to be a practical, working document. He often provided internal references directing a reader to surveys of holdings he had already completed so that a complete picture of an individual's possessions could be achieved. For example, after describing the rights of Stephen, bailiff of Vic, to one-third of the Mercatel mill, Guimann steered the reader to the previous description of Mercatel and the mill itself, supplying a precise cross-reference.[144] Finally, Guimann himself encouraged the use of his work in his introduction. In his remarks on the veracity and accuracy of the *brevia*, Guimann asserted: "For example, if the reader should find Saint-Vaast to have this much or that much in a certain possession, he may diligently investigate immediately who owes and what they owe and how much each owes and why they owe it because he will find it before his eyes, and what is said to be combined in a total he will verify to be accurately divided in its parts."[145] In effect, Guimann invited his reader, either Abbot Martin, the dedicatee of his work, or another monk, to use his work when making such inquiries. Such an invitation demonstrated the confidence of someone who had assembled information exhaustively.

Although Guimann's writings do not provide any obvious annual calculations of what was paid versus what was owed (and, therefore, do not comprise an actual "account"), clearly Guimann intended the surveys to be used in performing such calculations. In particular, the section of his cartulary on *hostagia* and districts could be used to check on bailiffs. In his prologue to this section, Guimann indicated that the records of payments by individuals might be particularly useful for monitoring entry and exit fines which bailiffs were supposed to transmit to the monastery:

Concerning those reliefs, entry and exit: if the bailiffs (*villici*) by concealing anything or in any other way should dare to defraud or reduce them, the monk who collects *hostagia* should take careful precaution against [this practice]; and if he should see anyone pay rent for any house or *curtil* who in the past term did not pay, and it is not written in his charter, he should diligently inquire how and in what fashion he entered into that house or curtil and having discovered the concealment thus, let him extract his entry or exit relief from his bailiff (*villicus*).[146]

Although the problem of reliefs was similar to that of *hostagia*, namely that the frequent division and transmission of lands often outstripped written records, the problem of reliefs was also one of discipline.[147] Therefore, Guimann provided a way to check on both individual tenants and on bailiffs. Guimann must have been aware of the difficulties caused by men of the monastery who got out of hand and he intended his work to be a tool for preventing them from absorbing the monks' revenues. Since his lists recorded the monk who received payments, it could also be used for internal discipline. It is this prospective, practical aspect of Guimann's *brevia* that separated them from comparable earlier surveys. Guimann intended them to be used as the written basis of a regular audit, as a tool to compare what was owed with what was actually paid. They represented, albeit on a grander scale, the goal to which Abbots Hugh of Saint-Germain, Udo of Saint-Père, and even Suger were aspiring in their own record-keeping.

Discipline and Writing

Efforts to survey more descriptively and write down oaths of lay servitors formed critical parts of a larger attempt by abbots to redefine their service: to make them functional agents who served more responsibly. The occasional aspects of traditional discipline, such as the lordly audience and the one-time promise of fidelity, could only check lay agents to a limited degree. More thorough and regular methods of discipline and control were needed to curb abuses and monitor agents. Writing helped reinforce new techniques of discipline such as the oath of office (by providing a record of its terms) and audits (by providing a record against which to measure performance). When it came to disciplining and controlling their lay subordinates, abbots used all tools which came to hand. Thus, they employed a variety of measures in concert: oaths of office, monastic oversight, and audits (either oral or based on written records).

Such measures were valuable alternatives to traditional means of asserting the abbot's lordship (through force, claims of unfreedom, fidelity) and could be combined with them if necessary to achieve results.

Such innovative methods, however, should not be viewed in isolation from attempts at reform. Nor should they be separated from broader economic changes, especially the new opportunities for mayors to establish proto-lordships, which forced reaction by monastic reformers. The reorganization of estates for better exploitation could not be achieved without disciplining mayors and bailiffs, who sought to dominate them for their own profit. Surveys of estates could not be completed without the testimony and at least the nominal cooperation of such men. Monastic officers could not use revenues allocated to particular offices if they could not collect those revenues. Monastic oversight by provosts was not effective if those monks did not possess their own understanding of proper service. All of these activities were predicated on relatively peaceful and secure possession of estates by monks, whether that meant freedom from external threat or internal dissension by mayors.

Abbots who sought to effect reforms had to contend with all these matters at once. What is significant about these disciplinary measures in the twelfth century is not simply that they were attempted, since "reform" in various senses had always been a part of medieval monasticism, but that they were attempted programmatically by certain abbots. Abbots such as Suger of Saint-Denis, Martin of Saint-Vaast, Hugh V of Saint-Germain, Udo of Saint-Père, and even Lambert of Saint-Bertin had a broader, more insistent, and more practical view of reform than their predecessors. They sought to augment their monasteries' wealth by better management of extant resources and thus shared a vision of their monasteries which was economic. To do so, they had to pursue new management techniques as alternatives or supplements to their traditional authority, in order to persuade or force their men to behave as responsible servitors and to hold them accountable for their actions. These attempts, repeated again and again, were remembered, gradually written down, and eventually more consistently applied. These abbots gradually overcame resistance by insisting on better service and better behavior and thus slowly applied new ideas of their authority over lay agents in practice.

But the persistence of quasi-lordship and the continuing need for discipline and resubordination of lay agents reveals how difficult a situation most abbots faced. The constant repetition of the prohibition against inheritance by agents masks the almost universal concession of office by abbots to sons of mayors, ministerials, and bailiffs to insure fidelity. Inheritance was only one aspect of the problem of lay service. The inability of abbots to force their men to pay what they owed, even when armed with extensive records, shows how frequent evasion must have been. Every mayor or bailiff wanted to escape his dependent status and behave like a lord. The need to produce elaborate genealogies of mayors shows how hard it was to keep track of these men and their families. Complaints about the ever shifting possession of land by a burgeoning population provide evidence of how difficult it was to keep current records of status, who owed what, and whether agents had transmitted adequate revenues to the monastery. It was hard for abbots to keep pace with a society on the move. Ultimately, the lack of regular accounts and accounting probably frustrated the aims of many reform-minded northern French abbots.

To judge the ability and achievements of twelfth-century abbots by the continuation of such problems of discipline and control of agents is a mistake. Reform-minded abbots achieved valuable concessions, especially in their increasingly precise definition of the duties of lay agents. In addition, the pursuit of reform had a dramatic impact on the wealth, prosperity, and orderliness of most monastic communities. Rebuilding the church of Saint-Denis out of the *incrementum* achieved by Suger was only one dramatic example of what financial reforms could achieve. Between them, Abbot Martin and Guimann the cellarer secured the wealth and power of Saint-Vaast in one of the most dynamic cities in Europe. Abbots William and Udo of Saint-Père transformed what was once a small cell of monks into a substantial monastery. Even at monasteries where abbatial plans flew in the face of their servitors' ambitions, the reorganization of lands, increased produce of estates, and greater certainty of delivery of revenues for specific purposes was more than worth the trouble. Hugh of Saint-Germain managed to reestablish his monastery, whose influence had been eclipsed since Carolingian times, as a major and independent force in the Parisian region despite continuing attempts by mayors to escape his rule. The monks of Saint-Bertin, even though their abbots remained embroiled in election struggles, managed to regularize relations with some of the most powerful men who had dominated their estates.

Furthermore, the varied countermeasures to lay aggrandizement, successful or not, left traces in thought and writing which provided a new generation of monks with a basis for administrative action. By the late twelfth and early thirteenth century, many monasteries produced new, more extensive cartularies which went well beyond the traditional need to copy confirmations or compose history. Guimann's cartulary was a notable forerunner of these cartularies. These new cartularies had organizational structures adapted to the new demands of internal and external administration. At Saint-Denis, in addition to a known twelfth-century book of privileges, a now lost cartulary may have been produced toward the end of Suger's abbacy or slightly later.[148] The monks there also eventually produced the monumental *Cartulaire blanc*, in which the entries were organized by offices of the cloister or estate group.[149] The dates of the acts in this cartulary are quite revealing, as Giles Constable has observed: "While Suger did not initiate the tendency for the various monastic offices at Saint-Denis to become increasingly independent, it is no accident that so many of the sections in the *Cartulaire blanc* begin with documents dating either from his abbacy or just before or after."[150] At Saint-Germain-des-Prés, Hugh's successors, in addition to collecting his administrative documents at the end of the cartulary of three crosses, began to create a wholly new cartulary, organized by the geography of estates.[151] The earliest substantial cluster of documents in this cartulary dates from the mid-twelfth century, with a substantial increase in numbers during Hugh's abbacy (1162–82).[152] The *Codex Argenteus* of Saint-Père, produced in the last quarter of the twelfth century, had a section for documents relating to the cellary, including many of Abbot Udo's documents, and three others organized by provostships.[153] Even the thirteenth-century cartulary of Saint-Bertin, which does not have as rigid an organizational structure as these other cartularies, eschews traditional arrangement of privileges in favor of estate geography.[154] The explosion of overall monastic cartulary production in the thirteenth century, along with the widespread adoption of organization by estate geography or monastic office shows that administrative concerns were becoming widely diffused.[155] Cartularies were becoming practical tools of power.[156]

Conclusions

The new organizational schemes in late twelfth- and early thirteenth-century cartularies directly reflected an administrative mindset, which arose out of the efforts of twelfth-century reforming abbots and their confidantes. They are not only the proof of such attempts but were the goal of them as well. Abbatial initiatives—attempts to rule in a new, more associative fashion and to make monks and lay servants behave more officially—not only left written traces in their own time, but transformed monastic record-keeping afterward. The new style of record-keeping, emphasizing discipline and accountability instead of commemoration, history, and title, was consciously prospective. Monks like Guimann wrote not simply to be remembered, but in order to arm their successors with increasingly necessary information. New organizational schemes by estate geography or revenues of offices slowly took their place alongside (literally in Guimann's case) the older memorial and legal records, *gestae* and dossiers. The systematic and instrumental use of written records helped later abbots disciple and control their lay and monastic servitors—to achieve a more effective accountability—that allowed them to realize their administrative schemes. Thus, the successors of Suger, Martin, Udo, Hugh V, Lambert and other French abbots of the twelfth century could not just claim their rights, but administer their lands and people more effectively.

Conclusion: Accountability, Writing, and Rule by 1200

BY 1200, ALL FIVE OF THE monasteries examined in this study had developed new ways of organizing documents in books concerning their patrimonies. These books included new, more descriptive instruments of administration, which could be used to monitor the doings of monks and men who served them on estates. With these instruments, ranging from marginal notations to handlists to full-blown surveys, abbots could exploit lands more efficiently, allocate revenues, fund colossal building projects, find men who got "out of hand" and extract promises of more responsible behavior; ultimately, they could hold them accountable. But was monastic administration institutionalized at this time? If one defines institutionalized governance by change from ad hoc practices to the routine, by systematic adoption of repetitive procedures, written or otherwise, then the answer may be no. Some twelfth-century abbots at the five monasteries I consider certainly did begin to discipline their monks and lay agents more forcefully and more frequently. Slowly, they turned the traditional days on which men rendered produce and paid rent into occasions to examine the service and income they received. But abbots such as Suger, Martin, Udo, Lambert or Hugh do not seem to have called their monks or men to "account" in any systematic way. They dealt with problems as they arose through audits and audiences. Expectations were raised, but the gap between expectation and service was still substantial and countermeasures to bad or unacceptable service were still occasional.

If one is looking for specialized descriptive accounts that served *only* fiscal purposes as evidence of an institutionalized accountability, one may also be disappointed. The monastic *descriptio bonorum*, or monastic cartularies in their various organizing schemes, were still influenced by the older commemorative, pious, and historical forms out of which they grew. Likewise, monks' ideas about their land were always tempered by social and religious notions of space and influenced by the reform rhetoric of a fixed, inviolate patrimony. Holy space remained contested. Not surprisingly, many Benedictine monks were traditionalists. Many cartularies contained older fiscal records, preserved for historical reasons, which could be used to maintain the traditional patrimonial management system. But they described only what was ideally owed or possessed, not what was gathered or held in actuality. These older documents were in effect static and their contents had been made obsolete by the pace of social and economic change after the late Carolingian period. Abbots needed current descriptions to run the new revenue-based systems of administration and to share power with subordinates. They required updated instruments for dynamic management of changing resources. Even though monks started making more current and more descriptive records of their possessions, they were still heavily influenced by the old inventories and ideas associated with them. They treated some books, like the *Vetus Folquinus* at Saint-Bertin, more like treasures than tools.[1] As its name indicates, the *Codex Argenteus* of Saint-Père was bound in silver and encrusted in gems in the twelfth century, a treasure in itself.[2]

Despite such traditionalism, certain aspects of monastic administration became more firmly established by the end of the twelfth century. Monks made new, current surveys and leased, exchanged, and reorganized estates for efficiency of exploitation. They organized and assembled old and new documents in books, such as Guimann's cartulary, which were intended (at least in part) for the purpose of managing land resources and disciplining men. Monks thus brought the ideal and the real into sharper contrast during the twelfth century. Older commemorative forms eroded under the pressure of practical managerial considerations, so that the difference between what should be collected and what was actually received could be more easily determined. Abbots extracted promises from monks and mayors to behave responsibly, to do only what they should. Then they wrote these promises down and they, or their successors, sought to hold men to them. Suger could write an entire work, devoted to *augmentatio* and the *incrementum* he raised during the years of his administration and how he spent it. But a series of yearly accounts, as the kings of France and the counts of Flanders possessed by the turn of the thirteenth century, does not seem to have existed. Moreover, like contemporary kings and counts, twelfth-century monks did not have a balance sheet, to match income and outgo. Any balance had to be struck in their minds. Budgeting as such was a later phenomenon in northern France. In this sense, monastic administration was still not institutionalized.

But if one is looking for a group with the budding expertise to create such a balance sheet, with a body of continuous and communally held ideas about responsible service, remembered from generation to generation, this did exist. By the eleventh century, monks were already the "religious professionals" charged with the duty of remembering.[3] Their culture was explicitly a memorial one.[4] They remembered family relations, the dead, their patrons, and the confirmations they received in books. Only a small mental modification was needed to start remembering promises of payment or of service in written form. By the twelfth century, monks increasingly produced written instruments for administration, and counting (and accounting) became more common. Monks were becoming more professional, more like the *clerici*, the clerks who could be found serving lords everywhere. The transformation of the internal administration of monasteries, the new style of abbatial rule, and the increased expectation of responsible behavior from monks and laymen all provided a continuing body of ideas and practices which could be called institutional.

Inside the cloister, change had to proceed as reform and under the direction of a strong abbot. The reason for this is that monks, especially in older monasteries, were conservative. They preserved documents simply because they viewed them as part of the patrimony or the saint's treasures, and often did so for their own polemical ends. Monks had learned to resist transactions that would diminish any aspect of their part of the patrimony. Abbots also had to have opportunity. An abbot who had the power and authority to control both monks and laymen needed time to effect changes. Monks often did not want an abbot with that much power or so long a rule. As Gregorian reform made it possible for monks to have influence in the selection of the abbot, they could play it safe by choosing the oldest member of the house, knowing his rule would be short. A younger, vigorous abbot was a daring choice.[5] Choosing forty-year-old Suger, without consulting the king, was not easy for the monks of Saint-Denis. Martin of Saint-Vaast (1155–84) had nearly thirty years of rule, but only set Guimann to preparing his codex in 1170. The customary of Saint-Vaast, which regulated the monks' lifestyle and duties, could only be changed in 1175.

The greatest impact of the new administrative ideas and practices could be found inside the monastery itself. While some monastic officers were named in the Rule and while estates were allocated for particular needs in Carolingian reform, by the twelfth century these activities were becoming departmentalized in offices. An abbot could delegate authority to monks as officers, such as Guimann the cellarer. Increasingly, abbots expected and received responsible service from these monks: they were accountable for their behavior, even fiscally accountable. Abbot Udo of Saint-Père could order a yearly payment from every officer and provost of the monastery to improve the library. Moreover, once the arrangement was made, Udo had the specific payments written down in a list so that the *armarius* could not change the terms with the other *administratores*.[6] All sides had to be accountable: the abbot, the *armarius*, and the other officers.

Abbots faced greater problems externalizing new notions of service and discipline beyond the cloister. Throwing a mayor in prison, as Udo's predecessor Abbot William did, was an act of lordly power and could not always be the answer. Not every abbot could call upon a king, as Suger did with Louis VI, to check the abuses of self-aggrandizing local lords. Abbots began to rely increasingly on their monks, who could monitor the activities of lay agents and even record them. At the same time, the development of a consultative and shared power structure within the monastery necessarily diminished some of the independent power of an abbot to discipline. The new style of rule had its advantages and disadvantages. Likewise, record-keeping was a two-edged sword, which could cut abbots as well as those outside the cloister. Even the abbot could be held accountable, not just by God, but also by his brothers.

Day of Reckoning

And I saw the dead, great and small, standing before the throne, and books were opened. Also another book, which is the book of life. And the dead were judged by what was written in the books, by what they had done. (Revelation 20: 12)

In the apostle John's *Book of Revelation*, Jesus holds an audience at which the living and the dead are held accountable for their earthly actions. This apocalyptic story, well known to every medieval man and monk, presented in starkest terms how a person's afterlife would be determined. This final reckoning—accounting for all mortal transgressions—was repeatedly used as a cautionary tale about the wages of sin. Mortal actions could lead to Heaven or Hell. Kings and clerics knew, and feared, the Day of Reckoning, literally, the day of rendering accounts.[7]

With this biblical judgment in the offing, monastic accountability could never be a purely fiscal exercise. Accurate renders were for the glory of God, and not merely for the abbot. Abbots reminded their mayors and *villici* that failure to deliver what they owed the monastery constituted an offense against the saints and God. The moral, biblical dimension of accountability was ever present among monks and extended to laymen as well. Secular lords may have used the complementary teaching of Jesus for their own benefit: "Render therefore to Caesar the things that are Caesar's, and to God the things that are God's" (Matthew 22: 21). But medieval accountability, whether by abbot or king, could not totally separate the mundane from the divine. Administering was never without an element of ministering. Given this context, it would be a mistake to exclude monks from a larger discussion of lordship and accountability. Reflecting on the character of twelfth-century Benedictine accountability and administration, it is easy to see how these ideas and practices relate to other monks, other clerics, and secular rulers. It is worth thinking about Benedictine monks' relations with those outside their houses to put their thoughts and actions into proper perspective.

Just as with Carolingian and Cluniac reform, Benedictine monks have sometimes been seen as resistant to (and targets of) twelfth-century waves of monastic reform. The more strict Cistercian interpretation of the Rule and criticisms based on it encouraged Benedictine abbots such as Suger to reform their own lifestyles and those of their monks. The Benedictine response was to get back to the basics of Benedict of Aniane's Rule, not to adopt the new Cistercian interpretation evolving in the 1120s and 1130s. New economic ideas about land, however, could and did fit into this kind of reform and this fact has been overlooked previously. Assuming that stodgy black monks were the least likely candidates to engage in innovative economic practices, scholars have looked elsewhere to locate the roots of more flexible economic thinking. They believed that the most progressive economic behavior must be found in the newer orders. Many scholars point to the Cistercians as the true economic innovators. The Cistercians, besides emphasizing manual

labor and direct farming of their lands, also made active use of exchanges, pawning, and leasing of lands. They became adept financial
managers, assembling economically coherent granges, thereby taking
advantage of twelfth-century economic growth directly.[8] Indeed, as Dietrich Lohrmann has shown, Cistercian activities, like those of regular
canons, were a driving force in dividing and reshaping older estate patterns in twelfth-century northern France.[9] Constance Bouchard has argued,
furthermore, that no conflict existed between Cistercian spiritual ideals
and developing twelfth-century economic practices; indeed, these monks
were "prime movers in their evolution" as holy entrepreneurs.[10]

This focus on Cistercian innovation has obscured important economic developments at older Benedictine houses. The Cistercians were
not alone in using conveyances for economic purposes. Leasing, pawning, and exchanging required partners, neighbors willing to give or
cede land to the new orders. The local lay landholders were not the only
ones willing to be "neighbors" of Cluny or Cîteaux.[11] Older Benedictine houses also became willing partners in these economic processes.
As seen at Saint-Vaast, they took advantage of the opportunity to raise
income from previously unproductive lands, to consolidate or cede lands
which they found difficult to manage, and to secure stable supplies of
key foodstuffs. The occasion of exchanging or leasing land to other
ecclesiastical groups also provided the opportunity to reduce or throw
off the customary payments extracted by mayors or other laymen, a process of interaction which Lohrmann observed between older and newer
foundations in the Vermandois.[12] The explosive growth of priories in
Flanders and northern France had much the same effect. Indeed, Cistercians were not the only holy entrepreneurs in the twelfth century.
Perhaps we should see them, rather, as providing the "sweat equity" or
labor for a mutually beneficial exercise, while older Benedictine houses
contributed the "capital": lands which did not fit into an increasingly
perceived scheme of exploitation for gain.[13] Moreover, if no conflict
existed between spirituality and economic practices among Cistercians,
how could there be one for their older brethren, like Suger, for whom
all gain was Saint Denis' gain?

Outside the cloister, but still in the Church, the role played by secular clergymen as bearers of new ideas of administration or accountability grew in importance. A *gesta episcoporum* could function in the same
manner as a *gesta abbatum*; episcopal cartularies changed just as monastic ones did in the twelfth century.[14] A good example is the *Gesta Pontificum*

Autissiodorensium, the "Deeds of the Bishops of Auxerre," which repeatedly emphasized the successful (or unsuccessful) administrative qualities of the six twelfth-century bishops.[15] In the first half of the twelfth century, two out of three bishops of Auxerre had previously been abbots.[16] Episcopal rule, probably always more lordly than abbatial rule, was likewise transformed by Gregorian reform, and twelfth-century bishops in northern France showed a renewed interest in reordered domains and exploiting their economic power base.[17] They often contended more directly with kings, counts, and lesser lords.

On a broader level, *clerici* became ever more ubiquitous throughout the church and society. This phenomenon was linked to two important trends in the twelfth century: the burgeoning use of money and the growing appreciation of literacy and counting ability. Those who could write and count possessed a practical skill which made them valuable to rulers, offering them the possibility of social climbing through service. Meanwhile, the increased use of money, while creating the possibility of mobile wealth in a society based largely on immovable economic resources, also forced rulers to keep track of ever larger amounts.[18] Monks participated in these developments, but their talents usually remained within the cloister. Secular clerks became the translators of ecclesiastical notions of accountability, placing useful skills and techniques in the hands of kings and great magnates. Philip Augustus, in particular, relied on clerics to run his fiscal and judicial central administration.[19] The counts of Flanders increasingly relied on such men in the later twelfth century, but they had used the provost of the church of Saint-Donatian of Bruges as the *susceptor et exactor* of their income since the late eleventh century.[20] Other rulers, such as the kings of England, also employed clerics as part of the personnel of their central administration.[21] While these *clerici* were not monks, they drew on the same broad cultural tradition and used similar practices.

Other rulers, outside the Church, also shared in this common culture of power. Medieval historians have explored royal and princely institutions of administration in detail. What those historians have discovered is that despite some regional variations, such institutions were remarkably similar.[22] Studies of the rise of royal and princely power have revealed a triumphant, dynastic lordship, reinforced both by an increasingly elaborate ideology and an increasingly effective structure of governance and administration, chiefly the creation of institutions of justice and finance.[23] The importance of these institutions in the history of the state has long been acknowledged.[24] Studies of French royal power are no exception. Judicial and financial institutions, the story goes, provided the sinews of the later French monarchy, which rose from a small territorial power to a triumphant lord-kingship during the reign of Philip Augustus (1180–1223).[25] But did the ending of this story help to shape the story itself? In the search for antecedents of royal (or state) power, scholars sought to discover them only in the doings of kings. One wonders if royal institutions had precursors in other settings.

One piece of this larger story of royal administration is the story of accountability: how kings made their men (or agents) account for their actions while ostensibly exercising the royal power to tax and judge. Accountability, especially fiscal accountability, could be shown to have existed only when documents which pertained to it (accounts) could be shown to exist. Such appearances could be dated very precisely: in France, the date was 1202/3, the date of the first surviving account.[26] Although the loss of the king's baggage train in 1194 at the battle of Fréteval included the loss of any earlier household accounts, John Baldwin traced the origin of these accounts (and accounting) to the Ordinance of 1190, which outlined the governance of the realm prior to Philip's departure on Crusade.[27] In Flanders, the date was 1187, the moment at which the first surviving *Gros Brief* of the counts could be found.[28] From these and subsequent documents the later fiscal apparatus of royal and princely power could be explained.[29] Before these dates, a documentary void seemed to exist. But one need not be limited by the absence of royal evidence or let the end of the story overwhelm its beginning.

The prevailing story of royal and princely administration is one which twelfth-century monks would recognize, though it does not use words exactly as they would. In Flanders, the *minister* of the story was a subordinate officer of the count, his *ministerium* just his area of collection. The *clerici*, the clerks or receivers, were just *notarii* (notaries) by another name. The *redeninge* (reckoning) was a special yearly auditing session of the count's court.[30] In France, as elsewhere, the *praepositus* (provost) was the *prévôt*, a royal agent charged with a geographic circumscription, a *prévôté*.[31]

For contemporaries, there was no possibility of removing the story of accountability from its religious context. Everyone certainly knew the contours of this larger religious story, such as the parable of the steward being called to account (Luke 16:2). They also knew its end, from the

Book of Revelation, when Jesus would use the book of life to mete out justice, a different, more final day of reckoning. Monks, in particular, had a special understanding of accountability: the brothers were to obey and answer to their abbot. Likewise, according to the Rule, the abbot would be held responsible: "whatever the number of brothers he has in his care, let him realize that on judgment day he will surely have to submit a reckoning to the Lord for all their souls—and indeed for his own as well."[32] The idea of dividing the secular and religious aspects of accountability would not have occurred to them, or, at least, such ideas were new in 1100. The idea of separating secular and ecclesiastical power was a product of eleventh-century reform, in which the driving force was monastic ideas about the ordering (or reordering) of the world. These reforming monks possessed a new view of the world, based on a different interpretation of the past and different concepts of power and authority.

The ideas and practices of twelfth-century abbots and monks afford useful perspective on the doings of the counts of Flanders and kings such as Philip Augustus. Monks had a strong continuing consciousness of the religious context of accountability, which they shared with laymen. Ministering had always been, and would continue to be, linked to administering. Judging was linked to revenue collection in the development of monastic administration. Accountability was not merely fiscal or judicial or moral, but a combination of all three. Thus, it may be a mistake to separate prematurely institutions of "justice" and "finance" from the larger context of accountability, as some historians of royal administration do when they anticipate later developments.[33] Abbots, like kings and counts, began to monitor their men by summoning them to great ritual assemblies, in which, with increasing frequency, they counted money and judged agents' conduct.

In these "days of reckoning" lay the origins of both the judicial and financial aspects of later medieval government. These occasions were fraught with anxiety and tension, implied forthcoming punishment, and were displays of lordly power all at once. In Flanders, when the castellans and *échevins* of the count were summoned to the annual *redeninge* (reckoning), high justice accompanied fiscal business.[34] Richard fitz-Nigel, in his *Dialogue of the Exchequer*, described the sheriff sitting at the end of the Exchequer table, waiting for the judgment of the court, as clerks moved counters across the checkered cloth.[35] The best-known medieval land survey, the *Domesday Book*, implied by its very title the element of final judgment implicit in every reckoning.[36] When a monk, mayor, or provost in northern France came before his abbot to account for his actions, even as books were increasingly consulted, he knew that the state of his soul as well as his conduct was being reviewed. Punishment could be fiscal (a payment), judicial (an oath), moral (religious sanctions), or a combination of all of these.

The techniques of accounting were not merely related to justice, but were essentially the same practices implemented by men who shared a common, usually ecclesiastical, education in the twelfth century. The same men could sit at the counting board and on the king's court and often did. Abbot Suger could be regent of France. The doing of justice was profitable and the counting of the profits of lordship was a matter of judging. From this perspective, justice and finance, hallmark institutions of the nation-state, were at root the same institution. Only the increasing sophistication of technique and burgeoning workload began to differentiate the records of these activities.[37] This fact suggests that justice and finance deserve to be studied in tandem, as two of the many elements comprising the larger culture of days of reckoning. Judgment and punishment were implied in all the rituals of accountability and the medieval mind linked these rituals to broader notions of justice—in particular, Judgment Day, the ultimate day of reckoning.

Reckoning with the Past

Everyone then knew that eternal judgment was the end of the medieval story of accountability; however, that is only one story this book tells. Modern historians can draw broader conclusions about documents, record-keeping, and history from medieval monastic "reckonings."

Certainly, the documents produced by monastic archives changed in the twelfth and thirteenth centuries. The new types of books and written instruments of administration were only one part of archival transformation. Charters that recorded transactions also changed. The social, commemorative context of documents, so crucial in the eleventh century, was increasingly left out of the text: the more succinct notice was the chosen form for the practical-minded monk by the turn of the thirteenth century.[38] Notices, by their very nature, have seemed to many historians to imply a decline of the old gift-exchange system in favor of what appears to be a "commercial" mode of operation.[39] The rich narrative preambles, so revealing of monastic ideas, disappeared as those ideas shifted.

For the historian concerned with changes in monastic thought and behavior such evidentiary trends are both fascinating and frustrating. While literacy and numeracy have been studied for their religious and cognitive implications, especially in regard to rationality, the practical aspects of accountability have largely been consigned to economic history (the narrow study of accounts) or legal history (court rolls).[40] Although most historians accept the broad importance of what I call the shift from oral culture to scribal culture, evaluating the specific significance of changes within the new scribal culture is more problematic. Common sense suggests that new documentary forms imply new ideas and practices, but one must always beware asserting that documentary change is tantamount to social or intellectual change. At the same time, changes in the storage, arrangement, or organization of documents (regardless of any formal changes) more strongly suggest new attitudes and methods. These changes may have had less to do with the act of writing itself (or its relation to memory), than the uses to which written records were put. Archives and books reflect the intentions or actions of their organizers in ways that the internal structure of documents may not. Also, it is possible to see increased "cartularization" from the eleventh century on as provoked by the abundance of documents, rather than as an illusory *mutation documentaire*.[41] Nevertheless, a mere counting of documents does not suffice to understand them.

New means of record-keeping had transformed monastic archives by the thirteenth century. In the eleventh and twelfth centuries, monks were constantly mining their archival materials not just to (re)construct their history but to assert their place in the world. How they created, destroyed, and reorganized their records, when the historian can perceive it, provides good evidence of their goals. From this perspective, even forgeries are excellent evidence because they show the mind of the forger at work. A useful source for studying the use of the written word, forgeries have generally been underestimated, even though they were just as good a means of "organizing" archives or books as selecting and rearranging texts physically without inventing them.[42]

The new culture of reckoning was important not only because it foreshadowed institutions of finance and justice, but also because it governed how monks selected, organized, copied, and stored their written records. Monks had strong ideas about how "reckonings" would occur

and the need for written records in the process. On the ever more frequent occasions of accounting or judging, documents played an increasingly vital role. The *Gros Brief* of Flanders, Philip Augustus's accounts,
the Exchequer rolls, monastic cartularies, even the biblical "book of life"
were all written records for "reckoning" and, thus, shared common
attributes. By the twelfth century, monastic books and archives had new
organizational forms, which corresponded to new thoughts and behaviors.[43] Moreover, by the thirteenth century, the proliferation of so-called
"pragmatic literacy," especially the instrumental use of writing in law
and commerce, shows that such thoughts and behaviors were widely
disseminated throughout Europe.[44]

The new culture of power not only had a larger role for writing and
counting, but particular kinds of record-keeping. To label the new forms
of organization is difficult, perhaps even more difficult than trying to
label documentary forms. As argued above and pointed out by many
medievalists, narrative charters, pancartes, and inventories were both
more and less than notices, title deeds, and surveys. Likewise, lists of
wrongs and payments were both more and less than court rolls and
account books. A similar problem of interpretation exists when one
considers medieval methods of book-writing and record-keeping. Foundation stories, saints' lives, cartularies and *gestae* were both more and
less than modern histories. In an age before the concept of plagiarism or
forgery, monks could edit or select their documentary strands very
freely. Unconstrained by the demands of modern historical science, they
also could weave them together using many methods. All medieval
monks "reckoned" with their past, but not as today's historians can or
should; however, the two groups are linked by the changed nature and
role of monastic archives. The demands of the scribal culture that produced them must be remembered in any final reckoning we wish to
make of those times.

Appendix A: The Cartularies
of Saint-Bertin

THE DESTRUCTION AND RELOCATION of the archives of Saint-Bertin during the French Revolution caused the loss of many cartularies and original charters of the monastery. The archives had been divided between the library, accessible to scholars, and the treasury, which was restricted to members of the house and contained all of the oldest and most valuable pieces (including the *Vetus Folquinus*). Although the library was relocated to the departmental archives at Boulogne-sur-mer, everything in the treasury was lost. The early history of Saint-Bertin would have remained virtually unknown except for Dom Charles-Joseph DeWitte, who exhaustively recopied all the ancient charters and cartularies immediately prior to the Revolution and preserved his copies until his death in 1807. His volumes of copies are the best source of many acts of Saint-Bertin. The description of the prerevolutionary archives and DeWitte's copies can be found in the preface to Haigneré 1: v–lxvi. The following is a list of the early cartularies of Saint-Bertin and their various copies. The relationship between cartularies and editions is also explained. The most important relationships are presented visually in the chart of manuscript relationships at the end of the appendix (Table A1). Manuscripts are lettered in order of their creation, with letters in parentheses () indicating a now lost manuscript. Consult the bibliography for full publication information about editions.

Lost and Extant Cartularies of Saint-Bertin

(A). *Vetus Folquinus*. Written in 961–62 by Folquin of Saint-Bertin, later Abbot of Lobbes, in the form of a *gesta abbatum* including transcriptions of whole charters and notices. Original manuscript lost but it resided in the treasury at Saint-Bertin until the Revolution. Contained copies of *brevia* of polyptych of Adalard, compiled ca. 855–59. The *gesta* covered the period from the foundation of the monastery by Saint-Bertin until early 962. Known from F, below.

(B). Simon's first *gesta abbatum*. Written between 1095 and 1123 by Simon of Saint-Bertin, later Abbot of Auchy and of Saint-Bertin from 1131 until his removal by the pope in 1136. Original manuscript lost but it existed until at least the late twelfth century and possibly longer in the treasury of the monastery. According to the description in *Histoire Littéraire de la France* 13 (1814), 80–81, the manuscript contained a *gesta abbatum* for the four abbots between 1021 and 1095, two books of rents, a catalogue of the library, and genealogy of the kings of France, as well as intermixed copies of original charters. Known from D, below.

(C). Simon's second *gesta abbatum*. Written between 1137 and 1148 by Simon of Saint-Bertin, during his retirement in Ghent. Original manuscript lost but it existed in the late twelfth century and possibly longer in the treasury of the monastery. Contained a *gesta abbatum* for the time of Lambert and his successors until 1145 and intermixed copies of charters, but omitted discussion of Simon's own rule. The work was incomplete upon Simon's death in 1148. Known from D, below.

D. Combined *Gesta abbatum Sithiensis*. Compiled between 1148 and 1163 by anonymous monks of Saint-Bertin, based on (A), (B), and (C). Written in a uniform script. Original manuscript resided in the library of Saint-Bertin until the Revolution, but was divided after 1512 into two parts: Folquin's *gesta abbatum*, D1, and Simon's, D2. The *Gesta abbatum Sithiensis* contained copies of (A), (B), and (C) with interpolations, additions, and a continuation until 1187. Certain portions of (B), notably the sections on rents, books, and the kings of France, were removed to integrate (B) and (C) together. D2 was eclipsed in the early nineteenth century until it was found by François Morand in the 1860s. D1 is now BM Boulogne-sur-mer ms. 146b and D2 is BM Boulogne-sur-mer ms. 146a.

E. Copy of D by Alard Tassart. Copied in 1512, based on D before its division. Contains variants of D. Now BM St. Omer ms. 750.

F. Incomplete copy of (A) by Dom Portebois. Copied in 1693. Contains a list of added chapters in D which copyist claimed were not in the original script of (A). Now BnF nouv. acq. lat. 275.

G. *Grand Cartulaire* of Dom Charles-Joseph DeWitte. 15 volumes compiled in 1775–90 based on original charters, (A), D, and other now lost manuscripts at Saint-Bertin and verified as accurate by notaries. Contains acts of the monastery from foundation to 1790. The work consists of 10 volumes of charter copies and a volume of cartulary copies with indices, such that many acts have both a charter version, G1, and cartulary copy version, G2. Unknown to most nineteenth-century editors, DeWitte's work is now BM Boulogne-sur-mer mss. 803–15.

Editions and Their Relation to Cartulary Manuscripts

1. Benjamin Guérard, ed., *Cartulaire de l'abbaye de Saint-Bertin*. Published in 1840. Based on D1 and E. Contains a full edition of Folquin's and Simon's cartularies as known to Guérard.

2. François Morand, ed., *Appendice au cartulaire de l'abbaye de Saint-Bertin*. Published in 1867 as a supplement to Guérard, printing corrections of his text using D2. Contains some acts omitted in Guérard.

3. Oswald Holder-Egger, ed., *Gesta abbatum S. Bertini sithiensium*, MGH SS 13: 600–673. Published in 1881. Contains only the narrative sections of Folquin's and Simon's cartularies, based on G2 (BM S. Omer ms. 815), D1, and D2.

4. Daniel Haigneré, ed., *Les Chartes de Saint-Bertin*. Published in 1887. Based on G1, G2, D1, D2, E, F, and surviving originals. Contains a catalogue of acts only, with a few editions of unpublished acts. Does not contain narrative sections of cartularies.

5. François-Louis Ganshof, ed., *Le polyptyque de l'abbaye de Saint-Bertin*. Published in 1975. Contains the text of the polyptych of Adalard as recorded by Folquin, based on D1, F, G1, G2.

TABLE A1. Extant and Lost Cartularies of Saint-Bertin

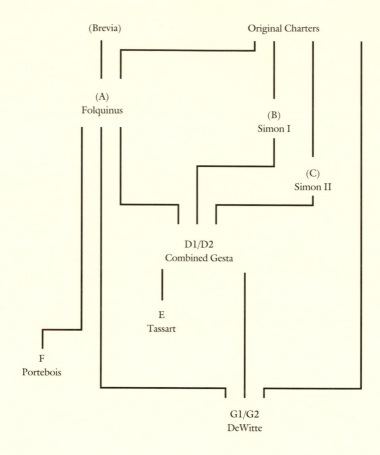

Appendix B: The Cartulary of Three Crosses

The "CARTULARY OF THREE CROSSES" of Saint-Germain was dated by its handwriting in Henri Stein's *Bibliographie générale des cartulaires français* (Paris: Picard, 1907), 394, no. 2870 as a twelfth-century manuscript, containing documents from the sixth to the twelfth century. While this dating reflects the work as a whole, like many cartularies the "cartulary of three crosses" is composed of a central section that was the subject of later additions and continuations. Complicating matters further, some of the original folios were altered and interpolated prior to reassembly in the early thirteenth century. A fifteenth-century rebinding added end-sheets to the existing manuscript and may have accidentally reordered some folios that had previously been numbered. The content and structure of the cartulary reveal that the majority of it was composed in the late twelfth century, probably starting in the last years of Abbot Hugh V (1162–82). This main section then accumulated additions and interpolations through the first quarter of the thirteenth century.

The following tables show the structure and content of the cartulary. Table B1 shows the structure of the cartulary based on an investigation of the gatherings of AN LL 1024, available for direct inspection during my research because of the decayed binding. This investigation revealed that the late twelfth-century manuscript contained at least nine quires (1–9), with several additions made soon after the initial composition (10–14). The main body of nine quires was prepared together; each was signed at the bottom of the recto of the last folio with a number in the same script as the text. Quires 4, 7, 8, and 9 had a memory word accompanying the quire number at the bottom edge of the folio to indicate the beginning of the subsequent quire, which was found there in each case. Other similar words may have been trimmed off of the edges of the other quires. There was a new script beginning on folio 24r, where a later scribe inserted a charter copy in a blank space; three folios were interpolated here, prior to the beginning of the original fourth quire, which was missing its first page.

Most of the added quires (10, 10bis, 11–13) were grouped with the main text slightly after its composition, quire 10 in particular, since it continues the text and script of the previous quire. However, substantial rearrangement of folia, probably a result of various insertions and rebindings, make the original order of folia hard to determine. It was

TABLE B1.   Structure of Cartulary of Three Crosses

Quire	Folios	Dates of acts	Remarks
n/a	a–g	1492	Fifteenth-century endsheets and preface
1	1–8	566–1153	Quaternion, signed "Ius"
2	9–16	1158–76	Quaternion, signed "IIus"
3	17–24	588–1176	Quaternion, signed "IIIus"
(3bis)	25–26	846–1240?	Single sheet, inserted in thirteenth century
(3ter)	27–30	Unknown	Bifolium, forged in ninth century or later
4	31–37	845–1031	Quaternion, signed "IVus" and "cartinam," missing 1st folio
5	38–45	1031–1168	Quaternion, signed "Vus"
6	46–53	697–1170	Quaternion, signed "VIus"
7	54–61	979–1176	Quaternion, signed "VIIus" and "pontificalis"
8	62–69	1116–68	Quaternion, signed "VII-Ius" and "filio"
9	70–75	1063–1182	Trifolium, signed "IXus" and "suo"
(10)	76–79, 82–83, 89	Ante 1182	Originally a quaternion but divided and reordered, sheets missing
(10bis)	80–81	1176–82	Single sheet inserted in the midst of former 10th quire
(11)	84–88	1176–82	Bifolium, loosely attached
(12)	90–93	1063–82	Bifolium
(13)	94–101	1159–85	Quaternion, followed fol. 89 in late twelfth century
(14)	102–4	1176–1229	Damaged bifolium, continues from quire 12
n/a	j–p	1492	Fifteenth-century endsheets and tables

certainly substantially different. For example, prior to the thirteenth century, what is now folio 94r was a direct continuation of the text of folio 89v. These added quires contain the majority of the "administrative" documents and were practical supplements, collecting documents relevant to the holdings of Saint-Germain. The last of the added quires (14) contained leaves that were originally blank and were filled by later continuators. Table B2 summarizes the contents of the manuscript and shows that the original organization of the cartulary was hierarchical by grantor, but that this scheme was modified by the added quires, which were organized by estates.

TABLE B2.   Content of the Cartulary of Three Crosses

Quire	Folios	Dates of acts	Charters or acts
n/a	a–g	1492	Fifteenth-century endsheets and preface
1	1–8	566–1153	Papal charters
2	9–16	1158–76	Royal charters
3	17–24	588–1176	Royal charters
(3bis)	25–26	846–1240?	Royal and miscellaneous charters (interpolated)
(3ter)	27–30	Unknown	Royal charters (forged)
4	31–37	845–1031	Royal charters
5	38–45	1031–1168	Royal charters
6	46–53	697–1170	Ducal/comital charters
7	54–61	979–1176	Episcopal charters
8	62–69	1116–68	Ecclesiastical charters
9	70–75	1063–1182	Ecclesiastical charters
(10)	76–79	Ante 1182	Abbatial charters, primarily of Saint-Germain
(10bis)	80–81	1176–1182	Estate of Samoreau
(10ctd)	82,83,89	Ante 1182	Estate of Samoreau and acts about Bourg Saint-Germain
(11)	84–88	1176–82	Holdings of Saint-Germain
(12)	90–93	1063–1182	Holdings of Saint-Germain
(13)	94–101	1159–85	Holdings of Saint-Germain, lists and miscellaneous acts
(14)	102–4	1176–1229	Papal acts, estate of Samoreau, notes
n/a	j–p	1492	Fifteenth-century endsheets and tables

Appendix C:
Enumerations in Papal Confirmations

The following tables provide an analysis of the property lists (*enumeratio bonorum*) in papal confirmations for the five northern French monasteries examined in Chapter 2. The dates and references to the confirmations can be found at the head of the table for each monastery along with a note about the opening phrase of the *enumeratio*, in either the old style (*videlicet*) or the new style (*propriis nominibus*). The tables show the increasing specificity and length of these lists over time. For this reason, the tables provide lists of place names in parallel columns exactly in the order they appear in the confirmations. Descriptive phrases are placed in notes when relevant (e.g., donor's name, locational information) and omitted if not, as is *de*, unless it appears as part of a name. No attempt has been made to normalize spellings of place names; since one cannot count on the orthography of printed editions, certain obvious confusions between ae/e, c/t, i/j, in/im, and n/u/v remain.

Key to Tables of Enumerations

The following abbreviations have been employed for commonly repeated words and phrases:

&	cum
a	altare(ia)
c	capella(m, s)
cae	cum appenditiis earum
cas	cum appenditiis suis
ccs	cum capella(is) sua(is)
coas	cum omnibus appenditiis suis
cps	cum pertinentiis suis
coepa	cum omnibus earum pertinentiis seu appenditiis
cospa	cum omnibus suis pertinentiis seu appenditiis

cps	cum pertinentiis suis
d	decima(m, e, s)
e	ecclesia(m, s)
oae	omnibus appenditiis earum
s	sanctus, sancta
v	villa(m, s)

Tables C1 and C2: Saint-Bertin, 1095–1139

A   Urban II, 1095 (PU *Frankreich* 3: 368, no. 4. JL 5600a)
    Style: *videlicet*

B   Pascal II, 1107 (CSB, 214–16. JL 6201)
    Style: *scilicet*

C   Calixtus II, 1119 (CSB, 260–62. JL 6769)
    Style: *videlicet*

D   Innocent II, 1139 (CSB, 310–12. JL 8016)
    Style: *In quibus hec propriis duximus exprimenda vocabulis*

TABLE C1.   Saint-Bertin, 1095–1119

A (1095)	B (1107)	C (1119)
e videlicet Stenkerka in Taruanensi	In Taruanensi parrochia e s Margarete	Omnis terris . . . in castellaria de Broburg[1]. . .
e Graveninga	e s Johannis	terram de Culhem
e Broburg ccs	s Martini	et Flechmel
e s Margaritae	e Harbela	et Helescolke . . .
s Iohannis	e Petrenessa	. . . a Helcin et cs[2] . . .
s Martini	e Torbodeshem[3] . . .	In Taruannensi quoque parrochia e Oxelare
e Pitarnesse	e Broburg ccs	et Warnestim
e Longanessa	e Graveninga	et Haveskerke
e Chelmes	et de Lo	a Merchem
e Poparingahem & ipsa villa	e Arkes & eadem villa	e Eggafridi c
e Arcas & ipsa villa	e Poperingehem & eadem villa	In Tornacensi parrochia e Coclara
e Arbela & ipsa villa	e Stenkerka	Ruslethe
e Coica & ipsa villa	e Brusele	et Runbecca ccs
e Helcin & ipsa villa	e Scales	e Lisgnege
e Weserna & ipsa villa	e Boveringhem & villis earum	Snelgerkerke
e Aquina & ipsa villa	v Aldenfort	et Hermingehem
e Tarbodeshem	et Ostresela	et Bovenkerke

A (1095)	B (1107)	C (1119)
e Bosrihem & eadem villa	et Rokestor[4] . . .	in Attrebatensi parrochia a Anesim
e Scalas & eadem villa	allodium quod Clarembaldus dedit in v Lustingehem	in Coloniensi e Frequena
e Hunela & eadem villa	e Coieka	et Wildestorp
in Noviomensi parrochia e Calamunt	e Helcin & villis earum	in Belvacensi terram Hubertuisin dictam cospa
in Tornacensi parrochia e Rukeshem	et partem e Walnas	terram quoque Claremnbaldi de Lustingehem
e Hetlingehem	e Locanes	terram quam comes Robertus . . . dedit
Hinninkehem	et Aquina	berquariam quam comes Balduinus . . . dedit
Wastkerke	e Hunela & eadem villa	berquariam pro commutatione villa Ostresele datam
in Coloniensi parrochia e Frekenai Gildestop	altare Merchem[5] . . . in Noviomensi parrochia Kanetecurtim	et duas portiones d Brucsele
in Cameracensi parrochi v Ostrosela coepa	In Tornacensi e Rokeshem	
	e Hetlingehem	
	e Hitlingehem	
	Westkerke	
	et d Clemeskerke	
	In Coloniensi parrochia e Frekena	
	e Gildestorp cae . . .	
	e quoque Coclers . . .	
	. . . una cum altari Rusletha . . .	
	. . . monasterium sancti Silvini apud Alciacum . . .	
	. . . piscariis Mera et Grath, Mardic et Strangnerh, et Laugha et terris adjacentibus	

[1] Includes agreement with count of Flanders, including phrases from Arques forgery; see Chapter 2.
[2] "quas per episcoporum derationis."
[3] "sicut retroactis temporibus, ab omni episcopali redditu liberas"
[4] "cum terra quam emisti ab Arnoldo de Wneti et aliis terris adjacentibus."
[5] "quod venerabilis Johannes episcopus vobis concessit."

Table C2.   Saint-Bertin, 1095–1139

A (1095)	C (1119)	D (1139)
e videlicet Stenkerka in Taruanensi	Omnis terris . . . in castellaria de Broburg[1] . . .	in Taruanensi parrochia e s Margarete
e Graveninga	terram de Culhem	e s Johannis
e Broburg ccs	et Flechmel	s Martini
e s Margaritae	et Helescolke . . .	e Harbela
s Iohannis	. . . a Helcin et cs[2] . . .	e Petrenesse
s Martini	In Taruannensi quoque parrochia e Oxelare	e Torbessem[3] . . .
e Pitarnesse	et Warnestim	e Broburg ccs[4]
e Longanessa	et Haveskerke	e Archas & eadem villa
e Chelmes	a Merchem	e Popringhem & eadem villa
e Poparingahem & ipsa villa	e Eggafridi c	e Steenkerka
e Arcas & ipsa villa	In Tornacensi parrochia e Coclara	e Bruxele
e Arbela & ipsa villa	Ruslethe	e Scales
e Coica & ipsa villa	et Runbecca ccs	e Bovrinkehem & villis earum
e Helcin & ipsa villa	e Lisgnege	v Aldefort
e Weserna & ipsa villa	Snelgerkerke	et Ostresela
e Aquina & ipsa villa	et Hermingehem	et Rokestoir & cum terram emit ecclesia[5]
e Tarbodeshem	et Bovenkerke	allodium[6] . . . in v Lustinghem
e Bosrihem & eadem villa	in Attrebatensi parrochia a Anesim	e Coeka
e Scalas & eadem villa	in Coloniensi e Frequena	et e Helcim & villis earum
e Hunela & eadem villa	et Wildestorp	et partem e Vualnas
in Noviomensi parrochia e Calmunt	in Belvacensi terram Hubertuisin dictam cospa	e Locanes
in Tornacensi parrochia e Rukeshem	terram quoque Claremnbaldi de Lustingehem	et Aquina
e Hetlingehem	terram quam comes Robertus . . . dedit	e Hunela & eadem villa
Hinninkehem	berquariam quam comes Balduinus . . . dedit	a Merchem[7] . . .
Wastkerke	berquariam pro commutatione villa Ostresele datam	In Noviomensi parrochia Canetekurtim id est Calmunt
in Coloniensi parrochia e Frekenai	et duas portiones d Brucsele	In Tornacensi e Rokeshem

A (1095)	C (1119)	D (1139)
Gildestop		e Hedinghem
in Cameracensi parrochi		Westkerke
v Ostrosela coepa		
		et d Clemeskerke
		e Hitinghem
		e Lisimega
		e Snelguekerke
		e Erninghem
		e Bovenkerke
		In Atrebatensi parrochia
		e Werkin
		e Salomones
		e Hautay
		In territorio Furnensi
		berquariam . .
		et terram de Buri . . . in
		Belvacensi pago
		In Colloniensi parrochia
		e Frekena
		e Gildestorp cae[8] . . .
		e quoque Coclers[9] . . .
		una cum a Rusleta[10] . . .
		Iterum in Parrochia
		Taruanensi e Oxelara
		e Warnestim
		e s Marie que dicitur
		Eggafridi c
		e Haveskerke
		Alciacum[11] . . .

[1] Includes agreement with count of Flanders, including phrases from Arques forgery; see Chapter 2.

[2] "quas per episcoporum derationis."

[3] "sicut antiquitus, ab omni episcopali redditu liberas"

[4] "duos eciam manipulos decime nove terre, ubicunque accreverit in tota parrochia de Broburg, que extenditur usque ad terminos vicinarum parrochiam" and clauses about Count Baldwin of Flanders as grantor.

[5] "ab Arnulpho de Venti et aliis terris adjacentibus"

[6] "quod Clarembaldus dedit"

[7] "quod venerablis Johannes episcopus vobis concessit"

[8] "Ex quibus precipimus ut nulla per episcopos vel eorum ministros exactio quibuslibet occasionibus exigatur, salvis episcoporum annuis redditibus."

[9] "quam Baldricus, tornacensis ecclesie episcopus, Lamberto, bone memorie abbati, suisque successoribus ordinandam"

[10] Long explanation of fishing rights along river and adjacent areas.

[11] "Subrogationem etiam abbatis in monasterio sancti Silvini apud Alciacum, justa preteriti temporis morem, in vestra semper concedimus dispositionem"

Table C3.   Saint-Germain-des-Prés, 1122–76

A   Calixtus II, 1122 (CSG 1: 126–27, no. 80. JL 6947)
    Style: *In quibus hec propriis duximus nominibus annotanda, videlicet*
B   Alexander III, 1176 (CSG 1: 238–40, no. 165. JL 12741)
    Style: *In quibus hec propriis duximus exprimenda vocabulis*

A (1122)	B (1176)
in pago Pictavensi e s Germani de Nentriaco	in episcopatu Senonensi e Emant
in pago Bituricensi e Catherigiaco	e Montis Machou
& aliis ecclesiis quas vestrum monasterium possidet	e Matricolis
	e beati Germani juxta Musteriolum
	e Laval
	e s Petri de Veteribus Matriolis
	e Balneolis
	in episcopatu Parisiensi
	e s Germani Veteris infra urbem
	e Villa Nova
	e Crona
	e Valentone
	e Theodasia
	e Pirodio
	e Antoniaci
	e Verrariis
	e Avremvilla
	e Surismis
	in episcopatu Carnotensi e s Martini de Drocis
	e beate Marie Magdelene de Monte Calvulo
	e domni Martini
	e Laoniarum
	e Neelfleta
	e Septulia
	in episcopatu Rothomagensi e s Leodegarii
	e Vilers
	e Longuessa
	in Suessionensi episcopatu e Novigento
	in Meldensi episcopatu e Colii
	e beati Marie de Ramainvillare
	e Monteri
	e Abeli
	in Eduensi episcopatu e Gilli
	e Vilerbichet

A (1122)	B (1176)
	e Marri
	In Bituricensi episcopatu e Britiniaco
	e Nove Ville
	e Lemauso
	in Pictavensi episcopatu e Naintriaco
	e s Johannis de Foro Castri Eraudi[1]

[1] "Predicta autem ecclesias cum omnibus ad eas pertinentibus sicut eas canonice possidetis . . . confirmamus."

TABLE C4.   Saint-Denis, 1131–48

A   Innocent II, 1131 (PU Frankreich 9(2): 148–51, no. 35. JL 7472)
Style: *In quibus haec propriis nominibus duximus exprimenda*
B   Eugenius III, 1148 (PU Frankreich 9(2): 163–67, no. 44. JL 9247)
Style: *In quibus haec propriis nominibus duximus exprimenda*

A (1131)	B (1148)
In pago Metensi cellam novam coas videlicet Hulsperc, Ansminge, Enmelingas	In pago Metensi cellam novam coas videlicet Hulsperc, Ansminge, Eumelingas
e Fulcreia	e Fulcreia
salinas ac patellas salinarum apud Marsalciam	salinas ac patellas salinarum apud Marsatiam
monasterium Argentolium quod situm est in pago Parisiensi super fluvium Sequanam cps	monasterium Argentolium quod situm est in pago Parisiensi super fluvium Sequanam cps
In episcopatu Aurelianensi campum Mainerii	In episcopatu Aurelianensi campum Manerii
Villare	Villare
Uendrous	Vendrous
Villammeium	V Meium
Feiems	Feiems
Linus	Liuns
ad haec comitatum Vilcassini[1] . . .	In episcopatu Laodunensi a Cardursa
	a s Goberto
. . . villam Sancti Dionysii[2] . . .	a Pirolis
	a Sairiaco cc s Dionisii qui est apud Ribomontum in Iusana valle
	a Sorbais
	a Altrepia
	a Rosbais
	a Rochiniis
	a Serenis fontibus

A (1131)	B (1148)
	In episcopatu Cameracensi a Solemio
	a Vertiniolo & decimis et oae
	e Calvomonte cas[3] . . .
	cellam beatae Marie prope Corbolium super fluvium Esona sitam cas
	. . . [4]v Trapis . . .
	et talliam quam apud Cergiacum in Vilcassino
	et apud Cormelias . . .
	. . . [5]a Monarvilla
	et Rubrido
	. . . [6]a Anechin
	. . . [7]Derhestiam super fluvium Sabrinae sitam
	Tantoniam
	et Moram
	ad haec comitatum Vilcassini[8] . . .
	. . . villam Sancti Dionisii[9] . . .

[1] "qui juris Beati dionisii est, quem karissimus filius noster Lodoicus rex Francorum, per te a beato Dionisio in beneficium et feodum suscepisse cognoscitur."

[2] The rights of jurisdiction, markets, etc. over the town, whose boundaries are specified: "a fluvio videlicet Sequanae, a molendino quod vulgo appelatur Bayard, usque as supremum caput villae quae vocature Halbervillare."

[3] "quam venerabilis frater noster Hugo Rothomagensis archiepiscopus, consentiente karissimo filio nostro Ludouico rege Francorum vobis donavit."

[4] "Ex dono praedicti regis"

[5] "Ex dono bonae memoriae Gaufridi Carnotensis episcopi"

[6] "Ex dono Aluisi Atrebatensis episcopi`"

[7] "Ex dono illustris memoriae Eduardi scilicet et Guillelmi regum Angliae"

[8] "qui juris Beati dionysii est, quem karissimus filius noster Lodoicus rex Francorum, per te a beato Dionisio in beneficium et feodum suscepisse cognoscitur."

[9] Jurisdiction, markets, and other rights over the town, whose boundaries are specified: "a fluvio videlicet Sequanae, a molendino quod vulgo appelatur Baiard, usque as supremum capud ville que vocatur Halbervillare."

Tables C5 and C6. Saint-Vaast, 1102–70

A   Pascal II, 1102 (CSV, 70–73. JL 5896)

Style: *quorum videlicet altarium nomina sunt hec*

B   Innocent II, 1135 (CSV, 75–78. JL 7699)

Style: *In quibus his propriis nominibus annotanda subjunximus*

C   Eugenius III, 1153 (CSV, 81–82. JL 9688)

Style: *In quibus his propriis duximus vocabulis exprimenda*

D   Alexander III, 1164 (PU *Frankreich* 3: 116–19, no. 58)

Style: *In quibus hec propriis duximus exprimenda vocabulis*

E   Alexander III, 1170 (CSV, 91–98. JL 11709)

Style: *In quibus hec propriis duximus exprimenda vocabulis*

The enumerations in A, B, and C have been combined in the first column because they are nearly the same, except for small differences in
orthography and a reversal, noted below. B and C mention the priories
of Haspres, Berclau, and Gorres, before proceeding to a separate list of
altars, which were also listed separately in D and E.

TABLE C5.   Saint-Vaast, 1102–70

B/C (1135/53)[1]	D (1164)	E (1170)
. . . villam Hasprensem	e videlicet et v Asprensem & altaribus et eiusdem e appenditis	e videlicet et v Asprensem & altaribus et eiusdem e appenditis
e Bercloensem	videlicet altare Moncellis	videlicet altare Moncellis
e Gorrea cae	altare Halcim Monstrelli curia	altare Alci de Monstrelli curia
et terram juxta mare sitam . . .	altare Gisennis et duas et duas garbas decimales in eius altaribus & d Fossis	altare Giseniis et duas garbas decimales & d Fossis
	altare Novennis	altare Lomnis
	altare Oneliis	altare Oneliis
	et Onisel	et Ouysel
	altare Mulli cc	altare Nuilli
	altare Haumale	altare Haysmocaisnoit
	d Iuur	altare Haumala
	in Robecuncultura	d Ilbrie in Rotberti cultura
	et Gaultericultura	et in Gualteri cultura
	. . . theloneum . . . in Atrebatensi civitate	. . . theloneum . . . in Atrebatensi civitate
	in Anzinio duo molendina	in Anzinio duo molendina

B/C (1135/53)[1]	D (1164)	E (1170)
	in Dominica curte tria molendia & vivario	in Dominica curte tria molendina & vivario
	apud Melenz quatuor molendina & vivario	in Meaullens quatuor molendina & vivario
	apud Blangi quatour molendina & vivario	in Blangy quatour molendina & vivario
	apud Ateias quatuor molendina & vivario	in Atheiis quatuor molendina & vivario
	apud Pabulam unum molendinum & vivario	apud Pabulam unum molendinum & vivario
	apud Bigartium quatuor molendinum & vivario	In Biacre duo molendina & vivario duo quoque molendina infra muros Atrebate . . .
	e Bercloensem & altaribus suis	e Bercloensem & altaribus suis
	Vicelicet Duurim	videlicet Dovrim
	Billi	Billi
	Baluim	Baluin
	Prouim	Prouvy
	Marchelgis	Marchielles
	Merenniis	Merenies
	Serchingehem & berberia	Serchinguehem & berberia
	e Gorrea cas	e Gorea cas
	duas quoque e beati Petri et beate Marie virginis infra castrum sitas . . .	c s Mauritii
	e s Michaelis cas	altaria duo in Moriensi episcopo sita, Leghem
	vicelicet	
	terram iuxta mare sitam . . .	et Rumbli & aliis possessionibus
	altaria duo in Morinensi episcopo sita, Linghem videlicet	et has villas cas Montes in Pabula
	et Rumbli & aliis possessionibus . . .	Ransart
	et e Wilfara cas cambas & aliis bonis in Badia trans Renum citra	Puteasaquas
		Anolinum
		Buhircurt
		Berny
		Meurchin

B/C (1135/53)[1]	D (1164)	E (1170)
		Moylens
		Valles super Summan fluvium
		Sernin
		Harnem
		Campaniolas
		Mares
		Angilcurt
		Tilloy
		Ponz
		medietatem vinee in suburbio Atrebate . . .
		cambas et e Wulfara in Batua cas
		medietatem de Rischesburch
		et terram juxta mare sitam . . .
		Duas quoque e beati Petri
		et beate Marie infra castrum sitas . . .
		et c duas in Atrebato videlicet s Crucis
		et s Marie in horto

[1] B and C mention Haspres, Berclau, and Gorres explicitly in a separate section, begun with variants of the standard phrasing. A contained no mention of properties other than altars.

TABLE C6.   List of Altars at Saint-Vaast, 1102–70

A/B/C (1102–53)[1]	D (1164)	E (1170)
Salgi	Salgi	Salgi
Hamesels	Florbais	Farbu
Hamblen	Leventiis	Basilice
Florbais	Felci	Florbais
Colummunt	Vi	Hendencurt
Fraisnes	Conteham	Boinvileirs
Leventie	Remi	Leventies
Dainville	Hendecurt	Asceel
Noveville	Aschehel	Hamesaez
Felci	Hadas	Felci
Novevillule	Mons	Hadas
Mooville	Noveville	Columnum

A/B/C (1102–53)[1]	D (1164)	E (1170)
Vici	Pabule	Vis
Berneville	Basilice	Mons
Yser	Boinvileir	Dainville
Contehem	Hamesels	Contehem
Warlus	Daginville	Noveville
Theulet	Guarlus	Warlus
Remit/Fissau[2]	Fissau	Remmy
Fissau/Remmi	Bairi	Pabule
Farbu	Fontenellis	Fissau
Hendencurt	Ateias	Fontenelles
item Hendencurt	Baliul	Betricourt
Moflanas	Gaverlle	Yser
Ascehel	Fuscarias	Baillol
Fontenelles	Bertricurt	Bigartii
Ymercurt	Bigartii	Thelut
Hadas	Hamblain	Atheias
Atheias	Fraisne	Hamblen
Merlecastel	Novivillule	Mofflanas
Mons	Iser	Gaverelle
Baillol	Teuluth	Frasne
Huluz	Moiflaines	Ymercurt
Noveville	Imercurt	Illies
Gaverelle	Berneville	Foscarias
Billi	Illiis	Novevillule
Pabule	in pago Atrebatensi	Berniville
	Bigartiam	
Foscarias	Teuluth cas	
Doverin	Buhercurt cas	
Basilice	Hadas cas	
Bertricurt		
Illiis		
Buinviller		
Bigartii		
Marchelliis		

---

[1] The altars listed in A, B, and C were the same except for one reversal in B, noted below, and the spelling of names.

[2] Remit and Fissau appeared in reversed order in B.

TABLE C7.   Saint-Père-de-Chartres, 1106–27

A   Pascal II, 1106 (CSP 2: 257–59. JL 6067)
     Style: *In quibus hec propriis visa sunt nominibus annotanda*
B   Honorius II, 1127 (CSP 2: 260–63. JL 7285)
     Style: *In quibus hec propriis nominibus duximus exprimenda*

A (1106)	B (1127)
e s Hylari	e videlicet s Germani de Alogia
	cc Domna Petra
s Leobini	e s Leobini de Braiaco
Campi Fauni	e s Romani de Braiaco
Manuvillaris	e s Petri de Arro ccs
Mitani Villaris	e s Marie de Evorea
Verni	e Ville Villonis
Alone Boas v	e s Marie de Stellionibus
Reclainvillaris	e Luigniaco
Imonis v	e Domna Petra
Germenonis v	e s Leobini Castro Duni
Ursi v	e s Stephani Spelterolis
Alpedani	e Tornesiaco
c Regie . . .	e de capella Osane
item altaria sex videlicet altare	e Verrigniaco
videlicet Bruerolis	
et Armentariis	e Billoncellis
et Roheria	e Senonchiis
et Buxeto	e Puteosa cc
et Cruciaco	e Mansellaria
et Castellaris[1] . . .	e Resuntis
e Gisiaco	e Mori Villari
et e Fontaneto in pago Vilcassini in	e Mutionis Villari
parrochia Rothomagensi . . .	
et in Carnotensi e beate Marie	e capella Fortini
prebendas VI[2]	
	e Rivellonio
	e Fursonis Villari
	e Vitriaco
	e Belchia
	e Rudeto
	e Alneto
	e Monasteriolo
	e s Martini de Firmeri Curia
	e Nantilliaco
	e Olins
	e Aneto
	e Saleeto

A (1106)	B (1127)
	e s Marie de Moncellis & c Sorel
	e Calgeto
	e Vi
	redditum prebende e s Martini de Valle in episcopatu
	quoque Aurelianensi e s Paterni
	e Niz
	in episcopatu quoque Ebroicensi e Bello Loco
	e s Christofori
	e Canziaco
	e Illeis
	e s Georgii
	e Purliaco
	in episcopatu Sagiensi e Plachiis
	e s Laurentii
	e Broglio Amaro
	et in Rothomagensi episcopatu e Leonis Curia
	e Gueriaco
	e Aldonei villa
	e Gundeli curia
	preterea in preafato Carnotensi episcopatu e Treione
	e s Germani de Guastina
	e Isis[3]

[1] "sicut a venerabili fratre nostro Ivone episcopo institutem est"
[2] "sicut . . . Rainfredo, Carnotensium episcopo, eidem vestro monasteri contributae sunt."
[3] The last three churches were free of any exaction, "salvo jure episcopali, in sua permanente libertate."

Appendix D:
Abbatial and Monastic Acts:
Saint-Vaast, Saint-Bertin, and Saint-Denis

TABLE D1. Abbatial Acts (ca. 1000–1200)

Abbots of Saint-Vaast		
Abbot	*Rule*	*Known acts*
Aloldus	1068–1104	6
Henry	1104–30	6
Walter	1130–47	4
Wéry	1147–55	7
Martin	1155–84	21
Abbots of Saint-Bertin		
Roderick	1018–43	1
Bovo	1043–65	2
Heribert	1065–81	1
Jean I	1081–95	2
Lambert	1095–24	4
Jean II	1124–31	2
Simon I	1131–36	0
Leo	1136–63	5
Godescalc	1163–70	1
Simon II	1170–86	8
Jean III	1186–1230	19

TABLE D2. Form of Abbatial Charters and Other Acts, Abbot Martin of Saint-Vaast (1155–84)

Date	Title of abbot	Assent	Officers	Perm?[1]
Known charters (18)				
1161	Indignus minister		Etc.[2]	Y
1161	Abbas	Y		Y
1161	Humilis minister	Y		
1162	Dei gratia ecclesia beati vedasti . . . servus	Y	Y	Y
1167	Abbas		Y	Y
1168	Humilis minister	Y	Y	Y
1175	Abbas	Y	Y	Y
1175	Abbas		Etc.	
1176	Abbas	Y		
1176	Indignus minister	Y	Etc.	Y
1176	Humilis minister	Y	Y	Y
1178	Minister humilis	Y		
1179	Abbas		Y	
1179	Abbas	Y[3]	Y	Y
1179	Humilis minister		Y	Y
Post-1177	Humilis minster			
Pre-1184	Humilis minister		Etc.	Y
Pre-1184	unknown[4]			
Notices[5] (3)				
1169	Abbas	Y[6]	Etc.	Y
1177	Ecclesia	Y	Etc.	Y
1178	Ecclesia	Y	Etc.	Y

[1] Does act permanently transfer lands or revenues, see Chapter 3.
[2] "etc." indicates the witness list abbreviated in later cartulary copy.
[3] "Abbas atque . . . universam capitulum."
[4] Act survives only in fragmentary form.
[5] These acts were dated during Martin's rule, but he was not the author of the acts.
[6] Notice of gift given "in presentibus fratribus nostris."

TABLE D3.   Form of Abbatial Charters and Other Acts, Abbot Suger of
             Saint-Denis (1122–51)

ID	Date	Title of abbot	In chapter	Assent	Officers
Known charters and acts (16)					
1	1122–24	Humilis minister	Y	N	N
2	1125	Humilis minister	Y	N	Y
3	1125	Abbas	N	N	N
4	1133	Abbas	N	Y	N
5	Pre-1135	Abbas	N	Y	Y
6	1135–36	Abbas	Y	N	Y
7	1122–36	Abbas	N	N	N
8	1137	Humilis minister	Y	Y	Y
9	1137	Abbas	Y	Y	Y
10	1122–37	Humilis minister	N	Y	N
11	1137–38	Abbas	Y	Y	N
12	1140	Abbas	Y	Y	N
13	1145	Abbas	N	Y	Etc.[1]
14	1148–49	Minister et abbas indignus	Y	Y	N
15	1149	Abbas	N	Y	N
16	1150	Abbas	Y	N	Y

ID is the number of the act in Gasparri.

[1] "etc." indicates the witness list abbreviated in later cartulary copy.

TABLE D4.   Officers in Witness Lists to Suger's Charters

ID	Date	PR	SP	PC	HP	TH	CX	CT	CC	CE
1	1122–24									
2	1125	X	X			X		X		
3	1125									
4	1133									
5	Pre-1135	X					X			
6	1135–36	X	X	X		X	X			
7	1122–36									
8	1137	X	X	X	X	X	X		X[1]	X
9	1137	X		X	X	X	X			
10	1122–37									
11	1137	X		X		X	X			
12	1140									
13	1145[2]									
14	1148–49									
15	1149									
16	1150	X								

PR = Prior, SP = Subprior, PC = Precentor, HP = Hospitarius/Infirmarius, TH = Thesaurarius, CX = Capicerius, CT = Cantor, CC = Cancellarius, CE = Cellararius.
X = present in witness list.
Officers have been placed in the order most commonly used in acts.
ID is the number of the act in Gasparri.
[1] Listed in his other capacity, "cartographer."
[2] The witness list was not copied in the later cartulary.

Abbreviations

AD	Archives départementales (followed by département name)
AN	Archives nationales, Paris
Annales: ESC	*Annales: Économies, sociétés, civilizations*
ASB	*Annales de Saint-Bertin*, ed. Félix Grat, Jeanne Vielliard, and Suzanne Clémencet, Paris: C. Klincksieck, 1964.
BCRH	*Bulletin de la Commission royale d'histoire*
BEC	*Bibliothèque de l'École des Chartes*
BHL	*Bibliotheca hagiographica latina antiquae et mediae aetatis*, ed. Société des Bollandistes, 2 vols. 1898–99; reprint, Brussels: Société des Bollandistes, 1949. *Novum supplementum*, ed. Henry Fros, Brussels: Société des Bollandistes, 1986. (followed by document number)
BM	Bibliothèque municipale (followed by city)
BnF	Bibliothèque Nationale de France, Paris, Département des manuscrits lat.: manuscrits latins nouv. acq. lat.: nouvelles acquisitions latines
CEA	*Les chartes des évêques d'Arras (1093–1203)*, ed. Benoît-Michel Tock, Paris: CTHS, 1991.
ChLA	*Chartae latinae antiquiores*, ed. Albert Bruckner and Robert Marichal, vols. 13–18, *France I-VI*, ed. Hartmut Atsma and Jean Vezin, Olten: U. Graf, 1981–86.
CSB	*Cartulaire de l'abbaye de Saint-Bertin*, ed. Benjamin Guérard, Paris: Crapelet, 1840.
CSG	*Recueil des chartes de l'abbaye de Saint-Germain-des-Prés: des origines au début du XIIIe siècle*, ed. René Poupardin, 2 vols. Paris: H. Champion, 1909–32.
CSP	*Cartulaire de l'abbaye de Saint-Père de Chartres*, ed. Benjamin Guérard, 2 vols. Paris: Crapelet, 1840.
CSV	*Cartulaire de l'abbaye de Saint-Vaast rédigé au XIIe siècle*

	par Guimann, ed. Eugène Van Drival, Arras: A. Courtin, 1875.
Gasparri	Suger, *Oeuvres*, ed. Françoise Gasparri, 2 vols. Paris: Belles Lettres, 1996–2001.
Haigneré	*Les chartes de Saint-Bertin d'après le Grand Cartulaire de Dom Charles-Joseph Dewitte*, ed. Daniel Haigneré, 4 vols. Saint-Omer: H. D'Homont, 1886–99.
JL	*Regesta pontificum Romanorum ab condita ecclesia ad annum post Christum natum MCXCVIII*, ed. Philip Jaffé, Samuel Loewenfeld, et al., 2nd ed., 2 vols. Leipzig: Veit, 1885–88; reprint, Graz: Akademische Druck-U. Verlagsanstalt, 1956.
La Neustrie	*La Neustrie: Les pays au nord de la Loire de 650 à 850*, ed. Hartmut Atmsa, 2 vols. Sigmaringen: J. Thorbecke, 1989.
Les cartulaires	*Les cartulaires: Actes de la Table ronde organisée par l'École nationale des chartes*, ed. Olivier Guyotjeannin, Laurent Morelle, and Michel Parisse, Paris: École des Chartes, 1993.
MGH	Monumenta Germaniae Historica
	Capitularia
	Concilia
	Epistolae Karolini Aevi
	Schriften
	SS: Scriptores
	Scriptorum rerum Merovingicarum
Morand	*Appendice au Cartulaire de l'abbaye de Saint-Bertin*, ed. François Morand, Paris: Imprimerie Impériale, 1867.
PL	*Patrologiae cursus completus . . . Series latina*, ed. Jacques-Paul Migne, 221 vols. Paris, 1844–64.
PU	*Papsturkunden* (in Frankreich or Niederlanden, see bibliography)
Tardif	*Monuments historiques: Cartons des rois*, ed. Jules Tardif, Paris: J. Claye, 1866; reprint, Nendeln: Kraus, 1977.

Notes

Introduction

1. BnF ms. lat. 12194, fol. 219r, edited in CSG 1: 298–99, no. 214: "Guido, major de Surinis, astu malignitatis negabat se hominem nostrum et ecclesie nostre esse."

2. CSG 1: 298, no. 214: "Proinde nos submonuimus eum de jure et ad diem statutum undequaque congregavimus in curia nostra utriusque sexus fere quinquaginta de parentela predicti Guidonis."

3. CSG 1: 298, no 214: "Qui omnes homines nostri de corpore parati essent approbare quod idem Guido sicut et ipsi homo noster esse debebat."

4. BnF ms. lat. 12194, fol. 219v, edited in CSG 1: 318, no. 226(i).

5. For more on this matter, see Chapter 4.

6. Jean-Pierre Poly and Eric Bournazel, *La mutation féodale: Xe–XIIe siècles*, rev. ed. (Paris: Presses Universitaires de France, 1991), trans. Caroline Higgitt, *The Feudal Transformation: 900–1200* (New York: Holmes and Meier, 1991).

7. Georges Duby, *La société aux XIe et XIIe siècles dans la région mâconnaise*, 2nd ed. (Paris: J. Touzot, 1971). See also Duby's discussion of the "feudal revolution" in his *Les trois ordres ou l'imaginaire du féodalisme* (Paris: Gallimard, 1978), trans. Arthur Goldhammer, *The Three Orders: Feudal Society Imagined* (Chicago: University of Chicago Press, 1980), 147–66.

8. The most radical statement of the "mutationiste" position can be found in Guy Bois, *La mutation de l'an mil: Lournand, village mâconnais de l'antiquité au féodalisme* (Paris: Fayard, 1989).

9. See Thomas N. Bisson, "The Feudal Revolution," *Past and Present* 142 (1994): 6–42; the responses of Dominique Barthélemy "Debate: The 'Feudal Revolution' I," *Past and Present* 152 (1996): 196–205; Stephen D. White, "Debate: The 'Feudal Revolution' II," *Past and Present* 152 (1996): 205–23; Timothy Reuter, "Debate: The 'Feudal Revolution' III," *Past and Present* 155 (1997): 177–95; Chris Wickham, "Debate: The 'Feudal Revolution' IV," *Past and Present* 155 (1997): 196–208; and Thomas N. Bisson, "The 'Feudal Revolution': Reply," *Past and Present* 155 (1997): 208–25.

10. Susan Reynolds, *Fiefs and Vassals: The Medieval Evidence Reinterpreted* (Oxford: Oxford University Press, 1994).

11. Dominique Barthélemy, *La mutation de l'an mil a-t-elle eu lieu? Servage et chevalerie dans la France des Xe et XIe siècles* (Paris: Fayard, 1997), 29–56. See also his documentary studies in *La société dans le comté de Vendôme: de l'an mil au XIVe siècle* (Paris: Fayard, 1993), 19–116.

12. A notable exception is Dirk Heirbaut, "Flanders: A Pioneer of State-Oriented Feudalism? Feudalism as an Instrument of Comital Power in Flanders During the High Middle Ages (1000–1300)," in *Expectations of Law in the Middle Ages*, ed. Anthony Musson (Woodbridge: Boydell, 2001), 23–34.

13. Elizabeth Eisenstein, *The Printing Press as an Agent of Social Change: Communications and Cultural Transformation in Early-Modern Europe*, 2 vols. (Cambridge: Cambridge University Press, 1979).

14. Michael Clanchy, *From Memory to Written Record: England 1066–1307*, 2nd ed. (Oxford: Blackwell, 1993).

15. Brian Stock, *The Implications of Literacy: Written Language and Models of Interpretation in the Eleventh and Twelfth Centuries* (Princeton, N.J.: Princeton University Press, 1983), 88–92. See later refinements in Brian Stock, *Listening for the Text: On the Uses of the Past* (Philadelphia: University of Pennsylvania Press, 1996), 140–58.

16. Patrick Geary, *Phantoms of Remembrance: Memory and Oblivion at the End of the First Millennium* (Princeton, N.J.: Princeton University Press, 1994). See also the important qualification of Laurent Morelle, "Histoire et archives vers l'an mil: Une nouvelle 'mutation'?" *Histoire et archives* 3 (1998): 119–41.

17. Georges Declercq, "Originals and Cartularies: The Organization of Archival Memory (Ninth-Eleventh Centuries)," in *Charters and the Use of the Written Word in Medieval Society*, ed. Karl Heidecker (Turnhout: Brepols, 2000), 147–70. For northern France in particular, see Laurent Morelle, "The Metamorposis of Three Monastic Charter Collections in the Eleventh Century (Saint-Amand, Saint-Riquier, Montier-en-Der)," in *Charters and the Use of the Written Word*, ed. Heidecker, 171–204.

18. Robert F. Berkhofer III, "Inventing Traditions: Forgery, Creativity, and Historical Conscience in Medieval France" (forthcoming).

19. Mary Carruthers, *The Book of Memory: A Study of Memory in Medieval Culture* (Cambridge: Cambridge University Press, 1990), esp. ch. 6, "Memory and Authority," 189–220.

20. Henk Teunis, "Negotiating Secular and Ecclesiastical Power in the Central Middle Ages: A Historiographical Introduction," in *Negotiating Secular and Ecclesiastical Power: Western Europe in the Central Middle Ages*, ed. Arnoud-Jan A. Bijsterveld, Hank Teunis, and Andrew Wareham (Turnhout: Brepols, 1999), 1–18.

Chapter 1. A Fragmentary Past: Monastic History, Memory, and Patrimony

1. For example, Elisabeth Magnou-Nortier, "La gestion publique en Neustrie: Les moyens et les hommes (VIIᵉ–IXᵉ siècles)," in *La Neustrie* 1: 271–320, and her edited volumes, *Aux sources de la gestion publique*, 3 vols. (Lille: Presses Universitaires de Lille, 1993–97). See also Jean Durliat, *Les finances publiques de Dioclétien aux Carolingiens (284–889)* (Sigmaringen: J. Thorbecke, 1990), 189–285.

2. See Jean Durliat, "Le polyptyque d'Irminon et l'impôt de l'armée,"

BEC 116 (1983): 183–208 and subsequent debate in *La Neustrie*, and also Durliat, *Les finances publiques*, 222–30, 244–51, 264–67.

3. Jean-Pierre Devroey, "Un monastère dans l'économie d'échanges," *Annales: ESC* 39 (1984): 570–89.

4. Janet Nelson, *Charles the Bald* (London: Longman, 1992), 23–29. See also her remarks about Charles's "taxation," 188, 207, 213, 250–51.

5. MGH Concilia 2(1): 464–66, no. 40.

6. For the traditional version, see Emile Lesne, *Histoire de la propriété ecclésiastique en France du VIIIe à la fin du XIe siècles* (Lille: R. Giard, 1910–43) 2(2): 185–502. For more recent suggestions, see Franz Felten, *Äbte und Laienäbte im Frankreich: Studie zum Verhältnis von Staat und Kirche im früheren Mittelalter* (Stuttgart: Anton Hiersemann, 1980), 143–287 and Laurent Morelle, "Les 'actes précaire,' instruments de transferts patrimoniaux (France du Nord et de l'Est, VIIIe–XIe siècle," *Mélanges de l'École française de Rome. Moyen Age* 111, 2 (1999): 607–47.

7. A diploma of Louis the Pious, January 13, 829, edited in CSG 1: 43–47, no. 88 established the number of monks at Saint-Germain. The *partitio bonorum*, AN K9 no. 5, fixed it at Saint-Denis.

8. Otto Gerhard Oexle, *Forschungen zu monastischen und geistlichen Gemeinschaften im westfränkischen Bereich* (Munich: W. Fink, 1978), 15–22 (edition) and 96–111 (analysis). The number of religious at Saint-Germain may have peaked at 212 around 800; see Konrad Elmshäuser and Andreas Hedwig, *Studien zum Polyptychon von Saint-Germain-des-Prés* (Köln: Böhlau, 1993), 9.

9. CSG 1: 43–46, no. 28. Hilduin was one of many Saint-Denis abbots who served as archchaplain, see Josef Fleckenstein, *Die Hofkapelle der deutschen Könige*, MGH Schriften 16(1): 39, 45–48.

10. MGH Concilia 2(2): 683–87, no. 52. See Léon Levillain, "Études sur l'abbaye de Saint-Denis à l'époque mérovingienne II: Les origines de Saint-Denis," *BEC* 86 (1925): 5–99, esp. 35–43 (hereafter "Les origines de Saint-Denis") and the revisions of Oexle, *Forschungen zu monastischen und geistlichen Gemeinschaften*, 23–34, 112–19.

11. AN K9 no. 6, edited in Tardif, 87–88, no. 124, "regulariter . . . sed minus perfecte."

12. For the identification of Mours, see Levillain, "Les origines de Saint-Denis," 37. See also Georges Tessier, ed., *Recueil des actes de Charles II le Chauve, roi de France* 3 vols. (Paris: Imprimérie nationale, 1943–55) 2:65, no. 247.

13. Oexle, *Forschungen zu monastischen und geistlichen Gemeinschaften*, 25–26 (edition), 118 (analysis).

14. MGH Concilia 2(2): 683–87, no. 52. See Levillain, "Les origines de Saint-Denis," 5–99, esp. 35–43 and Oexle, *Forschungen zu monastischen und geistlichen Gemeinschaften*, 23–34, 112–19.

15. As implied by the preamble of Hilduin's *partitio bonorum*, discussed below. See Oexle, *Forschungen zu monastischen und geistlichen Gemeinschaften*, 115 n63.

16. *Flodoardi Historia Remensis Ecclesiae*, MGH SS 13: 475. Much of this information came from Hincmar, who had been a member of the convent who

did not go to Mours. See Oexle, *Forschungen zu monastischen und geistlichen Gemeinschaften*, 32–33.

17. Tardif, 88, no. 124. See Levillain, "Les origines de Saint-Denis," 40.

18. MGH Concilia 2(2): 689, no. 53. A charter of Landry, Bishop of Paris, who supposedly founded Saint-Denis and abandoned episcopal control, is specifically mentioned, see Tardif, 8–9, no. 10.

19. Tardif, 88, no. 124.

20. AN K9 no. 5, edited in Michel Félibien, *Histoire de l'abbaye royal de Saint-Denys en France.* . . . (Paris: F. Leonard, 1706), lxix–li, no. 72 and partially in Tardif, 86–89, no. 124.

21. AN K9 no. 6, edited in Tardif, 86–89, no. 124.

22. See analysis (with facsimile) by Jean-Pierre Brunterc'h, "Acte constitutif de la mense conventuelle du monastère de Saint-Denis établie par l'abbé Hilduin le 22 janvier 832," in *Un village au temps de Charlemagne: Moines et paysans de l'abbaye de Saint-Denis du VIIe siècle à l'An Mil*, ed. Jean Cuisenier and Rémy Guadagnin (Paris: Réunion des musées nationaux, 1988), 125–28, no. 33.

23. AN K8 no. 12³, edited by Léon Levillain, "Un état de redevances dues à la mense conventuelle de Saint-Denis (832)," *Bulletin de la Société de l'histoire de Paris et de l'Ile-de-France* 36 (1909): 79–90. A forged charter of Dagobert was written on the reverse of the original document around 900.

24. Wheat and wine were treated separately in later acts of Abbot Louis and Charles the Bald, suggesting that this apparent omission was deliberate.

25. The trimming of the document by later forgers probably explains the discrepancy.

26. Jean-Pierre Devroey, "Problèmes de critique autour du polyptyque de l'abbaye de Saint-Germain-des-Prés," in *La Neustrie* 1: 442–44, esp. n111. See also Elmshäuser and Hedwig, *Studien zum Polyptychon von Saint-Germain-des-Prés*, 8–9.

27. Devroey, "Problèmes de critique autour du polyptyque," 452–53.

28. See Devroey, "Problèmes de critique autour du polyptyque," 445–46, 452 and Dieter Hägermann, ed., *Das Polyptychon von Saint-Germain-des-Prés*, i–xxix.

29. Hägermann, ed., *Das Polyptychon von Saint-Germain-des-Prés* (Köln: Böhlau, 1993), 217.

30. Bernard Delmaire, "Cartulaires et inventaires de chartes dans le nord de la France" in *Les cartulaires*, 305, found no other "cartulary" before 1100, but see below. For the transmission of Folquin's work, see appendix A.

31. BM St. Omer ms. 815, 295 (election) and 298–99. See also below.

32. BM St. Omer ms. 815, 119: "Nantharius interea abba, junior, migrans a seculo, regularis vitae primum destructorem sibi reliquit successorum, Fridegisum videlicet, nec ipso nomine dignum abbatem."

33. For Fridugis's role at court, see Georges Tessier, *Diplomatique royale française* (Paris: Picard, 1962), 44. See also *Gesta Abbatum S. Bertini Sithiensium*, MGH SS 13: 614 n5.

34. BM St. Omer ms. 815, 119: "Nam cum hactenus sacra monachorum regula, miseratione Dei, in hoc cenobio foret conservata, crescente rerum

opulentia, monachis ordinatione monasterii sui, abstracta abbatia regali beneficio in externas personas est beneficiata."

35. BM St. Omer ms. 815, 120–21: "Nam in capitaneo apostolorum seu
sancti Bertini loco, ubi LXXXIII monachi deserviebant Domino, LX, pro
humana potius laude quam pro Dei amore, retinuit; reliquos districtioris vitae
viros, quos suae perversitati putavit non consentire, de monasterio expellens
abire permisit. In sancti Audomari quoque monasterio, ubi regulariter viventes
aderant XL monachi, XXX canonicos ibidem ad serviendum deputavit in monasterio Christi."

36. BM St. Omer ms. 815, 121: "Ac post haec, totius abbatiae circuiens
villas, et quia duplex extabat monachorum numerus, dupplam eis portionem vil-
larum est largitus. Canonicis autem, quia pauciores erant numero, simpla contra monachis est data portio."

37. BM St. Omer ms. 815, 121: "Ipse ea quae sibi maxime placuerunt, ad
suae perversitatis usum reservavit." See Raoul Van Caenegem, "Le diplôme de
Charles le Chauve du 20 juin 877 pour l'abbaye de Saint-Bertin," *Revue d'histoire
du droit* 31 (1963): 413–15.

38. Nelson, *Charles the Bald*, 61–62.

39. MGH Epistolae Karolini Aevi 3: 325–27, no. 19 (BHL 2172). See J. M.
Wallace-Hadrill, "History in the Mind of Archbishop Hincmar," in *The Writing
of History in the Middle Ages: Essays presented to Richard William Southern*, ed.
R. H. C. Davis and J. M. Wallace-Hadrill (Oxford: Clarendon Press, 1981),
45–47, and Gabrielle Spiegel, *The Chronicle Tradition of Saint-Denis* (Brookline,
Mass.: Classical Folio Editions, 1978), 23.

40. *Post beatem et salutiferam*, PL 106, cols. 23–50 (BHL 2175). See also
Hilduin's response to Louis, *Exultavit cor meum*, MGH Epistolae Karolini Aevi
3: 327–35, no. 20 (BHL 2173); and his letter prefacing the work, *Cum nos Scrip-
tura*, MGH Epistolae Karolini Aevi 3: 335–37 (BHL 2174).

41. David Luscombe, "Denis the Pseudo-Areopagite in the Middle Ages
from Hilduin to Lorenzo Valla," in *Fälschungen im Mittelalter: Internationaler
Kongress der Monumenta Germaniae Historica* (Hannover: Hahnsche Buchhandlung, 1988–90) 1: 133–52.

42. *Gesta Dagoberti I. Regis Francorum*, MGH Scriptores rerum Merovingicarum 2: 396–425. There is no complete edition of the *Miracula*, see BHL
2193–2202 and supplement 2202a for bibliography.

43. Léon Levillain, "Études sur l'abbaye de Saint-Denis à l'époque mérovingienne I: Les sources narratives," *BEC* 82 (1921): 5–116. (Hereafter "Les sources
narratives") See also Luscombe, "Denis the Pseudo-Areopagite," 140–43.

44. See Levillain, "Les sources narratives," 58–72. Twenty-four Merovingian charters were produced for the *Gesta Dagoberti*, mostly forgeries. For an
enumeration and description, see Bruno Krusch, "Über die *Gesta Dagoberti*,"
Forschungen zur deutschen Geschichte 26 (1886): 161–91. For more recent bibliography, see Hartmut Atsma, "Le fonds des chartes mérovingiennes de Saint-
Denis: Rapport sur une recherche en cours," *Paris-et-l'Ile-de-France* 32 (1981):
259–72.

45. Tessier, ed., *Actes de Charles II* 2: 56–67, no. 247.

46. See Tessier's remarks, *Actes de Charles II* 2: 60.

47. For the importance of wine, see Jean Durliat, "La vigne et le vin dans le région parisienne au début du IXe siècle d'après le polyptyque d'Irminon," *Le Moyen Age* 24 (1968): 387–419.

48. These documents were later altered; see Georges Tessier, "Originaux et pseudo-originaux carolingiens du chartrier de Saint-Denis," *BEC* 106 (1946): 62–67.

49. ASB, 134–35.

50. Marie LaMotte-Collas, "Les possessions territoriales de l'abbaye de Saint-Germain-des-Prés du début du IXe au début du XIIe siècle," *Revue d'histoire de l'Église de France* 43 (1957): 49–80.

51. See maps in Elmshäuser and Hedwig, *Studien zum Polyptychon von Saint-Germain-des-Prés*, 531ff.

52. Elmshäuser and Hedwig, *Studien zum Polyptychon von Saint-Germain-des-Prés*, 10. See also Nelson, *Charles the Bald*, 50–53.

53. Tessier, ed., *Actes de Charles II* 2: 305–12, no. 363. See also Elmshäuser and Hedwig, *Studien zum Polyptychon von Saint-Germain-des-Prés*, 21 n173 for a table comparing the polyptych and acts of 829 and 872.

54. For a list see LaMotte-Collas, "Les possessions territoriales de Saint-Germain," 62.

55. The annals of Saint-Bertin say only that Charles received Saint-Vaast "in return for mutually convenient arrangements agreed between them," ASB, 128, trans. Janet Nelson, *The Annals of Saint-Bertin* (Manchester: Manchester University Press, 1991), 132. Ferdinand Lot, "Une année du règne de Charles le Chauve: Année 866," *Le Moyen âge* 15 (1902): 404–5, infers Charles used Lothar's divorce as leverage. Compare Nelson, *Charles the Bald*, 212.

56. CSV, 5, and see below.

57. ASB, 132.

58. Tessier, ed., *Actes de Charles II* 2: 170–76, no. 304.

59. Tessier, ed., *Actes de Charles II* 2: 213–14, no. 324 and CSV, 28.

60. BM Arras ms. 1266, fol. 4v and CSV, 35–38 (JL 3022). The contents of this charter should be regarded with suspicion.

61. Robert-Henri Bautier, ed., *Recueil des actes d'Eudes, roi de France (888–898)* (Paris: Imprimérie nationale, 1967), 85–98, no. 20.

62. See Lesne, *Histoire de la propriété ecclésiastique* 2(3). See also Jan Dhondt, *Études sur la naissance des principautés territoriales en France (IXe–Xe siècles)* (Bruges: De Tempel, 1948), 27–29, 50–61.

63. BM St. Omer ms. 815, 132–33. For Gundbert's career, see Nicolas Huyghebaert, "Le comte Baudouin II de Flandre et les *custos* de Steneland: A propos d'un faux précepte de Charles le Chauve pour Saint-Bertin (866)," *Revue bénédictine* 69 (1959): 49–53.

64. BM St. Omer ms. 815, 133, "Descripsit et compotum, quem et nobis concessit habendum." See J. M. de Smet, "Geen *Stylus Paschalis* in Vlaanderen tijdens de IXde eeuw," *De Leiegouw* 8, 1 (1966): 227–38 and Alexander Murray, *Reason and Society in the Middle Ages*, rev. ed. (Oxford: Oxford University Press, 1990), 141–61.

65. BM St. Omer ms. 815, 319–24.

66. BM St. Omer ms. 815, 315: "Quod si quisquam de rectoribus predicti monasterii hoc ab eis auferre, propter malivolentiam, vel inde debitum eorum supplere voluerit, tunc omnimodis, absque ulla contradictione, ad nostros legitimos heredes revertere debeat."

67. BM St. Omer ms. 815, 325.

68. BM St. Omer ms. 815, 326: "His omnibus, fili, te superstitem confirmo, quatinus et Dei hanc domum meamque ac antecessorum meorum etiam et tuam elemosinam, dum advixeris, congrua cura custodias."

69. See the list of *missi* in the Capitulary of Servais of 853, MGH Capitularia 2: 274. For his work as an emissary, see Nelson, *Charles the Bald*, 183–84, 187, 192. For his nobility, see BM St. Omer ms. 815, 164–65, 206–8 and also G. Coolen, "Guntbert de Saint-Bertin, chronique des temps carolingiens," *Revue du Nord* 40 (1958): 213–24.

70. When Gundbert wrote and subscribed as *praepositus* a charter of Adalard's concerning the *prestaria* of Odwin, the monastery's advocate, BM St. Omer ms. 815, 167–69.

71. Canons and monks coexisted at Saint-Bertin under Fridugis and Gundbert's exact status is unclear; see Huyghebaert, "Le comte Baudouin II de Flandre et les *custos* de Steneland," 50 n2. Folquin, however, certainly portrayed him as a monk (*monachus*).

72. François-Louis Ganshof, ed., *Le polyptyque de l'abbaye de Saint-Bertin (844–859): Édition critique et commentaire* (Paris: Klincksieck, 1975), 2.

73. Ganshof, ed., *Le polyptyque de Saint-Bertin*, 130–31 and compare Robert Fossier, *La terre et les hommes en Picardie jusqu'à la fin du XIIIe siècle* (Paris: B. Nauwelaerts, 1968) 1: 210–27.

74. Ganshof, ed., *Le polyptyque de Saint-Bertin*, 9–10, 129–30. Fossier, *La terre et les hommes en Picardie* 1: 217–8.

75. For the supposed foundation charter, see BM St. Omer ms. 815, 5–8 and Jean-François Lemarignier, *La France médiévale: Institutions et société* (Paris: A. Colin, 1970), 59, 84–85.

76. BM St. Omer ms. 815, 174. Ganshof showed that the polyptych was current and not a prescriptive (and thus outdated) list of estates, as previously thought: Ganshof, ed., *Le polyptyque de Saint-Bertin*, 133–34. Compare Fossier, *La terre et les hommes en Picardie* 1: 226–27.

77. BM St. Omer ms. 815, 327–30 and de Smet, "Geen *Stylus Paschalis* in Vlaanderen tijdens de IXde eeuw," 227–38.

78. BM St. Omer ms. 815, 335–41.

79. BM St. Omer ms. 815, 331–34. See Tessier, ed., *Actes de Charles II* 2: 623–24, no. 489. This act was a later forgery; see below.

80. See BM St. Omer ms. 815, 236–38, death of Hilduin and 238–43, charter of 877.

81. BM St. Omer ms. 815, 340, "Post haec, ego Gundbertus . . . dedi . . ." Another possible clue is that the first *brevis* used the *annus domini*, as did Adalard's confirmation, subscribed by Gundbert, see de Smet, "Geen *Stylus Paschalis* in Vlaanderen tijdens de IXde eeuw," 227–38.

82. BM St. Omer ms. 815, 335–41.

83. Tessier, ed., *Actes de Charles II* 2: 623–24, no. 489. The clumsy forgery suggests someone of inferior ability or working at some remove, see Coolen, "Guntbert de Saint-Bertin, chronique des temps carolingiens," 223–24. Nicolas Huyghebaert argued compellingly that the forgery was undertaken in 910–18, in response to Baldwin II's assumption of the lay abbacy of Saint Bertin: "Le comte Baudouin II de Flandre et les *custos* de Steneland," 60–67.

84. Tessier, ed., *Actes de Charles II* 2: 458–62, no. 430. See also BM St. Omer ms. 815, 236–43.

85. Tessier, ed., *Actes de Charles II* 2: 461, no. 430.

86. Van Caenegem, "Le diplôme de Charles le Chauve," 403–4.

87. Ganshof, ed., *Le polyptyque de Saint-Bertin*, 19–20 (text) and 91–98 (commentary) and BM St. Omer ms. 815, 329 for Wizernes. There is a Gundbert mentioned in the polyptych as holding lands in Moringhem, Ganshof, ed., *Le polyptyque de Saint-Bertin*, 14, 41, but it may not be the same man.

88. Of the sixteen places mentioned in the *brevia* of 867, thirteen were among the thirty-four places mentioned in the 856 confirmation of Adalard.

89. Folquin's version, see BM St. Omer ms. 815, 238–42. See also Tessier, ed., *Actes de Charles II* 2: 622–25, no. 489 and Maurits Gysseling and A. C. F. Koch, eds., *Diplomata Belgica ante annum millesimum centesium scripta* (Brussels: Belgisch Inter-Universitair Centrum voor Neerlandistiek, 1950) 1: 76–8, no. 44. Van Caenegem, "Le Diplôme de Charles le Chauve," 410–13 demonstrated the inadequacy of both editions' geographic information.

90. Or as many as seven, according to Folquin.

91. Haigneré 1: vi–v.

92. See Chapter 3.

93. The decline of long distance transport services may have abetted this measure, see Devroey, "Un monastère dans l'économie d'échanges," 570–89.

94. The mass of forgeries at Saint-Denis makes reconstructing its *mensa conventualis* from 877 to 1050 a very difficult enterprise. See Tessier, "Originaux et pseudo-originaux de Saint-Denis," 35–69 and Chapter 3.

95. Nelson, *Charles the Bald*, 255–57.

96. Thomas Waldman, "Saint-Denis et les premiers Capétiens" in *Religion et culture autour de l'an mil*, ed. Dominique Iogna-Prat and Jean-Charles Picard (Paris: Picard, 1990), 191–7.

97. LaMotte-Collas, "Les possessions territoriales de Saint-Germain," 59–60.

98. Robert-Henri Bautier, "Paris au temps d'Abélard" in *Abélard en son temps: Actes du colloque international organisé à l'occasion du 9ᵉ centenaire de la naissance de Pierre Abélard, 14–19 mai 1979* (Paris: Belles Lettres, 1981), 22; and Albert D'Haenens, *Les invasions normandes en Belgique au IXᵉ siècle: Le phénomène et sa répercussion dans l'historiographie médiévale* (Louvain: Publications Universitaires de Louvain, 1967), 106–11.

99. Charter of Philip I (1061), CSG 1: 103–6, no. 64: "accidit tempore Hugonis ducis, qui Magnus cognominabatur, ut ipse dux, sicut alias ecclesias attenuaverat multis prediis, ita quaque hanc ecclesiam mutilaret ablatione multarum possessionum."

100. LaMotte-Collas, "Les possessions territoriales de Saint-Germain," 60–65; Elmshäuser and Hedwig, *Studien zum Polyptychon von Saint-Germain-des-Prés*, 11–23.

101. LaMotte-Collas, "Les possessions territoriales de Saint-Germain," 60–61, 73–74.

102. CSV, 5: "Quod ex descriptione illa...vix nos omnium decimam habere non jam ex libro conjicimus, sed experientia sentimus."

103. The destruction of the original manuscript and a twelfth-century copy in 1944 leaves only the 1840 edition of Benjamin Guérard (CSP) as the source for the work's content, supplemented from originals by Réné Merlet in the *Inventaire sommaire des archives départementales antérieures à 1790. Eure-et-Loir*, H1 (Chartres: Garnier, 1897).

104. CSP 1: 5 and ASB, 75.

105. CSP 1: 9–10: "Praedictus ergo praesul, nacta [sic] occasione, praeciosa quae ibi repperit ornamenta vasaque diversa aurea vel argentea, quae concupivit, absportavit atque distraxit, terras quoque sanctuarii quas religiosorum virorum munificentia dederat, in quibus extendere manum potuit, propriis usibus stipendiariis mancipere non timuit, suisque domesticis, ausu temerario, in beneficio dividere praesumpsit."

106. CSP 1: 44.

107. CSP 1: 15: "Set quia fidelium donaria, scriptorum penuria, illo in tempore aut non scripta, aut si sunt scripta, neglegentia archiscriniorum, prae nimia vetustate sunt aboleta; ideo de antiquis cartis nullam praeter istam invenire valui." Olivier Guyotjeannin, "*Penuria Scriptorum*: le mythe de l'anarchie documentaire dans la France du nord (Xe-première moitié du XIe siècle)," BEC 155 (1997): 12, 41–42 interpreted "penuria scriptorum" as a lack of writers more than documents but emphasized the perceived lack of late Carolingian texts; the sole document was a charter Bishop Aimery of Chartres from 889–90.

108. CSP 1: 3 n1, 19 n1, for titles; only the *liber agani* and the *liber ragenfredi* had original titles, see CSP 1: 55 n1.

109. CSP 1: 35, 51.

110. CSP 1: 19–21.

111. CSP 1: 21–25. Only two charters survived from the time of Aganon, CSP 1: 26–27, 27–28, and see André Chédeville, *Chartres et ses campagnes (XIe–XIIIe siècles)* (Paris: Klincksieck, 1973), 117–18.

112. CSP 1: 11–12, 51.

113. CSP 1: 28–30, 49–54.

114. CSP 1: 35: "Res denique quas scriptas inveni et ad canonicos pertinere videbantur, deinde res quae ad luminaria aecclesiae et ad victum editui delegatae erant, et quae postea ab episcopis additae sunt, Agano videlicet atque Ragenfredo, monachi modo nequaquam possident." This comment only existed in copy B of the *Vetus Aganon* according to Guérard, CSP 1: 35 n1.

115. CSP 1: 35–39.

116. CSP 1: 40–43.

117. CSP 1: 48: "Deinde res possessas ab illis [canonicis] quas scriptas repperi in duobus rotulis, atque consuetudines quas ab agricolis accipiebant, quae multum discrepant a consuetudinibus nostri temporis."

118. Compare Chédeville, *Chartres et ses campagnes*, 361–63, who treats the two documents as one "polyptyque."

119. Chédeville speculates that the charters may have been interpolated after 1078, *Chartres et ses campagnes*, 409 n69.

120. CSP 1: 19–20.

121. Barbara Rosenwein, *To Be the Neighbor of Saint Peter: The Social Meaning of Cluny's Property, 909–1049* (Ithaca, N.Y.: Cornell University Press, 1989), 79 n4 observed that at Cluny between 909 and 1049, exchange transactions (including precarial gifts) were 11 percent of all known transactions.

122. Baudouin de Gaiffier, "Les revendications de biens dans quelques documents hagiographiques du XIᵉ siècle," *Analecta Bollandiana* 50 (1932): 123–38.

123. See examples in Patrick Geary, *Furta Sacra: Thefts of Relics in the Central Middle Ages*, rev. ed. (Princeton, N.J.: Princeton University Press, 1990), 85–86 and de Gaiffier, "Les revendications de biens," 128–30.

124. Martin Heinzelmann, *Translationsberichte und andere Quellen des Reliquienkultes*, Typologie des sources du moyen âge occidental 33 (Turnhout: Brepols, 1979); Karine Ugé, "Relics as Tools of Power: The Eleventh-Century *Inventio* of St. Bertin's Relics and the Assertion of Abbot Bovo's Authority," in *Negotiating Secular and Ecclesiastical Power: Western Europe in the Central Middle Ages*, ed. Arnoud-Jan A. Bijsterveld, Henk Teunis, and Andrew Wareham (Turnhout: Brepols, 1999), 51–72.

125. Lester Little, *Benedictine Maledictions: Liturgical Cursing in Romanesque France* (Ithaca, N.Y.: Cornell University Press, 1993), 218–29.

126. Georges Declercq, "Originals and Cartularies: The Organization of Archival Memory (Ninth–Eleventh Centuries)," in *Charters and the Use of the Written Word in Medieval Society*, ed. Karl Heidecker (Turnhout: Brepols, 2000), 170.

127. BM St. Omer ms. 815, 2: "In hoc codice gesta abbatum Sithiensis coenobii depromere cupientes, vel possessionum traditiones, quae a fidelibus, sub uniuscujusque illorum tempore, sacro huic loco, cum cartarum inscriptione, sunt concessae, describere volentes, a primo ipsius loci structore, domno Bertino abbate; operis hujus exordium sumamus Christo."

128. BM St. Omer ms. 815, 5: "Hunc tantummodo codicem de membranulis in unius libri cumulavimus corpus, ut, si forsan quis istius loci possessionum investigandarum fuerit avidus, ad hunc recurrat," trans. Patrick Geary, *Phantoms of Remembrance: Memory and Oblivion at the End of the First Millennium* (Princeton, N.J.: Princeton University Press, 1994), 102.

129. BM St. Omer ms. 815, 299: "Explevi jam, auxiliante Domino, quae jusseras, domne et beatissime, necnon et amantissime pater, Adalolphe, comprehendens in uno codice traditiones fidelium cum cartis earum, necnon et gesta abbatum."

130. BM St. Omer ms. 815, 299: "Fateor autem ipsa veritate, teste me, nihil hic aliud scripsisse nisi quod in exemplariis antiquorum potui reperire aut strenuis viris narrantibus agnoscere."

131. Karine Ugé, "Creating a Useable Past in the Tenth Century: Folcuin's *Gesta* and the Crises at Saint-Bertin," *Studi Medievali* 37 (1996): 887–903.

132. BM St. Omer ms. 815, 297. For Folquin's life career see Émile Brou-ette, *Dictionaire d'histoire et de géographie ecclésiastique* 17 (1971), cols. 744–49.

133. Michel Sot, *Gesta episcoporum, gesta abbatum,* Typologie des sources du moyen âge occidental 37 (Turnhout: Brepols, 1981), 22–23.

134. BM St. Omer ms. 815, 284–87. For Gerald of Brogne, see the memo-rial volume of *Revue bénédictine* 70 (1960).

135. Declercq, "Originals and Cartularies," 156–57 for Ghent and Saint-Bertin and the importance of reform as a stimulus.

136. BM St. Omer ms. 815, 297: "ne raptoris incurisse videretur notam." I translate *raptor* as thief, although the word indicates considerably more violence.

137. BM St. Omer ms. 815, 132–33: "Nam monasterii hujus libraria, quae pene omnia vetustate erant demolita, quoniam peritus erat scriba, propria ren-ovavit industria."

138. Haigneré 1: xii.

139. Guyotjeannin, "*Penuria Scriptorum*," 29–30.

140. For example, he left original dating formulas intact, see Guérard, CSB, iv.

141. Ugé, "Creating a Useable Past," 887–92.

142. As shown by the charter he had written for Arnulf, BM St. Omer ms. 815, 297, which included a witness list and his own subscription.

143. The list of monks closely follows Folquin's assertion of truthfulness, BM St. Omer ms. 815, 300.

144. BM St. Omer ms. 815, 313: "Hic etiam villulas ad elemosinae minis-terium a fidelibius contraditas, non meo parcens labori, sed monasterii pros-piciens utilitati, cum cartis suis, scribere aggrediar." The word *ministerium* had many meanings (a minister, ministering, a ministry), see Franz Blatt and Yves Lefèvre, eds., *Novum glossarium mediae latinitatis: ab anno DCCC usque ad annum MCC* (Hafniae: Munksgaard, 1957–), cols. 543–44, s.v., esp. 8B–D. I have avoided using the translation "office," since it is confusing and anachronis-tic; see Chapter 4.

145. BM St. Omer ms. 815, 282: "Reliquas vero kartas per diversorum min-isteriorum officio deputatas curavi separatim inscribere, ut quod unicuique min-isterio distributum erat, faciliori inquisitione posset inquirens indagare."

146. The section on alms (Gundbert's dossier) was separated from Folquin's narrative by an interpolated continuation in the *Vetus Folquinus*, BM Boulogne-sur-Mer ms. 815, 301–12. Folquin composed this section himself: he referred to its content explicitly in his narrative, BM St. Omer ms. 815, 136.

147. Ganshof, ed., *Le polyptyque de Saint Bertin*, 13: "Abbas igitur Adalar-dus villas ad fratrum usus pertinentes, vel quicquid exinde sub qualicumque servitio videbatur provenire, absque his quae in aliis ministeriis erant distribu-tae vel quae militibus et cavallaris erant beneficiatae, tali jussit brevitate describere." See also Ganshof's analysis, 25.

148. Compare Geary, *Phantoms of Remembrance,* 96–98, 102–3, who stressed *memoria* of the abbots instead of possessions.

149. For example, the Capitulary of Servais (853), MGH Capitularia 2: 274,

ordered each *centenarius* to swear to the *missi dominici* that he would collect a list of *franci homines* in his jurisdictional area (*in meo mynisterio*). By analogy, monastic officers eventually came to be charged with a special *ministerium*, see Emile Lesne, *L'origine des menses dans le temporal des églises et des monastères de France au XIe siècle* (Lille: R. Giard, 1910), 32 n1 (Saint-Vaast) and n2 (Saint-Denis).

150. Declercq, "Originals and Cartularies," 157, noted that both the complete copying of diplomas and the high proportion of private charters was a departure from previous forms.

151. Ugé, "Relics as Tools of Power," 51–72.

152. The twelfth-century continuator, the monk Simon, even recopied the *Vetus Folquinus* (with modifications) to serve as the first book of his own work, now BM St. Omer ms. 146a (Simon's cartulary) and 146b (Folquin); see appendix A.

153. Declercq, "Originals and Cartularies," 150–51 stressed the distinction between the probative value of the royal *preceptum* and the private *carta* and its reflection in archival memory.

154. Louis confirming Charlemagne, BM St. Omer ms. 815, 127–32; Charles, Tessier, ed., *Actes de Charles II* 2: 322–25, no. 370; Lothar, Louis Halphen and Ferdinand Lot, eds., *Receuil des Actes de Lothaire et Louis V, rois de France* (Paris: Klincksieck, 1908), 32–35, no. 15.

155. Philippe Lauer, ed., *Recueil des actes de Charles III le Simple, roi de France (893–923)* (Paris: Imprimérie nationale, 1949), 15–17, no. 10.

156. See Tessier, "Originaux et pseudo-originaux de Saint-Denis," 35–69, esp. 57–58.

157. Saint-Germain (829), CSG 1: 46, no. 28; Saint-Denis (832), AN K9 (6), edited in Tardif, 86–89, no. 124.

158. BM St. Omer ms. 815, 128–29: "percenseremus, ut omnes cellas et villas, seu ceteras possessiones . . . nullus succedentium nostrorum dividere aut in alios usos convertere presumeret." See also Louis' later reconfirmation in 835, BM St. Omer ms. 815, 138–43.

159. Tessier, ed., *Actes de Charles II*, nos. 247 and 304 (Saint-Denis), 363 (Saint-Germain), and 370 (immunity of Saint-Bertin). Note that Charles's act altering the *mensa conventualis* of Saint-Bertin did not contain such a clause.

160. Carlrichard Brühl, "Diplomatische Miszellen zur Geschichte des ausgehenden 9. Jahrhunderts," *Archiv für Diplomatik* 3 (1957): 9 esp. n11, where he identifies such clauses at eight monasteries.

161. Tessier, ed., *Actes de Charles II*, 175, no. 304.

162. In both acts: "ut nemo abbatum per successiones . . . subtrahere vel minuere audeat."

163. See Bautier, ed., *Actes d'Eudes*, 97, no. 20. Brühl, "Diplomatische Miszellen," 11 n23, suggested this confusion resulted from the fact that the formulas *comes et abbas* or *dux et abbas* became more commonplace as lay abbacy spread.

164. Brühl, "Diplomatische Miszellen," 11–13.

165. CSB, 195, "ea scilicet inviolabili interposita ratione, ut neque ego in vita mea, necque aliquis post me futurus abbas, neque aliqua quaelibet persona, inde audeat aliquid usurpare"

166. Barbara Rosenwein, *Negotiating Space: Power, Restraint, and Privileges of Immunity in Early Medieval Europe* (Ithaca, N.Y.: Cornell University Press, 1999), 156–62.

167. Jean-François Lemarignier, "L'exemption monastique et les origines de la réforme grégorienne," in *A Cluny: Congrès scientifique . . . en l'honneur des saints abbés Odon et Odilon* (Dijon: Société des Amis de Cluny, 1950), 288–340. See also Marco Mostert, "Die Urkundenfälschungen Abbos von Fleury," in *Fälschungen im Mittelalter* 4: 287–318.

168. Auguste Bernard and Alexandre Bruel, eds., *Recueil des chartes de l'ab-baye de Cluny* (Paris: Imprimérie nationale, 1876–1903) 5: 384–88, no. 2255. See also Rosenwein, *To Be the Neighbor of Saint Peter*, 87–88.

169. Harald Zimmermann, ed., *Papsturkunden, 896–1046* (Vienna: Öster-reischischen Akademie der Wissenschaften, 1984–89) 1: 682–86, no. 351.

170. Abbo's collection, PL 139, cols. 473–508. Lemarignier, "L'exemption monastique," 301–15, traced the adoption of Abbo's texts. For Abbo's program, see Marco Mostert, *The Political Theology of Abbo of Fleury: A Study of the Ideas About Society and Law of the Tenth-Century Monastic Reform Movement* (Hilver-sum: Verloren, 1987).

171. Lemarignier, "L'exemption monastique," 308. See also Waldman, "Saint-Denis et les premiers Capétiens," 191–97.

172. For the conflict see *Gesta pontificum Cameracensium*, MGH SS 7: 446 and 452, chs. 107 and 116. For Stephen II's bull see CSV, 22–25 (JL 2328). There are two texts of Vindicianus' act, one copied by Guimann, CSV, 18–22, and the other from the eleventh century, BM Douai ms. 753, in *Chronicon Vedastinum*, MGH SS 13: 697–98. See Lemarignier's analysis of both acts, "L'exemption monastique," 335–40.

173. CSV, 20 and Bautier, ed., *Actes d'Eudes*, 95–96, no. 20.

174. Lemarignier, "L'exemption monastique," 312, 315. The letter collec-tion, from the early tenth century, now BnF ms. lat. 2278, contains marginalia from Fleury in Abbo's time, see Lemarignier's analysis, 305–6.

175. Bernard and Bruel, eds., *Recueil des chartes de l'abbaye de Cluny* 3: 384–88, no. 2255.

176. Rosenwein, *To Be the Neighbor of Saint Peter*, 163–69, esp. map 5. See also Rosenwein, *Negotiating Space*, 168–73.

177. Rosenwein, *To Be the Neighbor of Saint Peter*, 172: "The force of these documents was not the threat of police power but of publicity." For the letters of Benedict, Zimmermann, ed., *Papsturkunden, 896–1046* 2: 1007–10, no. 530 (JL 4013).

178. Rosenwein, *To Be the Neighbor of Saint Peter*, 176–79, 205.

179. Rosenwein, *To Be the Neighbor of Saint Peter*, 78–108, esp. tables, 85–95, and map, 101; Georges Duby, *La société aux XIe et XIIe siècles dans la region mâconnaise*, 2nd ed. (Paris: J. Touzot, 1971).

180. Rosenwein, *To Be the Neighbor of Saint Peter*, 199.

181. Rosenwein, *Negotiating Space*, 173–83.

182. Cartulary A, BnF nouv. acq. lat. 1497. Dominique Iogna-Prat, "La geste des origines dans l'historiographie clunisienne des XIe–XIIe siècles," *Revue*

bénédictine 102 (1992): 153–70 and "La confection des cartulaires et l'historiographie à Cluny (XIe–XIIe siècles)," in *Les cartulaires*, 27–44; compare Geary, *Phantoms of Remembrance*, 103–7.

183. Bernard and Bruel, eds., *Recueil des chartes de l'abbaye de Cluny* 5: 844: "Igitur exordium nostrae narrationis tempus et gesta domni continebit Bernodus . . ."

184. Compare Declercq, "Originals and Cartularies," 159 and Geary, *Phantoms of Remembrance*, 105.

185. See Geary, *Phantoms of Remembrance*, 106, where the alterations are summarized.

186. Joseph Schmale, "Synoden Papst Alexanders II (1061–1073): Anzahl, Termine, Entscheidungen," *Annuarium historiae conciliorum* 11 (1979): 307–38. Roman synods occurred in 1063, 1065–70, and 1072–73.

187. Lemarignier, "L'exemption monastique," 310 n3.

188. CSB, 180–83 (JL 4367). See also Lemarignier, "L'exemption monastique," 332.

189. Forged Saint Germain charter, CSG 1: 4–7, no. 2; papal exemption CSG 1: 117–18, no. 73 (JL 6128). For the connection see Jean Derens, "Les origines de Saint-Germain-des-Prés: Nouvelle étude sur les deux plus anciennes chartes de l'abbaye," *Journal des savants* (1973): 45–60, esp. 55.

190. BnF nouv. acq. lat. 326.

191. Léon Levillain, "Études sur l'abbaye de Saint-Denis à l'époque mérovingienne III: *Privilegium et Immunitates* ou Saint-Denis dans l'Église et dans l'État," *BEC* 87 (1926): 245–346, esp. 298–99 (hereafter "*Privilegium et Immunitates*"). This initial dossier consisted of the texts now in BnF nouv. acq. lat. 326, fols. 1–18v.

192. Waldman, "Saint-Denis et les premiers Capétiens," 192.

193. See Lemarignier, "L'exemption monastique," 332. These included the Stephen II bull created at Saint-Vaast, for example. Leo IX's bull, AN L 220, no. 7 (JL 4182), pseudo-original; BnF nouv. acq. lat. 326, fol. 16v, dossier copy, both edited in PU *Frankreich* 9(2): 107–113, nos. 16a–b

194. AN L 222 no. 1 (JL 4565); BnF nouv. acq. lat. 326, fol. 24r, dossier copy, both edited in PU *Frankreich* 9(2): 116–17, no. 18a.

195. The *Praeceptum Dagoberti de fugitivis* was copied with a fabricated immunity of Dagobert on the first two folios, BnF nouv. acq. lat. 326, fols. 1v and 2r. Henri Omont, "Le *Praeceptum Dagoberti de fugitivis* en faveur de l'abbaye de Saint-Denis," *BEC* 61 (1900): 75–82. See also Geary, *Phantoms of Remembrance*, 109.

196. In particular, an act into which an immunity had been written around 1008, Tessier, ed., *Actes de Charles II* 2: 593–97, no. 479.

197. AN K 20, no. 4, original; BnF nouv. acq. lat. 326, fol. 73r, copy. Edited in Maurice Prou, ed., *Recueil des actes de Philippe Ier de France, 1059–1108* (Paris: Imprimérie nationale, 1908), 114–17, no. 40. The monks had already obtained less definitive statements about their *libertas* from Robert the Pious in 1008, AN K 18, no. 3, edited in Tardif, 158–59, no. 250.

198. Jean Vezin and Hartmut Atsma, "Le dossier suspect des possessions

de Saint-Denis en Angleterre revisté (VIIIᵉ–IXᵉ siècles)," in *Fälschungen im Mittelalter* 4(2): 210–36.

199. For the effect on Saint-Denis' archives, see Geary, *Phantoms of Remembrance*, 107–13.

200. Sot, *Gesta episcoporum, gesta abbatum*, 20–21, points out that such concerns were common in *gesta*; see also de Gaiffier, "Les revendications de biens," 136–38.

201. Amy G. Remensnyder, *Remembering Kings Past: Monastic Foundation Legends in Medieval Southern France* (Ithaca, N.Y.: Cornell University Press, 1995), esp. ch. 6. For England and Normandy, see Marjorie Chibnall, "Forgery in Narrative Charters," *Fälschungen im Mittelalter* 4(2): 331–46.

202. Foundation charter, CSG 1: 1–4, no. 1; *Vita Droctrovei Abbatis Parisiensis Auctore Gislemaro*, MGH Scriptores rerum Merovingicarum 3: 535–43.

203. BnF ms. lat. 12711. See Jean Derens, "Gislemar, historien de Saint-Germain-des-Prés," *Journal des savants* (1972): 228–31.

204. CSG 1: 117–9 (JL 6128). See Chapter 2.

205. CSP 2: 257–59, no. 1 (JL 6067).

206. Often they contained similar materials, see Sot, *Gesta episcoporum, gesta abbatum*, 18–19.

207. Declercq, "Originals and Cartularies," 160.

208. Rosenwein, *Negotiating Space*, 179–83.

209. For example, mayors are mentioned eighteen times in the polyptych of Saint-Germain. See Hägermann, ed., *Das Polyptychon von Saint-Germain-des-Prés*, 271. See also CSP, lxxiv–lxxvii.

210. Georges Duby, *L'économie rurale et la vie des campagnes dans l'occident médiévale: France, Angleterre, Empire, IXᵉ–XVᵉ siècles*, 2 vols. (Paris: Aubier, 1962), trans. Cynthia Postan, *Rural Economy and Country Life in the Medieval West* (Columbia: University of South Carolina Press, 1968), 175–76: "As in Carolingian times only one thing mattered to the administrators of a monastery or chapter: how to support the 'family' in plenty without pinching or fear of shortage."

211. Chédeville, *Chartres et ses campagnes*, 117, observed the importance of vineyards, which the monks of Saint-Père did not farm out as they did other holdings.

212. Rosenwein observed the decline, *To Be the Neighbor of Saint Peter*, 199–200, and attributed it to "the birth of the seigneurie and the solidification of the patrilinear family."

213. CSP 1: 96–98.

214. For a summary of hands, see Hägermann in *Das Polyptychon von Saint-Germain-des-Prés*, x–xviii.

215. CSP 1: 3: "Privilegiis quae in nostri coenobii sacris scriniis invenire potui." See also Guyotjeannin, "*Penuria Scriptorum*," 31 for other instances.

216. Elisabeth Magnou-Nortier, "Remarques générales à propos du manse," *Aux sources de la gestion publique* 1: 196–207.

217. CSV, 5: "vix nos omnium decimam habere non jam ex libro conjicimus, sed experientia sentimus."

218. CSB, 171–73.

219. Declercq, "Originals and Cartularies," 147: "Not only did archival memory undergo a profound transformation during this period with the introduction of cartularies and other types of copy books, but the nature and use of documents themselves changed considerably." See also chapter 2.

220. Laurent Morelle, "The Metamorphosis of Three Monastic Charter Collections in the Eleventh Century (Saint-Amand, Saint-Riquier, Montier-en-Der)" in *Charters and the Use of the Written Word*, ed. Heidecker, 172–73, esp. n5. Declercq, "Originals and Cartularies," 151.

221. Geary, *Phantoms of Remembrance*, 81–87 and Declercq, "Originals and Cartularies," 153–56. For an example see Charles Edmond Perrin, *Recherches sur la seigneurie rurale en Lorraine d'après les plus anciens censiers (IXᵉ–XIIᵉ siècle)* (Paris: Les Belles Lettres, 1935), 589–690.

222. Cluny was exceptional in this regard because new donations made careful management unnecessary and spending reached profligate levels by the end of the eleventh century, see Georges Duby, "Le budget de l'abbaye de Cluny entre 1080 et 1155: Économie domaniale et économie monétaire," *Annales: ESC* 7(2) (1952): 155–71, reprint Georges Duby, *Hommes et structures du moyen âge: Recueil d'articles* (Paris: Mouton, 1973), 66–70.

223. Giles Constable, *Monastic Tithes, from Their Origins to the Twelfth Century* (Cambridge: Cambridge University Press, 1964), 85–88. Note that Leo IX forbade the possession of ecclesiastical revenues and ordered laymen to return them in 1049–50.

Chapter 2. *Written Comprehension of Land and Signs of an Administrative Mentality*

1. For example, Robert Fossier, *Polyptyques et censiers* (Turnhout: Brepols, 1978).

2. See Chapter 3.

3. Olivier Guyotjeannin, "*Penuria Scriptorum*: Le mythe de l'anarchie documentaire dans la France du nord (Xe–première moitié du XIe siècle)," *BEC* 155 (1997): 29–30 and see below.

4. Patrick Geary, *Phantoms of Remembrance: Memory and Oblivion at the End of the First Millennium* (Princeton, N.J.: Princeton University Press, 1994), 81–114, 177–81.

5. Laurent Morelle, "The Metamorphosis of Three Monastic Charter Collections in the Eleventh Century (Saint-Amand, Saint-Riquier, Montier-en-Der)," in *Charters and the Use of the Written Word in Medieval Society*, ed. Karl Heidecker (Turnhout: Brepols, 2000), 175. Laurent Morelle, "Histoire et archives vers l'an mil: Une nouvelle 'mutation'?" *Histoire et archives* 2 (1998): 119–41, rebuts Geary in detail.

6. Morelle, "The Metamorphosis of Three Monastic Charter Collections," 172–76, 203–4.

7. Laurent Morelle, "Les chartes dans la gestion des conflits (France du nord, XIe–début XIIe siècle)," *BEC* 155 (1997): 269–71, esp. n18.

8. Barbara Rosenwein, *To Be the Neighbor of Saint Peter: The Social Meaning of Cluny's Property, 909–1049* (Ithaca, N.Y.: Cornell University Press), 170–73.

9. Rosenwein, *To Be the Neighbor of Saint Peter*, 205–7. In her view, the territorial aspect of the patrimony became more important toward 1049.

10. Dietrich Lohrmann, "Formen der *Enumeratio bonorum* in Bischofs-, Papst- und Herrscherurkunden (9.–12. Jahrhundert)," *Archiv für Diplomatik* 26: 283–86.

11. Giles Constable, "Les listes de propriétés dans les privilèges pour Baume-les-Messieurs aux XIᵉ et XIIᵉ siècles," *Journal des Savants* (1986): 105. See also Lohrmann, "Formen der *Enumeratio bonorum*," 285.

12. Constable, "Les listes de propriétés," 110–11, esp. n41. Lohrmann, "Formen der Enumeratio bonorum," 285–86, traced the earliest example to 1053, a precocious example Constable rejects as a forgery. For the overall importance of Urban's trip, see Barbara Rosenwein, *Negotiating Space: Power, Restraint, and Privileges of Immunity in Early Medieval Europe* (Ithaca, N.Y.: Cornell University Press), 181–83.

13. Constable, "Les listes de propriétés," 111, attributes this change to the influence of Bolognese legal forms on the curia through Jean de Gaete. Lohrmann, "Formen der *Enumeratio bonorum*," 285–99, argued that the formula was standardized in the 1130s.

14. Lohrmann, "Formen der *Enumeratio bonorum*," 303–7. For *ex dono* clauses and provenience, see also Dietrich Lohrmann, *Kirchengut im nördlichen Frankreich: Besitz, Verfassung und Wirtschaft im Spiegel der Papstprivilegien des 11.–12. Jahrhunderts* (Bonn: L. Rohrscheid, 1983), 72–90.

15. Lohrmann, "Formen der *Enumeratio bonorum*," 302.

16. Constable, "Les listes de propriétés," 102–5. Lohrmann, "Formen der *Enumeratio bonorum*," 389–96.

17. Lohrmann, "Formen der *Enumeratio bonorum*," 283. Constable, "Les listes de propriétés," 109–10.

18. Constable, "Les listes de propriétés," 108. Even more slippery, in his view, were terms such as *libertas* and *pertinentia*, which could include many rights and holdings.

19. Constable, "Les listes de propriétés," 110: "Les listes sont moins un guide de la propriété et de la possession réelles que d'une revendication de certains propriétés."

20. Rosenwein, *To Be the Neighbor of Saint Peter*, 170, noted the importance of the monastic petition. This fact also explains the purpose and efficacy of many forged dossiers.

21. As shown by references in the *narratio* of some papal charters to information supplied, see below. For Saint-Denis, see Chapter 1.

22. The lists of lands at Cluny in 998, therefore, seem exceptionally early. Cluny was, however, the innovator in the quest for exemptions.

23. CSB, 180–83 (JL 4367).

24. See Jean-François Lemarignier, "L'exemption monastique et les origines de la réforme grégorienne," in *A Cluny: Congrès scientifique . . . en l'honneur des saints abbés Odon et Odilon* (Dijon: Société des Amis de Cluny, 1950), 332 n9.

25. CSB, 181: "Pariter quoque confirmamus tibi tuisque successoribus, sicut dictum est, imperpetuum, cuncta eidem cenobio juste pertinentia . . . in arvis, campis, pratis, pascuis, silvis, aquis aquarumve decursibus, molendinis, piscariis, villis, ecclesiis, comitatibus, familiis, vineis, pomeriis, cunctisque suis mobilibus vel immobilibus, cultis vel incultis."

26. PU *Frankreich* 3: 368, no. 4 (JL 5600a) and CSB, 214–16 (JL 5628). The second, very similar in content, may have been interpolated later; it mentions land at Humbertutsin, the object of an equally dubious charter, BM St. Omer ms. 815, 298.

27. See appendix table C1.

28. CSB, 217–20 (JL 6201).

29. CSB, 258–60 (JL 6374a). The text made clear the petition of Lambert: "Quamobrem nos petitionibus vestris annuimus, et commutationem inter vos et Balduinum, Flandrensium comitem, factam, quia utilem monasterio credimus, scripti presentis assertione firmamus."

30. CSB, 260–62 (JL 6769).

31. CSB, 320–21 (JL 8740). See appendix table C2.

32. CSG 1: 117–19, no. 73 (JL 6128): "Per presentis itaque privilegii paginam tibi tuisque successoribus in perpetuum confirmamus ut quecunque libertas, quecunque dignitas privilegio beati Germani, scriptis Childeberti, Clotharii, atque aliorum regum Francorum vestro monasterio collata est, quecunque bona, quecunque possessiones concessione pontificum, liberalitate principum vel oblatione fidelium ad idem cenobium pertinere noscuntur."

33. See text of exemption in note above. These charters continue to be mentioned in subsequent confirmations. See the charter of Saint Germain supposedly from 566 in CSG 1: 4–6, no. 2. For analysis of the forgery, see Jean Derens, "Les origines de Saint-Germain-des-Prés: Nouvelle étude sur les deux plus anciennes chartes de l'abbaye," *Journal des savants* (1973): 45–60, esp. 55.

34. CSG 1: 126–27, no. 80 (JL 6947). See appendix table C3. Note the churches are introduced by the phrase "in quibus hec propriis duximus nominibus annotanda."

35. CSG 1: 163–64, no. 107 (JL 9381) and 190–92, no. 128 (JL 10822), concerning the church of Montchauvet and the lands at Dammartin, which confirmed previous episcopal and royal acts; see below.

36. CSG 1: 238–40, no. 165 (JL 12741).

37. See CSG 1: 182–83, no. 122 (JL 10738), a bull of Alexander III from 1162 taking Saint-Germain under his protection, in which he mentions several predecessors: "ad exemplum predecessorum nostrorum beate memorie Paschalis, Innocentii, Lucii, Eugenii, Anastasii et Adriani, Romanorum pontificum, sub beati Petri et nostra protectione suscipimus, et presentis scripti privilegio communimus." The bull goes on to repeat verbatim many clauses of the bull of Anastasius IV from 1154, CSG 1: 171–73, no. 115 (JL 9825).

38. BnF nouv. acq. lat. 326, fol. 16v, edited in PU *Frankreich* 9(2): 107–13, no. 16a (JL 4182).

39. PU *Frankreich* 9(2): 116–24, nos. 18a-b (JL 4565). See also BnF nouv. acq. lat. 326, fol. 24r.

40. BnF nouv. acq. lat. 326. See Chapter 1.

41. AN L 221, no. 1; BnF nouv. acq. lat. 326, fol. 18v, edited in PU *Frankreich* 9(2): 113–16, no. 17 (JL 4456); see Rolf Grosse's apparatus for bibliography on this act.

42. PU *Frankreich* 9(2): 131–33, no. 25 (JL 5902) and 137–39, no. 29 (JL 6749).

43. AN LL 1156, fol. 79r, edited in PU *Frankreich* 9(2): 139–41, no. 30 (JL 6946).

44. PU *Frankreich* 9(2): 144–46, no. 33 (JL 7372) and 146–47, no. 34 (JL 7426). See Thomas Waldman, "Abbot Suger and the Nuns of Argenteuil," *Traditio* 41 (1985): 239–72.

45. PU *Frankreich* 9(2): 148–51, no. 35 (JL 7472). See appendix table C4. This list was introduced by "in quibus haec propriis nominibus duximus exprimenda." This charter mixes the older and newer forms of geographical division, suggesting the *enumeratio* is a composite list.

46. PU *Frankreich* 9(2): 163–67, no. 44 (JL 9247).

47. Harald Zimmermann, ed., *Papsturkunden, 896–1046* (Vienna: Österreichische Akademie der Wissenschaften, 1984–9) 2: 1101–13, no. 532 (JL 4033).

48. Léon Voet, "Étude sur deux bulles de Benoît VIII pour Saint-Vaast-d'Arras," *BCRH* 109 (1944): 187–242.

49. Such as "in ministerio camere," "ad matriculam ecclesie" and so on. See Émile Lesne, *Histoire de la propriété ecclésiastique en France du VIIIe à la fin du XIe siècles* (Lille: R. Giard, 1910–43) 6: 163 n1 (matricula) and 254 (camera). For the original pieces of the text see Zimmermann, ed., *Papsturkunden, 896–1046* 2: 1012–13, no. 532.

50. For example, the mills at Anzin, the subject of a charter of Abbot Henry (1104–30), CSV, 317–18, or the mills at Blangy, CSV, 340–41 (1141).

51. Jean-François Lemarignier, "Le prieuré d'Haspres, ses rapports avec l'abbaye de Saint-Vaast d'Arras et la centralisation monastique au début du XIIe siècle," *Revue du Nord* 29 (1947): 261–68. Possibly the document was subsequently interpolated, since the known copy is from Guimann's codex (1170), which may also explain its detail.

52. Zimmermann, ed., *Papsturkunden, 896–1046* 2: 1041–43, no. 549 (JL 4056).

53. CSV, 70–73 (JL 5896). For a comparison of the enumerations of confirmations mentioned in this paragraph, see appendix table C5. For a comparison of the altar lists, see appendix table C6.

54. A confirmation of Pascal II in 1112 resolved a dispute between the canons and monks over the chapels of Saint-Croix and Saint-Maurice, CSV, 150–1 (JL 6311). In 1119, the church of Saint-Michel and five places between the river and the city gate were listed, PU *Frankreich* 3:53–4, no. 14.

55. CSV, 75–78 (JL 7699).

56. CSV, 81–82 (JL 9688).

57. PU *Frankreich* 3: 116–19, no. 58.

58. CSV, 91–98 (JL 11709).

59. CSP 2: 257–59, no. 1 (JL 6067). See appendix table C7.

60. CSP 2: 260–63, no. 3 (JL 7285).

61. Colin Morris, *The Papal Monarchy: The Western Church from 1050 to 1250* (Oxford: Oxford University Press, 1989), 57–64.

62. Haigneré 1: 23–24, no. 70.

63. CSB, 192–94.

64. CSB, 242–44. The order of the papal confirmation can be found in appendix table C1.

65. Auguste Bernard and Alexandre Bruel, eds., *Recueil des chartes de l'abbaye de Cluny* (Paris: Imprimérie nationale, 1876–1903) 5: 64, no. 3718 (JL 5725).

66. CSB, 295–96. Pascal originally confirmed seven churches and the episcopal charter makes explicit reference to his confirmation.

67. Fernand Vercauteren, ed., *Actes des comtes de Flandres, 1071–1128* (Brussels: Palais des Académies, 1938), 46–47, no. 14 and 194–97, no. 87.

68. Vercauteren, ed., *Actes des comtes de Flandres*, 85–87, no. 29. See also P. Bernard, "Études critiques sur les chartes des comtes de Flandre pour l'abbaye de Saint-Bertin," *Positions des thèses*, École Nationale de Chartes (Paris: Picard, 1923), 5–13.

69. Thérèse de Hemptinne and Adrian Verhulst, eds., *De oorkonden der graven van Vlaanderen (juli 1128–september 1191)* (Brussels: Commission royale d'histoire, 1988) 2(1): 174–78, no. 109.

70. CSB, 184–87, no. 14 and 203–4, no. 29. See also critical remarks in de Hemptinne and Verhulst, eds., *De oorkonden der graven van Vlaanderen* 2(1): 175.

71. CEA, 11–13, no. 6.

72. CEA, 31–32, no. 21.

73. CSV, 75, 81–82. See appendix table C6.

74. AD Pas-de-Calais 9 J/AA, no. 572.

75. de Hemptinne and Verhulst, eds., *De oorkonden der graven van Vlaanderen* 2(1): 179–212, no. 111.

76. BnF nouv. acq. lat. 326, fol. 73r. Maurice Prou, ed., *Recueil des actes de Philippe Ier de France, 1059–1108* (Paris: Klincksieck, 1967), 114–17, no. 40. Note that both dossiers were combined in the same codex.

77. Tardif, 254, no. 466.

78. Jean Dufour, ed., *Recueil des actes de Louis VI, roi de France (1108–1137)* (Paris: De Boccard, 1992–94), nos. 40, 59, 70, 74, 87, 89, 91, 135, 142, 163, 189, 210, 220, 227, 281, 300, 359, 409, 410. Some grants such as Toury (no. 135) and Cergy (no. 163) were made even before 1122.

79. Dufour, ed., *Recueil des actes de Louis VI*, 1: 392–97, no. 189.

80. Dufour, ed., *Recueil des actes de Louis VI*, 1: 458–66, no. 220.

81. See appendix table C4, where the grants at Cergy, Reuil, and the taking of the county of Vexin as benefice are mentioned. See also Dufour, ed., *Recueil des actes de Louis VI* 1: 463–64.

82. See chapter 3 for details.

83. Renunciation of 1073, CSG 1: 110–11, no. 67.

84. See CSG 1: 179–80, no. 120 (1156/7); 188–90, no. 127 (1163/4); 203, no. 137 (1164/5); 205–6, no. 139 (1167); 217, no. 147 (1168/9); 224–25, no. 154 (1173/4); 248–49, no. 172 (1176/7); 249–51, no. 173 (1176/7); 266–67, no. 188 (1179/80).

85. CSG 1:133–34, no. 86. A charter of the bishop of Chartres from 1134 concerning the church of Montchauvet.

86. CSG 1: 162–63, no. 106 (1149/50); 174, no. 116 (1149–55); 201–2, no. 135 (1156–64); 213–14, no. 144 (1168).

87. Of the nine royal charters, eight concerned a small group of properties: Dammartin, Montchauvet, Antony, Thiais, Villeneuve-Saint-Germain, the eastern fair at Saint-Germain, and Samoreau. All except Samoreau (acquired 1176) and the heavily disputed Dammartin were mentioned in the 1176 charter. The episcopal charters concerned Montchauvet, Septeuil, and Gilly, all of which appeared in 1176.

88. CSP 1: 244–45, and CSP 2: 265–66, no. 6.

89. Dufour, ed., *Actes de Louis VI* 1: 221–22, no. 104, and CSP 2: 263–64, no. 4.

90. CSP 2: 266–67, no. 7.

91. See appendix table C7.

92. CSP 1: 4: "Oportet enim omnes scire res quibus victus et vestitus eis administratur, ut sacrilegorum ambitio, quae litibus et minis semper simplices viros, ut ab eis aliquid extorqueat, exterret, possint repellere."

93. Paul's work was added to by continuators, but he foreshadows the end of his labors around 1087, CSP 1: 226, "Nunc ad ea quae ab abbate Eustachio jam per octo annos sunt patrata, subcinctus scribere maturabo."

94. Bernard and Bruel, ed., *Recueil de chartes de l'abbaye de Cluny* 5: 64, no. 3718, and 838, no. 3806bis.

95. CSB, 252–53. Lambert was alienated by the aggressive stance of the new abbot of Cluny. See Guérard, CSB, lx–lxi.

96. CSB, 251 (JL 6537).

97. PL 166, col. 1227, no. 7 (JL 7194).

98. PL 166, col. 1229, no. 9 (JL 7196).

99. PL 179, col. 134, no. 97 (JL 7561).

100. CSB, 304.

101. CSB, 310–13 (JL 8016).

102. See Simon's remarks on the monks' conduct, CSB, 268–71.

103. CSB, 194–96.

104. See discussion in Giles Constable, "Suger's Monastic Administration," in *Abbot Suger and Saint-Denis: A Symposium*, ed. Paula L. Gerson (New York: Metropolitan Museum of Art, 1986), 19.

105. Lindy Grant, *Abbot Suger of St-Denis: Church and State in Early Twelfth-Century France* (London: Longman, 1998), 185–87. See also Chapter 3.

106. Michel Parisse, "Les pancartes: Étude d'un type d'acte diplomatique," in *Pancartes monastiques des XIe et XIIe siècles*, ed. Michel Parisse, Pierre Pégeot, and Benoît-Michel Tock (Turnhout: Brepols, 1998), 26–35.

107. Morelle, "The Metamorphosis of Three Monastic Charter Collections," 173 n5.

108. Declercq, "Originals and Cartularies," 158.

109. Geary, *Phantoms of Remembrance*, 87.

110. Michel Parisse, "Écriture et réécriture des chartes: Les pancartes aux XIe et XIIe siècles," *BEC* 155 (1997): 258–60.

111. Declercq, "Originals and Cartularies," 165–67.

112. Compare Morelle, "The Metamorphosis of Three Monastic Charter Collections," 194 and Declercq, "Originals and Cartularies," 170, who both stress the importance of individual choices and local tradition.

113. CSB, 289.

114. See Morand, vii and appendix A.

115. See Guérard's introduction, CSB, lxi–xliv.

116. Morand, viii.

117. Eugène Van Drival, ed., *Nécrologe de l'abbaye de St-Vaast d'Arras* (Arras, 1878), 21. He held the important position of *praepositus aquarum* and in 1190 he became *praepositus* of Gorres.

118. CSV, 8.

119. See appendix B.

120. CSP 1: 3–4, 48.

121. See Paul's discussion of his own work, CSP 1: 226. See also Guérard's speculations, CSP 1: cclxix, that Paul continued his work until 1096.

122. CSP 2: 258: "et, in Carnotensi ecclesia beate Marie, prebendas VI, ita libere et integre possidendas, sicut a bone memorie Rainfredo, Carnotensium episcopo, eidem vestro monasterio contribute sunt."

123. Suger's *gesta*, BnF lat. 13835, edited in Gasparri 1: 54–155. This work has customarily been referred to by the sixteenth-century editor's title *De rebus in administratione sua gestis*, or *De administratione* for short, though the sole manuscript bears only a late medieval (fourteenth- or fifteenth-century) title, "Gesta Suggerii Abbatis," see Gasparri 1: lx–lxii. I will use *De administratione* following convention, though the work is clearly a *gesta* in format and execution.

124. Michel Bur, *Suger: Abbé de Saint-Denis, régent de France* (Paris: Perrin, 1991), 172–76 argued that the writing was accomplished in 1144–45 and "retouched" in 1147–49. Grant, *Abbot Suger of St Denis*, 33–36, argued it was begun in 1145 and remained incomplete at Suger's death in 1151.

125. Constable, "Suger's Monastic Administration," 23 n101.

126. CSB, 169: "Quorum [abbatum] etiam gestis breviter summatimque descriptis, cartas nichilominus separatim in uno volumine a mea exiguitate describi voluistis, quas, tam principum quam diversorum presulum auctoritate, ad utilitatem devitande controversie vel pacis continue, de traditionibus et diversis fidelium commutationibus, vel de qualicunque utilitate ecclesie, posteris confirmatas reliquerent, ut futurorum incuria, cognita eorum vivaci industria, memoriale bonorum operum non lateret in secula."

127. BM Boulogne-sur-mer ms. 146a. See appendix A.

128. *Histoire littéraire de la France* (Paris: Firmin Didot, 1814) 13: 80–81. The two books on the estates were described as "livres des cens."

129. Morand, 2 (text) and vii–viii (analysis).

130. See Chapter 1.

131. Morand, ix.

132. See CSP 1: 17. See also Geary, *Phantoms of Remembrance*, 103.

133. See CSP 1: cclxviii–cclxxii for Guérard's "plan d'édition," the best source for the organization of the text, given the loss of the original manuscript in 1944.

134. See appendix table B2.

135. See Van Drival's description, CSV, xvi–xvii.

136. CSV, 18 (Vindicien) and 91–98 (Alexander) (JL 11709). The section as a whole can be found in CSV, 9–98.

137. CSV, 105–95.

138. CSV, 111, "ut omnia compleamus."

139. CSV, 141. This section also was an attempt to assert the monks' jurisdiction over the "old" town against the canons.

140. CSV, 165–91.

141. CSV, 197–241.

142. This pattern can be followed on the map following CSV, 451.

143. CSV, 243–400.

144. AD Pas-de-Calais 1 H1 and AD Pas-de-Calais 9 J/AA.

145. See Gasparri, plate 8, for a map of local holdings and Bur, *Suger*, 137 for distant holdings in Suger's time.

146. The only two exceptions to the route outlined above, Berneval on the Norman coast (ch. 30) and Celles near Metz (ch. 28) in Lorraine, are explicable in terms of Suger's personal concerns; he had been *praepositus* of the first before becoming abbot and had visited the second soon after, and made dispositions concerning it in his testament, see Gasparri, 206–7, no. 8.

147. AN LL 1157, 240–42. See Constable, "Suger's Monastic Administration," 25 and Grant, *Abbot Suger of St-Denis*, 218–20.

148. *De Administratione*, ch. 18, Gasparri, 88–89.

149. See Chapter 3.

150. See Dieter Hägermann, ed., *Das Polyptychon von Saint-Germain-des-Prés: Studienausgabe* (Köln: Böhlau, 1993), 28, 36–39, 52, 102–3, 138, 146, and 159 and also Olivier Guyotjeannin, "*Penuria Scriptorum*," 29–30.

151. CSG 1: 308–16, nos. 222–24. See also Chapter 3.

152. For example, CSG 1: 266–67, no. 188 (1179/80), in which Louis VII confirms Peter of Samois' renunciation of rights over the monks' land at Samoreau, described in a handlist, CSG 1: 312–13, no. 222.

153. See appendix A.

154. CSP 1: 21–25.

155. CSP 1: 43–45.

156. CSP 1: 44–45.

Chapter 3. Ministering and Administering: Abbots as Catalysts of Change

1. One exception might be the charters concerning the disputed possession of Chapel-Aude, though several of these have dubious authenticity. See C. Van der Kieft, *Étude sur le chartrier et la seigneurie du prieuré de la Chapel-Aude (XIᵉ–XIIIᵉ siècle)* (Assen: Van Gorcum, 1960).

2. Barbara Rosenwein, *To Be the Neighbor of Saint Peter: The Social Meaning of Cluny's Property, 909–1049* (Ithaca, N.Y.: Cornell University Press, 1989), 202–3.

3. There are numerous works on the economic boom. The seminal work is Robert S. Lopez, *The Commercial Revolution of the Middle Ages, 950–1350* (Cambridge: Cambridge University Press, 1976). For changes in thought related to money, accounting, and education see Alexander Murray, *Reason and Society in the Middle Ages*, rev. ed. (Oxford: Oxford University Press, 1990).

4. For monastic reaction, see Lester Little, *Religious Poverty and the Profit Economy in Medieval Europe* (Ithaca, N.Y.: Cornell University Press, 1978), 61–68. Compare Constance Bouchard, *Holy Entrepreneurs: Cistercians, Knights, and Economic Exchange in Twelfth-Century Burgundy* (Ithaca, N.Y.; Cornell University Press, 1991), 31–65. By this time, traditional strictures in the Rule of Saint-Benedict against greed and fraud had also eroded somewhat. See Benedict of Nursia, *Regula*, ch. 57, in *La règle de Saint-Benoît*, ed. Jean Neufville and Adalbert de Vogüé (Paris: Cerf, 1972) 2: 624.

5. Laurent Morelle, "The Metamorphosis of Three Monastic Charter Collections in the Eleventh Century (Saint-Amand, Saint-Riquier, Montier-en-Der)," in *Charters and the Use of the Written Word in Medieval Society*, ed. Karl Heidecker (Turnhout: Brepols, 2000), see tables of acts, 178–79, 192–93, and analysis, 200.

6. See appendix table D1.

7. See appendix table D3.

8. See appendix table D1. Perhaps these acts were omitted by later continuators, who had primarily historical concerns.

9. See appendix table D2.

10. Only three of the eighteen acts survive in copies of Guimann's work; most survive in later cartulary copies (esp. BM Arras ms. 1266).

11. Simon Lloyd, "The Crusading Movement, 1096–1274" in *The Illustrated History of the Crusades*, ed. Jonathan Riley-Smith (Oxford: Oxford University Press, 1997), 54–58; Little, *Religious Poverty and the Profit Economy*, 64–65.

12. The first was an act of Martin from 1176, Alexandre Pruvost, ed., *Chronique et cartulaire de l'abbaye de Bergues-Saint-Winoc: De l'ordre de Saint-Benoît* (Bruges: D'Aime de Luttere, 1875–78), 139; the second was from an undetermined time in his rule, BM Amiens ms. 1077, fol. 60v, edited in Benoît-Michel Tock, ed., *Monumenta Arroasiensia* (Turnhout: Brepols, 2000), 297, no. 166.

13. *De administratione*, part 1, chs. 1, 7, 18, 21 in Gasparri 1: 56–58 (lands in Saint-Denis), 60 (house in Paris), 71 (a tithe), 87–88 (land at Toury), 93 (vineyard at Beaune-la-Rolande).

14. For example, Gasparri 2: 180–83, no. 5, in which Suger approves a sale and enlarges a grant. There are examples also at Saint-Vaast: in two of Martin's charters, BM Arras ms. 1266, fol. 55v ter and fol. 53v bis; the prior transactions also recorded how the land was acquired in order to prevent future disputes.

15. Indeed, the vehemence with which monks and all churchmen insisted on the ultimate inalienability of their patrimonial land inclined Susan Reynolds to be suspicious of the rhetoric of their charters, *Fiefs and Vassals: The Medieval Evidence Reinterpreted* (Oxford: Oxford University Press, 1994), 59–63, 122–23.

16. Rosenwein, *To Be the Neighbor of Saint Peter*, 132 notes that between 909 and 1049 donations made to Saint Peter or God were different from more "commercial" transactions like sales and exchanges, which were made with the monks.

17. Dominique Barthélemy, *La mutation de l'an mil: A-t-elle eu lieu? Servage et chevalerie dans la France des Xe et XIe siècles* (Paris: Fayard, 1997), 13–56, and Dominique Barthélemy, *La société dans le comté de Vendôme de l'an mil au XIVe siècle* (Paris: Fayard, 1993), 19–116. See also his partial retraction "Une crise de l'écrit? Observations sur des actes de Saint-Aubin d'Angers (XIe siècle)" *BEC* 155 (1997): 97.

18. Olivier Guyotjeannin, Jacques Pycke, and Benoît-Michel Tock, eds., *Diplomatique médiévale* (Turnhout: Brepols, 1993), 76–79, 103–4, 111–12; Georges Declercq, "Originals and Cartularies: The Organization of Archival Memory (Ninth-Eleventh Centuries)," in *Charters and the Use of the Written Word in Medieval Society*, ed. Karl Heidecker (Turnhout: Brepols, 2000), 165–66.

19. BM Arras ms. 1266, fol. 48r bis: "terram . . . quamvis curti nostre de Ponz subjacentem, tamen eidem curti propter remotionem ad colendum minus habilem."

20. Note, however, that the verb *cedo* was often used for sales (or to disguise sales).

21. BM Arras ms. 1266, fol. 48r bis: "eadem terram eis ad colendum habilior et necessaria erat."

22. BM Arras ms. 1266, fol. 52v bis. Sometimes the religious motivation dominated. In such cases, it was not always the monastery which benefitted directly. In 1179, Martin allowed a man of Saint-Vaast, one Robert, to give infertile land to the Hospitalars in the hope they could use it for their own profit since it was "suited to their uses" (*eorum usibus accomodatu*). Whether Saint-Vaast profitted is unclear, but the Hospitalars certainly had a recognized economic interest in the land, AN S 5208, no. 19.

23. See a charter of Wéry, which concerns a dispute about rights at Halmaal (attached to Haspres) which were recovered, in Charles Piot, ed., *Cartulaire de l'abbaye de Saint-Trond*, 2 vols. (Brussels: F. Hayez, 1870–74) 1: 74–77.

24. BM Arras ms. 1266, fol. 53v ter (Neder-Overhembeek) and CSV, 412 (Kattem). Note both were leased to the monastery of Grimbergen near the holdings themselves.

25. Pruvost, ed., *Chronique et cartulaire de l'abbaye de Bergues-Saint-Winoc*, 139.

26. BM Arras ms. 1266, fol. 55v. This act was essentially a permanent acquisition from Saint-Vincent, as language of the charter indicates: "eternaliter tenendum contradidit." Those abbatial acts which contained similar language of permanency are listed in the last column of appendix table D2.

27. BM Arras ms. 1266, fol. 49v and AD Pas-de-Calais 1 H2, fol. 133r. Both were intended to be perpetual.

28. See Dietrich Lohrmann, "Répartition et création de nouveaux domaines monastiques au XIIe siècle," in *Villa-Curtis-Grangia: Économie rurale entre Loire et Rhin de l'époque Gallo-Romaine au XIIe–XIIIe siècles*, ed. Wilhelm

Janssen and Dietrich Lohrmann (Munich: Artemis, 1983), 242–57. See also Bouchard, *Holy Entrepreneurs*, 53–65.

29. Later on, this practice also evaded the canonical prohibition against alienating goods of the church, a practice which the Cistercians encouraged, see Lohrmann, "Répartition et création de nouveaux domaines monastiques," 252.

30. In 1153, lands near Grévillers (21 km south of Saint-Vaast) were given to the nearby church of Avesnes-lès-Bapaume for two *muids* of wheat and another *muid* of oats; CSV, 281–82. In 1175, Abbot Martin ceded all the lands the monastery possessed between Lépine-Avernoise and Wailly (6–7 km from Saint-Vaast) to the monks at Longvillers in return for an annual rent of one hundred cheeses. The delivery site was specified as Campigneulles or Montreuil. BM Arras 1266, fol. 40v bis.

31. CSV, 269.

32. BM Arras ms. 1266, fol. 53r: "de proprio supplebit."

33. For example, an act from 1168, CSV, 276, acquiring a tithe for mortgage, at Hendecourt-les-Cagnicourt.

34. These exploits are well known. The most famous example is at Toury, where Suger had been provost, and where King Louis VI helped to remove the "tyranny" of Hugh of Le Puiset. See *De administratione*, part 1, ch. 18 in Gasparri 1: 82–89 and Suger, *Vie de Louis VI le Gros*, ed. Henri Waquet (Paris: H. Champion, 1929), 128–50, ch. 19.

35. Suger calculated the "incrementum" as ninety *muids* to account for rent paid to the count, which he valued at a rate of one pound per *muid*. See *De administratione*, part 1, ch. 2 in Gasparri 1: 60–63 and calculations in Lindy Grant, *Abbot Suger of St-Denis: Church and State in Twelfth-Century France* (London: Longman, 1998), 230.

36. *De administratione*, part 1, ch. 17 in Gasparri 1: 82–83. See also Suger's ordinance of 1140/1 in Gasparri 2: 255, no. 12.

37. *De administratione*, part 1, chs. 1, 10, 21 in Gasparri 1: 60–61 (Saint-Lucien at Saint-Denis and comments about Lagny), 70–71 (Louveciennes), and 90–93 (Saint-Loup-des-Vignes at Beaune-la-Rolande).

38. *De administratione*, part 1, chs. 1, 12 in Gasparri 1: 56–61 for Saint-Denis and 72–73 for Vaucresson. Grant, *Abbot Suger of St-Denis*, 226–29.

39. For Suger's exact gains, see chart in Grant, *Abbot Suger of St-Denis*, 230.

40. Suger's first ordinance, AN K22, no. 6, 1122–24, edited in Gasparri 2: 156–67, no. 1. Bernard's letter of 1127 in Bernard of Clairvaux, *Opera*, ed. Jean Leclercq, C. H. Talbot, and H. M. Rochais (Rome: Editiones Cisterciensis, 1957-) 7: 201–10, no. 78. See also Grant, *Abbot Suger of St-Denis*, 185–87.

41. N. K. Rasmussen, "The Liturgy at Saint-Denis: a Preliminary Study," in *Abbot Suger and Saint-Denis: A Symposium*, ed. Paula L. Gerson (New York: Metropolitan Museum of Art, 1986), 41–47.

42. Constable, "Suger's Monastic Administration" in *Abbot Suger and Saint-Denis*, ed. Gerson, 20.

43. Constable, "Suger's Monastic Administration," 18.

44. Constable, "Suger's Monastic Administration," 21–22.

45. Gasparri 1: 230–31, trans. Erwin Panofsky, *Abbot Suger on the Abbey*

Church of St.-Denis and Its Art Treasures, 2nd ed. (Princeton, N.J.: Princeton University Press, 1979), 122.

46. Trans. Constable, "Suger's Monastic Administration," 19.

47. Gasparri 2: 265, no. 16: "Certum est, servi Dei, vos de laboribus tantum et de nutrimentis vivere, aut de elemosinis sustenari. Vita et substantia vestra, quanto est artior, tanto debet esse liberior." Trans. Constable, "Suger's Monastic Administration," 22.

48. For Hilduin's acts, see Chapter 1. Fulrad's Testament of 777 edited in Michel Félibien, *Histoire de l'abbaye royal de Saint-Denys en France.* . . . (Paris: F. Léonard, 1706), xxxviii, no. 56. See also Grant, *Abbot Suger of St-Denis*, 185–89, 232.

49. Grant, *Abbot Suger of St-Denis*, 215 n33, noted eight estates Hilduin had allocated to the *mensa conventualis* as being in Suger's hand.

50. Lohrmann, "Répartition et création de nouveaux domaines monastiques," 252 n31, noted the general importance of exchanges with religious communities to create the occasion to throw off lay control.

51. See Ulysse Berlière, "Notes pour servir à l'histoire des monastères bénédictins de la province de Reims," *Revue bénédictine* 11 (1894): 36–37, which gives the text of the legate's report to the pope. For details of the visit, see Wilhelm Janssen, *Die päpstlichen Legaten in Frankreich: Von Schisma Anaklets II. bis zum Tode Coelestins III (1130–1198)* (Cologne: Böhlau, 1961), 35–36.

52. See appendix table D2.

53. CSV, 91–98.

54. The rent had been customarily received "de bono cellararie" and the whole transaction had been "absque advocato et absque assensu capituli." See CSB, 244 corrected in Haigneré 1: 36, no. 94.

55. The abbot reclaimed the use of the land for himself and the brothers, CSB, 241, no. 29: "post discessum illius, nullus heredum, nullus successorem suorum quicquam ex eisdem terris exigere vel vendicare presumat, sed ex integro ad usus abbatis et fratrum omnino redirent."

56. CSB, 242, no. 30.

57. CSB, 195.

58. *De administratione*, prologue, Gasparri 1: 54, trans. Panofsky, *Abbot Suger on the Abbey Church of St.-Denis*, 41, with my corrections.

59. Presumably following Benedict of Nursia, *Regula*, ch. 3, in *La règle de Saint-Benoît*, ed. Neufville and de Vogüé, 1: 452.

60. Grant, *Abbot Suger of St-Denis*, 207, argued that the document is "essentially internal propaganda" for the monks and that this passage was to disguise authoritarian aspects of his rule.

61. Grant, *Abbot Suger of St-Denis*, 23 argued about Suger's use of the *Celestial Hierarchies* that "The one concept that he extracted from it was that of anagogy, of using the material to understand the immaterial."

62. Grant, *Abbot Suger of St Denis*, 35–36, pointed out that this two-part division was typical of contemporary deeds of abbots and bishops.

63. Indeed, he used the word or variants of it seven times in the prologue and first chapter of *De administratione*. See Gasparri 1: 54–61.

64. Primarily the work of Hilduin, described in Chapter 1.

65. *De administratione*, part 1, ch. 3 in Gasparri 1: 64. Compare Michel Bur, *Suger: Abbé de Saint-Denis, regent de France* (Paris: Perrin, 1991), 33–40 and Grant, *Abbot Suger of St-Denis*, 80–81.

66. AN LL 1157, 240–42: "Notum sit omnibus tam presentibus quam futuris quod ego Matheus bellushomo ligius existens sancti dyonisii et eius abbatis rogatu domni Sugerii abbatis et totius conventus omnes feodos meos quorum de sancto dyonisio in proprium possideo et quos ceteri mei feodati computavi nullum pretermittens." Note that this passage shows Suger consulting the convent, see Constable, "Suger's Monastic Administration," 26, n171.

67. For a discussion of the nature of these men as military dependents, see Grant, *Abbot Suger of St-Denis*, 218–20.

68. Marcel Aubert, *Suger* (Paris: Fontenelle, 1950), 25: "Dès 1125, Suger ordonne un recensement du temporel de l'abbaye dont nous avons conservé le souvenir dans le rôle présenté pour son fief par Matthieu le Bel, homme-lige de l'abbaye dans le Vexin français."

69. AN LL 1156, fols. 85–86v.

70. *De administratione*, part 2, ch. 1 in Gasparri 1: 110: "His igitur reddituum incrementis taliter assignatis, ad aedificiorum institutionem memorandam manum reduximus."

71. See *De administratione*, part 2, chs. 4–5, 7, 9–11, and 19 in Gasparri 1: 116, 120 (in, on, and around the doors); 120–22 (on the upper choir); 124–30 (on altars); 153 (on altar vases).

72. *De administratione*, part 2, ch. 19 in Gasparri 1: 155, trans. Panofsky, *Abbot Suger on the Abbey Church of St.-Denis*, 81.

73. See Constable's discussion of Suger's piety and concern with display, "Suger's Monastic Administration," 19–20 and compare Grant, *Abbot Suger of St-Denis*, 24–26.

74. See Bur, *Suger*, 176.

75. For one particularly detailed example, see *De administratione*, part 1, ch. 10 in Gasparri 1: 70, where Suger described abandoning the traditional rent of 15 pounds at Louveciennes and imposing wine production.

76. Bur, *Suger*, 175–76. My translation from French.

77. Constable, "Suger's Monastic Administration," 22.

78. Constable, "Suger's Monastic Administration," 22.

79. Grant, *Abbot Suger of St-Denis*, esp. 33–36.

80. The two surviving manuscript copies of Guimann's original (AD Pas-de-Calais 1 H1 and AD Pas-de-Calais 9 J/AA) are edited inadequately in CSV.

81. Perhaps on display prominently? See CSV, 112–23.

82. Payers were listed in groups based on streets or areas within the town. Van Drival reconstructed the street plan of Arras-town based on the headings of these groups; see CSV, 451–55, esp. map following 455.

83. CSV, 102–3: "De hostagiis autem, id est censibus domorum, quoniam inolevit nequitia ut plerumque post longos temporum decursus et generationum permutationes hi qui hostagia debent ea ab Ecclesia abalienare et sciscitantes unde ea debeant, libertatem quam nec habent nec habere debent, sibi usurpare contendunt, dignum ac necessarium duxi, loca ipsa in quibus et de

quibus debentur, eos quoque qui debent nominatim discernere, obsecrans qua-
tenus hec nomina que scribuntur modo nequaquam eradantur, ut futuris temporibus idem redditus quantum detrimenti vel crementi susceperint edoceant.
Porro qui breves habeat secundum generationum discessiones vel successiones
debentium nomina in suis carthulis permutent ut quidquid de habitatoribus vel
per decessionem, vel per venditionem, vel per transmutationem seu divisionem
contingerit cartha presens in omnibus consulta loca ipsa denominet et distin-
guat, nullusque de cetero errori vel fraudulentie locus remaneat."

84. A very brief continuation and poetic prologue and epilogue were
probably added after Guimann's death in 1192 by his fellow monk Lambert. See
Van Drival's speculations, CSV, xi–xii. Guimann's intended ending point cannot
be determined from the manuscript copies.

85. For Guimann see CSV, 105–12 (relics and sacred vessels) and 112–23
(*miracula*). For Suger, see *De administratione*, part 1, chs. 25–26 (*miracula*), part
2, chs. 15 (relics) and 19 (vessels) in Gasparri 1: 98–105, 140–45, and 151–55.

86. Some charters also show revenue allocation, such as BM Arras ms.
1266, fol. 32r, in which the renders of Atheis are allocated to the *camerarius* and
then to the prior (for the chapter) upon the donor's death.

87. AN LL 1024, fol. 94r, edited in CSG 1: 308–13, no. 222. See appendix
B for further details.

88. For the acquisition of Samoreau, see CSG 1: 249–51, no. 173.

89. CSG 1: 313–4, no. 223.

90. BnF lat. 13056, fol. 2r. The list is edited in CSG 1: 306–8, no. 221.
Poupardin dated this document 1176–82.

91. CSG 1: 315–16, no. 224.

92. CSG 1: 317–19, no. 226 (1–3). See Chapter 4.

93. BM Auxerre ms. 212. The manuscript (with later copies) is superbly
edited by Robert-Henri Bautier and Monique Gilles in *Chronique de Saint-
Pierre-le-Vif de Sens, dite de Clarius* (Paris: CNRS, 1979).

94. See Bautier and Gilles, eds., *Chronique de Saint-Pierre-le-Vif de Sens*,
x–xvii for details of content and structure.

95. The lists of rents are in Bautier and Gilles, eds., *Chronique de Saint-
Pierre-le-Vif de Sens*, 285–301, appendix 2, where they are numbered as fifteen
separate "censiers." The editors do not edit the relic list but provide a note about
it, xvi.

96. Bautier and Gilles, eds., *Chronique de Saint-Pierre-le-Vif de Sens*, 285–92.
The groups correspond to document nos. 1–3, 4–5, 6–15.

97. See Bautier and Gilles, eds., *Chronique de Saint-Pierre-le-Vif de Sens*, x,
where the editors argue Arnaud provided a first-person recitation of the events
in the "annals" 1100–1108. See also the introduction, xxviii–xix, where they discussed the "third hand" which wrote this and other sections of the manuscript.

98. Bautier and Gilles, eds., *Chronique de Saint-Pierre-le-Vif de Sens*,
293–95, nos. 1–3. The first was entitled: "Minuti census sancti Petri qui sunt in
manu abbati [sic]." Bautier, 285, characterized the first two of these documents
as "un relevé comptable précis des revenus en cens, gros et menus, de la mense
abbatiale."

99. The monks almost certainly had eighth- and ninth-century documents in their possession in the early twelfth century and the monastery existed at the time of Carolingian reforms. See Bautier and Gilles, eds., *Chronique de Saint-Pierre-le-Vif de Sens*, 239–51.

100. Bautier and Gilles, eds., *Chronique de Saint-Pierre-le-Vif de Sens*, 295–96, no. 4: "Census qui venit ad manus donni [*sic*] ar(naldi) abbat's."

101. Bautier and Gilles, eds., *Chronique de Saint-Pierre-le-Vif de Sens*, 301, no. 15. Note there are no sums in the survey.

102. Bautier and Gilles, eds., *Chronique de Saint-Pierre-le-Vif de Sens*, 294–95, no. 3: "Hoc scriptum, sicut hic continetur, fecit subscribere quidam servus sancti Petri, Gauterius nomine, cognomento Rufus, qui diu majoriam eiusdem ville tenuerat et ad ultimum gravi infirmitate correptus, antequam moreretur, ita esse in veritate testatus est."

103. See Bautier and Gilles, eds., *Chronique de Saint-Pierre-le-Vif de Sens*, 291, where the editors speculate there might have been a sale or alienation.

104. Document no. 10 records only a lump sum from an estate held by Saint-Germain-d'Auxerre instead of a breakdown by payees, Bautier and Gilles, eds., *Chronique de Saint-Pierre-le-Vif de Sens*, 299. No. 14 (page 301) consists entirely of the "summa census vogredii."

105. For example, the editors suggest that overlapping efforts by different surveyors produced the double entries recorded in the second and third sections of the survey of Travances. See Bautier and Gilles, eds., *Chronique de Saint-Pierre-le-Vif de Sens*, 289.

106. Bautier and Gilles, eds., *Chronique de Saint-Pierre-le-Vif de Sens*, 298, no. 9. The end of the entry for this list seems to include a fragmentary portion of the closing formulae of the proposed charter.

107. Bautier and Gilles, eds., *Chronique de Saint-Pierre-le-Vif de Sens*, 188, "Hec enim summa omni tempore fuit intentio sue mentis subtrahi sibi fere omnia secularia negocia."

108. BnF ms. lat. 10101. See also Guérard's partial edition, CSP 2: 257–620.

109. For more of the role of *praepositi*, see chapter 4.

110. CSP 2:352. Several of these descriptions were grouped by Guérard into a "panagraphum," CSP 2: 377–82.

111. For example, space for additions seems to have been left at the end of book one on the cellary, BnF ms. lat. 10101, fol. 29v, where at least two blank pages were cut out in later rebinding.

112. CSV, 5. See also Chapter 1.

113. Bernard Delmaire, "Cartulaires et inventaires de chartes dans le nord de la France," in *Les cartulaires*, 301–24. See also Michel Parisse, "Les cartulaires: copies ou sources originales?" in *Les cartulaires*, 503–12.

114. AN LL 1157–58. The first stage of this work was completed in 1277–78, see Guyotjeannin, "*Penuria Scriptorum*," BEC 155 (1997): 15.

115. AN LL 1025.

116. Among the many examples is the cartulary copied in BnF lat. 5439 and BnF Duchesne 22.

117. Notably BM Arras ms. 1266.

118. See Bernard Delmaire, *Le diocèse d'Arras de 1093 au milieu du XIVᵉ siècle: Recherches sur la vie religieuse dans le nord de la France au moyen âge* (Arras: Commission départementale d'histoire et d'archéologie du Pas-de-Calais, 1994) 1: 69–90, esp. 74–75 (parishes) and Roger Berger, *Littérature et société arrageoises au XIIIᵉ siècle: les chansons et dits artésians* (Arras: Commission départmentale des monuments historiques du Pas-de-Calais, 1981), 38 (roads).

119. Technically speaking, the diocese was "restored" out of the larger diocese of Cambrai. For details, see Delmaire, *Le diocèse d'Arras*, 39–60.

120. For further details about the physical landscape of Arras, see Berger, *Littérature et société arrageoises*, 32–38. Unsurprisingly, in 1113 a dispute arose between the cathedral canons and the monks over the parishes divided by the new walls, which was not settled until 1144. See Delmaire, *Le diocèse d'Arras*, 55.

121. Disputes over tolls in the market, which was controlled by Saint-Vaast, occurred throughout the 1140s and were settled temporarily by a comital charter in 1148 (BM Arras ms. 1266 fol. 22v). See Berger, *Littérature et société arrageoises*, 66.

122. *De administratione*, part 1, chs. 1, 11 in Gasparri 1: 56–59, 72–73.

123. *De administratione*, part 1, ch. 21 in Gasparri 1: 90–93.

124. See Georges Duby, "Le budget de l'abbaye de Cluny," 61–82.

125. *De administratione*, part 1, chs. 2, 23–24 in Gasparri 1: 60–63, 94–97. See also Bur, *Suger*, 106 n12, where six separate instances are listed.

126. *De administratione*, part 1, ch. 4 in Gasparri 1: 66–69.

127. CSB, 269–270. See also Guérard's introduction, CSB, liii–liv.

128. Suger, *Vie de Louis VI le Gros*, ed. Waquet, 212–15, ch. 27.

Chapter 4. Discipline and Service Inside and Outside the Cloister

1. Roger Reynolds, "The *De officiis vii graduum*: Its Origins and Early Medieval Development," *Medieval Studies* 34 (1972): 113–51, reprint in Roger Reynolds, *Clerical Orders in the Early Middle Ages: Duties and Ordination* (Aldershot: Ashgate, 1999).

2. Gasparri 2: 199, no. 8: "hoc etiam a toto capitulo obtinuimus, ut de capicio capiciarius frater, quicumque sit ille, refectionem fratribus in refectorio . . . procuret."

3. Gasparri 2: 212–17, no. 9. Note that Suger remarks on his predecessors' poor endowment of the treasury.

4. Gasparri 2: 228–57, no. 12.

5. See Giles Constable, "Suger's Monastic Administration," in *Abbot Suger and Saint-Denis: A Symposium*, ed. Paula Gerson (New York: Metropolitan Museum of Art, 1986), 25–26.

6. The only exception was a dubious notice from the eleventh century, CSP 2: 297.

7. Claude Gaier, "Documents relatifs aux domains hesbigans de l'abbaye de Saint-Denis en France," *BCRH* 127 (1961): 185–88, no. 2. See also 181–82, no.

1, where the bishop of Liège grants Suger's request conveyed by Peter, "petitione quam habuit apud nos quendam fidelissimum fratrem Petri nomine et ecclesiae beati Dyonisii camerarium."

8. Lindy Grant, *Abbot Suger of St-Denis: Church and State in Early Twelfth-Century France* (London: Longman, 1998), 204–6.

9. See appendix table D3. See also Michel Bur, *Suger: Abbé de Saint-Denis, regent de France* (Paris: Perrin, 1991), 206.

10. Constable, "Suger's Monastic Administration," 26.

11. Gasparri 2: 156–67, no. 1 and 216–19, no. 10.

12. CSP 2: 359: "consilio et rogatu fratrum assentiens" (William); CSP 2: 392: "communi assensu et benevolentia omnium" (Udo).

13. There is a close (but not exact) correspondence of acts giving capitular assent and the use of the term "minister." See appendix table D3.

14. Compare Constable, "Suger's Monastic Administration," 26 n170, who stressed the frequent mention of capitular assent and Grant, *Abbot Suger of St-Denis*, 207, who stressed the lack of monastic witnesses to charters. For changes in the abbot's role generally, see Giles Constable, "The Authority of Superiors in Religious Communities," in *La notion d'autorité au Moyen Age*, ed. George Makdisi, Dominique Sourdel, and Janine Sourdel-Thomine (Paris: Presses universitaires de France, 1982), 202–3.

15. Gasparri 2: 173, 209 (testament), 215, 227, nos. 2, 8, 9, 11.

16. For example, an act allocating the revenues of Berneval to the treasury for the ornamentation of the church. See appendix table D4, no. 9. Compare to Suger's testament, no. 8.

17. Gasparri 2: 209. Constable, in "Suger's Monastic Administration," 25, offers a complete list of officers in the order in which they usually subscribed charters: abbot, prior, subprior, precentor, infirmarian, treasurer, capicerius, chanter, chancellor, cellarer, and almoner. I have adopted this order in appendix table D4.

18. Nine of eighteen acts. See appendix table D2.

19. CSV, 317–8.

20. Charles Duvivier, *Actes et documents anciens intéressant la Belgique* (Brussels: n.p., 1898), 338–39.

21. See appendix table D2. Such "permanent" land transactions are noted in the last column.

22. For the economic implications of this act, see Chapter 3.

23. Although the original document was lost in 1917, a summary exists in Henri Loriquet and Jules Chavanon, eds., *Inventaire sommaire des archives départementales antérieures à 1790. Pas-de-Calais* H1 (Arras: Société du Pas-de-Calais, 1902), 126, no. 141, which makes this aspect of the reform clear: "*Consuetudines ministeriorum sancti Vedasti* Réglement édicté en chapitre en présense de Pierre . . . par Martin, abbé de Saint-Vaast (1 mai 1175?) fixant le role spécial les revenus et la reddition des comptes des offices claustraux de son abbaye: l'abbé, le cellérier, le prévôt, l'hospitalier, le chambrier, le portier, l'aumônier, l'infirmier."

24. There are two notices of these acts from 1177 (BM Arras ms. 1266 fol. 41v) and 1178 (AD Pas-de-Calais 1H 2, fol. 139r). Note that these notices were granted by the *ecclesia* of Saint-Vaast and had witness lists (unknown because of abbreviation in later copies).

25. CSP 2: 393: "totius capituli nostri benivolentia et assensu communi."

26. CSP 2: 393: "Hunc autem redditum reddent ei annuatim, in festivitate omnium sanctorum, administratores obedientiarum nostrarum; et, ne aliquis nimis hoc facto gravetur, parvissimum quid unicuique impositum est, ut scripto presenti monstratur." The document then proceeds to list 41 monks by title rather than name, paying a total of 76 *solidi*. The list included the chamberlain, almoner, provosts, cellarer, sacristan and monks who oversaw particular lands. Note that the abbot himself also had to contribute ten *solidi*.

27. CSP 2: 379–80.

28. Note that the term *ministerium* was used in various contexts until Folquin's time and had a long history of Carolngian use at Saint-Bertin and elsewhere. See Chapter 1.

29. CSB, lxii-lxiii.

30. See Félix Henri D'Hoop, ed., *Recueil des chartes du prieuré de Saint-Bertin, à Poperinghe* (Bruges: Vandecasteele-Werbrouck, 1870), 13 n11 (hereafter cited as *Poperinghe*).

31. The charter used the term *mensa* to refer to the meals the monks receive, but the double meaning of *mensa conventualis* could not have been far from their minds.

32. Assent was mentioned in later acts sparingly: acts of 1150 and 1185, which were acts of the prior written in absence of an abbot (crusade and vacancy), an act establishing an abbatial anniversary in 1161, and an act concerning assarting and forest law in 1177. Haigneré 1: 91, no. 207 (1150); CSB, 362 (1185); CSB, 329 (1150); Robert Fossier, *Chartes de coutume en Picardie: XIᵉ-XIIᵉ siècle* (Paris: Bibliothèque Nationale, 1974), 111–12, no. 25 (1165).

33. For the pervasiveness of such "bad lordship" in the twelfth century, see Thomas N. Bisson, "The Feudal Revolution," *Past and Present* 142 (1994): 28–34.

34. Ludolf Kuchenbuch, *Bäuerliche Gesellschaft und Klosterherrschaft im 9. Jahrhundert: Studien zur SozialStruktur der Abtei Prüm* (Wiesbaden: Steiner, 1978), 271–79, argued that the unfree status of Carolingian mayors was a product of their office.

35. CSP 2: 274–77, no. 17.

36. For law and marriage of the unfree, see Robert F. Berkhofer III, "Marriage, Lordship, and the Greater Unfree in Twelfth-Century France," *Past and Present* 173 (2001): 3–27.

37. CSG 1: 186–87, no. 125 (Thibaut): "concesserunt fieri ancillam ecclesie beati Germani, et in eam legem servitutis transire in qua est maritus suus Johannes." CSG 1: 187–8, no. 126 (Odo): "ut fieret ancilla beati Germani et in eam legem servitutis in qua maritus suus est Johannes transiret concessimus."

38. Early instances of exchange at Saint-Germain in charters include CSG

1: 145–46, no. 92 (1140), 168–69, no. 112 (1152), and 169–70, no. 113 (1152), the first two of which concern mayors or their children.

39. CSP 2: 382, no. 166: "quia eum suspicabamus quod de dominio nostro vellet exire."

40. Robert's pledges included Albert, mayor of Emprenville, Rainier the vicarius, Arnulf the sacristan, and several others, CSP 2: 382–83, no. 166. Could Robert have been planning to leave (exire) Saint-Père entirely?

41. CSP 2: 461, no. 67: "Gallesius, filius Ribaldi de Artenaico, priusquam filiam Alberti, majoris Imprenville, uxorem duceret, in capitulum nostrum venit, et, cum eodem patre suo Ribaldo, ecclesiae et capitulo nostro super sanctorum reliquias hujusmodi fidelitatem juravit." This charter may date from either Udo's time, or that of his predecessor, William (1101–29).

42. CSP 2: 462, no. 67: "Predicta quoque puella, ejusdem Gallesii uxor mox futura, hoc idem post eum, sicut hic determinatum est, juravit jusjurandum; in eodem sacramento suo addens hoc, quod, si forte eidem marito suo superstes foret, non nisi consilio, voluntate et licentia capituli nostri, alteri se viro in matrimonium copularet."

43. CSP 2:372, no. 160: "ob multimodas contumelias quas nobis ingerebat, Mascelinum de Reconvillari, nostrum famulum, cum fratre suo Teidardo in carcerem trusimus."

44. CSP 2: 372, no. 160: "Ligavimus ergo eum juramenti vinculo."

45. André Chédeville, Chartres et ses compagnes (XIᵉ–XIIIᵉ siècles) (Paris: Klincksieck, 1973), 387ff., in discussing the mayors of Saint-Père, argued that the size of this sum reflected Mascelinus' importance.

46. The notices were written on LL 1024 fols. 84r–85v. The list of Geoffrey Pooz's fief is in the same bifolium (fols. 84–88) and various lists of acquisitions in adjoining quires; see appendix tables B1 and B2 for the structure of the cartulary.

47. CSG 1: 294–95, no. 209. This phrase was typical for unfree men in northern France at this time.

48. CSG 1: 295–96, no. 210.

49. CSG 1: 296, no. 211.

50. CSG 1: 297, no. 212.

51. BM ms. lat. 12194, fol. 219r; edited in CSG 1: 298–99, no. 214. This volume of sermons on John dates from the eleventh century, but it was rebound in the very early thirteenth century with the late twelfth-century endsheets.

52. CSG 1: 298, no. 214: "Guido, major de Surinis, astu malignitatis negabat se hominem nostrum et ecclesie nostre esse. Proinde nos submonuimus eum de jure et ad diem statutum undequaque congregavimus in curia nostra utriusque sexus fere quinquaginta de parentela predicti Guidonis." This may be a Continental instance of "suit of kin," known in later medieval England; see Paul Hyams, King, Lords, and Peasants in Medieval England: The Common Law of Villeinage in the Twelfth and Thirteenth Centuries (Oxford: Clarendon Press, 1980), 171–81.

53. CSG 1: 298, no. 214: "Qui omnes homines nostri de corpore parati essent approbare quod idem Guido sicut et ipsi homo noster esse debebat."

54. CSG 1: 298, no. 214: "At ille videns in abnegatione dominii nostri se minus provide ac sapienter egisse."

55. BnF ms. lat. 12194, fol. 219v; edited in CSG 1: 318, no. 226(i).

56. The number of relations may have been large. The notice claims they met in the abbot's court with fifty of Guy's relatives (*utriusque sexus fere quinquaginta de parentela predicti Guidonis*). This number may have been exaggerated, but the genealogy lists ninety-nine relatives in five generations and the fact that the status of the whole family was at issue would have provided incentive to appear. For an analysis of this and the other genealogies, see Nathaniel L. Taylor, "Monasteries and Servile Genealogies: Guy of Suresnes and Saint-Germain-des-Prés in the Twelfth Century," in *Genèse médiévale de l'anthroponymie moderne* 5.1, *Serfs et dependants au Moyen Âge*, ed. Monique Bourin and Pascal Chareille (Tours: Université de Tours, 2002), 249–68.

57. AN LL 1024, fol. 86v, BnF ms. lat. 13056, fol. 125v, and BM ms. lat. 13882, fol. 93v; edited in CSG 1: 318–9, no. 225(ii and iii) and CSG 2: 235, no. 226bis.

58. Dieter Hägermann, ed., *Das Polyptychon von Saint-Germain-des-Prés* (Köln: Böhlau, 1993), 28, 36–39, 138, 146. See also the argument for dating by Olivier Guyotjeannin, "*Penuria Scriptorum*: Le mythe de l'anarchie documentaire dans la France du nord (Xe–première moitié du XIe siècle)," *BEC* 155 (1997): 29 n43.

59. Guimann preserved several genealogies to keep track of "liege men" (*legius homo*); see CSV, 239–41. These men included lesser fief-holders as well as more important men like the castellan of Arras.

60. CSG 1: 294, no. 209: "Noverit universitas vestra quod Willelmus major de Emancto fecit fidelitatem ecclesie beati Germani in presentia nostra sicut homo de corpore, ubi interfuerunt isti: [list of 4 monks and 10 men]."

61. CSG 1: 295, no. 209: "Post longum vero tempus, cum quadam die a nobis citatus sui nobis presentiam fecisset, et nos ei diceremus ut super quibusdam injuriis, quas nobis fecerat, sicut homo de corpore responderet, hominium et fidelitatem quam prescriptis audientibus et videntibus nobis fecerat, denegavit, eamque postea amicorum suorum usus consilio pariter et hominium recognvoit." Note that throughout this notice the fidelity receives greater stress than the homage, probably because it was mentioned explicitly in the first instance.

62. CSG 1: 295, no. 209: "Milo . . . prius ad mandatum nostrum facere recusavit."

63. Rijksarchief te Gent Sint-Bertijns, Poperinghe 3, in D'Hoop, ed., *Poperinghe*, 5–6, no. 3. Cartulary copy, BM Boulogne-sur-Mer ms. 146A, fol. 41; edited in CSB, 248.

64. D'Hoop, ed., *Poperinghe*, 5: "in magna pace fuit usque ad tempus quo Odo de Rinegelles ministerium obtinuit, qui pravas consuetudines in eadem villa elevavit."

65. D'Hoop, ed., *Poperinghe*, 5, no. 3: "Post mortem siquidem Odonis, Lambertus, filius ejus, venit ad abbatem Lambertum rogans eum ut quod pater suus ab eo tenuerat, scilicet quoddam feodum in terris et ministerium de Poperingehem, ei redderet, offerans pecuniam pro ministerio."

66. D'Hoop, ed., *Poperinghe*, 5, no. 3: "Abbas vero communicato consilio cum capitulo ecclesie et hominibus suis feodum quidem terre ei concedens

ministerium reddere noluit, propter magnas injustitias et forisfacturas quas pater eius fecerat."

67. D'Hoop, ed., *Poperinghe*, 5, no. 3: ". . . eidem Lamberto ministerium ad custodiendum tantummodo commendavit et nullum donum ei aliquatenus inde fecit, ita tamen ut tamdiu hanc custodiam haberet quamdiu abbati placeret."

68. D'Hoop, ed., *Poperinghe*, 5–6, no. 3. See also D'Hoop's description of these promises, xxiv.

69. That Lambert had to offer the abbot money for the *ministerium*, but seemed to receive his fief as a matter of course, suggests that certain profiteering may still have been expected. The document does not mention if the abbot took the money.

70. This was certainly true in the Carolingian period, when the *villa* was more than twice the size of any other; see François-Louis Ganshof, ed., *Le polyptyque de Saint-Bertin (844–859): Édition critique et commentaire* (Paris: Klincksieck, 1975), 135. For Poperinghe in the twelfth century, see D'Hoop, ed., *Poperinghe*, xviii–xxi.

71. Rijksarchief te Gent Sint-Bertijns, Poperinghe 17, edited in Thérèse de Hemptinne and Adrian Verhulst, eds., *De oorkonden der graven van Vlaanderen (juli 1128–september 1191)* (Brussels: Palais des Arádémies, 1988) 2(1): 213–15, no. 131.

72. Profits of justice were probably the Count's main concern, since he shared in them through his *scabini*. See D'Hoop, ed., *Poperinghe*, xxi–xxii.

73. PU *Frankreich* 3: 138–39, no. 81 (JL 12836).

74. Rijksarchief te Gent, Sint-Bertijns, Poperinghe 24; edited in D'Hoop, ed., *Poperinghe*, 24, no. 24. A later cartulary copy also exists, BM Boulogne-sur-Mer ms. 144, fol. 96v, edited in CSB, 366.

75. D'Hoop, ed., *Poperinghe*, 24, no. 24: "eandemque legem de ceteris ministerialibus ecclesiae tenendam autorizamus, ut scilicet nullus eorum vel per hereditariam successionem vel in feodum habeat suum ministerium, nec alio modo quam abbati vel ecclesiae dare placuerit."

76. D'Hoop in *Poperinghe*, xxiii, n1 defines his terms (somewhat overly precisely) as follows: "Le *ministerialis* administrait plusieurs villages en commun, d'après un même droit: ces *villae* formaient un métier (en latin, *ministerium*, *officium*, en flamand *ambacht*). The idea of office was latent in the term *ministerium* since Carolingian times, see the discussion of Gundbert and Folquin, chapter 1.

77. The terminology of the newly developed concept was understandably loose and based on previous connotations of the word. The term *officium* could bear many of the same meanings as *ministerium*.

78. BM Arras, ms. 1266, fol. 49r; edited in Adolphe Guesnon, "Un cartulaire de l'abbaye de Saint-Vaast d'Arras, codex du XIIe siècle," *Bulletin historique et philologique du Comité des travaux historiques et scientifiques* (1896): 271–73, no. 2: "[Theodoricus] se nunquam Atrebatensi abbati extra terminos ministerii sui justiciam prosecuturum respondit" (hereafter cited as "Un cartulaire de Saint-Vaast").

79. For example, CSP 2: 484, no. 24. After granting the *majoratum terre*, the abbot then mentioned the land separately: "terram ad unam carrucam de eadem terra, convenienti loco, ei delegavi."

80. CSP 2: 389, no. 175. See the quotation below.

81. CSP 2: 430, no. 39: "Ego Eustachius, abbas Sancti Petri, hujus descriptionis testimonio ad noticiam sequentium reducere studui, Martino de Empregni Villa et filio ejus Alberto soli, si patri superstes fuerit, majoratus villicationem in vita sua, et dimidium camparti masure quam tenuit pater, nisi, reatu exigente, perdiderit, me pari assensu fratrum commendasse." N.B. the *villicationem* may refer to either the lands administered by the mayor, his dwelling, or his charge.

82. CSP 2: 461, no. 67.

83. CSP 2: 389, no. 175: "Ego frater Udo, monasterii sancti Petri Carnoti humilis abbas . . . nosse volumus omnes . . . quod Berengarius, filius Godescalli, recognovit in capitulo nostro, et super sanctas reliquias ibidem juravit, quia in majoratu ville nostre Campo Fauni nichil hereditarium clamaret, nichil feodaliter aut ex patrimonio reposcere deberet vel habere. Cui nos ejusdem majoratus officium tantummodo ad vitam suam commendavimus; eo tenore, ut nichil hereditatis, nichil patrimonii vel ipse vel posterorum suorum aliquis possit unquam in eodem officio feodaliter clamare."

84. CSP 2: 381: "Item apud Achiacum de terra IIIIor boves, cujus partem, cum majoria, Garnerius tenet ad vitam tantummodo suam." This note was part of the *panagraphum* of Udo's notices, see below.

85. CSP 2: 507–8, no. 51: "nichil prorsus nobis prejudicii retinemus, nisi ut ipsa nec heres suus, in predicti patris sui Mascelini hereditate, nulla possit occasione hereditarie quicquam reclamare."

86. CSV, 401 (Esclusiers) and 407 (Bihucourt). In both cases, one of two arbiters was Wibert, an important mayor of Saint-Vaast. For more on Achard, mayor of Esclusiers, see below.

87. CSP 2: 484–85, no. 24. The charter mentions that the land had just been given in alms to the monastery.

88. The language of the charter was particulary insistent about the latter, CSP 2: 484–85, no. 24: "Placita causarumque discussiones omnes ante monachum, qui eidem terre prefuerit, adducet, et, ad voluntatem monachi jussionemque omnia placita adterminabuntur, differentur, discutientur, vel definientur, districture sue jure in omnibus salvo."

89. CSP 2: 485, no. 24: "Memorandum quoque, quia Gaufridus quem voluerit servientem in eadem terram habebit: de omni autem forisfacto quod fecerit serviens G., tercio ammonitus, si non emendaverit, ejiciatur serviens." Note that *serviens* could mean anything from servant (or serf) to sergeant.

90. AD Eure-et-Loir H 450. René Merlet in *Inventaire sommaire des archives départementales antérieures à 1790: Eure-et-Loir* H1 (Chartres: Garnier, 1897), 59, dates the swearing of fidelity around 1140.

91. CSP 2: 464, no. 71: "Ipse itaque Odo, quia plurima sub pretextu feodi super ecclesiam nostram occupaverat . . ."

92. The chirograph makes the connection between the fief and peace explicit, CSP 2: 464, no. 71, "Cui nos tam ipsi quam heredi suo ea que subter annotata sunt, pacis et concordia causa, concessimus in feodum et concedimus: XX scilicet solidos de pastibus."

93. CSP 2: 464, no. 71: "utque eosdem XX solidos, vel quod minus forte fuerit, non nisi de manu monachi eidem loco prepositi accipiat, et hoc in assumptione sancte Marie."

94. CSP 2: 465, no. 71: "His majori a nobis in feodum communi assign-atis, definitum est et adjudicatum, ipso cum suis omnibus assentiente, nichil amplius vel ipsum vel heredem suum super ecclesiam nostram feodaliter ulterius posse clamare."

95. Jean Dufour, ed., *Receuil des actes de Louis VI, roi de France (1108–1137)* (Paris: De Boccard, 1992–94) 1: 193–94, no. 87. For the battles with Hugh, see Suger, *Vie de Louis VI le Gros*, ed. Henri Waquet (Paris: H. Champion, 1929), 128–80, ch. 19–21.

96. Gasparri 1: 82–89.

97. Grant, *Abbot Suger of St-Denis*, 92–93 argued that Suger exaggerated his own role in these events. Compare Suger's comments about the mayors of Beaune-la-Rolande, below.

98. AN LL 1158, 220, edited in Annie Dufour-Malbezin, ed., *Actes des évêques de Laon des origins à 1151* (Paris: CNRS, 2001), 252–53, no. 156.

99. AN LL 1158, 24–25. See also Grant, *Abbot Suger of St-Denis*, 213–14.

100. CSP 2: 500–501, no. 44.

101. CSP 2: 657–58, no. 53: "Habebit autem majoratum eo modo quo pater suus habuit; id est hospitium, in quo habitat, sine censu tenebit, et jarbam solummodo reddet de terra quam colit. Si sacrista famulum suum, messis tem-pore, ad numerandum et ad recipiendum terragium suum miserit, Milo de pastibus medietatem solummodo habebit. Eo autem anno quo sacrista terrag-ium suum ad modiationem ipsi tradiderit, tunc Milo omnes pastus, id est duos solidos et decem denarios, habebit. Quando censum nostrum afferet, panis et vinum ei dabitur, sicut et ceteris majoribus nostris quando ab ipsis nostri census nobis afferuntur."

102. BM Arras ms. 1266, fol. 49r; edited in Guesnon, "Un cartulaire de Saint-Vaast," 271–73, no. 2.

103. Guesnon, "Un cartulaire de Saint-Vaast," 271–72: "In pago Bathuano, sub tutela advocatie nostre, ecclesia S. Vedasti beneficium quoddam a regibus sibi collatum antiquitus possederat, cui ministrum quendam Theodoricum ut servum ecclesie prefecerat, et viginti solidos Tillensis monete, qui libra vocantur, pro feodo quotannis eidem assignaverat. Sed cum is, male tractando res domi-norum suorum, pro huiusmodi [delictis] responsurus ad ecclesiam a dominis suis vocaretur." Note the brackets indicate a missing word suggested by Guesnon.

104. Guesnon, "Un cartulaire de Saint-Vaast," 272: "[Theodoricus] quod servum ecclesie se omnino denegavit et se nunquam Atrebatensi abbati extra ter-minos ministerii sui justiciam prosecuturum respondit."

105. Guesnon, "Un cartulaire de Saint-Vaast," 272: "Nos eum audire dis-tulimus donec clamoribus, calliditatibus, promissionibus ejus aliquantulum decepti ministerio eum restituimus."

106. William produced letters of Godfrey, Duke of Brabant, who had resolved the conflict in the time of Arnold's father; see Guesnon, "Un cartu-laire de Saint-Vaast," 272: "Statim gravis clamor ecclesie vestre nos insequitur.

Guillelmus, vester prepositus, cum vestris precibus et litteris domini ducis nos impetit, suadet, hortatur ut ab hoc proposito desistamus."

107. The money seems to have been some sort of pay-off by the Count to Theodore for forgoing any claim: Guesnon, "Un cartulaire de Saint-Vaast," 272: "super hoc depactus est illi duodecim libras nostre monete."

108. Guesnon, "Un cartulaire de Saint-Vaast," 273: "Quatuor mansos et dimidium ab ecclesia censualiter, ut quilibet rusticus de familia, suscepit, quorum investituram a Theodorico nepote suo, modo vestro ministrio, vellet nollet, accepit."

109. Louis Ricouart, *Les biens de l'abbaye de St-Vaast dans les diocèses de Beauvais, de Noyon, de Soissons et d'Amiens* (Anzin: Ricouart-Dugour, 1888), 178: "Quod si usque ad prefatum terminum Acardus et sui successores praedictas anguillas non solverent, ecclesia sancti Eligii monacho de Vaus non esse solutas intimabit. Monachus vero de Vaus praedictum Acardum et ejus successores ad solutionem anguillarum infra quindecim dies a praescripto termino complendam districtius compellet. Quas si solvere contempserit, curia de Vaus ecclesiae sancti Eligii persolvet sine contradictione aut molestia dilationis . . ." Note that Guimann witnessed this charter.

110. CSV, 401: "idem major [Achardus] asserebat se debere habere in domo nostra de Vallibus corredium sicut monachus."

111. A Raoul (perhaps the same or his son) is mentioned in a charter of 1192 (D'Hoop, ed., *Poperinghe*, 31, no. 32). Another Lambert de Reningelst took over in 1208 and in 1226 Daniel de Reningelst, the "justicier" of Poperinghe, passed on his holdings to his son, Lambert. See D'Hoop, ed., *Poperinghe*, 23–25 for details.

112. BM Boulogne-sur-Mer ms. 144, fol. 97r. D'Hoop summarizes the conditions in *Poperinghe*, xxiv.

113. For example, CSP 2: 476, no. 10.

114. CSP, 2: 441–43, no. 49. Such negotiating continued well into the thirteenth century at Saint-Père, see CSP 2: 693–94, no. 118 (1243).

115. Gasparri 1: 54: "cum in capitulo generali, quadam die, conferendo cum fratribus nostris tam de hominibus quam de privatis negotiis consederemus." See also Chapter 3.

116. AN LL 1157, 240: "ego Matheus bellushomo . . . rogatu domni Sugerii abbatis et totius conventus." See also chapter 3.

117. Gasparri 1: 92: "usurpatas et alienatas tam a majore quam ab aliis terras nobis retraximus."

118. Grant, *Abbot Suger of St-Denis*, 89–96.

119. Gasparri 1: 80: "Easdem enim consuetudines quas de Monarvilla enumeravimus, vicelicet talliam annona, porcorum, ovium, agnorum, anserum, gallinarum, pullorum, lignorum, ab eadem terra more antecessorum suorum abripuerant, et ex hoc ipso tam nobis quam sibi infructuose jacentem omnino inutilem reddiderat."

120. According to Suger in *De Administratione*, Gasparri 1: 78, Monnerville (*Monarvilla*) lay below the castle of Méréville (*Merevilla*), which was itself listed in Abbot Hilduin's 832 *partitio bonorum*, AN K 9 n. 6. The renders in

kind Suger listed (see above note) were somewhat similar to those Hilduin used in his calculations. See Chapter 1.

121. CSP 2: 377–82, no. 165. Clearly, the *panagraphum* was assembled by later monks and copied into the cartulary from notes made in Udo's time. Guérard, CSP 2: 377, dates these pieces 1135–43.

122. CSP 2: 380: "Mascelinus de Reconvillari debet camere nostre VI denarios census de platea in qua sedet grangia ejus, festo Sancti Petri de more reddendos."

123. CSP 2: 380: "De reditu capicerie nostre debet major Mendre Ville XXVII solidos census, et VIII denarios festo Sancti Remigii, itemque V solidos census festo omnium sanctorum reddendos; sed et campipartem, quam capiceria nostra in ejusdem ville territorio habet, major idem et colligit nobis quandiu voluerimus et reddit." Compare the crop-sharing arrangement in 1180, above.

124. CSP 2: 381: "Ad eandem obedientiam pertinet Pomerata, cum omnibus exitibus suis; quod est parte decime, campiparte tota, tota avena de oblivionibus, et XII solidis de obliviis, et VI solidis de censu festo sancti Mauricii."

125. CSP 2: 381, a rent of 8 *denarii* and 1 *obolus*.

126. For example, the description of Céreville, CSP 2: 382.

127. Guimann consistently used the terms *homo legius*, *vavassores*, and *feodus* in his descriptions of these men and their holdings. For one of many examples, see the entry for Mercastel, CSV, 259–61.

128. See Chapter 3.

129. For Guimann's mention of the polyptych of 866, see CSV, 5.

130. Some as high as five and one-half *solidi* and eleven chickens for one *curtil*. See CSV, 243–47.

131. There were also *majores* at Saint-Vaast. Guimann used the term similarly, if not synonymously.

132. CSV, 265–66. Not all of the rights were evenly divided; Stephen, for example kept one-third of the mill.

133. CSV, 255–56.

134. See Chapter 3.

135. CSV, 256–58.

136. CSV, 257: "In hoc itaque generali placito presidente abbate seu preposito, circunsedentibus [sic] etiam scabinionibus, si quis adversus alterum habet querelam stabit, et clamorem suum faciet legitime super illum, audieturque clamor ejus et diligenter discutietur, ac secundum legem placiti, res inter utrumque juste dijudicabitur."

137. CSV, 257: ". . . et hujus fredi due partes erunt prepositi, tertiam vero partem habebit major placiti. Si autem lex abbatis vel prepositi fuerit, totum fredum major placiti habebit." For more information on allodial lands in Flanders, the age of these customs, and the "Pays d'alleu" of Saint-Vaast, see Ernest Warlop, *De Vlaasme Adel voor 1300* (Handzame: Familia et Patria, 1968), trans. J. B. Ross, *The Flemish Nobility Before 1300* (Kortrijk: G. Desmet-Huysman, 1975) 1: 284–85, esp. n330.

138. Baldwin's *villicatio* was described separately under Simoncourt, CSV, 307.

139. CSV, 305–6: "Huic ville adjacet viculus Gorghechunz qui est Balduini de Simoncurt in quo cum idem Balduinus longo tempore oblationes denariorum et panum et minutam decimam curtiliorum, pullorum, agnorum, vellerem et eorum que ad altare venire solent tenuisset et de feodo suo esse contenderet, venerabilis abbas Martinus ei negavit."

140. CSV, 306: "Unde idem Balduinus ad Christianam justiciam summonitus, timore Dei et consilio amicorum suorum quia illegitimum et contra rationem erat, ut laica de ecclesiasticis se intromitteret persona, eamdem decimam super altare sancti Vedasti episcopi ramum et cespitem reddidit."

141. For example, after treating the nearby village of Dainville, the *brevia* treated estates up the northern bank of the river Crinchon, looped back through inland estates to the river Scarpe, and proceeded down the south bank of that river, returning to Arras itself, a circuit of 25–30 kms.

142. CSV, 376: "Quamvis in villa de Ballol, diversitas consuetudinum in terris et redditibus sancti Vedasti plurimam pariat confusionem, eo quod sanctus Vedastus nullum nisi tantum in liberis alodiis suis districtum habeat, nos tamen que juris ecclesiae nostre sunt conservantes, ad liquidum disquisitam et majorum testimonio probatam redditum et consuetudinum veritatem litteris mandamus." N.B. The *majors* referred to could be either mayors or just elders, but usage elsewhere in the document suggests "mayors." For fines of justice, see above.

143. CSV, 378–80.

144. CSV, 266: "et tertia pars molendini, cujus molendini tertia pars est de feodo de Senous, cujus feodi descriptionem superius in titulo Meruli castelli sive Harcicurt invenies." See also CSV, 335 and 355 for similar references.

145. CSV, 6: "Verbi gracia, si in illa possessione, sanctum Vedastum tantum vel tantum habere lector invenerit, mox qui et quid debeant et quantum singuli et unde debeant quia pre oculis inventurus est, diligenter disquirat, et quod in summa complexim dictum est, in partibus divisum determinatum esse comprobabit."

146. CSV, 194–95: "De quibus relevationibus, introitibus atque exitibus: si quid villici vel concelando, vel alio quolibet modo, defraudere vel imminuere presumpserint, monachus qui hostagia colligit caute provideat; et si quem pro aliqua domo vel curtilio redditum solvere viderit qui in preterito termino non solverit, et in sua charta scriptus non sit, per quam et quomodo in illam domum vel curtilium intraverit, diligenter sciat, sicque deprehensa concelatione, relevationem sive introitum et exitum suum a villico suo exquirat."

147. For Guimann's remarks concerning this problem and the *hostagia* within Arras, see Chapter 3. The provosts for the estates outside of the city also collected *hostagia* and it is these monks to whom the passage refers.

148. See the speculations of Rolf Grosse, based on his analysis of the extant codex (AN LL 1156), in his "Remarques sur les cartulaires de Saint-Denis aux XIIIᵉ–XIVᵉ siècles," in *Les cartulaires*, 279–89, esp. 282–84.

149. AN LL 1157–58 (*Cartulaire blanc*). For a description of the contents consult the electronic edition of the Ecole Nationale des Chartes, an ongoing project, located online at http://www.enc.sorbonne.fr/cartulaireblanc/.

150. Constable, "Suger's Monastic Administration," 25.

151. AN LL 1025. A dossier describing the contents of the cartulary is in preparation at the Institut de Recherche et d'Histoire des Textes.

152. Of the 95 acts attributed to the period before 1200 by the dossier at the Institut de Recherche et d'Histoire des Textes, 71 are dated and of these only 14 come from the period from 1077 to 1162 (most after 1140), while 30 come from the period 1162–82.

153. BnF ms. lat. 10101.

154. BM Boulogne-sur-Mer ms. 144.

155. For a count of cartularies in northern France, see Bernard Delmaire, "Cartulaires et inventaires de chartes dans le nord de la France," in *Les cartularies*, 305, 310.

156. For a contemporary secular example, see Adam J. Kosto, "The *Liber feudorum maior* of the counts of Barcelona: the cartulary as an expression of power," *Journal of Medieval History* 27 (2001): 1–22.

Conclusion: Accountability, Writing, and Rule by 1200

1. Compare Patrick Geary, *Phantoms of Remembrance: Memory and Oblivion at the End of the First Millennium* (Princeton, N.J.: Princeton University Press, 1994), 102–3.

2. See Guérard's description, CSP, cclxxv.

3. Geary, *Phantoms of Remembrance*, 179.

4. See Mary Carruthers, *The Book of Memory: A Study of Memory in Medieval Culture* (Cambridge: Cambridge University Press, 1990), 14, 259–60, about *memoria* as a "modality" of medieval culture, especially for monks.

5. Giles Constable, "The Authority of Superiors in Religious Communities," in *La notion d'autorité au Moyen Age*, ed. George Makdisi, Dominique Sourdel, and Janine Sourdel-Thomine (Paris: Presses Universitaires de France, 1982), 195–96, noted that there seems to have been a tendency for strong, prestigious houses to choose young abbots. Cluny, for example, had only nine abbots between 909 and the mid-twelfth century.

6. CSP 2: 393–94, no. 178: "Hunc autem redditum reddent ei annuatim, in festivitate omnium sanctorum, administratores obdientiarum nostrarum; et, ne aliquis nimis hoc facto gravetur, parvissimum quid unicuique impositum est, ut scripto presenti monstratur."

7. For ideas of the Last Judgment, see Hervé Martin, *Mentalités médiévales II: Représentations collectives du XIe au XVe siècle* (Paris: Presses Universitaires de France, 2001), 174–90.

8. Constance Bouchard, *Holy Entrepreneurs: Cistercians, Knights, and Economic Exchange in Twelfth-Century Burgundy* (Ithaca, N.Y.: Cornell University Press, 1991), 31–65, 187–98. See also Constance H. Berman, *Medieval Agriculture, the Southern French Countryside, and the Early Cistercians: A Study of Forty-Three Monasteries* (Philadelphia: American Philosophical Society, 1986).

9. Dietrich Lohrmann, "Répartition et création de nouveaux domaines monastiques au XIIe siècle," in *Villa-Curtis-Grangia: Économie rurale entre Loire*

IIe siècles, ed. Wilhelm Janssen and , 242–57.

bor of Saint Peter: The Social Mean-
.: Cornell University Press, 1999),
o–84. Both authors understandably
as neighbors.

n de nouveaux domaines monas-
ploitation de leur terrres, l'implan-
n serait restée confinée à un niveau
le transfert de terres de d'église à
t l'occasion de réduire les droits des

me Activity: Reassessing Benedictine
;" *Revue bénédictine* (forthcoming).
abbatum (Turnhout: Brepols, 1981),

iothèque historique de l'Yonne (Aux-
stance Bouchard, *Spirituality and*
-Century Auxerre (Cambridge, Mass.:
43–50, 53–63, 135–39. Note that the
.

) had been abbot of Saint-Germain-
), had been abbot of the Cistercian
ut the latter: "Redditus episcopales
ampliavit." Duru, ed., *Bibliothèque*

annin, *Episcopus et comes: Affirmation*
royaume de France (Beauvais-Noyon,
Xᵉ–début XIIIᵉ siècle (Geneva: Droz, 1987), esp. 123–30 on the monk-bishops of Beauvais. Note that regular clergy became bishops frequently in the wake of Gregorian reform.

18. For the social importance of counting, money, and the role of clerics, see Alexander Murray, *Reason and Society in the Middle Ages*, rev. ed. (Oxford: Oxford University Press, 1990), 162–210.

19. John Baldwin, *The Government of Philip Augustus: Foundations of French Royal Power in the Middle Ages* (Berkeley: University of California Press, 1986), 115–22.

20. Bryce Lyon and Adriaan Verhulst, *Medieval Finance: A Comparison of Financial Institutions in Northwestern Europe* (Providence, R.I.: Brown University Press, 1967), 24–29. The arrangement was instituted in 1089; see Fernand Vercauteren, ed., *Actes des comtes de Flandres, 1071–1128* (Brussels: Palais des Académies, 1938), 23–32, no. 9.

21. For the role of clerks in financial administration in England, see Lyon and Verhulst, *Medieval Finance*, 53–78, passim. Curial clerks often ended up as bishops under the Angevins, see Ralph Turner, *Men Raised from the Dust:*

Administrative Service and Upward Mobility in Angevin England (Philadelphia: University of Pennsylvania Press, 1988), 7–8, 20–34. See also the cautionary remarks of Michael Clanchy about "clerics" in *From Memory to Written Record: England, 1066–1307*, 2nd ed. (Oxford: Blackwell, 1993), 226–30. By contrast, Thomas N. Bisson, *Fiscal Accounts of Catalonia Under the Early Count-Kings (1151–23)* (Berkeley: University of California Press, 1984) 1: 60–66, emphasized the importance of "working knights" who played a role in the north as well.

22. Lyon and Verhulst, *Medieval Finance*, stressed shared features. The papacy should also be considered as part of this group. See Paul Fabre and L. Duchesne, eds., *Le Liber Censuum de l'Église Romaine*, 3 vols. (Paris: Fontemoing, 1889–1952); for a brief summary of the place of the *Liber Censuum* in papal administration, see Colin Morris, *The Papal Monarchy: The Western Church from 1050 to 1250* (Oxford: Oxford University Press, 1989), 164–69, 210–19.

23. On Capetian dynasticism see Andrew Lewis, *Royal Succession in Capetian France: Studies on Familial Order and the State* (Cambridge, Mass.: Harvard University Press, 1981). On French royal historiography see Gabrielle M. Spiegel, *The Chronicle Tradition of Saint-Denis: A Survey* (Brookline, Mass.: Classical Folia Editions, 1978).

24. Joseph R. Strayer, *On the Medieval Origins of the Modern State* (Princeton, N.J.: Princeton University Press, 1970); Heinrich Mitteis, *Der Staat des höhen Mittelalters*, 4th ed. (Weimar: H. Bohlaus, 1953), trans. H. F. Orton, *The State in the Middle Ages* (Amsterdam: North-Holland, 1975).

25. The definitive study is Baldwin, *The Government of Philip Augustus*; see in particular his discussions of justice and finance, chapters 3, 7, 10, 15. See also previous studies of the French royal domain and finance, Marcel Pacaut, *Louis VII et son royaume* (Paris: SEVPEN, 1964), 119–60 and William M. Newman, *Le domaine royal sous les premiers Capétiens (987–1180)* (Paris: Receuil Sirey, 1937), 1–66, 161–201.

26. Ferdinand Lot and Robert Fawtier, eds., *Le premier budget de la monarchie française: Le compte général de 1202–1203* (Paris: H. Champion, 1932).

27. Baldwin, *Philip Augustus*, 44–58, 137–75, 405–7. See also the suggestions about the household accounts in Thomas N. Bisson, "Les Comptes des domaines au temps de Philippe Auguste: Essai comparatif," in *La France de Philippe Auguste: Le temps de mutations*, ed. Robert-Henri Bautier (Paris: CNRS, 1982), 525–28.

28. Adriaan Verhulst and M. Gysseling, *Le compte général de 1187, connu sous le nom de "Gros Brief," et les institutions financières du comté de Flandre au XIIe siècle* (Brussels: Palais des Académies, 1962).

29. Baldwin, *Philip Augustus*, 407, described the first known attempt of the French kings to estimate total receipts and expenses, from 1221, which was a precursor of the later *Magna recepta et expensa*, 1227–28. Ellen Kittell, *From Ad Hoc to Routine: A Case Study in Medieval Bureaucracy* (Philadelphia: University of Pennsylvania Press, 1991), despite the *Gros Brief* of 1187, dated the routine budgeting in Flanders to the thirteenth-century.

30. Lyon and Verhulst, *Medieval Finance*, 25–29, 36, 43, 66–67, 72–75.

31. Baldwin, *Philip Augustus*, 35–36, 43–44, 125–28.

32. The Rule, ch. 2, *La règle de Saint-Benoît*, ed. Jean Neufville and Adalbert de Vogüé (Paris: Cerf, 1972) 1:450, trans. Timothy Fry, *The Rule of Saint Benedict* (New York: Vintage, 1998), 11. See also the Rule, ch. 64, and Giles Constable, "The Authority of Superiors in Religious Communities," 192.

33. For example, Lyon and Verhulst, *Medieval Finance*, excluded almost all judicial matters from consideration (save the income they generated). One of the strengths of Baldwin's *Philip Augustus* is that he treated both subjects together. Kittell, *From Ad Hoc to Routine*, 8, noted that the judicial functions of the General Receiver of Flanders began to separate from the financial around 1262, but the two were not formally divided until 1372.

34. Lyon and Verhulst, *Medieval Finance*, 27–29.

35. Richard fitzNigel, *Dialogus de scaccario*, ed. and trans. Charles Johnson, *The Course of the Exchequer*, rev. ed. (Oxford: Clarendon, 1983), 7–8.

36. Clanchy, *From Memory to Written Record*, 32

37. Clanchy, *From Memory to Written Record*, 145–62, suggested that the initial impulse to archive such records emerged from ecclesiastical, specifically monastic, practices of cartulary and *descriptio* production.

38. Olivier Guyotjeannin, Jacques Pycke, and Benoît-Michel Tock, *Diplomatique médiévale* (Turnhout: Brepols, 1993), 115–19 succinctly outline the development of the notice in France.

39. Richard Keyser, "La transformation de l'échange des dons pieux: Montier-la-Celle, Champagne, 1100–1350," *Revue historique* (forthcoming) offers a concise review of the problem. See also Rosenwein, *To Be the Neighbor of Saint Peter*, 176–79, who notes the increasing preoccupation with economic (as opposed to social) concerns in later Cluny confirmations, which heralded twelfth-century economic reforms.

40. Brian Stock, *The Implications of Literacy: Written Language and Models of Interpretation in the Eleventh and Twelfth Centuries* (Princeton, N.J.: Princeton University Press, 1983) and Murray, *Reason and Society in the Middle Ages* both stress religious and cognitive implications of literacy. Murray, 110–37, does consider "Reason and Power" but from an intellectual, not a practical perspective. See also the cautionary remarks of Carruthers, *The Book of Memory*, 200–201 about reason.

41. Laurent Morelle, "The Metamorphosis of Three Monastic Charter Collections in the Eleventh Century (Saint-Amand, Saint-Riquier, Montier-en-Der)," in *Charters and the Use of the Written Word in Medieval Society*, ed. Karl Heidecker (Turnhout: Brepols, 2000), 203: "It is not the cartulary that produces an image of abundance, it is the accumulation of writings that stimulates 'cartularization.'" Morelle, however, cautions against drawing firm conclusions from quantitative measures.

42. Robert F. Berkhofer III, "Inventing Traditions: Forgery, Creativity, and Historical Conscience in Medieval France," (forthcoming).

43. In addition to books, monastic archives were themselves reorganized. For an example, see Donatella Nebbiai-Dalla Garda, *La Bibliothèque de l'abbaye de Saint-Denis en France du IXe au XVIIIe siècle* (Paris: CNRS, 1985). For the

importance of archival formation and its long-term implications, see Roger Chartier, *The Order of Books: Readers, Authors, and Libraries in Europe Between the Fourteenth and Eighteenth Centuries* (Stanford, Calif.: Stanford University Press, 1994).

44. Richard Britnell, "Pragmatic Literacy in Latin Christendom," in *Pragmatic Literacy East and West, 1200–1330*, ed. Richard Britnell (Woodbridge: Boydell Press, 1997), 3–24. See also Jean Favier, *Gold and Spices: The Rise of Commerce in the Middle Ages*, trans. Caroline Higgitt (New York: Holmes and Meier, 1998), 258–79.

Bibliography

PRINTED SOURCES

The following list contains some secondary or reference works useful for the primary documents printed in them.

Bautier, Robert-Henri, ed. *Recueil des actes d'Eudes, roi de France (888–898)*. Chartes et diplômes relatifs à l'histoire de France. Paris: Imprimérie nationale, 1967.

Bautier, Robert-Henri and Monique Gilles, eds. *Chronique de Saint-Pierre-le-Vif de Sens, dite de Clarius*. Sources d'histoire médiévale. Paris: CNRS, 1979.

Benedict of Nursia. *Regula*. 3 vols. Ed. Jean Neufville and Adalbert de Vogüé. *La règle de Saint-Benoît*. Paris: Cerf, 1972. Trans. Timothy Fry, *The Rule of Saint Benedict*. New York: Vintage, 1998.

Bernard, Auguste and Alexandre Bruel, eds. *Recueil des chartes de l'abbaye de Cluny*. 6 vols. Collection de documents inédits sur l'histoire de France, publiés par les soins du ministre de l'instruction publique, 1e sér, Histoire politique. Paris: Imprimérie nationale, 1876–1903.

Bernard of Clairvaux, Saint. *Opera*. 9 vols. to date. Ed. Jean Leclercq, C. H. Talbot, and Henri Rochais. Rome: Editiones Cistercienses, 1957–.

Bethmann, L. C., ed. *Gesta pontificum Cameracensium*. MGH SS 7 (1846): 393–525.

Blatt, Franz and Yves Lefèvre, eds. *Novum glossarium mediae latinitatis: ab anno DCCC usque ad annum MCC*. 5 vols. to date. Hafniae: Munksgaard, 1957–.

Bruckner, Albert and Robert Marichal, eds. *Chartae latinae antiquiores: facsimile edition of the Latin charters prior to the ninth century*. 25 vols. to date. Olten, Lausanne: U. Grat, 1954–.

de Hemptinne, Thérèse and Adrian Verhulst, eds. *De oorkonden der graven van Vlaanderen (juli 1128–september 1191)*. 1 vol. to date. Brussels: Commission royale d'histoire, 1988–.

Devroey, Jean-Pierre, ed. *Le polyptyque et les listes de biens de l'abbaye Saint-Pierre de Lobbes: IXe–XIe siècles*. Brussels: Palais des Académies, 1986.

D'Hoop, Félix Henri, ed. *Recueil des chartes du prieuré de Saint-Bertin, à Poperinghe, et de ses dependances à Bas-Warneton et à Couckelaere, déposées aux archives de l'état, à Gand*. Recueil de chroniques, chartes et autres documents concernant l'histoire et les antiquités de la Flandre-Occidentale. Bruges: Vandecasteele-Werbrouck, 1870.

Dufour, Jean, ed. *Recueil des actes de Louis VI, roi de France (1108–1137)*. 4 vols. Chartes et diplômes relatifs à l'histoire de France. Paris: De Boccard, 1992–94.

Dufour-Malbezin, Annie, ed. *Actes des évêques de Laon des origines à 1151*. Paris: CNRS, 2001.

Duru, Louis Maximilien, ed. *Bibliothèque historique de l'Yonne; ou, Collection de légendes, chroniques et documents divers pour servir à l'histoire des differentes contrées qui forment aujourd'hui ce departement.* 2 vols. Auxerre: Perriquet, 1850–1863.

Fabre, Paul and L. Duchesne, eds. *Le liber censuum de l'Église romaine.* 3 vols. Bibliothèque des Écoles Françaises d'Athènes et de Rome, 2ᵉ sér., no. 6. Paris: Fontemoing, 1889–1952.

Félibien, Michel. *Histoire de l'abbaye royal de Saint-Denys en France.* . . . Paris: F. Leonard, 1706.

fitzNigel, Richard. *Dialogus de scaccario: Constitutio domus regus.* Ed. and trans. Charles Johnson, with corrections by F. E. L. Carter and D. E. Greenway, *The Course of the Exchequer: the Establishment of the Royal Household.* Rev. ed. Oxford: Clarendon Press, 1983.

Fros, Henry, *Bibliotheca hagiographica latina antiquae et mediae aetatis novum supplementum.* Subsidia hagiographica, no. 70. Brussels: Société des Bollandistes, 1986.

Ganshof, François-Louis, ed. *Le polyptyque de l'abbaye de Saint-Bertin (844–859): Édition critique et commentaire.* Mémoires de l'Académie des Inscriptions et Belles-Lettres 45. Paris: Klincksieck, 1975.

Grat, Félix, Jeanne Vielliard and Suzanne Clémencet, eds. *Annales de Saint-Bertin.* Société de l'histoire de France. Série antérieure à 1789, no. 470. Paris: Klincksieck, 1964. Trans. Janet Nelson. *The Annals of Saint-Bertin.* Ninth-Century Histories 1. Manchester: Manchester University Press, 1991.

Guérard, Benjamin, ed. *Cartulaire de l'abbaye de Saint-Bertin.* Collection de documents inédits sur l'histoire de France 1ᵉ sér, Histoire politique. Collection des cartulaires de France, 3. Paris: Crapelet, 1840.

——, ed. *Cartulaire de l'abbaye de Saint-Père de Chartres.* 2 vols. Collection des cartulaires de France 1–2. Paris: Crapelet, 1840.

——, ed. *Le polyptyque de l'abbé Irminon; ou, Denombrement des manses, des serfs et des revenus de l'abbaye de Saint-Germain-des-Prés sous le règne de Charlemagne.* 2 vols. Paris: Imprimérie royale, 1844.

Gysseling, Maurits and A. C. F. Koch, eds. *Diplomata Belgica ante annum millesimum centesimum scripta.* 2 vols. Bouwstoffen en studien voor de geschiedenis en de lexicografie van het Nederlands 1. Brussels: Belgisch Inter-Universitair Centrum voor Neerlandistiek, 1950.

Hägermann, Dieter, ed., with assistance of Konrad Elmshäuser and Andreas Hedwig. *Das Polyptychon von Saint-Germain-des-Prés: Studienausgabe.* Köln: Böhlau, 1993.

Haigneré, Daniel, ed. *Les chartes de Saint-Bertin d'après le Grand Cartulaire de Dom Charles-Joseph DeWitte.* 4 vols. Saint-Omer: H. D'Homont, 1886–99.

Halphen, Louis and Ferdinand Lot, eds. *Recueil des actes de Lothaire et Louis V, rois de France (954–987).* Chartes et diplômes relatifs à l'histoire de France. Paris: Klincksieck, 1908.

Heller, J. and G. Waitz, eds. *Flodoardi Historia Remensis Ecclesiae.* MGH SS 13 (1881): 405–519.

Histoire littéraire de la France. [de Pastouret] Commission dans la Classe d'Histoire et de la Littérature 13 (suite du douzième siècle). Paris: Firmin Didot, 1814.

Holder-Egger, Oswald, ed. *Chronica monasterii sancti Bertini auctore Iohanne Longo de Ipra.* MGH SS 25 (1880): 736–866.

——, ed. *Gesta Abbatum S. Bertini Sithiensium.* MGH SS 13 (1881): 600–673.

——, ed. *Vita Folquini Episcopi Morinensis.* MGH SS 15:1 (1857): 423–30.

Jaffé, Philip, Samuel Loewenfeld, et al., eds. *Regesta pontificum Romanorum ab condita ecclesia ad annum post Christum natum MCXCVIII.* 2nd ed. 2 vols. Leipzig: Veit, 1885–88. Reprint, Graz: Akademische Druck-U. Verlagsanstatt, 1956.

Kehr, P., ed. *Die Urkunden Arnolfs.* MGH Diplomata ex stirpe Karolinorum 3 (1955).

Krusch, Bruno, ed. *Gesta Dagoberti I. Regis Francorum.* MGH Scriptores rerum Merovingicarum 2 (1888): 396–425.

——, ed. *Vita Droctrovei Abbatis Parisiensis Auctore Gislemaro.* MGH Scriptores rerum Merovingicarum 3 (1906): 535–43.

Lauer, Philippe, ed. *Recueil des actes de Charles III le Simple, roi de France (893–923).* Chartes et diplômes relatifs à l'histoire de France. Paris: Imprimérie nationale, 1949.

Lebel, Germaine, ed. *Catalogue des actes de l'abbaye de Saint-Denis relatifs à la province ecclésiastique de Sens, de 1151 à 1346.* Paris: Imprimérie administrative centrale, 1935.

Longnon, Auguste, ed. *Polyptyque de l'abbaye de Saint-Germain-des-Prés, rédigé au temps de l'abbé Irminon.* 2 vols. Société de l'histoire de Paris et de l'Ile-de-France, Paris. Documents 11–12. Paris: H. Champion, 1886–95.

Loriquet, Henri and Jules Chavanon, eds. *Inventaire sommaire des archives départementales antérieures à 1790. Pas-de-Calais.* Archives ecclésiastiques H1. Arras: Société du Pas-de-Calais, 1902.

Lot, Ferdinand and Robert Fawtier, eds. *Le premier budget de la monarchie française: Le compte général de 1202–1203.* Bibliothèque de l'École des Hautes Études, Sciences historiques et philologiques, no. 259. Paris: H. Champion, 1932.

Merlet, René, ed. *Inventaire sommaire des archives départementales antérieures à 1790. Eure-et-Loir.* Archives ecclésiastiques H1. Chartres: Garnier, 1897.

Migne, Jacques-Paul, ed. *Patrologiae cursus completus . . . Series latina.* 221 vols. Paris, 1844–64.

Morand, François, ed. *Appendice au Cartulaire de l'abbaye de Saint-Bertin.* Collection de documents inédits sur l'histoire de France. 1e sér. Histoire politique. Paris: Imprimérie imperiale, 1867.

Pertz, G. H., ed. *Gesta Abbatum Lobiensium.* MGH SS 4 (1841): 52–74.

Piot, Charles, ed. *Cartulaire de l'abbaye de Saint-Trond.* 2 vols. Publication of Académie royale des sciences, des lettres, et des beaux-arts de Belgique, Brussels. Commission royale d'histoire. Brussels: F. Hayez, 1870–74.

Poupardin, René, ed. *Recueil des chartes de l'abbaye de Saint-Germain-des-Prés: des origines au début du XIIIe siècle.* 2 vols. Paris: H. Champion, 1909–32.

Prou, Maurice, ed. *Recueil des actes de Philippe Ier de France, 1059–1108.* Chartes et diplômes relatifs à l'histoire de France. Paris: Imprimérie nationale, 1908.

Pruvost, Alexandre, ed. *Chronique et cartulaire de l'abbaye de Bergues-Saint-Winoc: de l'ordre de Saint Benoît*. Recueil de chroniques, chartes et autre documents concernant l'histoire et les antiquités de la Flandre, 1e sér. Bruges: D'Aime de Luttere, 1875–78.

Ramackers, Johannes, ed. *Papsturkunden in den Niederlanden Belgien, Luxemburg, Holland und Franzosisch-Flandern*. 2 vols. Abhandlungen der Gesellschaft der Wissenschaften zu Göttingen. Philologisch-historische Klasse 3, nos. 8–9. Berlin: Weidman, 1933–34.

Ramackers, Johannes, Dietrich Lohrmann, and Rolf Grosse, eds. *Papsturkunden in Frankreich. Neue Folge*. 9 vols. to date. Abhandlungen der Gesellschaft der Wissenschaften zu Göttingen. Philologisch-historische Klasse 3, nos. 3–4, 21, 23, 27, 35, 41, 95, 174, 225. Göttingen: Vandenhoeck and Ruprecht, 1932–.

Société des Bollandistes, ed. *Bibliotheca hagiographica latina antiquae et mediae aetatis*. 2 vols. 1898–99. Subsidia hagiographica 6. Reprint, Brussels: Société des Bollandistes, 1949.

Suger, Abbot of Saint-Denis. *Oeuvres*. Ed. Françoise Gasparri. 2 vols. Paris: Belles-Lettres, 1996–2001.

———. *Oeuvres complètes de Suger*. Ed. Albert Lecoy de La Marche. Société de l'histoire de France. Paris: Mme. ve. J. Renouard, 1867.

———. *Vie de Louis VI le Gros*. Ed. Henri Waquet. Les Classiques de l'histoire de France au moyen âge, 11. Paris: H. Champion, 1929

Tardif, Jules, ed. *Monuments historiques: Cartons des rois*. Paris: J. Claye, 1866. Reprint, Nendeln: Kraus, 1977.

Tessier, Georges, ed. *Recueil des actes de Charles II le Chauve, roi de France*. 3 vols. Chartes et diplômes relatifs à l'histoire de France 8. Paris: Imprimérie nationale, 1943–55.

Tock, Benoît-Michel, ed. *Les chartes des évêques d'Arras (1093–1203)*. Collection de documents inédits sur l'histoire de France 21. Paris: CTHS, 1991.

———, ed. *Monumenta Arroasiensia*. Corpus Christianorum, Continuatio Mediaevalis 175. Turnhout: Brepols, 2000.

Van Drival, Eugène, ed. *Cartulaire de l'abbaye de Saint-Vaast, rédigé au XIIe siècle par Guiman*. Documents inédits concernant l'Artois 6. Arras: A. Courtin, 1875.

———, ed. *Nécrologe de l'abbaye de St-Vaast d'Arras*. Documents inédits concernant l'Artois 7. Arras: n.p., 1878.

Vercauteren, Fernand, ed. *Actes des comtes de Flandres, 1071–1128*. Commission royale d'histoire. Recueil des actes des princes Belges. Brussels: Palais des Académies, 1938.

Verhulst, Adriaan, and M. Gysseling. *Le compte général de 1187, connu sous le nom de "Gros Brief," et les institutions financières du comté de Flandre au XIIe siècle*. Académie royale de Belgique. Commission royale d'histoire. Brussels: Palais des Académies, 1962.

Waitz, G., ed. *Chronicon Vedastinum*. MGH SS 13 (1881): 674–715.

Zimmermann, Harald, ed. *Papsturkunden, 896–1046*. 3 vols. Österreichische Akademie der Wissenschaften. Philosophisch-Historische Klasse, Denkschriften 174, 177, 198. Vienna: Verlag der Österreichischen Akademie der Wissenschaften, 1984–89.

SECONDARY WORKS

Atsma, Hartmut. "Le fonds des chartes mérovingiennes de Saint-Denis: Rapport sur une recherche en cours." *Paris-et-l'Ile-de-France* 32 (1981): 259–72.

——, ed. *La Neustrie: Les pays au nord de la Loire de 650 à 850: colloque historique international*. 2 vols. Beihefte der Francia 16. Sigmaringen: J. Thorbecke, 1989.

Aubert, Marcel. *Suger*. Paris: Fontenelle, 1950.

Baldwin, John M. *The Government of Philip Augustus: Foundations of French Royal Power in the Middle Ages*. Berkeley: University of California Press, 1986.

Barthélemy, Dominique. "Une crise de l'écrit? Observations sur des actes de Saint-Aubin d'Angers (XIe siècle)." *BEC* 155 (1997): 95–118.

——. "Debate: The 'Feudal Revolution' I." *Past and Present*, no. 152 (1996): 196–205.

——. "La mutation féodale a-t-elle eu lieu?" *Annales: ESC* 47 (1992): 767–77.

——. *La mutation de l'an mil a-t-elle eu lieu? Servage et chevalerie dans la France des Xe et XIe siècles*. Paris: Fayard, 1997.

——. *La société dans le comté de Vendôme: de l'an mil au XIVe siècle*. Paris: Fayard, 1993.

Bautier, Robert-Henri. "Paris au temps d'Abélard." In *Abélard en son temps: Actes du colloque international organisé à l'occasion du 9e centenaire de la naissance de Pierre Abélard, 14–19 mai 1979*. Paris: Belles Lettres, 1981.

Berger, Roger. *Littérature et société arrageoises au XIIIe siècle: Les chansons et dits artésians*. Mémoires de la Commission départementale des monuments historiques du Pas-de-Calais 21. Arras: Commission départementale des monuments historiques du Pas-de-Calais, 1981.

Berkhofer, Robert F. III. "Inventing Traditions: Forgery, Creativity, and Historical Conscience in Medieval France." Forthcoming.

——. "Marriage, Lordship and the 'Greater Unfree' in Twelfth-Century France." *Past and Present* 173 (2001): 3–27.

Berlière, Ulysse. "Notes pour servir à l'histoire des monastères bénédictins de la province de Reims." *Revue bénédictine* 11 (1894): 36–37.

Berman, Constance H. *Medieval Agriculture, the Southern French Countryside, and the Early Cistercians: A Study of Forty-Three Monasteries*. Philadelphia: American Philosophical Society, 1986.

Bernard, P. "Études critiques sur les chartes des comtes de Flandre pour l'abbaye de Saint-Bertin." *Positions des thèses*, École Nationale de Chartes. Paris: Picard, 1923.

Bijsterveld, Arnould-Jan A., Hank Teunis, and Andrew Wareham, eds. *Negotiating Secular and Ecclesiastical Power: Western Europe in the Central Middle Ages*. Turnhout: Brepols, 1999.

Bisson, Thomas N. "Les Comptes des domaines au temps de Philippe Auguste: Essai comparatif." In *La France de Philippe Auguste: Le temps de mutations: actes du colloque international*, ed. Robert-Henri Bautier. Colloques internationaux du Centre National de la Recherche Scientifique 602. Paris: CNRS, 1982.

———. "The 'Feudal Revolution'." *Past and Present* 142 (1994): 6–42.

———. "The 'Feudal Revolution': Reply." *Past and Present* 155 (1997): 208–25.

———. *Fiscal Accounts of Catalonia Under the Early Count-Kings (1151–23)*. 2 vols. Berkeley: University of California Press, 1984.

Bloch, Marc. *La société féodale*. Paris: A. Michel, 1949. Trans. L. A. Manyon. *Feudal Society*. Chicago: University of Chicago Press, 1963.

Bois, Guy. *La mutation de l'an mil: Lournand, village mâconnais de l'antiquité au féodalisme*. Paris: Fayard, 1989.

Bouchard, Constance. *Holy Entrepreneurs: Cistercians, Knights, and Economic Exchange in Twelfth-Century Burgundy*. Ithaca, N.Y.: Cornell University Press, 1991.

———. *Spirituality and Administration: The Role of the Bishop in Twelfth-Century Auxerre*. Speculum Anniversary Monographs 5. Cambridge, Mass.: Medieval Academy of America, 1979.

Britnell, Richard, ed. *Pragmatic Literacy East and West, 1200–1330*. Woodbridge: Boydell Press, 1997.

Broutte, Émile. "Folquin." *Dictionnaire d'histoire et de géographie ecclésiastique* 17 (1971): cols. 744–49.

Brühl, Carlrichard. "Diplomatische Miszellen zur Geschichte des ausgehenden 9. Jahrhunderts." *Archiv für Diplomatik* 3 (1957): 1–19.

Brunterc'h, Jean-Pierre. "Acte constitutif de la mense conventuelle du monastère de Saint-Denis établie par l'abbé Hildiun le 22 janvier 832." In *Un village au temps de Charlemagne: Moines et paysans de l'abbaye de Saint-Denis du VIIe siècle à l'An Mil: Musée national des acts et traditions populaires, 29 novembre 1988–30 avril 1989*, ed. Jean Cuisenier and Rémy Guadagnin, 125–28, catalogue no. 33. Paris: Réunion des musées nationaux, 1988.

Bur, Michel. *Suger: Abbé de Saint-Denis, régent de France*. Paris: Perrin, 1991.

Carruthers, Mary. *The Book of Memory: A Study of Memory in Medieval Culture*. Cambridge: Cambridge University Press, 1990.

Chartier, Roger. *The Order of Books: Readers, Authors, and Libraries in Europe Between the Fourteenth and Eighteenth Centuries*. Stanford, Calif.: Stanford University Press, 1994.

Chédeville, André. *Chartres et ses campagnes (XIe–XIIIe siècles)*. Publications de l'Université de Haute-Bretagne 1. Paris: Klincksieck, 1973.

Chibnall, Marjorie. "Forgery in Narrative Charters," In *Fälschungen im Mittelalter: Internationaler Kongress der Monumenta Germaniae Historica, München, 16.–19. September 1986* 4(2): 331–46. MGH Schriften 33. Hanover: Hanhsche Buchhandlung, 1988–1990.

Clanchy, Michael. *From Memory to Written Record: England, 1066–1307*. 2nd ed. Oxford: Blackwell, 1993.

Constable, Giles. "The Authority of Superiors in Religious Communities." In *La notion d'autorité au Moyen Age: Islam, Byzance, Occident: Colloques internationaux de La Napoule, session des 23–26 octobre 1978*, ed. George Makdisi, Dominique Sourdel, and Janine Sourdel-Thomine. Paris: Presses Universitaires de France, 1982. Reprint, Giles Constable, *Monks, Hermits, and Crusaders in Medieval Europe*. London: Variorum, 1988.

———. "Les listes de propriétés dans les privilèges pour Baume-les-Messiers aux XIᵉ et XIIᵉ siècles." *Journal des Savants* (1986): 97–131.

———. *Monastic Tithes, from Their Origins to the Twelfth Century.* Cambridge Studies in Medieval Life and Thought, new series, 10. Cambridge: Cambridge University Press, 1964.

———. "Suger's Monastic Administration." In *Abbot Suger and Saint-Denis: A Symposium*, ed. Paula L. Gerson, 17–32. New York: Metropolitan Museum of Art, 1986.

Coolen, G. "Guntbert de Saint-Bertin, chronique des temps carolingiens." *Revue du Nord* 40, 158 (1958): 213–24.

Cuisenier, Jean and Rémy Guadagnin, eds. *Un village au temps de Charlemagne: Moines et paysans de l'abbaye de Saint-Denis du VIIᵉ siècle à l'An Mil: Musée national des acts et traditions populaires, 29 novembre 1988–30 avril 1989.* Paris: Réunion des musées nationaux, 1988.

de Gaiffier, Baudouin. "Les revendications de biens dans quelques documents hagiographiques du XIᵉ siècle." *Analecta Bollandiana* 50 (1932): 123–38.

de Smet, J. M. "Geen *Stylus Paschalis* in Vlaanderen tijdens de IXde eeuw." *De Leiegouw* 8, 1 (1966): 227–38.

Declercq, Georges. "Originals and Cartularies: The Organization of Archival Memory (Ninth–Eleventh Centuries)." In *Charters and the Use of the Written Word in Medieval Society*, ed. Karl Heidecker, 147–70. Turnhout: Brepols, 2000.

Delmaire, Bernard. "Cartulaires et inventaires de chartes dans le nord de la France." In *Les cartulaires: Actes de la Table ronde, organisée par l'École nationale des chartes et le G.D.R. 121 du C.N.R.S. (Paris, 5–7 décembre 1991)*, ed. Olivier Guyotjeannin, Laurent Morelle, and Michel Parisse, 301–24. Mémoires et documents de l'École des chartes 39. Paris: École des Chartes, 1993.

———. *Le diocèse d'Arras de 1093 au milieu du XIVᵉ siècle: Recherches sur la vie religieuse dans le nord de la France au moyen âge.* Mémoires de la Commission départementale d'histoire et d'archéologie du Pas-de-Calais 31. Arras: Commission départementale d'histoire et d'archéologie du Pas-de-Calais, 1994.

Derens, Jean. "Gislemar, historien de Saint-Germain-des-Prés." *Journal des savants* (1972): 228–32.

———. "Les origines de Saint-Germain-des-Prés: Nouvelle étude sur les deux plus anciennes chartes de l'abbaye." *Journal des savants* (1973): 28–60.

Devroey, Jean-Pierre. "Un monastère dans l'économie d'échanges: les services de transport à l'abbaye de Saint-Germain-des-Prés au IXᵉ siècle." *Annales: ESC* 39 (1984): 570–89.

———. "Problèmes de critique autour du polyptyque de l'abbaye de Saint-Germain-des-Prés." In *La Neustrie: Les pays au nord de la Loire de 650 à 850: colloque historique international*, ed. Hartmut Atsma, 1: 441–66. Sigmaringen: J. Thorbecke, 1989.

D'Haenens, Albert. *Les invasions normandes en Belgique au IXᵉ siècle: Le phénomène et sa répercussion dans l'historiographie médiévale.* Louvain: Publications Universitaires de Louvain, 1967.

Dhondt, Jan. *Études sur la naissance des principautés territoriales en France (IXᵉ–Xᵉ siècles)*. Rijksuniversiteit te Gent. Werken uitgegeren door de Faculteit van de wijsbegeerte en letteren 102. Bruges: De Tempel, 1948.

Duby, Georges. "Le budget de l'abbaye de Cluny entre 1080 et 1155: Économie domainale et économie monétaire." *Annales: ESC* 7, 2 (1952): 155–71. Reprint, George Duby, *Hommes et structures du moyen âge: Recueil d'articles*, 61–82. Paris: Mouton, 1973.

———. *L'économie rurale et la vie des campagnes dans l'occident médiévale: France, Angleterre, Empire, IX–XV siècles*. 2 vols. Paris: Aubier, 1962. Trans. Cynthia Postan, *Rural Economy and Country Life in the Medieval West*. Columbia: University of South Carolina Press, 1968.

———. *La société aux XIᵉ et XIIᵉ siècles dans la région mâconnaise*. 2nd ed. Paris: J. Touzot, 1971.

———. *Les trois ordres ou l'imaginaire du féodalisme*. Paris: Gallimard, 1978. Trans. Arthur Goldhammer, *The Three Orders: Feudal Society Imagined*. Chicago: University of Chicago Press, 1980.

Durliat, Jean. *Les finances publiques de Dioclétien aux carolingiens (284–889)*. Beihefte der Francia 21. Sigmaringen: J. Thorbecke, 1990.

———. "Le polyptyque d'Irminon et l'impôt de l'armée." *BEC* 116 (1983): 183–208.

———. "La vigne et le vin dans le région parisienne au début du IXᵉ siècle d'après le polyptyque d'Irminon." *Le Moyen Age* 24 (1968): 387–419.

Duvivier, Charles. *Actes et documents anciens intéressant la Belgique*. Belgium: n.p., 1898.

Eisenstein, Elizabeth. *The Printing Press as an Agent of Social Change: Communications and Cultural Transformation in Early-Modern Europe*. 2 vols. Cambridge: Cambridge University Press, 1979.

Elmshäuser, Konrad, and Andreas Hedwig. *Studien zum Polyptychon von Saint-Germain-des-Prés*. Köln: Böhlau, 1993.

Fälschungen im Mittelalter: Internationaler Kongress der Monumenta Germaniae Historica, München, 16.–19. September 1986. 6 vols. MGH Schriften 33. Hanover: Hahnsche Buchhandlung, 1988–90.

Favier, Jean. *Gold and Spices: The Rise of Commerce in the Middle Ages*. Trans. Caroline Higgitt. New York: Holmes and Meier, 1998.

Felten, Franz. *Äbte und Laienäbte im Frankreich: Studie zum Verhältnis von Staat und Kirche im früheren Mittelalter*. Monographien zur Geschichte des Mittelalters 20. Stuttgart: Anton Hiersemann, 1980.

Fleckenstein, Josef. *Die Hofkapelle der deutschen Könige*. 2 vols. MGH Schriften 16. Stuttgart: Hiersemann, 1959–66.

Fossier, Robert. *Chartes de coutume en Picardie: XIᵉ–XIIIᵉ siècle*. Collection de documents inédits sur l'histoire de France. Paris: Bibliothèque Nationale, 1974.

———. *Polyptyques et censiers*. Typologie des sources du moyen âge occidental 28. Turnhout: Brepols, 1978.

———. *La terre et les hommes en Picardie jusqu'à la fin du XIIIe siècle*. 2 vols. Publications de la Faculté des lettres et sciences humaines de Paris-Sorbonne. Série "Recherches" 48–49. Paris: B. Nauwelaerts, 1968.

Gaier, Claude. "Documents relatifs aux domains hesbigans de l'abbaye de Saint-Denis en France." *BCRH* 127 (1961): 163–202

Geary, Patrick. *Furta Sacra: Thefts of Relics in the Central Middle Ages.* Rev. ed. Princeton, N.J.: Princeton University Press, 1990.

———. *Phantoms of Remembrance: Memory and Oblivion at the End of the First Millennium.* Princeton, N.J.: Princeton University Press, 1994.

Grant, Lindy. *Abbot Suger of St-Denis: Church and State in Early Twelfth-Century France.* London: Longman, 1998.

Grosse, Rolf. "Remarques sur les cartulaires de Saint-Denis aux XIIIe–XIVe siècles." In *Les cartulaires: Actes de la Table ronde, organisée par l'Ecole nationale des chartes et le G.D.R. 121 du C.N.R.S. (Paris, 5–7 décembre 1991)*, ed. Olivier Guyotjeannin, Laurent Morelle, and Michel Parisse, 279–90. Paris: École des Chartes, 1993.

Guesnon, Adolphe. "Un cartulaire de l'abbaye de Saint-Vaast d'Arras, codex du XIIe siècle." *Bulletin historique et philologique du Comité des travaux historiques et scientifiques* (1896): 240–305.

Guyotjeannin, Olivier. *Episcopus et comes: Affirmation et déclin de la seigneurie épiscopale au nord du royaume de France (Beauvais-Noyon, X^e–début XIIIe siècle).* Mémoires et documents 30. Geneva: Droz, 1987.

———. "*Penuria Scriptorum*: le mythe de l'anarchie documentaire dans la France du nord (X^e-première moitié du XIe siècle)." *BEC* 155 (1997): 11–44.

Guyotjeannin, Olivier, Laurent Morelle, and Michel Parisse, eds. *Les cartulaires: Actes de la Table ronde, organisée par l'Ecole nationale des chartes et le G.D.R. 121 du C.N.R.S. (Paris, 5–7 décembre 1991).* Mémoires et documents de l'École des Chartes 39. Paris: École des Chartes, 1993.

———. *Pratiques de l'écrit documentaire au XIe siècle. BEC* 155 (1997).

Guyotjeannin, Olivier, Jacques Pycke, and Benoît-Michel Tock. *Diplomatique médiévale.* L'atelier du mediéviste 2. Turnhout: Brepols, 1993.

Heinzelmann, Martin. *Translationsberichte und andere Quellen des Reliquienkultes*, Typologie des sources du moyen âge occidental 33. Turnhout: Brepols, 1979.

Heirbaut, Dirk. "Flanders: A Pioneer of State-oriented Feudalism? Feudalism as an Instrument of Comital Power in Flanders During the High Middle Ages (1000–1300)." In *Expectations of Law in the Middle Ages*, ed. Anthony Musson, 23–34. Woodbridge: Boydell, 2001.

Holder-Egger, Oswald. "Folcwin von St. Bertin und Folcuin von Lobbes." *Neues Archiv der Gesellschaft für ältere deutsche Geschichtskunde* 6 (1881): 417–38.

Huyghebaert, Nicolas. "Le comte Baudouin II de Flandre et les *custos* de Steneland: A propos d'un faux précepte de Charles le Chauve pour Saint-Bertin (866)." *Revue bénédictine* 69 (1959): 49–67.

Hyams, Paul. *King, Lords, and Peasants in Medieval England: The Common Law of Villeinage in the Twelfth and Thirteenth Centuries.* Oxford: Clarendon Press, 1980.

Iogna-Prat, Dominique. "La confection des cartulaires et l'historiographie à Cluny (XIe–XIIe siècles). In *Les cartulaires: Actes de la Table ronde, organisée par l'Ecole nationale des chartes et le G.D.R. 121 du C.N.R.S. (Paris, 5–7 décembre*

1991), ed. Olivier Guyotjeannin, Laurent Morelle, and Michel Parisse, 27–44. Paris: École des Chartes, 1993.

———. "La geste des origins dans l'historiographie clunisienne des XIᵉ–XIIᵉ siècles." *Revue bénédictine* 102 (1992): 135–91.

Janssen, Wilhelm. *Die päpstlichen Legaten in Frankreich: von Schisma Anaklets II. bis zum Tode Coelestins III (1130–1198).* Kölner historische Abhandlungen 6. Cologne: Böhlau, 1961.

Jordan, Erin. "Separate Rule, Same Activity: Reassessing Benedictine Economic Activity in the Thirteenth Century." *Revue bénédictine,* forthcoming.

Keyser, Richard. "La transformation de l'échange des dons pieux: Montier-la-Celle, Champagne, 1100–1350." *Revue historique,* forthcoming.

Kittell, Ellen. *From Ad Hoc to Routine: A Case Study in Medieval Bureaucracy.* Philadelphia: University of Pennsylvania Press, 1991.

Kosto, Adam J. "The *Liber feudorum maior* of the Counts of Barcelona: The Cartulary as an Expression of Power." *Journal of Medieval History* 27 (2001): 1–22.

Krusch, Bruno. "Über die *Gesta Dagoberti.*" *Forschungen zur deutschen Geschichte* 26 (1886): 161–91.

Kuchenbuch, Ludolf. *Bäuerliche Gesellschaft und Klosterherrschaft im 9. Jahrhundert: Studien zur SozialStruktur der Abtei Prüm.* Wiesbaden: Steiner, 1978.

LaMotte-Collas, Marie. "Les possessions territoriales de l'abbaye de Saint-Germain-des-Prés du début du IXᵉ au début du XIIᵉ siècle." *Revue d'histoire de l'Église de France* 43 (1957): 49–80.

Lemarignier, Jean-François. "L'exemption monastique et les origines de la réforme grégorienne." In *A Cluny: Congrès scientifique: fêtes et cérémonies liturgiques en l'honneur des saints abbés Odon et Odilon, 9–11 juillet, 1949; travaux du congrès; art, histoire, liturgie.* Dijon: Société des Amis de Cluny, 1950.

———. *La France médiévale: Institutions et société.* Collection U. Sér. Histoire médiévale. Paris: A. Colin, 1970.

———. *Le gouvernement royal aux premiers temps Capétiens, 987–1108.* Paris: Picard, 1965.

Lemarignier, Jean-François. "Le prieuré d'Haspres, ses rapports avec l'abbaye de Saint-Vaast d'Arras et la centralisation monastique au début du XIIᵉ siècle." *Revue du Nord* 29 (1947): 261–68.

Lesne, Emile. *Histoire de la propriété ecclésiastique en France du VIIIe à la fin du XIe siècles.* 6 vols. Mémoires et travaux des facultés catholiques de Lille, 6, 19, 30, 34, 44, 46, 50, 53. Lille: R. Giard, 1910–43.

———. *L'origine des menses dans le temporel des églises et des monastères de France au IXᵉ siècle.* Mémoires et travaux des facultés catholiques de Lille 7. Lille: R. Giard, 1910.

Levillain, Léon. "Un état de redevances dues à la mense conventuelle de Saint-Denis (832)." *Bulletin de la Société de l'histoire de Paris et de l'Ile-de-France* 36 (1909): 79–90.

———. "Études sur l'abbaye de Saint-Denis à l'époque mérovingienne I: Les sources narratives." *BEC* 82 (1921): 5–116.

———. "Études sur l'abbaye de Saint-Denis à l'époque mérovingienne II: Les origines de Saint-Denis." *BEC* 86 (1925): 5–99.

———. "Études sur l'abbaye de Saint-Denis à l'époque mérovingienne III: *Privilegium et Immunitates* ou Saint-Denis dans l'église et dans l'état." Pt. 1–2. *BEC* 87 (1926): 20–97, 245–346.

Lewis, Andrew. *Royal Succession in Capetian France: Studies on Familial Order and the State*. Harvard Historical Studies 100. Cambridge, Mass.: Harvard University Press, 1981.

Little, Lester. *Benedictine Maledictions: Liturgical Cursing in Romanesque France*. Ithaca, N.Y.: Cornell University Press, 1993.

———. *Religious Poverty and the Profit Economy in Medieval Europe*. Ithaca, N.Y.: Cornell University Press, 1978.

Lloyd, Simon. "The Crusading Movement, 1096–1274." In *The Illustrated History of the Crusades*, ed. Jonathan Riley-Smith, 34–65. Oxford University Press: Oxford, 1997.

Lohrmann, Dietrich. "Formen der *Enumeratio bonorum* in Bischofs-, Papst- und Herrscherurkunden (9.–12. Jahrhundert)." *Archiv für Diplomatik* 26 (1980): 281–311.

———. *Kirchengut im nördlichen Frankreich: Besitz, Verfassung und Wirtschaft im Spiegel der Papstprivilegien des 11.–12. Jahrhunderts*. Bonn: L. Rohrscheid, 1983.

———. "Répartition et création de nouveaux domaines monastiques au XIIe siècle." In *Villa-Curtis-Grangia: Économie rurale entre Loire et Rhin de l'époque Gallo-Romaine du XIIe–XIIIe siècles*, ed. Wilhelm Janssen and Dietrich Lohrmann. Beihefte der Francia 11. Munich: Artemis, 1983.

Lopez, Robert S. *The Commercial Revolution of the Middle Ages, 950–1350*. Cambridge: Cambridge University Press, 1976.

Lot, Ferdinand. "Une année du règne de Charles le Chauve: Année 866." *Le Moyen âge* 2e sér, 15, 6 (1902): 394–438.

Luscombe, David. "Denis the Pseudo-Areopagite in the Middle Ages from Hilduin to Lorenzo Valla." In *Fälschungen im Mittelalter: Internationaler Kongress der Monumenta Germaniae Historica, München, 16.–19. September 1986*, 1: 133–52. MGH Schriften 33. Hanover: Hahnsche Buchhandlung, 1988–90.

Lyon, Bryce and Adriaan Verhulst. *Medieval Finance: A Comparison of Financial Institutions in Northwestern Europe*. Providence, R.I.: Brown University Press, 1967.

Magnou-Nortier, Elisabeth, ed. *Aux sources de la gestion publique*. 3 vols. Lille: Presses Universitaires de Lille, 1993–1997.

———. "La gestion publique en Neustrie: Les moyens et les hommes (VIIe–IXe siècles)." In *La Neustrie: Les pays au nord de la Loire de 650 à 850: colloque historique international*, ed. Hartmut Atsma, 1: 271–320. Sigmaringen: J. Thorbecke, 1989.

———. "Remarques générales à propos du manse." In *Aux sources de la gestion publique*, ed. Elisabeth Magnou-Nortier, 1: 196–207. Lille: Presses Universitaires de Lille, 1993–7.

Martin, Hervé. *Mentalités médiévales II: Représentations collectives du XIe au XVe siècle*. Paris: Presses Universitaires de France, 2001.

Mitteis, Heinrich. *Der Staat des hohen Mittelalters: Grundlinien einer vergleichenden Verfassungsgeschichte des Lehnszeitalters*. 4th ed. Weimar: H. Bohlaus,

1953. Trans. H. F. Orton. *The State in the Middle Ages: A Comparative Constitutional History of Feudal Europe*. North-Holland Medieval Translation 1. Amsterdam: North-Holland, 1975.

Morelle, Laurent. "Les 'actes précaire,' instruments de transferts patrimoniaux (France du Nord et de l'Est, VIIIᵉ–XIᵉ siècle." *Mélanges de l'École française de Rome: Moyen Age* III, 2 (1999): 607–47.

——. "Les chartes dans la gestion des conflits (France du nord, XIe-début XIIe siècle)." *BEC* 155 (1997): 267–98.

——. "Histoire et archives vers l'an mil: Une nouvelle 'mutation'?" *Histoire et archives* 2 (1998): 119–41.

——. "The Metamorphosis of Three Monastic Charter Collections in the Eleventh Century (Saint-Amand, Saint-Riquier, Montier-en-Der)." In *Charters and the Use of the Written Word in Medieval Society*, ed. Karl Heidecker, 171–211. Turnhout: Brepols, 2000.

——. "Moines de Corbie sous influence sandionysienne? Les préparatifs corbéians du synod romain de 1065." In *L'église de France et la papauté (Xᵉ–XIIIᵉ siècle): Actes du XXVIᵉ colloque historique franco-allemand*, ed. Rolf Grosse, 197–218. Études et documents pour servir à une Gallia Pontificia. Bonn: Bouvier, 1993.

Morris, Colin. *The Papal Monarchy: The Western Church from 1050 to 1250*. Oxford History of the Christian Church. Oxford: Oxford University Press, 1989.

Mostert, Marco. *The Political Theology of Abbo of Fleury: A Study of the Ideas About Society and Law of the Tenth-Century Monastic Reform Movement*. Hilversum: Verloren, 1987.

——. "Die Urkundenfälschungen Abbos von Fleury." In *Fälschungen im Mittelalter: Internationaler Kongress der Monumenta Germaniae Historica, München, 16.–19. September 1986*, 4(2):287–318. 6 vols. MGH Schriften, Bd. 33. Hanover: Hahnsche Buchhandlung, 1988–1990.

Murray, Alexander. *Reason and Society in the Middle Ages*. Rev. ed. Oxford: Oxford University Press, 1990.

Musson, Anthony, ed. *Expectations of Law in the Middle Ages*. Woodbridge: Boydell, 2001.

Nebbiai-Dalla Guarda, Donatella. *La Bibliothèque de l'abbaye de Saint-Denis en France du IXe au XVIIIe siècle*. Paris: CNRS, 1985.

Nelson, Janet. *Charles the Bald*. The Medieval World. London: Longman, 1992.

Newman, William M. *Le domaine royal sous les premiers Capétiens (987–1180)*. Paris: Recueil Sirey, 1937.

Oexle, Otto Gerhard. *Forschungen zu monastischen und geistlichen Gemeinschaften im westfränkischen Bereich*. Munstersche Mittelalter-Schriften 31. Munich: W. Fink, 1978.

Omont, Henri. "Le *Praeceptum Dagoberti de fugitivis* en faveur de l'abbaye de Saint-Denis." *BEC* 61 (1900): 75–82.

Pacaut, Marcel. *Louis VII et son royaume*. Bibliothèque générale de l'École Pratique des Hautes Études. 6th section. Paris: SEVPEN, 1964.

Panofsky, Erwin, trans. *Abbot Suger on the Abbey Church of St.-Denis and its Art Treasures*. 2nd ed. Princeton, N.J.: Princeton University Press, 1979.

Parisse, Michel. "Les cartulaires: copies ou sources originales?" In *Les cartulaires: Actes de la Table ronde, organisée par l'Ecole nationale des chartes et le G.D.R. 121 du C.N.R.S. (Paris, 5–7 décembre 1991)*, ed. Olivier Guyotjeannin, Laurent Morelle, and Michel Parisse, 503–12. Paris: École de Chartes, 1993.

——. "Écriture et réécriture des chartes: Les pancartes aux XIe et XIIe siècles." In *Pratiques de l'écrit documentaire au XIe siècle*, ed. Olivier Guyotjeannin, Laurent Morelle and Michel Parisse. *BEC* 155 (1997): 247–66.

——. "Les pancartes: Étude d'un type d'acte diplomatique." In *Pancartes monastiques des XIe et XIIe siècles*, ed. Michel Parisse, Pierre Pégeot, and Benoît-Michel Tock, 11–62. Turnhout: Brepols, 1998.

——, Pierre Pégeot, and Benoît-Michel Tock, eds. *Pancartes monastiques des XIe et XIIe siècles*. Turnhout: Brepols, 1998.

Perrin, Charles Edmond. *Recherches sur la seigneurie rurale en Lorraine d'après les plus anciens censiers (IXe–XIIe siècle)*. Publications de la Faculté des lettres de l'Université de Strasbourg 71. Paris: Belles Lettres, 1935.

Poly, Jean-Pierre and Eric Bournazel. *La mutation féodale: Xe–XIIe siècles*. Rev. ed. Paris: Presses Universitaires de France, 1991. Trans. Caroline Higgitt, *The Feudal Transformation: 900–1200*. New York: Holmes and Meier, 1991.

Rasmussen, N. K. "The Liturgy at Saint-Denis: a Preliminary Study." In *Abbot Suger and Saint-Denis: A Symposium*, ed. Paula L. Gerson, 41–48. New York: Metropolitan Museum of Art, 1986.

Remensnyder, Amy. *Remembering Kings Past: Monastic Foundation Legends in Medieval Southern France*. Ithaca, N.Y.: Cornell University Press, 1995.

Reuter, Timothy. "Debate: The 'Feudal Revolution' III." *Past and Present* 155 (1997): 177–95.

Reynolds, Roger E. "The *De officiis vii graduum*: Its Origins and Early Medieval Development." *Medieval Studies* 34 (1972): 113–51. Reprint, Roger E. Reynolds, *Clerical Orders in the Early Middle Ages: Duties and Ordination*. Aldershot: Ashgate, 1999.

Reynolds, Susan. *Fiefs and Vassals: The Medieval Evidence Reinterpreted*. Oxford: Oxford University Press, 1994.

——. *Kingdoms and Communities in Western Europe, 900–1300*. Oxford: Oxford University Press, 1984.

Ricouart, Louis. *Les biens de l'abbaye de St-Vaast dans les diocèses de Beauvais, de Noyon, de Soissons et d'Amiens*. Anzin: Ricouart-Dugour, 1888.

Rosenwein, Barbara H. *Negotiating Space: Power, Restraint, and Privileges of Immunity in Early Medieval Europe*. Ithaca, N.Y.: Cornell University Press, 1999.

——. *To Be the Neighbor of Saint Peter: The Social Meaning of Cluny's Property, 909–1049*. Ithaca, N.Y.: Cornell University Press, 1989.

Schmale, Joseph. "Synoden Papst Alexanders II (1061–1073): Anzahl, Termine, Entscheidungen." In *Annuarium historiae conciliorum; internationale Zeitschrift für Konziliengeschichtsforschung* 11 (1979): 307–38.

Sot, Michel. *Gesta episcoporum, gesta abbatum*. Typologie des sources du moyen âge occidental 37. Turnhout: Brepols, 1981.

Spiegel, Gabrielle M. *The Chronicle Tradition of Saint-Denis: A Survey*. Medieval Classics, Texts, and Studies 10. Brookline, Mass.: Classical Folia Editions, 1978.

Stein, Henri. *Bibliographie générale des cartulaires français ou relatifs à l'histoire de France*. Manuels de bibliographie historique 4. Paris: Picard, 1907.

Stock, Brian. *The Implications of Literacy: Written Language and Models of Interpretation in the Eleventh and Twelfth Centuries*. Princeton, N.J.: Princeton University Press, 1983.

——. *Listening for the Text: On the Uses of the Past*. Philadelphia: University of Pennsylvania Press, 1996.

Stoclet, Alain. "*Evindicatio et petitio*: Le recouvrement de biens monastiques en Neustrie sous les premiers Carolingiens: L'exemple de Saint-Denis." In *La Neustrie: Les pays au nord de la Loire de 650 à 850: colloque historique international*, ed. Hartmut Atsma, 2: 125–50. Sigmaringen: J. Thorbecke, 1989.

——. "Le temporel de Saint-Denis du VIIᵉ au Xᵉ siècle: La constitution de patrimoine foncier dans le Parisis." In *Un village au temps de Charlemagne: Moines et paysans de l'abbaye de Saint-Denis du VIIᵉ siècle à l'An Mil: Musée national des acts et traditions populaires, 29 novembre 1988–30 avril 1989*, ed. Jean Cuisenier and Rémy Guadagnin, 94–105. Paris: Réunion des musées nationaux, 1988.

Strayer, Joseph R. *On the Medieval Origins of the Modern State*. Princeton, N.J.: Princeton University Press, 1970.

Taylor, Nathaniel L. "Monasteries and Servile Genealogies: Guy of Suresnes and Saint-Germain-des-Prés in the Twelfth Century." *Genèse médiévale de l'anthroponymie moderne* 5:1: *Serfs et dependants au Moyen Age*, ed. Monique Bourin and Pascal Chareille, 249–68. Tours: Université de Tours, 2002.

Tessier, Georges. *Diplomatique royale française*. Paris: Picard, 1962.

——. "Originaux et pseudo-originaux carolingiens du chartrier de Saint-Denis." *BEC* 106 (1946): 35–69.

Teunis, Henk. "Negotiating Secular and Ecclesiastical Power in the Central Middle Ages: A Historiographical Introduction." In *Negotiating Secular and Ecclesiastical Power: Western Europe in the Central Middle Ages*, ed. Arnoud-Jan A. Bijsterveld, Hank Teunis, and Andrew Wareham, 1–18. Turnhout: Brepols, 1999.

Turner, Ralph. *Men Raised from the Dust: Administrative Service and Upward Mobility in Angevin England*. Philadelphia: University of Pennsylvania Press, 1988.

Ugé, Karine. "Creating a Useable Past in the Tenth Century: Folcuin's *Gesta* and the Crises at Saint-Bertin." *Studi Medievali* 37 (1996): 887–903.

——. "Relics as Tools of Power: The Eleventh-Century *Inventio* of St. Bertin's Relics and the Assertion of Abbot Bovo's Authority." In *Negotiating Secular and Ecclesiastical Power: Western Europe in the Central Middle Ages*, ed. Arnoud-Jan A. Bijsterveld, Henk Teunis, and Andrew Wareham, 51–72. Turnhout: Brepols, 1999.

Van Caenegem, Raoul. "Le diplôme de Charles le Chauve du 20 juin 877 pour l'abbaye de Saint-Bertin." *Revue d'histoire du droit* 31 (1963): 403–26.

Van der Kieft, C. *Étude sur le chartrier et la seigneurie du prieuré de la Chapel-Aude (XIᵉ–XIIIᵉ siècle)*. Bibliothèque Historique 60. Assen, Netherlands: Van Gorcum, 1960.

Vezin, Jean. "Les manuscrits copiés à Saint-Denis pendant l'époque carolingi-enne." *Paris-et-l'Ile-de-France* 32 (1982): 273–87.

Vezin, Jean, and Hartmut Atsma. "Le dossier suspect des possessions de Saint-Denis en Angleterre revisté (VIIIe–IXe siècles)." In *Fälschungen im Mittelalter: Internationaler Kongress der Monumenta Germaniae Historica, München, 16.–19. September 1986* 4(2): 211–36. MGH Schriften 33. Hanover: Hanhsche Buchhandlung, 1988–90.

Voet, Léon. "Étude sur deux bulles de Benoît VIII pour Saint-Vaast-d'Arras." *BCRH* 109 (1944): 187–242.

Waldman, Thomas. "Abbot Suger and the Nuns of Argenteuil." *Traditio* 41 (1985): 239–72.

———. "Saint-Denis et les premiers Capétiens." In *Religion et culture autour de l'an mil: Royaume capétien et Lotharingie: actes du colloque Hugues Capet 987–1987, la France de l'an mil, Auxerre, 26 et 27 juin 1987, Metz, 11 et 12 septembre 1987*, ed. Dominique Iogna-Prat and Jean-Charles Picard. Paris: Picard, 1990.

Wallace-Hadrill, J. M. "History in the Mind of Archbishop Hincmar." In *The Writing of History in the Middle Ages: Essays presented to Richard William Southern*, ed. R. H. C. Davis and J. M. Wallace-Hadrill. Oxford: Clarendon Press, 1981.

Warlop, Ernest. *De Vlaamse Adel voor 1300*. 3 vols. Handzame: Familia et Patria, 1968. Trans. J. B. Ross, *The Flemish Nobility Before 1300*. 4 vols. Kortrijk: G. Desmet-Huysman, 1975.

Wickham, Chris. "Debate: The 'Feudal Revolution' IV." *Past and Present*, no. 155 (1997): 196–208.

White, Stephen D. "Debate: The 'Feudal Revolution' II." *Past and Present* 152 (1996): 205–23.

Wyss, Michaël. *Atlas historique de Saint Denis: Des origins au XVIIᵉ siècle*. Documents d'archéologie française 59. Paris: Maison des sciences de l'homme, 1996.

Index

abbatial lands, 11–13, 17–20, 22–23, 25, 27–29, 101, 114–15

Abbo, abbot of Fleury (988–1004), 43–45, 47, 58, 61, 73, 78

abbots, 3, 37, 74, 91–131, 138–40, 143, 157–63, 167; authority of, 104–5, 123–28, 130–31, 138–39, 143, 158, 161; lay, 12, 19, 21–22, 29–30, 32, 40–42, 47; as ministers, 91, 100, 105, 108, 122, 126–30, 163, 194–95. *See also* individual entries

Abelard, Peter, 100

accountability, 2–8, 11, 50, 52, 54, 112, 122–24, 131–33, 135, 139, 143–59, 161–70; and responsible service, 2–3, 123–24, 131–33, 135, 139, 143–47, 152, 154–59, 161–62

accounting, 85, 153–54, 156, 159–61, 166–67, 169–70. *See also* accountability

Adalard, abbot of Saint-Bertin (844–59, 860–64), 24–28, 39, 86, 171, 173

Adalolph, abbot of Saint-Bertin (961), 36, 38

Adam, abbot of Saint-Denis (1099–1122), 101, 120

administration. *See* administrative mentality; governance

administrative mentality, 2–3, 38–39, 49–50, 53–55, 76–80, 83–92, 103–24, 133, 143, 157–68, 208 n.149. *See also* abbots, as ministers; governance

Adrian IV, 131

advocates, 13, 101–2, 107, 120, 123–24, 139, 144–45, 205 n.70

Aganon, bishop of Chartres (ca. 930–54), 31–32, 80, 87

Aimoin of Fleury, 47

Albert, mayor of Emprenville, 140, 146

Alexander II, 45–46, 60, 68

Alexander III, 81

archives, 3, 7–9, 24, 29, 31–42, 44–52, 54–55, 73–77, 88–91, 108, 113, 115, 117, 162, 168–71, 210 n.153; *scriptoria*, 4, 51, 76

Argenteuil, nunnery, 61, 64, 83

Arnaud, abbot of Saint-Pierre-le-Vif of Sens (1096–1124), 113–17, 119

Arnold, count of Cleves, 139, 144–45

Arnulf I, count of Flanders, 36–38, 135

Arques, *villa* of Saint-Bertin, 65–66, 70

Arras, bishop of, 67, 119

Arras, town of, 67, 72, 81–83, 85, 97, 109–10, 113, 118–19, 150, 152, tolls of, 67, 82, 109, 229 n.121

audiences, 4, 104–5, 134, 139, 147–48, 151–52, 159, 167

audits, 4, 147–54, 159, 166

bailiffs, 123–24, 130–31, 150–56, 163; office of, 150

Baldwin V, count of Flanders, 44

Baldwin, John, 166

Barthélemy, Dominique, 95

Baume-les-Messieurs, monastery, 56

Benedict VIII, 44

benefices, 13, 17–20, 22–23, 25, 29–31, 41. *See also* feudalism; fiefs; *precaria*

Berclau, priory of Saint-Vaast, 62

Berengar, mayor of Champol, 140, 146, 149

Acknowledgments

In the preparation of this book, I have benefited from the advice and assistance of many persons and the support of several institutions. Research was supported in part by a J. William Fulbright Scholarship, with funds provided by the United States Information Agency (USIA). I have also received travel grants and other support from the Departments of History at Western Kentucky University and Western Michigan University.

I am deeply indebted to all the librarians and archivists who aided me in my research. All historians depend and rely on the work of these men and women, without whom our work would be less accurate and comprehensive. While in France, I had the good fortune to have full access to the Archives Nationales, the Bibliothèque Nationale de France, and numerous departmental and municipal archives, especially at Chartres, Arras, and Saint-Omer; I am extremely grateful to their professional staffs. I would also like to thank the librarians and staff of Widener Library (Harvard College) and Western Michigan University, Special Collections.

My work has also benefited from the advice of many colleagues in France. At various times I had the pleasure and privilege of speaking with members of the German Historical Institute in Paris, including Hartmut Atsma, who shared his knowledge of Carolingian surveys, and Rolf Grosse, who magnanimously shared his knowledge (and photographs) of papal confirmations. I will always appreciate Jean Vezin's tour of the back rooms of the Salle des Manuscrits and his willingness to discuss the *scriptorium* of Saint-Denis. The kind and generous guidance of Professor Olivier Guyotjeannin was of inestimable value; his enthusiasm and learning were inspirational models. Many thanks to Annie Dufour, head of the Parisian Section Diplomatique of the Institut de Recherche et d'Histoire des Textes (IRHT) for her aid in reviewing the most recent French computer databases on charters and cartularies (including ARTEM and the "Nouveau Stein") and for access to the Institute's vast microfilm holdings; I shall always remember our conversations at Avenue d'Ièna fondly. She was instrumental in placing me in contact with Jacques Pycke at the CETEDOC "Nouveau Wauters" project; he kindly sent me preliminary versions of their charter databases for Saint-Bertin and Saint-Vaast on diskette, which were an invaluable resource for my research.

The assistance of one's advisors is impossible to measure. From the beginning, Professor Thomas N. Bisson has guided me, both directly and with the exemplar of his own scholarship, in becoming a medieval historian. His belief in the project has been a neverending source of inspiration and encouragement. I am grateful to Professor Charles Donahue for the numerous conversations we have had about my work; his intellectual contributions were exceeded only by his honest friendship. Professor Michael McCormick has been a constant supporter over the years, willing to undertake meticulous reading of pages as well as providing numerous references. Though I am to be held accountable for any flaws that may remain in the work, it is my hope that this present book lives up to their high and rigorous standards of scholarship.

My colleagues have provided scholarly aid, without which the work could not have been brought to completion. A complete inventory would run to many manuscripts leaves, however, I especially wish to thank those who graciously offered advance copies of their work: Erin Jordan, Rick Keyser, Russell Martin, Jennifer Paxton, and Nathaniel Taylor. For his delight in Latinity and superb wit, Ted Lendon, "best of men," should hold a place of high honor. Patricia and Michael Minter have been both generous and steadfast in their support. Other than myself, no one has had to live as closely with the book as my wife, Sally; for her willingness to do so and patience in listening to many odd ideas about the medieval world no thanks can be enough. Most of all, I would like to thank my parents, Genevieve and Robert Berkhofer, my first and best history teachers.

notarius -166

De Securio ?